2nd edition

ETHICS AND SOCIETY

Peter A. Facione
California State University, Fullerton
Santa Clara University

Donald Scherer
Bowling Green State University

Thomas Attig
Bowling Green State University

Prentice Hall
Englewood Cliffs, New Jersey 07632

Library of Congress Cataloging-in-Publication Data

Facione, Peter A.
   Ethics and society / Peter A. Facione, Donald Scherer, Thomas
Attig. — 2nd ed.
      p.—cm.
   Rev. ed. of: Values and society. c1978.
   Includes bibliographical references and index.
   ISBN 0-13-291667-3
   1. Ethics. I. Scherer, Donald. II. Attig, Thomas, (date)
III. Facione, Peter A. Values and society. IV Title.
BJ1025.F15 1991
170—dc20

90-42046
CIP

Previously published as *Values and Society*.

Editorial/production supervision and
      interior design: KERRY REARDON
Cover design: BEN SANTORA
Pre-press buyer: HERB KLEIN
Manufacturing buyer: DAVID DICKEY

©1991, 1978 by Prentice-Hall, Inc.
A Division of Simon & Schuster
Englewood Cliffs, New Jersey 07632

Printed in the United States of America

10 9 8 7 6 5 4 3 2 1

ISBN 0-13-291667-3

PRENTICE-HALL INTERNATIONAL, INC., *London*
PRENTICE-HALL OF AUSTRALIA PTY. LIMITED, *Sydney*
PRENTICE-HALL HISPANOAMERICANA, S.A., *Mexico*
EDITORA PRENTICE-HALL DO BRASIL, LTDA., *Rio de Janeiro*
PRENTICE-HALL CANADA INC., *Toronto*
PRENTICE-HALL OF INDIA PRIVATE LIMITED, *New Delhi*
PRENTICE-HALL OF JAPAN, INC., *Tokyo*
SIMON & SCHUSTER ASIA PTE. LTD., *Singapore*

CONTENTS

PREFACE

Each day we make evaluations, judgments, and decisions. Among the most important are decisions concerning our goals and judgments concerning how to achieve those goals in an effective and yet ethical way. Individuals make these evaluations as they reflect on what they should or should not do. Corporations, institutions, and communities make them concerning both their communal or institutional purposes and the methods used to achieve them. Legislative bodies, judges, and government officials make them as they determine the direction of society, frame its laws, administer its policies, and adjudicate its conflicts.

Often it is not easy to decide what one ought to do: what is right, what is wrong, and where do our obligations, responsibilities, rights, and duties lie. Yet these decisions are an essential part of living. Goals must be clarified, reasons considered, relevant information brought to light, and universal ethical principles applied. To become responsible members of society we must learn what those principles are, how they apply, and how facts and reasons support ethical decisions.

In addition to presenting normative concepts and theories, *Ethics and Society* gives you the intellectual tools for dealing with ethical questions. Fictional case studies, real life examples, rich sets of exercises, and challenging discussion questions let you come to grips with ethical theories and concepts in a practical way. The book presumes most readers have no previous experience with philosophy and are interested primarily in acquiring practical as well as theoretical knowledge of ethics or social philosophy. Naturally, many discussions can be advanced to more sophisticated levels—and we encourage you to pursue them—however, reaching professional levels in this book is inconsistent with our chief goal: making ethical ideas accessible to college students and equipping students with the mental tools to make rational sense of ethical concerns in both the personal and social realm.

The book is organized around seven values: social utility, ethical egoism, rights and duties, freedom, justice, society, and law. The chapters that discuss these seven can be read in any grouping or order which suits your particular interests and needs. These middle seven are flanked with chapters aimed at providing a framework for understanding what ethics is about and for dealing rationally with ethical concerns. Chapter 1 explains how to justify normative claims, whereas Chapter 9 works on how to resolve divergent and conflicting values.

The book includes several features that students and instructors have found useful. Chapters are divided into sections, usually three in a chapter, each starting off by identifying the four or five most important things you should learn as you study that section. Use these short lists to focus your efforts. Next comes a case study—a fictional story that illustrates the chief ideas and techniques to be developed in that section. The explanatory text draws out theoretical points and describes philosophical techniques, both abstractly and by detailed use of the case study and other examples. Exercises and discussion questions, at the end of each section, give you the opportunity to apply what you are learning. We are proud of these exercises and questions and we know that they can reinforce your understanding of what you have read. Answers to selected exercises, along with references back to specific paragraphs, help to locate relevant material.

The Starting Point introduces ethics by focusing on how to express value judgments and justify claims regarding what one ought to do or ought not to do. Chapter 1 looks briefly at ethical nihilism, ethical skepticism, ethical emotivism, and the ever-troublesome ethical relativism. However, its goal is to stress the importance of using reasons to justify normative claims. It rejects unacceptable strategies such as rationalizing, self-excusing, and appealing to emotions, motivations, or the sources of one's views. This chapter discusses ways of applying conceptual analysis, factual information, and universal ethical principles to support normative reasoning.

Chapter 2, *Social Utility*, features a treatment of classical universalistic utilitarianism along with examples illustrating how this normative theory translates into twentieth century cost-benefit analysis. This chapter treats the evaluation of consequences as fundamental and the evaluation of practices leading to consequent states of affairs as derivative. In addition to concerns over the meaning of *the good*, and the difficulty of making requisite calculations, and the problems associated with either the rule-utilitarian or the act-utilitarian interpretation, this chapter notes the insensitivity of this theory to various kinds of human relationships and its inconsistency with values, such as, justice and respect for persons.

Ethical Egoism addresses the challenge of moving beyond the hypothesis that "Everybody does what they want anyway," to the normative question: "Should we act that way?" The case for pursuing one's own enlightened self-interest is made clearly and persuasively. This is balanced with objections to both psychological egoism and ethical egoism. The question "Why be moral?" is addressed as well as the question about what *the good life* is and what habits or virtues are most conducive to the good life.

Chapter 4, *Rights and Duties*, begins by outlining a wide variety of claims about rights with emphasis on the distinction between conventional and moral rights. Using examples from business and governmental affairs, it shows how the concept of rights, as entitlements, relates to other normative concepts, especially that of duty. Kant's ethical theory is used as an example of the view that some actions are intrinsically right or intrinsically wrong. This chapter outlines one possible justification of claims that indefeasible and inalienable rights and categorical duties exist. That justification is developed in terms of integrity and respect for persons.

The central questions for Chapter 5, *Freedom,* are how moral responsibility is related to autonomy and what justifications there might be for limiting a person's freedom in a free society? This chapter introduces the concept of freedom using the word *autonomy* defined in terms of rational, unconstrained decision making. After relating moral responsibility to autonomy, reward, and punishment, the chapter clarifies the differences among four notions of freedom: positive, negative, formal, and effective. It discusses how limiting one kind of freedom might lead to an expansion of other kinds of freedom for an individual and for a society.

Questions regarding the rightness or wrongness of particular policies often depend on whether or not they promote *justice.* Chapter 6 discusses how questions of justice arise and distinguishes between distributive, compensatory, and retributive justice. It analyzes the formal principle of justice: "Treat persons alike who are alike in morally relevant respects; treat persons proportionately differently to the extent that they differ in morally relevant respects." After clarifying the relation of the formal principle of justice to the concept of equality, this chapter addresses the practical question, "Exactly which differences among persons are the morally relevant ones?"

The *Society* chapter examines the conceptual progression from the right to rule, to the purposes of a society, and then to the puposes of states seen as one kind of society. This leads to the purposes of governments, as the agency to carry out the aims of a society. The term *society* (and, hence, the society's government) applies to a very broad spectrum of objects, including corporations, office staffs, clubs, religious communities, families, teams, companies, brigades, and so forth. Thus, philosophical issues concerning rightful authority, conflicts between individual and group interests, and the limits of government can be applied to one's own career and home life as well as to the state. Chapter 7 brings into focus the organic and the atomistic conceptualizations of a society, the root meaning of democracy, and the normative interpretation of the social contract theory.

Chapter 8, *Law*, presents an integrated application of many ethical concepts, particularly those developed in *Society* and in *Justice*. A good legal system promotes social stability, creates opportunities, and provides for cultural diversity, social complexity, and orderly ways to amend and transmit its own regulations. This chapter details the substantive, procedural, and practical prerequisites that must be met for the rule of law. It asks: What is the relationship between law and morality? Exactly how should we understand the concept of a legal obligation? In terms of the reasons that purport to justify them, how do the penalties imposed relate to those found guilty of breaking the law, those harmed by such offenses, and society in general?

Chapter 9, *Clashing Ethical Ideals*, responds to the crucial problem of how to rationally resolve those value tensions that are unavoidably part of living ethically in a complex society. This chapter distinguishes value conflicts and value divergences; then, it examines the kinds of value tensions we experience in personal ethics and in social ethics. Finally, it explains the assumptions, plausibility, and limitation of rational strategies, such as setting priorities, finding alternatives, and negotiating acceptable compromises.

We are grateful for the help many have given with this project. We thank our spouses and families for being patient, sensitive, and understanding while we labored at the word-processor or reflected on one of the many consuming problems or questions this book addresses. We thank our students for having worked through the ideas, examples, and exercises. We thank our colleagues and editors at Prentice Hall for their constructive comments. Special thanks to our reviewers: Bruce Landesman, *University of Utah*; Dr. David B. Fletcher, *Wheaton College*; John W. Copeland, *Drew University*; and G.A. Spangler and Dr. Paul C.L. Tang,*California State University*. Also, thank you for considering this book; please send us your comments.

Peter A. Facione
Donald Scherer
Thomas Attig

1 | THE STARTING POINT

Unless we're only in a yelling contest, you can't just say something's right or wrong. You got to give me your thinking behind it.

Koby's Reflections on Justice

Our success in any activity as serious as deciding matters of personal and social ethics requires that we strive to be objective, fair-minded, sensitive, prudent, informed, and rational. In coming to our positions we must consider relevant issues and questions, state our views and our reasons with care and precision, and be open to considering objections and alternatives. There is a strong correlation between higher-order thinking skills and the kind of reasoning we use in formulating and applying ethical principles. The thinking skills to cultivate include the ability to reason at a formal and abstract level; the ability to formulate broad principles; the ability to apply abstract principles to particular cases; the ability to define, compare and contrast abstract concepts and cases; the ability to evaluate inferences and draw conclusions logically; the ability to raise relevant questions; and the ability to put yourself in the mind set of another to see where that person's beliefs and reasons lead.

Very likely, you already have many of these dispositions and skills, even if you do not recognize our terminology. You can formulate claims expressing normative points of view, use conceptual analysis to clarify and interpret normative claims, and use good critical thinking to support these claims. In this chapter we will help you sharpen these skills. Terminology is important, for in something as vital as ethics people must be able to communicate with one another. The educational goal of this chapter is to introduce concerns of personal and social ethics, alternative ways those concerns can be interpreted, and how those concerns can be subjected to rational analysis and justification. In this chapter you will learn to identify normative issues, understand normative assertions in a variety of general ways, and categorize the kinds of reasons people offer in support of their normative claims.

Section 1
ETHICS—HOW WE OUGHT TO BEHAVE?

Let's start by seeing what ethics is all about. After clarifying the distinction between facts and values, we will focus on claims that express value judgments about how people ought or ought not to behave, either individually or collectively. Assertions about what we ought to do are called *normative statements*. The matters of human behavior they refer to are the principal concerns of the normative discipline of ethics. After studying Section 1, you should be able to:

- Distinguish normative statements from other assertions.
- Give examples of normative and non-normative statements.
- Compare and contrast value judgments and judgments of fact.
- Describe personal ethics and social ethics in terms of their normative concerns.
- Contrast ethical concerns with the similar yet different concerns of the social sciences, values-clarification, behavioral modification, and counseling.

THE CASE OF THE AMBIGUOUS ASSIGNMENT

There had been racial tensions at the school all during the spring. Mr. Hart, the social science teacher, decided that one way to keep the lines of communication open between various groups of students was to frankly discuss the racial issues in class. He gave the students the following assignment as a preliminary to the class discussion: "Write a short paragraph on the topic 'Racism Today.'" The following two papers were selected to be read in class:

Racism Today
by Judith Harris
Everybody says that it's wrong to be prejudiced. Even though anthropologists think we all had dark-skinned African ancestors over four million years ago, for at least the last several thousand years humans have been divided into groupings which often practiced ethnic and racial prejudice. You can see racists on the TV news even today. I think those TV news shows only encourage them. I know some people who hide their racism in public but at home they let it out. If kids hear their parents making racist remarks, they will probably become prejudiced bigots too. They become bigots without even realizing it. After all, you can't change how you were brought up.

Racism Today
by Louis Ross
People should stop being racists. Racism is immoral because it lacks respect for people in terms of their character or their ideas.   Racism is dumb, narrow-minded, unscientific, and self-serving. Racism is immoral because it often leads to tragic results like violence, misery, and harm to life and property. It's not fair to treat some people one way and other people other ways just because they are different colors. There is no place for racism in society, it should be rooted out.

1.1 Normative Statements

Normative statements are assertions that express value judgments. Accordingly, every normative statement expresses or implies that something is good or bad, better or worse, ought to be or ought not to be. Some normative statements, such as "The crimson leaves of a red maple are most beautiful during an autumn sunset," are about aesthetic concerns. Some normative statements express value judgments about logical concerns—for example, "Aristotle's argument is not acceptable." Some normative statements, such as "Arrows are better weapons than spears," express value judgments that do not necessarily have immediate behavioral implications. Others, such as "Informed consent laws should be revised," do have immediate behavioral implications about what should or should not be done. A broad spectrum of such statements with immediate and important behavioral implications expresses the concerns of ethics.

Here are some additional examples of normative claims:

- The musical *Phantom of the Opera* is delightful.
- Picasso's "Guernica" is magnificent.
- The headquarters building is an abomination.
- The wetlands must be saved to protect our human environment.
- You have drawn the wrong conclusions from your data sample.
- Your inference is not valid.
- Public nudity should be legalized.
- Free health care is a basic human right.
- Violence in children's television should be eliminated.
- Our employees don't deserve child care benefits.
- Adultery is a sin.

All of the statements that Louis Ross made in the previous case study are normative statements. Do you agree with him? Why?

1.2 Non-normative Statements

Non-normative statements are value-neutral, ones that do not express (or are not intended to express) value judgments. Non-normative statements include reports, descriptions, or assertions, either true or false, used to express matters of empirical or logical fact. For example:

- In 1990 America changed its policy on space exploration.
- Triangles have three sides.
- Most people now see abortion as a woman's right.
- People usually do what they are told without thinking about it.
- Violence is a socially disruptive force.
- A person can hold values which are in conflict with her parents'.
- Alcoholism and drug abuse are widespread diseases.
- Alzheimer's victims feel lost and confused.
- Small children enjoy being told stories.
- Interpersonal competition leads to decreased productivity.
- Irma thinks Steven King is a great writer.
- It's John's opinion that safety is more important than rights.
- Bill thinks that his fiancé is the most wonderful person alive.

All of these examples state judgments or opinions about facts, either empirical facts or conceptual (logical) facts. As you can see from the last three examples, we can make factual or descriptive judgments about what other people value. More examples of non-normative statements occur in the Judith Harris paragraph in the case study. Her essay on racism today is composed exclusively of non-normative, value-neutral statements. But are they true?

1.3 Classifying Assertions

If you contrast what Harris wrote with the Ross essay, you will see why this case is called "The Case of the Ambiguous Assignment." Both Ross and Harris followed the instructions, yet they came up with quite different essays. Harris wrote a non-normative essay that relied on her understanding of various facts, scientific theories, and also included a few of her own opinions about human behavior. Ross wrote a totally normative essay aimed at treating racism today as a normative issue with social dimensions. As the case study illustrates, many issues can be treated from both the normative and non-normative points of view. Consider alcoholism, for example. Normative statements can be made:

- Drinking is wrong.
- Don't drink and drive.

- There should be no minimum drinking age.
- It's all right to use alcohol in moderation.

Non-normative statements also can be made:

- Lowering the drinking age leads to increased traffic fatalities.
- The nominee was rejected because of his drinking problem.
- Alcoholism among the aristocracy contributed to Rome's fall.
- Teen-age alcoholism is increasing at a rate of 2% per year.
- Alcohol is both physically and psychologically addictive.
- Alcohol is destructive to normal liver function.

Understanding that we are simplifying matters for the sake of equipping you with some initial conceptual tools, we still should tell you that, as with any broad conceptual distinction, there are borderline cases. Some statements are difficult to categorize as either normative or non-normative. Consider, for example, the supervisor who puts these notes in the personnel file:

- Gerald is lazy.
- Brenda is industrious.

On the one hand, each of these statements seems to be non-normative in describing how eager some person is to work. In part, the assertions report that Gerald is not eager to work and that Brenda is. Yet clearly each says more than that. Gerald is being evaluated negatively, while Brenda is commended. *Lazy* does not simply mean *inclined to do a little*. A negative evaluation of that inclination is involved in the meaning of the term. Notice the similar situation with *industrious*. Throughout the text, we shall treat statements that have both descriptive components and evaluative components as normative statements. *The principle to follow is that a statement is considered normative whenever it says, implies, or was intended to assert, that something is good or bad, better or worse, for being the way it is.* Consider the general claim that TV coverage only encourages racists. Can you see both normative and non-normative dimensions in that statement?

1.4 Comparing Normative and Non-Normative Statements

Non-normative statements can be appraised as true or false. They can be used as the premises or conclusions of arguments. And, most importantly, non-normative statements are amenable to being argued for, and thus having their truth (or falsity) demonstrated by rational proof and appeal to relevant information. To argue in support of a non-normative statement one appeals to empirical and possibly logical information. For example, to show that "women consuming alcohol is correlated with higher incidents of breast cancer" one must conduct statistical studies of cancer patients and their personal drinking histories. To try to establish why that correlation exists, one must do research into biochemistry and medicine with a view toward developing and confirming an explanatory theory. One can run experiments and marshal evidence in order to confirm or disconfirm empirical non-normative statements. Descriptive studies and analyses of concepts and their implications reveals what is needed to support non-normative or value-neutral statements.

We have elected to treat normative claims or assertions as statements, although we recognize that this is a matter of some dispute. Many would argue that normative claims cannot be appraised as true or false; they would deny that normative assertions are statements at all. On the other hand, many others would contend that normative claims are like statements of the non-normative variety. We will continue to speak of normative claims as statements that can reasonably be called true or false because of certain practices relating to how people commonly treat them. First, as with other statements, people do, from time to time, offer arguments in support of normative claims. Second, people evaluate the adequacy of these kinds of arguments, calling some reasons offered in support of normative claims better and some weaker. Third, people recognize that certain combinations or sets of normative claims are consistent, whereas other sets are not. So, whatever the precise status of normative claims, whatever the exact character of their possible truth or falsity, there are certain important similarities between them and non-normative statements. We believe these similarities warrant our treating normative claims as statements.

Normative claims can often be supported by argumentation and appeal to relevant information. Some normative studies, such as logic, are rather rigorous and fully developed, so that there is considerable confidence in the normative statements they support. If the techniques of logic tell us that a particular argument is valid, there is little reason to doubt the truth of that normative conclusion. Other normative studies, such as aesthetics, are less fully developed, less rigorous in their procedures, or treat subjects which, by their nature, seem amenable to incontestable and definitive analyses. Nonetheless, one can still make reasonable arguments to the effect that one piece of sculpture is more beautiful, more balanced, more powerful, more sensitive or, in other words, better, than another. The normative study, *ethics*, falls someplace between aesthetics and logic in terms of how fully ethics is developed, how rigorously established (and widely accepted) its conclusions are, and how amenable its issues are to incontestable and definitive analyses.

Arguments in support of normative statements attempt to demonstrate, in non-trivial and non-fallacious ways, that their normative conclusions are true. Proof offered in support of statements, either normative or non-normative, are basically arguments; their premises can be listed, they can be examined for logical correctness, their premises can be evaluated as true or false. Let us look at two examples. First, we have the argument that Louis Ross offered in support of his normative statement that racism is immoral.

1. Racism leads to violence, misery, and harm to lives and property.

2. These consequences are tragic.

3. Anything which leads to tragic consequences is immoral.

---

4. So, racism is immoral.

Premise **3.** is needed (unspoken but implicit) in the original passage. It provides the value dimension Ross implicitly relies on to support his normative conclusion. Contrast this with an argument that Harris makes:

1. Parents express racism at home, where their children can see it.

2. Children imitate and learn from their parents.

---

3. So, children learn from their parents to be racist.

Premise **2.** is an unspoken premise in Harris' argument. Notice that neither it nor Premise **1.** is normative. Rightly so, for one need not use normative claims to support non-normative claims.

1.5 Fact and Opinion

It is customary to distinguish statements of fact from expressions of opinion. While this distinction can be quite useful, it is important that you realize the difference between it and the normative vs. non-normative distinction we have been discussing. When we distinguish statements of fact from matters of opinion, we have in mind that the *statements of fact can be known to be true or false* whereas the *matters of opinion are such that nobody is now in a position to know*. For example, someone might believe that professional soccer will have more fans in the year 2010 than American football will. Since no one today can know whether this will prove true, this assertion about the future popularity of soccer is a matter of opinion. But if we assert that in the U.S. more high school students participate in soccer than in basketball, that would be a statement of fact. We are in a position to find out if that claim is true or false.

Whether a normative statement should be regarded as a matter of opinion is, in the first place, a question of whether any reasons and relevant information can be advanced to establish or disestablish it. If a person asserts a normative statement without being in any position to know if it is true or justify it in any way, the assertion might be called a matter of opinion. But normative claims can be backed by facts and reasons. Moreover, there are several well-accepted standards by which the relevance and the strength of those facts and reasons can be evaluated. Ethics is in large part an attempt to define the criteria of relevance and strength more clearly. Accordingly, we should not consign all normative statements to the category of matters of opinion. In contrast to free standing matters of normative opinions we should be aware that there can be well reasoned and factually supported normative claims. We will discuss the standards for normative reasoning more fully in Section 3.

1.6 Concerns of Ethics: Personal and Social

Ethics focuses on those human concerns and those normative statements that have important and immediate implications for human conduct. As such, ethics is concerned with a range of value judgments regarding human behavior. Not all value judgments are correctly understood as having ethical significance. The following normative statements would not ordinarily be understood as having ethical force:

- Brush your teeth after every meal.
- Allow the machine to warm up before making a copy.
- We should leave open the parking places near the door for our customers.
- Allow your coffee to cool before drinking it.
- Don't use a standard screwdriver for a Phillips screw.
- Change the engine oil every 3,000 miles.
- I enjoy listening to 94.7 FM.

Though these statements have immediate behavior implications, they concern personal taste, prudence, etiquette, or good technique. In ordinary circumstances, such matters lack a certain moral seriousness or social weightiness. However, the ethicist is concerned with behavior that either entails significant harm or benefit for others or for oneself; is in accord with or in violation of duties; or involves matters of justice, autonomy, respect or disrespect for human or moral rights. Examples of statements expressing ethical concerns are the following:

- Real-estate fraud is irreparably harmful to retired persons.
- Murder is wrong, but not capital punishment.
- Deception by government is destroying democracy.
- You should almost always respond to a cry for help.
- Police services should be distributed equitably within the city.
- Alzheimer's victims should not be allowed to drive a car.
- Verbal contracts are obligations which ought to be kept.
- The right to live is a fundamental concern.
- Harmonizing one's abilities with one's desires is important.
- The state has no right to do what its citizens cannot do.
- No one should be made the object of a medical experiment.
- Nuclear power plants should never be licensed.

How, then, are personal ethics and social ethics to be distinguished? *Personal ethics* is the normative study of individual conduct, and *social ethics* is the normative study of communal conduct. If the question of euthanasia is treated as one about the possible behavior of an individual, as in "Would it be right for me to perform a mercy killing?", then the problem is one of personal ethics. On the other hand, if the normative issue is a possible communal act, as in "Should euthanasia be legalized?", then the problem is one of social ethics. In terms of content, then, there is a considerable overlap between personal ethics and social ethics. The difference comes in whether we are active collectively or as individuals. This, in turn, raises interesting questions regarding our personal responsibility for collective decisions.

1.7 Characterizing the Study of Ethics

Ethics is a disciplined study of normative problems from an unbiased, fair-minded, rational point of view. Its aim is to arrive at reasonable resolutions of normative issues through the use of clear thinking, rational argumentation and careful consideration of relevant information. In other words, ethics strives for well-thought-out, justifiable value judgments.

In pursuing these normative questions, ethics bridges the gap between theory and practice. Obviously it is desirable to reach a reasonable resolution to the moral problem presented by a given situation. There are practical concerns such as determining the obligations or responsibilities of people and groups: "What should I do?" and "What should we do?" But there is also the vital theoretical concern for finding those more general ethical principles or more universal moral standards which can be relied upon in a variety of situations: theories of moral obligation, theories of praise and blame, and theories about the meaning of individual good and social well-being.

Ethics has a very practical side, and yet it is not to be confused with other practical (and important) human activities that are also concerned with human behavior. Ethics is not advising; it is not counseling. Ethics is not concerned with telling people what is best for them; it is not concerned with helping people to deal in a more emotionally stable way with their personal problems. While the study of ethics can lead to emotionally agreeable, sound personal decisions, ethics is about the ways those decisions should be made and the principles they should be based on. But, if you approach the study of ethics expecting to be told what is best for you or expecting to have your emotional problems settled by examining some of the most powerful, life-shaping ideas in our civilization, you may be surprised to find that these hopes are not the ones which ethicists seek to fulfill.

Ethics is not values-clarification or psychoanalysis. These techniques can help people find out what they really value or prize. The concern of ethics, however, is not with what one *does* value or with what one *says* one values, but with what one *should* or *ought* value. Similarly ethics does not aim at saying what a corporation or a community *does* consider important, or what it *proclaims* to be important, but at what a corporation or a community *ought* to consider important.

Ethics should not be confused with *behavior modification*, which aims to alter how a person acts—often manipulating rewards and punishments to reinforce desired behaviors, or even using drug therapy. Ethics does not concern itself with forcing, causing, or encouraging people to act in certain ways, except in the sense that giving reasons should lead reasonable, objective people to form intelligent, informed decisions about how they ought to behave. The immediate goal of ethics is knowledge. Knowledge can guide behavior, but it does not program that behavior; nor does knowledge force or manipulate a person to do one thing rather than another.

Just as there are similar yet different concerns on the practical side, there are also similar yet different concerns on the theoretical side. Ethics is not to be confused with the social or behavioral sciences. Unlike sociology or anthropology, the concern of ethics is not with describing the values, norms, or customs of a given community. Unlike psychology, the concern is not with discovering motivations nor with explaining and predicting human behavior. Unlike history, economics, or political science, the concern is not with understanding the causes or factors that contributed to economic, social, or political phenomena past or present. The primary concerns of the scientist are with explanation and prediction in order to make possible knowledge and control. Scientists tell how the world is, why the world is that way, and how it is likely to be in the future if such-and-such happens or does not happen. In contrast, the primary concern of the ethicist is with how the world *should* be, what will make it *better*, how we *ought* to live.

The problems of ethics are problems about conduct. They are problems about what people *should do* and *how they ought to behave*. They may be questions about goals, such as, "Should legislation be passed to support the maxim of equal pay for equal work?" or "In the name of freedom of expression should a responsible book publisher produce a manuscript which millions regard as religiously offensive?" They may be questions about principles, such as, "Does the principle of professional confidentiality take priority over the principle of protecting innocent persons from harm?" They may be questions about the means to a goal, such as "Is domestic price fixing for higher profits justified in today's world market economy?" Whether they concern principles, goals or means, they remain questions about human behavior and whether or not it is moral, justified, or right.

EXERCISES

1. Which of the following are normative statements? (1.1-1.4)
   (a) Any action which produces emotional pain is wrong.
   (b) A person shot through the heart will likely die.
   (c) Racism is a function of ignorance.
   (d) American foreign policy is a product of political compromise.
   (e) Given two equally qualified candidates for a job, one a woman and the other a man, we should hire the woman.

(f) Always respect and obey your parents no matter what they say.

(g) Individual autonomy ought to be respected at all costs.

(h)There is nothing more important than human life.

(i) Polygamy is no longer openly practiced in New York.

(j) Life under communist rule is not worth living.

2. Below is a set of statements. If a statement is purely descriptive, mark it *PD*. If the statement is a normative statement that has descriptive implications, mark it *N* for normative and then state its descriptive implication. (1.4)

   (a) The architecture of the church is gothic.

   (b) Terry was rude to my parents.

   (c) Gerald came up with a clever way to solve that problem.

   (d) The corporate board of directors is oppressive.

   (e) The skilled crafts union is conducting a membership drive.

   (f) The new weapons system is dangerously unreliable.

   (g) Fluorescent light is cool light.

   (h) The cooler a light, the less wasteful it is of energy.

   In the above statements knowledge of the meanings of the terms involved is sufficient to determine if the statement is purely descriptive or if it has an evaluative component. The meaning of some words, however, is sufficiently unclear that reasonable persons might disagree about whether some statements using them were purely descriptive or contained an evaluative component. The following are examples:

   (i) Norma is healthy.

   (j) Centralized government is inefficient.

   (k) Herbert manipulates people.

   (l) Susan is an alcoholic.

3. Which of the following specific directives would properly fall within the scope of ethics? (1.6-1.7)

   (a) Use plutonium if you wish to build effective atomic weapons.

   (b) An antiabortion amendment should be added to the U.S. Constitution.

   (c) Bribery of foreign officials by international corporations should be prohibited.

   (d) Using anabolic steroids is a poor idea.

   (e) When bowling, only one's waist should bend.

   (f) Nuclear warfare kills innocent people and is, therefore, wrong.

   (g) Never break implicit promises.

   (h) Company property is not for your personal use.

   (i) Put savings aside regularly.

   (j) Funds should be set aside for non-fossil fuel development.

4. Which of the following expresses a general concern of ethics? (1.6–1.7)

   (a) A concern to determine whether a particular act is right or wrong.

   (b) A concern to list the values held by a given community.

   (c) A concern to help people learn what motivates their activity.

   (d) A concern to encourage people to act ethically.

   (e) A concern to discover standards or principles that justify moral evaluations.

   (f) A concern to describe how people behave in society.

   (g) A concern to determine how people ought to behave.

   (h) A concern to protect human life.

   (i) A concern to replace religion with humanism.

5. Write two normative statements and two non-normative statements about each of the following. (1.3) At least one normative statement in each set should express a concern of ethics.
   (a) National elections   (e) Defense spending
   (b) Consumerism   (f) Genetic control
   (c) Liberal education   (g) Pornography
   (d) American funeral practices   (h) Suicide

6. Compare and contrast normative statements that express value judgments with non-normative statements expressing factual judgments. Using examples from the case study, compare and contrast the fact vs. opinion distinction with the normative vs. non-normative distinction. (1.1–1.5)

7. Briefly state the chief concerns of personal ethics and social ethics. Give examples of the problems they would treat. (1.6–1.7)

8. Explain how ethics differs from both the behavioral sciences and counseling techniques. (1.7)

9. Write two paragraphs on the topic "Pornography Today." Compose one entirely of non-normative statements and the other entirely of normative statements.

DISCUSSION QUESTIONS

1. In the case study Judith claimed that a person cannot escape his upbringing. Clarify that claim and determine if it is true. If it is, what does that mean for the enterprise of ethics? If it is not, how should one go about forming one's ethical opinions?

2. To what extent is an individual responsible for the ethical decisions made by communities of which she is a member? For example, as a junior executive, would a person be responsible if the corporation she worked for knowingly engaged in a brutally harmful policy just for the sake of increased profit? What if the person were a senior executive who unsuccessfully argued against the policy?

3. Does the fact that the large majority of reasonable and responsible people agree on some normative view mean that this consensus view is right? If not, give a counter-example and defend it.

4. We mentioned general or universal ethical principles on which specific ethical decisions can be based. Can you think of any examples of what these principles might be? If not, how will you find out?

ANSWERS TO SELECTED EXERCISES

1. The normative statements are *a, e, f, g, h, j*.

2. (a) *PD.*
   (b) *N:* Terry's behavior offends people.

(c) *N:* Gerald figures things out.

(d) *N:* The Government restricts persons.

(e) *PD.*

(f) *N:* The weapons system breaks down in dangerous ways.

(g) *PD.*

(h) *N:* Cool lights use less energy than hot lights to produce the same amount of light.

3. The questions of ethics are *b, c, d, f, g, h, j.*

4. The questions of ethics are *a, e, g.*

5. Here are some examples of correct answers.

(a) Non-Normative: Voter registration is declining. Few people today value their right to vote. Normative: Good citizens should vote for the candidates of their choice. Presidential campaigning should be carefully regulated.

(c) Non-Normative: Fewer students today value a liberal education.   Critics are currently questioning the worth of the liberal arts. Normative: There is nothing more fulfilling than liberal education. Liberal education is a waste of time.

(f) Non-Normative: We still know little about genetic control.   The prospects of influencing character through genetic control frighten many. Normative: We should not tamper with nature's genetic code.   Genetic manipulation should be used to prevent birth defects.

(h) Non-Normative: Suicide is increasing in New York.   Addicts frequently commit suicide. Normative: Self-sacrificing suicide is permissible. All suicide is wrong.

Section 2
INTERPRETING NORMATIVE CLAIMS

Normative assertions can be interpreted in many conflicting ways. Using the philosophical tool of conceptual analysis, we will distinguish some of the possible meanings normative statements can have and distinguish among a number of kinds of values. In the process we will briefly sketch the positions of ethical nihilism, ethical skepticism, ethical emotivism and ethical relativism, and we will look at one descriptive theory of moral development to see what implications it might have for reasoning in ethics. After reading Section 2, you should be able to:

- Distinguish subjectivist and objectivist interpretations of normative statements.
- Distinguish normative statements about intrinsic or instrumental values.
- Distinguish normative statements about absolute or relative values.
- Give examples of each interpretation of normative statement listed above.
- Describe the strategies and the role of conceptual analysis in the interpretation of normative statements.
- Contrast normative and non-normative interpretations of Ethical Relativism, Ethical Skepticism and Ethical Nihilism.

THE CASE OF BOYCE SUGAR ENTERPRISES

C. J. Mogle, an executive vice-president of Boyce Sugar Enterprises, was asked to testify regarding the corporation's position on proposed legislation permitting trade with certain Latin American countries such as Cuba and Nicaragua. After the congressional hearing he agreed to an interview with a national TV anchor, Anita Vantage. Here is a transcript of the interview:

VANTAGE: What do you think about the proposed legislation to permit sugar importation from communist controlled Latin American countries?

MOGLE: It's a good policy.

VANTAGE: Could you be more specific? What do you mean?

MOGLE: I mean I like the policy. I feel good about it.

VANTAGE: Why? Are you saying you believe the legislation will benefit the balance of trade and that it will bring down domestic prices?

MOGLE: No. I like it because I generally favor legislation designed to benefit international business.

VANTAGE: Are there any other reasons why you think the legislation is good?

MOGLE: Certainly. I expect it will benefit Boyce Enterprises.

VANTAGE: Are you saying what's good for Boyce Sugar Enterprises is good for the country?

MOGLE: No, I didn't say it would be good for the country. I was talking about Boyce Sugar. It will be good for us.

VANTAGE: Do you feel that legislation should serve the public good or the good of only a few?

MOGLE: Why, the public good, of course, unless it puts certain businesses at a disadvantage in the international market.

VANTAGE: Like Boyce Sugar.

MOGLE: Yes, exactly.

VANTAGE: In your view, if the pending sugar legislation fails, will it disadvantage Boyce Enterprises in the international market?

MOGLE: Why yes, its failure would cut into our projected profits.

VANTAGE: But wouldn't it be to the advantage of domestic producers to keep Latin American sugar out of the U.S. market.

MOGLE: Yes, it might help the domestic companies, but that's not so good. The sooner we put domestic sugar producers out of business, the sooner we can more carefully regulate the sugar industry.

VANTAGE: What do you mean, Mr. Mogle? Are regulations needed?

MOGLE: Oh, I don't mean regulations in the sense of "laws"; I mean Boyce
Enterprises will be able to control sugar production, distribution,
and ultimately the sugar prices throughout the Western
Hemisphere.

VANTAGE: May I ask you a more personal question? What would you say if a
domestic producer tried to put Boyce out of business?

MOGLE: I wouldn't like it at all. It should be illegal! And I'm not happy with
your obvious efforts to embarrass Boyce Sugar on national TV!
Good day, Ms. Vantage. This interview is over!

2.1 Alternative Interpretations

In the case study Anita Vantage tries to interpret Mogle's normative claim that
the proposed legislation is good. She starts by trying to figure out what Mogle
means by saying that the legislation is good. To do this she suggests two possible reasons why Mogle might want to call the legislation good: that the legislation would benefit the balance of trade and that it would bring down domestic
prices. The implications are first, that these are desirable goals and, second, that
any policies which help to achieve these goals are, thereby, good. Mogle, on the
other hand, rejects these reasons and offers an alternative interpretation of his
claim. He asserts that when he said the policy was good he meant simply that he
liked it. Vantage, sensing that the answer is incomplete, presses him for his reasons. Only then does Mogle explain that he favors the policy because it would
benefit his corporation. The interview illustrates that a normative claim such as
"X is good" can be interpreted in a variety of ways.

If we are going to make any progress in deciding which normative claims
are more reasonable than others, we first must short-circuit the disagreements
that can arise over how normative statements such as "X is good" are to be
understood. We must begin, as Vantage did, by locating the speaker's intended
interpretation of his or her normative claims. Only when we understand what a
person means can we assess the strength of the person's reasons offered in
support of his claims.

To discover how Mogle intends his normative claim to be interpreted,
Vantage presses several times for clarifications. Only slowly does Mogle reveal his
position. Vantage is fully aware that the simple claim "It's a good policy" can be
difficult to interpret correctly. Out of fairness, we must strive to interpret a person's
claim the way the person intends it to be taken. It is not our goal to put words in the
mouths of others; nor, if we are being intellectually honest, should we allow
ourselves to misconstrue things out of laziness, inattention, carelessness, or because
we might want to disagree.

2.2 Conceptual Analysis

One of the chief tools used by philosophers, among others, to secure the needed clarifications of vague or ambiguous assertions is conceptual analysis. *Conceptual analysis is the methodical examination of words, ideas, and concepts with a view toward clarifying their meaning.* By examining various nuances of usage and meaning, and by comparing and contrasting possible instances, we can isolate the precise sense of a vague or ambiguous concept and so identify the exact meaning of a particular statement.

To take a normative example, suppose we are presented with the claim "Public nudity is obscene." First, it is not immediately clear whether this is a normative or non-normative claim. *Obscene* may be used here to mean *unchaste,* the implication being that public nudity is undesirable. Or *obscene* may be used here in a non-normative sense, as in "found to be offensive by at least 60 percent of the population." In this case the claim that public nudity is obscene becomes the non-normative sociological claim that at least 60 percent of the population finds public nudity offensive. Second, the term *nudity* needs clarification. How many articles of apparel and what kind should a person be wearing in order not to be described as nude? Is nude different than naked? Does the person's condition make a difference—for example, if the person has suffered an accident and the paramedics strip off garments to apply first aid? And then, there's the adjective, *public* Is standing nude in front of an uncurtained window, *public* nudity? How about taking a shower in a public bath? As the different but related cases begin to emerge, we can more clearly draw out their relevant similarities and differences. And understanding the matter more fully puts us in the position to make more careful and thoughtful normative claims.

In addition to the strategies of contrasting cases and exploring the nuances of a term's meaning, philosophers believe that it is often possible to remove problematic vagueness and ambiguity by analyzing complex, unfamiliar, and difficult concepts or ideas into their simpler, more familiar, better-understood constituent ideas. For example, the concept *hexagon* can be analyzed into the familiar ideas "being a closed figure," "having straight sides," "having sides of equal length," and "having exactly six sides." The hope is that through such analysis the original concept will be clarified.

Often the fruits of a systematic and complete conceptual analysis are presented in the form of a definition. For example:

> "*A* is a bachelor at time *t*" is definitionally equivalent to "*A* is a male, *A* is an adult, *A* is not married at time *t,* and there is no time *t′* such that *t′* is earlier than *t* and *A* was married at *t′.*"

The conditions set forth in the definition are usually viewed as those that must be met if the term being defined is to be used correctly. Thus, each of the conditions is seen to be an essential or necessary prerequisite; the conditions taken as a group are intended to be complete or sufficient for the proper use of the term. For example, you cannot be a bachelor unless you satisfy all four of the conditions given, and further, you are a bachelor if you do satisfy all four.

One way conceptual analysis is in personal and social ethics is as a means to achieving full and precise definitions of key concepts. For example, here is the analysis of the normative concept of a *supererogatory virtuous act* in terms of simpler component ideas:

> "A performs a supererogatory virtuous act by doing X at time t" is definitionally equivalent to "A performs X at time t, X is a virtuous act, and the performance of X by A at t is over and above any of A's duties at time t."

Another strategy conceptual analysis uses is to relate two equally complex ideas to each other. This can be done by tracing each of the complex ideas back to their common conceptual roots, thus, establishing their connection to each other. For example, one might ask whether or not it is possible to be free in an unjust society. The concepts of freedom and justice are both relatively complex. However, we can establish important connections between these ideas using conceptual analysis. We can, thereby, argue that genuine freedom cannot exist in a completely unjust society. To prove this we would have to show that there is a conceptual inconsistency between genuine freedom and total injustice. The primary data in this proof would not be the empirical information that can be gained through social psychology. Rather it would be the conceptual information available through a careful analysis of the two concepts.

We can profitably employ conceptual analysis in ethics. Starting with problematic normative words, such as *good* or *right*, and moving on to the variety of justifications offered for normative claims, and the pros and cons of various normative positions, we will have plenty of opportunities to root out troublesome vagueness and ambiguity, draw detailed comparisons of cases, state careful definitions, and explore conceptual connections. As a start, let's look at some different interpretations of "X is good."

2.3 Subjectivist and Objectivist Interpretations

One important step in understanding normative statements is to find out whether a particular claim is meant to be taken subjectively or objectively. In the case study, Vantage uses conceptual analysis as a way of determining whether Mogle's position is *subjectivist* or *objectivist*. The reasons she first suggests, (promoting trade and lowering domestic prices), are objectivist. In general, an objectivist interpretation of "X is good" is that X possesses some characteristic that makes it worthy of preference, desire, or value, independently of the actual preferences or desires of the speaker. One can express the objectivist interpretation using statements such as "X is a worthy goal," "X is really the just thing to do even though we would not like it," "X is our duty." *On the objectivist interpre-*

tation a normative claim becomes a statement about what in or about X makes X worthy of being preferred independently of the speaker's actual personal preferences or feelings concerning X.

Mogle, however, finds neither of the interpretations offered by Vantage to his liking, and instead he offers a subjectivist interpretation of his position. The subjectivist interpretation of "X is good" is that the speaker prefers or values X. This preference can be expressed in many ways—for example, "I like X," "I approve of X," "I favor X," or "I feel good about X." *On the subjectivist interpretation a normative claim becomes a claim about the speaker and what that speaker in fact desires or prefers.*

2.4 Ethical Emotivism, Ethical Nihilism, and Ethical Skepticism

How one would go about justifying a normative assertion taken in its objectivist sense is the topic of Section 3 of this chapter. As to the subjectivist interpretation, being entitled to make the claim is largely a matter of coming to understand and express how one feels. In most cases we do not fault people for feeling the way they feel. (Although we certainly do not agree that everyone always has the right to feel as they do, nor do we approve of people always acting on their feelings or giving free reign to their expression.) But if normative claims are nothing more than expressions of feelings, then it is easy to see why some thinkers came to the view that such claims were without intellectual substance or significance. Earlier in this century the subjectivist interpretation of normative claims led some to *Ethical Emotivism*, the view that normative claims were simply curious ways of ventilating one's emotional responses to actions, policies, persons or situations or else ways of evoking emotional responses in others. Holders of ethical emotivism argued that, as explosions of feelings, ethical claims were nonsensical and, as such, could never be justified or refuted. Happily, a fuller understanding and appreciation of the subtlety and richness of language and the nuances of human interaction has led us past myopic ethical emotivism. But it did teach us an important lesson. There is a sense in which, when people say something is good or bad, they often may also be saying that they feel positively or negatively toward it. However, we know of many cases when we must say "X is good, but I don't like it." Think of going on a diet, putting off a vacation, cleaning the bathroom, obeying a strict company policy, freeing a known criminal because of a legal technicality, or undergoing a stressful but necessary interpersonal confrontation.

While we are on the topic of non-standard views, we should mention two more. *Ethical Nihilism* is the view that any normative claim that something is or is not desirable cannot be true. Taken as a descriptive statement about human psychology, ethical nihilism is obviously false. There are plenty of counter-examples, things people willingly classify as desirable or undesirable. But *as a normative theory, ethical nihilism asserts that there is nothing which we ought to desire or not desire.* As such, it is a claim about how we should conduct our lives as a result of an assumption about the nature of reality. It asserts that there is nothing in the universe, no state of affairs, no sensation, no person, no relationship which is worthy of being called good or bad. If a person gets sick and dies of an infection, that is not bad. It is simply a case where the germ species prevailed over the human species. If a person falls in love, that is simply a social-psychological phenomenon, but in itself, it is neither good nor bad. Ethical nihilism in its normative sense presupposes a deep, unbridgeable fissure between the realm of existence and the realm of value, such that nothing in existence has either positive or negative value. This conceptual and metaphysical assumption is contrary to the assumptions which one might find in those theories about reality which begin by asserting that existence is fundamentally good or fundamentally bad. While we do not have the time to go into the relationship between metaphysical assumptions and normative theories, is important to know that there are such relationships. Every world view says something about the nature of reality and the nature of value and how they relate. Ethical nihilism is one such view.

Whereas ethical nihilists say there is nothing which is worthy of being called good or bad, and ethical emotivists say that normative claims make no objective sense, *ethical skeptics think that normative claims make sense but simply cannot be justified.* The skeptics say they can understand "X is good" in its objectivist interpretation, and, having done so, they doubt that one can ever prove such a claim no matter what X is. Ethical skepticism, like the other brands of skepticism, trades on the idea that proof requires absolute certainty. Knowledge, for skeptics, is more than an informed and well-considered judgment; it is more than certainty beyond reasonable doubt; it is more than scientific confirmation. The skeptics assume that knowledge means certainty beyond all possible (rational or irrational) doubt. Whether the standard of certainty which skepticism assumes, is a reasonable standard is itself a serious question. How can the skeptics prove they are not demanding too much? If scientific confirmation exists when the chances of events randomly turning out the way they did are less than 1 in a 100, and if the law allows that a criminal is guilty if a jury judges it to be so beyond a reasonable doubt, then why should the justifications for normative claims be held to a standard which other, very important non-normative claims are not held to?

If ethical skepticism is taken as a non-normative claim about the quality of proof required to establish a normative claim, then, except for repeating the assertion "That's still not proof enough," its position has yet to be clearly articulated and defended. On the other hand, if ethical skepticism is the normative claim that we ought not to accept anything as sufficient proof of a normative claim, then it is self-defeating, for, as such, it is a normative claim also. In effect it would be recommending that we not accept anything as sufficient proof of itself. Just as ethical nihilism makes some questionable assumptions about reality, we can say ethical skepticism makes its own questionable assumptions about what knowledge and justification are really about.

Below we give a second case study. We will be using it momentarily to illustrate how one can further interpret normative claims by noting the kinds of values they appeal to. But, as you read the case, ask yourself whether the normative claims made are best interpreted as subjectivist or objectivist.

THE CASE OF THE TROUBLESOME TRUTH

I leaned back in my swivel chair and pressed sweaty hands against my aching temples. What was I supposed to do? I looked at the phone, thinking of the conversation I had just finished. Why did he call me? I would have been happier not knowing. Or would I?

If what I had learned was true, then my company was in for trouble. A hostile takeover bid is going to be announced in just three hours. If I was smart I would get my stock broker on the phone and buy every share of stock I could get. Then I would just hang on while the price soared. Let the big boys fight it out—my short term gains could be as much as 30%. Let's see, 30% of twenty-five-thousand dollars—and in less than a week's time too.

The truth is good, right? I mean, there's no such thing as a bad truth. The truth is what people always want. So, what should I have said when I found out about the hostile takeover? "No, stop. Don't tell me any more truthful information. Keep the truth to yourself! I'm weird, I don't want to know what's going to happen. I don't like knowing the truth."

And now that I know, how could it be wrong for me to use the truth? They say the truth will set us free. Well I'll settle for the quick seven thousand five hundred. Thank you. It may not mean retirement city, but it sure will cover a year's lease on a BMW.

Oh, I know, I know—insider trading is illegal. But that's just in this country. It's perfectly legal in Japan! So why is it wrong on one side of the Pacific and right on the other side? Aren't both nations single-mindedly devoted to the private accumulation of wealth and to national economic growth? So tell me why the U.S. outlaws what Japan extols.

I reached toward the phone, but hesitated. This isn't Japan. And laws should be obeyed. What if everyone went around breaking laws whenever their interests and the laws came into conflict? Why, it wouldn't even make sense to have laws. The idea of a law you follow only if you have no interest in not following is absurd. We have laws because we have interests and must sort out what to do in peaceful and equitable ways. I knew nobody would ever catch me. But still...

A quick $7,500!

What to do?

2.5 Intrinsic vs. Instrumental Values

Many normative statements give reasons why things are desirable or undesirable. Generally speaking, people have classified most things into those which are desirable (undesirable) in and of themselves and those which are useful (detrimental) as means to achieving some goal or end. *Things which are desirable (undesirable) in and of themselves are said to be intrinsic values, or intrinsically good (bad).* For example, people have generally thought of things such as pleasure, honor, wisdom, intelligence, virtue, life, liberty, and harmony as intrinsically desirable. Intrinsically undesirable things might include pain, ignorance, boredom, frustration, terror, infamy, and discord.

Things that are viewed as desirable (undesirable) because they are useful (detrimental) as means to further ends are called instrumental values or instrumentally good (bad). Money is often considered to be the chief instrumental good (asset), and poverty, therefore, the greatest instrumental evil (liability). The same item can be both an asset and a liability, depending on your goals. Some things, such as health, peace, and wisdom, can be viewed in terms of both their intrinsic and instrumental value. Indeed, most anything which is viewed as intrinsically good can also be recognized to be instrumentally valuable, that is, as contributing to the realization of other things which are valuable. The reverse, however, is not true. A piece of used chewing gum might be instrumentally valuable in a given situation, but it is not generally regarded as having much intrinsic value. In the case study the speaker sees truth as both an intrinsic and an instrumental value. Can you identify which of his claims indicate each of these values?

2.6 Absolute vs. Relative Values

Driving safely is something most people in our society regard as desirable in an absolute sense. *Anything a society deems good or worthy of desire for its own sake is an absolute value (at least in that society).* In our society, for example, safe, efficient, and fast transportation appears as an absolute value along with maximizing individual liberty, preserving a rule of law, respecting other persons, and respecting property rights.

In order to achieve safety on the highways in North America we have adopted the convention of driving on the right side of the road. In some countries, such as Great Britain and Australia, safety on the highways is achieved by following the convention of driving on the left side of the road. In North America, then, driving on the right is desirable. It is a relative good; that is, it is good relative to Canadian, U.S., and Mexican conventions. In Great Britain and Australia driving on the right is undesirable. No one questions the absolute value of safety, and we agree that driving on the same side of the road is safer than driving on whichever side we feel like. But which side is the safe side is relative to which country you are driving in. *Anything a society deems desirable as a convention or means of realizing its absolute values can be called a relative value in that society.*

In the previous case study the speaker notes that both the U.S. and Japan prize the accumulation of personal wealth and national economic growth. But how are these to be achieved? In one country insider trading is expressly forbidden for it is thought to inhibit the achievement of these goals; in the other it is permitted with the idea that it contributes toward achieving these goals.

It is generally thought desirable that dinner guests show courtesy and gratefulness to their host. In Western civilizations this is done by following the convention of sampling all of the foods offered and being sure to eat everything that one takes. In Eastern civilizations this is done by following the convention of taking only a portion of what is served and by always leaving some food uneaten. In the West we show how good the food is by consuming it; in the East we show how bountiful the meal is by leaving some food uneaten. Eating all of one's meal can be viewed as both desirable and undesirable relative to the two contrary conventions. However, the conventions that elicit different behavior both aim at the same absolute value—that is, expressing respect for the other person, in this case one's host.

Obeying the laws of society can be viewed as an absolute good. In the case study the speaker argues that to make a universal practice out of disobeying laws which work against one's interests would be to make a shambles of the concept of law itself. What sense would there be to say something was a law if whenever a person's own interests were involved the person could disregard the law? In part we have laws just because we must regulate how people act when their personal interests are involved.

In the case study the speaker also values laws because they contribute to the equitable and peaceful resolution of conflicting interests. A very strong case for obeying the laws and conventions of one's society rests on seeing in them relative rather than absolute value. It is desirable to follow the laws and conventions not because they are intrinsically desirable in themselves but because laws are instrumentally desirable. They are the ways a given society or community has arrived at for achieving its further social or communal ends, which ends it views as absolutely desirable.

Some absolute values may be common to all or most civilized communities. Avoiding unnecessary harm, respecting persons, promoting communal security—these values or goals seem to be very widely shared. There are, however, vast differences in the conventions established by various communities as they try to pursue even these widely shared goals. That the conventions vary is an empirical fact. Whether there are basic human values that transcend all these various conventions is a question we have not tried to settle here. We also have not touched the question of why a society has selected any particular things as its absolute values. But it is clear that they have been selected.

When we call something relatively good or bad, one meaning is that it is good or bad relative to an established social convention for achieving some goal. The concept of *relative* value also has meaning when no conventions are involved. This occurs when instrumental value is being judged. The same means (say, starting on a trip at 11:00 A.M.) may be good relative to one goal (getting all our work done before we leave), yet bad relative to another (reaching our destination before the storm strikes). In this sense *relative* means *useful for some purpose*. This second meaning of *relative* should not be confused with the first, where *relative* meant *conventional*. When you speak of relative values, be sure to make it clear which kind you are referring to, *in accord with social conventions* or *useful for some purpose*.

2.7 Ethical Relativism

Discussion of the comparative desirability or undesirability of various practices suggests an interesting problem: *Are ethical principles, themselves, relative?* As we did with the claim "Public nudity is obscene," we must first notice that this question can be interpreted in both a normative and a non-normative way.

Taken as a non-normative question we would be asking: "Are there differences in the moral standards of various communities or societies?" To find out, we would do careful anthropological, historical, and social research. We might find that people generally value more or less the same things the world over—perhaps health, safety, family, autonomy, the society of other intelligent persons. Or we might find that there are important differences, for example, that one society values aggressive, competitive, individual self-aggrandizement at the expense of all else, whereas another society values social harmony and communal accord even to the extent of refusing to take needed action unless there is no dissent.

As a non-normative question, whether or not ethical principles extend universally or are relative to given historical and cultural eras is an empirical issue. The affirmative answer to this empirical question is called *sociological relativism*. In one sense sociological relativism is obviously true. We have cited examples of differences in relative values which confirm sociological relativism. In another sense it is as yet unresolved. If it is taken as a question about there being cultural differences in the basic underlying absolute values, then maybe the answer will turn out to be "No."

Some studies in cognitive psychology suggest very strongly that humans, for all their cultural and social differences, basically progress through the same stages of moral development the world over. According to Lawrence Kohlberg (1964, 1984), for example, in the first stage our reasons are limited to avoiding the immediate negative consequences of doing something wrong. In the second stage satisfaction of our own needs is our paramount concern. In the third stage we seek the approval of significant others. The fourth stage is about following rules and doing what is expected of us just because those are our duties. Most of the time adults, Kohlberg claims, make moral decisions based on stage three and four reasons. In the fifth stage we look past the duties and laws to the social principles and values on which they are based. If you could understand our discussion about laws and conventions being good relative to some further goals, such as safety, then you are capable of understanding what Kohlberg calls stage five moral reasoning. Stage six, which is where we intend to go, moves us past the limits of one's own society and into the realm of universal ethical principles and a profound respect for persons. At level six, (a level Kohlberg says few people ever reach), a person can appeal to ethical principles and standards beyond those of her own society. In the way that Mohandas Ghandi or Martin Luther King, Jr., or Jesus Christ pointed out the need for moral change, a person at level six can seek to improve her own society and infuse it with a higher sense of what is right. Ethics is the exploration of these universal principles for it helps us understand respect for autonomy, justice, honesty, respecting persons, concern for the good of society taken as a whole, and honoring one's commitments.

The question, "Are ethical principles relative?" might also be taken as a normative rather than empirical question. In raising the normative question a person might be asking, "Is it desirable that there should be differences in the moral standards of different communities or societies?" Here, too, there is a crucial ambiguity. We may want to say "Yes" to ethical relativism if we are only agreeing that within one's society it is better to follow its conventions rather than those of another society. In the U.S. it is better to drive on the right, but in Australia you should drive on the left. This kind of ethical relativism (restricted to the relative values of a given society) seems highly desirable, one could argue, because social stability and security are the intrinsic goods promoted by conformity to established relative values. So, a person who maintains that one's duty is always to live by the conventions of the society in which one finds oneself would be an ethical relativist in the weaker sense of the term. The person would be saying in effect, "When in Rome do as the Romans do," provided we are talking about relative rather than absolute values.

Weak-sense ethical relativism may be a prudent policy, depending on one's assessment of the absolute values which a society's laws and conventions are designed to serve. But to blindly follow conventions, to limit one's thinking by refusing to consider the values which those conventions are designed to serve or the broader ethical principles beyond, is to close one's eyes to the entire realm of ethics. When people have offered this kind of thinking, ("I was only following orders, doing what was expected of me, doing my job,") their claims have not been accepted as sufficient to offset their violating one of society's absolute values, let alone violating such basic ethical principles as respect for life, or human rights.

Ethical relativism might also be taken as the stronger normative claim: "There ought to be differences in the most fundamental moral principles viewed as absolutely valuable by different human communities." How one would argue this, without also arguing that ethical relativism (as a normative principle itself) is not thereby self-defeated, seems difficult.   We may also want to reject this interpretation of ethical relativism if it means that there should be differences in the most basic moral principles of human communities. At least, before embracing this view, we should be given some reasons to show why it is a wise and prudent normative position to take regarding how societies ought to behave. Why should different societies have different absolute values? If that's what the strong-sense ethical relativist is proposing ought to happen, let him prove his case.

To accept ethical relativism in this, its strongest sense, is to say that there ought to be differences in the basic moral standards of different communities—for example, that persons ought to be respected in some societies but ought not to be respected in others. One reason it would be hard to defend rationally is that there would be no moral principles beyond those of a given society to which its defenders could appeal. Then there are the practical problems of applying the view. How would we, as faithful relativists, decide how many members (or what percentage of the members) of a group would have to accept a moral principle for it to become operative for that group? Also, what if there was something about a society we did not approve of, say its criminal justice system? We would have a hard time justifying the desirability of any changes in the society's existing standards. Improvements would seem impossible, for the possibility of an improvement implies a standard outside the community against which those of the community are being judged, but strong-sense ethical relativism says there should be no such external criteria or principles. At this point, the case for ethical relativism as a normative theory about absolute values seems seriously flawed, conceptually self-defeating, unworkable, and wrong-headed.

EXERCISES

1. What is conceptual analysis? From what you have learned so far, state how it functions in ethics. (2.1, 2.2)
2. Provide subjectivist reasons that might be offered in support of each of the following normative claims. (2.3)
   (a) Cigarette smoking in public places should be prohibited by law.
   (b) It is wrong for public officials to take bribes.
   (c) Keep off the grass.
   (d) Prostitution should be legalized.
   (e) Irresponsible sexual activity is bad.
   (f) Avenge injuries done to you.
   (g) Never harm another—even in self-defense.
3. Provide objectivist reasons that might be offered in support of each of the normative claims in Exercise 2. (2.1)
4. State the difference between subjectivist and objectivist interpretations of normative claims. (2.1)

5. Give a normative and a non-normative interpretation of ethical nihilism and ethical skepticism. How would each of the four views describe the statement "Apartheid social policies are wrong?" (2.4)

6. Recall the listing in 2.5 of things that many have thought of as being intrinsically valuable: pleasure, honor, wisdom, intelligence, virtue, life, liberty, and harmony. Provide normative statements that give expression to the intrinsic value (or lack of it) of each of these things. (2.5)

7. Working with the list of things thought to be intrinsically valuable in Exercise 5, provide normative statements that express the instrumental value (or lack of it) of other things that may be thought of as means to those desirable ends. (2.5)

8. What is the difference between something intrinsically desirable and something instrumentally desirable? (2.5)

9. Suppose that justice, health, and safety are held to be of absolute value. Provide for each of these two conventions that may be understood as promoting these values in differing ways. (2.6)

10. Here are five arguments. Classify the normative principle operative in each as an appeal to absolute or relative normative concerns. (2.6)

    (a) Reverse discrimination procedures should be enacted into law because with proper safeguards they promote justice.

    (b) Polygamy should be considered seriously in circumstances where through warfare the male population has been severely reduced.

    (c) International corporations should respect the sovereignty of the states in which they do business lest international harmony be undermined.

    (d) Involuntary euthanasia should never be condoned, for it can never take appropriate account of the wishes of the person who is to die.

    (e) I exposed the corpse of my dead husband to the elements because that was the custom of the tribe with whom we were living.

11. What is the difference between something that is absolutely desirable and something that is relatively desirable in a given society? Give three examples of each. (2.6)

12. Define ethical relativism in both a non-normative and normative sense. Characterize the difference between weak-sense ethical relativism and strong-sense ethical relativism. In terms of the motto, "When in Rome do as the Romans do," what might a weak-sense ethical relativist not do?

DISCUSSION QUESTIONS

1. Make a list of at least ten values which are both instrumentally and intrinsically valuable. Justify each item on the list. Rank order the list in terms of intrinsic values. Have someone else do the same thing and compare lists. Now reconcile any differences which might exist between the list by giving reasons why one ordering is superior to the other.

2. We mentioned Kohlberg's theory about the six stages of moral development. His theory is not the only theory of how we learn to be moral and how we make moral decisions. Other psychologists, like Carol Gilligan (1982), who study how we do

make moral decisions emphasize that there is a personal/impersonal dimension which must be taken into account. We tend to treat our more intimate acquaintances one way and other people with whom we are not friends or associates with a different standard. What are the normative implications, if any, of such scientific facts and theories? Just because Kohlberg has identified six stages, ought we to strive to reach the highest level of reasoning or is it justifiable to remain at one of the lower levels?

3. We were rather critical of ethical emotivism, ethical nihilism, ethical skepticism and ethical relativism. How might a defender of one or more of these theories respond to our criticisms? Using conceptual analysis decide whether it makes sense to hold more than one of these four theories at the same time, or are they mutually exclusive?

4. Consider the speaker's moral quandary in the Case of the Troublesome Truth. In the objectivist sense, what ought the speaker to do?

ANSWERS TO SELECTED EXERCISES

2. Here are some examples of correct answers:
   (a) I don't like to have to put up with the foul odor.
   (b) I detest trampled lawns.
   (f) I approve of manly responses.

3. Here are some examples of correct answers:
   (a) Such smoking poses a serious threat to public health.
   (e) Such activity may well lead to serious post marital guilt feelings.
   (g) A world where this was accepted would be more peaceful.

5. EN non norm: "Apartheid has no value; we view it as neither good nor bad."
   ES norm: "Don't ascribe value to apartheid, it is worthy of none."
   ES non-norm: "It is not possible to prove apartheid has any value."
   ES norm: "You should not bother trying to prove apartheid has any value."

6. Here are some examples of such statements:
   (a) Only pleasure is a good in itself.
   (d) Wisdom is its own satisfaction.
   (e) Intelligence in and of itself is worth little. It has value only as a means to the good life.

7. Here are some examples of such statements:
   (b) Suicide is wrong because it is dishonorable.
   (e) Discipline is valuable in promoting the development of virtues.
   (g) Sex-role socialization is morally objectionable to the extent that it inhibits the free development of human potential.

9. Here are some examples of such conventions:
   (a) Justice: (1) Presume that the accused is innocent until proven guilty. (2) Presume that the accused is guilty unless proven innocent.
   (b) Health: (1) Provide emergency care first for those in greatest danger of death. (2) Provide emergency care first for those whom one has the best chance to aid.
   (c) Safety: (1) To prevent accidents with pedestrians require that bicyclists ride in the street. (2) To prevent accidents with cars require that bicyclists ride on the sidewalks.

10. In argument (b) the value of polygamy changes with the circumstances of the need to insure the future of the species. In (e) the exposing of the corpse is valued because it was the custom of the tribe with which the widow lived.

11. Here are some examples: (1) In Eskimo society exposing the elderly to the cold so that they might die was thought to be the best means of promoting the survival of the most members of the community. (2) In our society we value absolutely the health of mothers of newborn children. When medical knowledge was less valued than today, this absolute value was promoted by the custom of confining new mothers to bed for extended periods of time.

Section 3
JUSTIFYING NORMATIVE CLAIMS

Objective, fair-minded, rational people give reasons on behalf of their normative claims. Of course, some reasons are better than others. We begin Section 3 by characterizing justifications and distinguishing them from a number of pseudo-justifications. Then we focus on the ways in which justifications in personal and social ethics are susceptible to rational evaluation with emphasis on the matter of providing factual support. After reading this section, you should be able to:

- Compare and contrast offering a justification for a normative claim and doing any of the following: stating one's motivations, appealing to someone's emotions as a means to elicit certain behavior, rationalizing one's position, mentioning the source of one's views, and offering excuses.
- Give examples of each of the above.
- Distinguish ways in which attempted justification for a normative claim can fail such as by relying on false, irrelevant, or inconclusive factual support or relying on normative principles which are not universalizable.
- Give examples of the above.

3.1 Seeking Reasons

An important step toward understanding what people mean by their normative claims is to ask for reasons why we should accept their normative views. Vantage challenged Mogle in precisely this way in the case study at the beginning of Section 2. She tried to make Mogle reveal his reasons for preferring the pending sugar legislation. Besides offering us further insights into what people mean, hearing their arguments and reasons often helps us take some position on their normative claims ourselves. For example, one of Mogle's reasons for favoring the legislation was that it "was good for Boyce Sugar." We may not share the desire to benefit Boyce Enterprises; we may even be tempted to view that reason as grounds to reject the legislation.

However, until we hear a person's reasons, it is very hard to stake out our own rational response to the person's normative claims.

The goal of presenting reasons for normative claims is to develop arguments that establish the truth and wisdom of those claims. We should strive for *reasons that would persuade unbiased, informed, rational people that our normative claims are, beyond reasonable doubt, correct.* We shall call such reasons *justifications.* In the case study Vantage suggests some possible arguments in support of the view that the legislation is desirable for the country. Her arguments can be reconstructed as follows:

1. (a) Whatever improves the balance of trade is good for the country.
   (b) The pending legislation would improve the balance of trade.

   _____

   (c) So, the legislation is good for the country.

2. (a) Whatever lowers domestic prices is good for the country.
   (b) The legislation would lead to lower domestic sugar prices, and, in turn, to generally lower domestic food prices.

   _____

   (c) So, the legislation is good for the country.

3. (a) Whatever is good for Boyce Enterprises is good for the country.
   (b) The legislation, according to Mogle, is good for Boyce.

   _____

   (c) So, it is good for the country.

As you study ethics, you will encounter a wide variety of arguments. Not all of them will be structured like the three simple examples above. Actually there is considerable variation and subtlety in the structure of arguments people offer as proofs in support of their normative claims. However, it is reasonable to ask (a) whether that which is offered in support of a normative claim is in fact a justification or merely a pseudo-justification and (b) whether a purported justification meets the minimum requirements of inferential and factual adequacy applicable in ethics.

3.2 Pseudo-Justifications

Giving reasons is a response to the question: "Why should we accept your normative claim as true?" But, there are a number of other things that people confuse with giving solid reasons. That is, there are a number of other ways to understand the "Why?" question which have little or nothing to do with finding out why a claim is true. For example, people could give their motivations, appeal to emotions, make up excuses, cite the source of their views, or contrive something plausible to say which they really do not believe themselves. We will call these other kinds of responses *pseudo-justifications.* The temptation to use pseudo-justifications derives from many sources—all the way from innocence and intellectual ignorance to the fear, stubbornness, pride or deceit associated with wanting to cling to one's prejudices or avoid taking responsibility for one's actions. Know these; that way you can avoid confusion as you attempt to support your own views and avoid being misled as you attempt to understand and evaluate the support others offer for their views.

When we say something is a pseudo-justification, we mean it should not be taken as a justification at all. We are not saying it is a weak justification in contrast to a strong one, we are saying that *it does not even qualify to be evaluated as a justification, good or bad.* Whatever pseudo-justifications do socially, inter-personally or psychologically, they do not give rational grounds for believing that one's normative claims are (or might be) true. They are not arguments (strong or weak) in support of one's normative claims. Instead, they direct attention elsewhere, such as: why the speaker wants to believe the claim; where the claim originated; why the speaker should not be held accountable for the claim; why someone should act on the claim; or why the listener might want to believe the claim. Let's look at some commonly troublesome kinds of pseudo-justifications more closely.

3.3 Justifications vs. Motivations

Giving a justifying reason is not the same as explaining one's *motivations.* People are motivated to act by such things as ambition, anger, desperation, fear, friendship, grief, hope, jealousy, and love. It is possible to answer the question, "Why did you do X?" by citing one's motivations. For example, one might say, "I did it because I loved them," or, "I did it because I was afraid." Such a listing of one's motivations for acting is not to be confused, however, with giving reasons that justify normative claims. To give such reasons is to answer the question, "Why did you do X?" by citing the normative considerations that support the belief that the action is correct. The contrast is between providing an account of facts about oneself that led one to act as opposed to presenting a justification for the action itself. For example, a governor may be motivated out of political self-interest to sign an important bill. Be that as it may, the governor cannot justify signing the bill by appeal to her personal political motivation. The justification has to be in terms of reasons why the bill is a good bill and why it should be signed into law. Note that if the governor decides to sign the bill out of a motivation of political self-interest, that does not necessarily make the bill a bad law. Motivations in and of themselves do not count as justifications *for or against* the normative claim "X is not good."

Motivations are not entirely disconnected from justifications, however. For example, a manufacturer advertises products to sell them for profit. But when it claims its products are of good quality, pointing its profit motive will not justify such claims. "We want to make money" is not a reason in support of "this product is good." But, taking into consideration the manufacturer's motivations and interests is part of assessing its credibility. After examining the facts, we might decide that the manufacturer is very credible and come to believe its claims about the high quality of its products because we have learned the manufacturer operates on the policy that quality products come to be trusted by consumers, sell better, and hence, in the long run, generate more profits. In this case, its motivations lead the manufacturer to do a good job. Doing a good job leads to building good quality products. But even here, just explaining its good intentions does not justify its normative claim "Our products are good." Regardless of its intentions and regardless of its policies, to justify that claim the manufacturer must show that its products meet recognized standards or criteria of quality for products of their kind. In other words, only after the products are tested against accepted standards and criteria and found to be good, can the manufacturer justify its claim that they are good. And, apart from establishing its own credibility, justifying its claims means presenting the results of those tests, not appealing to its good intentions and sound business practices.

3.4 Justifications vs. Appeals to Emotion

Often we appeal to emotion to bring about action, but doing so does not constitute a justification for our normative claims. To justify a normative claim is to argue rationally (but not necessarily *coldly*) that the claim should be accepted. To prove a statement true is to argue that it should be believed. However, believing a statement or accepting a normative claim does not necessarily lead to engaging in some immediate activity. For example, we can believe cutting down on alcohol would be healthy without cutting down. We can agree that dumping toxic wastes into the water system is bad without picketing a local factory engaged in such dumping. We can accept the view that military intervention is warranted without running out to join the Army. Often it takes an emotional jolt to spur us into action. As fund raisers know, persuading people that their cause is good and getting people to open their checkbooks are two different things.

An emotional appeal aimed at getting someone to act a certain way is not a justification of the normative claim that the person should act that way. Frequently emotional appeals bypass justification altogether. Patriotic music, rousing appeals to school or community pride, vivid pictures illustrating threats to the safety of home and family, desperate or teary-eyed appeals for economic aid, coy suggestions that doing this or that will lead to prestige, peer envy or peer acceptance, calculated ad campaigns aimed at guilt induction, our pride, sense of snobbish elitism or our subtle need to feel superior to the rest of humankind, these are the tools people use to motive us to action. The ad might not say: "If you buy this, you're sexy!" But the images and the tone of the ad are aimed at our emotions, feelings and needs, not at offering rational justifications. If we are gullible and let ourselves be victimized by those who would manipulate our needs and emotions for their own interests, then to that extent we are acting irrationally and relieving them of the sensible demand that they present us with genuine justifications for their normative claims. To what degree is the advertising industry responsible—and how much is our own responsibility for not demanding more of ourselves as wise consumers?

Some philosophers would argue that there is a sense in which justifications—particularly good ones—appeal to one's feelings. One might regard one's sense of loyalty, duty, personal commitment, integrity, fair play or one's conscience as at least akin to the sentiments or emotions referred to above. So, for people with a keen sense of fairness and a profound respect for human life, a justification based on the principles of justice, autonomy and respect for persons, might do much more than establish that the claim being supported is, in an abstract and intellectual sense, true. It might also motivate such a person to action. We shall distinguish this sort of rational appeal from those crude appeals to our needs or emotions which bypass or ignore reasons and principles. A crude appeal to emotion aims directly at bringing about an action by triggering irrational attitudes or arousing strong feelings. On the other hand, no matter what emotions, attitudes or dispositions to action also might be aroused, a justification aims at showing that a normative assertion is true by rationally appealing to relevant facts and universal ethical principles.

3.5 Justifications vs. Rationalizations

At times we give a reason we think someone else might accept even if that reason was not what we had in mind originally. This practice, called *rationalizing*, amounts to choosing first and looking for reasons later. Even if our choices are in-tuitively correct, rationalizing is *not* the same as acting rationally. In fact, it can be the antithesis. When people ask us why we think something, they do not want to hear why *they should think it* or why *they should think we think it*. They want our straightforward reasons why we think it. They certainly do not want us to fabricate a bogus reason and present it as if it had been our reason all along. That kind of misleading prevarication is deceitful.

Rationalization is the process of adopting or rejecting reasons because they respectively do or do not support one's preconceived point of view. A clear historical example was former President Nixon's Watergate cover-up. Motivated by what looks like personal political ambition, he moved to cover up the Watergate break-in which occurred during his campaign for re-election. Later, when the news came out, he realized he needed a justification. He and his aides cooked up a likely-sounding story, which they hoped they could present as the justification they had been using all along. They invented the *national security* story. Knowing that revealing their true reasons would be disastrous, they rationalized what they had done. Notice that Nixon not only chose first, he also acted, and only afterwards did he and his aides try to find a normative principle that they could portray as their justification. Acting before seeking reasons, however, is not essential to rationalizing; one is rationalizing when one makes a decision about what is good or bad before taking into account the relevant facts and ethical principles.

3.6 Justifications vs. Excuses

When we do something wrong but we wish not to be held responsible, we offer an *excuse*. For example, we failed to make the car payment because we forgot what day it was, or we missed the important meeting because we were sick. A successful excuse gets us off the hook, it provides a reason why we should not be *held accountable*, blamed, or punished. It does not, however, change the ethical quality of what we did. It does not justify failing to make the car payment or missing the meeting. Nixon might have offered excuses for his cover-up. He could have said, "I realize it was wrong but I was under severe pressure and I did not, at that time, regard the Watergate affair as a very significant event." Perhaps no one would have accepted the excuses, but perhaps some would have. Accepting an excuse is far different from accepting a justification or a rationalization. To accept a person's justification (or rationalization) is to rationally agree (be deceived into agreeing) that the person did right. To accept an excuse is to say the person did wrong but should not be held fully responsible for the error.

Excuse giving and excuse accepting is a subtle and complex phenomenon. Suppose truthfully we tell our supervisor, "I didn't finish the report because a tragic thing happened and I was emotionally unable to do any work." But suppose our insensitive supervisor responds with "Sorry, it was your responsibility. I won't accept excuses. And, your failure will be noted in your performance evaluation." Does the supervisor's refusal mean we are accountable for our failure? Not necessarily. That the supervisor *is* going to hold us responsible is clear. Whether the supervisor *ought* to have accepted the excuse as exonerating our failure is another matter. But, what if people do accept our excuses? Suppose we are lazy, thoughtless persons who frequently fail to do our share of the household chores. Suppose on a given day we offer our typical excuse, "Sorry I forgot, I was so busy doing *XYZ*." The people in our household might say, "Fine, don't worry about it." Would that mean they accepted our excuse as justifying our failure, or would it mean our excuse was good enough to relieve us of responsibility? Not necessarily. They might actually have preferred not to have us around complaining and doing a poor job of things anyway; and they may not want the bother of discussing whether *XYZ* was really more important than our household chores. Thus, having one's excuses accepted or rejected does not imply that one is justified or not justified in doing what one did, and it may not imply that one is really excused or not excused either.

What about when we offer excuses to ourselves? In effect we are saying we should not blame ourselves and feel bad because we failed to meet one of our goals. There are times when this is reasonable and times when this is not. If saying "I didn't have enough time" really means "I did not value the project enough to put it ahead of anything else I was doing" that is something we should know about ourselves. *Akasia* is the chronic practice of making excuses to oneself. Suppose, for example, we always hear ourselves saying, "I'll start that exercise program as soon as the semester is over." If we are more or less regularly finding ourselves needing to make excuses to ourselves, we probably need to take a serious look at our real priorities and commitments. No matter how bad the akasiatic person feels about himself afterward, he finds tons of *reasons why not* all of which are aimed at letting himself off the hook for now. None of these reasons are justifications. Procrastination, denial, failure to pull together what is needed to do the job, and attention wasted on things of lesser priority are tactics of the chronic self-excuser. The difference between this person and the truly self-deceptive person is that the akasiatic person knows she is doing a poor job of covering herself with sorry excuses, but the self-deceptive person never recognizes his problem because he actually believes and accepts his own excuses!

3.7 Justifications vs. Sources

At times people respond to questions about justifications with statements about the source of their opinions. For example, to the question, "Why do you think abortion is wrong?" a person might say, "Well, that's just how I was raised." When pressed for a fuller explanation, the person might reply more firmly, "I was brought up to believe that." Several things might be happening here, but one of them is that the person is really saying "I don't want to talk about this. Leave me alone. I might have my reasons, but I do not intend to share them with you!" But, obviously, much more needs to be said to justify the claim "Abortion is wrong" or the claim "Abortion is right." Ethical principles like respect for persons and the importance of autonomous action must be considered. Biological, medical and technological facts are relevant. Different kinds of cases must be distinguished and their relevant similarities and differences brought to light. Closing off discussion by saying "I learned X once," is a kind of intellectual hiding. It is not the act of one who seeks to participate in the processes of rationally examining the issue and justifying a given normative position in regard to it.

Typical of the sources people try to hide behind when they want to close off rational discussion prematurely are features of their own background. A person might say their parents, their religion, their social or economic condition, their age, race, gender, or ethnicity, or their native culture, their political affiliation, or some event that happened earlier in their life makes them think what they think. But even if this were true, which is very doubtful, *such sources are not justifications.* People can question and disagree with any of those sources, they can change their minds; they can take a fresh look at situations, even painful ones. Above all, believing something does not put it beyond rational investigation and reconsideration. We can examine the reasons our parents, peer group, colleagues, or religious guides have for holding certain ethical views. We can question the values embodied in the standard and accepted practices of our workplace or our society. We can challenge how well any source of normative claims has done its homework. What universal ethical principles, relevant facts and good thinking has that source engaged in? Citing a source or authority is not a substitute for giving reasons; it is really only a way of identifying a place to look for the reasons which that authority, if it is good, should be able to muster to justify the views being presented.

Unsettling as it may be, in philosophy, naming sources proves almost nothing; rather it opens avenues for investigation and analysis. But then, that is why philosophy is such a liberating study. It frees us from an irrational bondage to others as the sole and unquestioned sources of our normative views. How else can our views really be considered our own but that we can rationally justify them ourselves?

3.8 Rational Criticism of Normative Arguments

Having clarified the differences between several varieties of pseudo-justification and genuine attempts at justification, let us now turn to consider how the latter may be susceptible to rational criticism. The arguments offered in defense of normative claims may be more or less adequate to the task. For example, normative arguments can be fallacious or non-fallacious. Perusal of any standard textbook of informal logic should acquaint you with the wide variety of errors of reasoning and other fallacies to which normative arguments are subject. Thus, contradicting those who hold that in ethics any opinion is as solid as any other, we maintain there are many ways normative arguments can fail to meet minimal requirements of rationality. Here we shall devote our attention to the need to properly marshal factual support where it is appropriate and to argue from universalizable moral principles.

3.9 The Need for Factual Support

Providing adequate factual support is often crucial in ethics. Simply not providing such support where it is appropriate is itself a failure to meet a minimal requirement in reasoning about normative concerns. In a trial, findings of fact are as vital as findings of guilt or innocence. Fact finding is a key part of negotiating settlements and establishing sound policies. Trials, settlements, and policies, just as ethics, involve assessing the reasonableness of normative claims. Let us briefly, though not exhaustively, note some of the circumstances where factual support is pertinent and relevant in assessing such claims.

(a) Normative reasoning commonly involves the evaluation of agents, actions, or practices in terms of normative principles. A fundamental prerequisite for the success of such evaluation is, then, the establishment of the fact that the agents, actions, or practices are of the types covered by the principles. Thus, for example, to argue that a particular person should not be appointed to a particular position because, in general, liars and those who abuse drugs should not be so appointed, requires that one establish that the person in question is indeed a liar or someone who abuses drugs. Or to argue that a particular act of disconnecting a human being from a life-support system is wrong because it is an act of willful homicide requires, in part, that one establish that the human being was not in fact dead prior to being removed from the life-support system.

(b) In seeking to justify actions or policies, appeal is frequently made to their purported consequences. Data supporting the predictions of consequences would then be vitally important. Thus, if one were to argue that lying to a particular person would prevent him from suffering unnecessarily, one would have to provide information about his personality to show that he was susceptible to being hurt by the truth in question. Or if one were to attempt to justify rehabilitation rather than punishment as a response to criminal behavior because it reduces the rate of recidivism, one would have to supply a factual demonstration concerning the rates of return to crime of those who had been treated in the different manners in question.

(c) Many questions in ethics concern the distribution of benefits and burdens; that is, they are matters of distributive justice. Facts about actual past or present distributions as well as accurate predictions of future distributions often are crucial in assessing the fairness of the distributions in question. For example, establishing the injustice of American slavery depends, in part, upon an accounting of the disproportionate distribution of benefits and burdens in slave states. In deciding how benefits and burdens ought to be distributed, it is generally agreed that they ought to be dispersed in proportion to the deserts of the persons involved. There is much disagreement over what makes a person deserving—whether it is, for example, his ability, actual contribution, effort, or need. In any case, facts pertaining to actual ability, contribution, effort, or need would have to be provided in order to justify distribution proportionate to any of them.

(d) In assessing responsibility and supporting claims that persons are deserving of praise or reward, blame or punishment, factual considerations are central in at least two ways. First, facts about the agent are important. Was the agent in fact free to do otherwise, or was she coerced or otherwise not at liberty? Was the agent of sound mind and in command of her faculties so that it is even appropriate to consider him or her a responsible agent? Second, facts about what actually was done are crucial. Who in fact did the deed in question? What exactly was done?

One can fall short of the minimal requirement in reasoning about normative concerns by not providing factual support where it is appropriate. One can also perceive the need for factual support for normative claims and yet fail in defending one's view by presenting *inadequate factual support*— factual claims that are either false, irrelevant, or inconclusive.

It should go without saying that no support is provided for a normative position by making a descriptive statement which is simply false. Thus, in the example of rehabilitation vs. punishment, if it is false that recidivism is reduced by rehabilitation, then making that false claim would lend no support to the argument that rehabilitation is preferable. Thus whenever factual information is relevant, as in the kinds of situations mentioned above, for example, the factual statements presented must be true, if they are to be of any rational use in establishing or disestablishing normative claims.

The kinds of pseudo-justifications listed earlier in this section offer us examples of how even the facts, truly stated, may not necessarily be relevant. For example, the citation of facts about the sources of the views that are being defined may not be relevant to proving the normative claim is true. However true it may be that a belief has the endorsement of parents, scripture, political authority, friends, supervisors, custom, and public opinion or is an outgrowth of one's strong feeling or emotion, citation of such facts is not equivalent to citation of reasons in support of their truth. Disclosing one's motives for wanting to defend a view is not the same as displaying a sound justification for the view one is defending. For example, while parents may well be the typical source for a belief that kindness is good, it is implausible to suppose that kindness is good *because* parents say it is or *because* one is motivated out of respect for them to accept what they have to say. Or, while it may well be that fear, pride and hatred contribute to the growth of racist belief, it is no clearer that racism is correct *because* of the strong feeling out of which it grows than it is clear that its opposite, anti-racism, is correct only *because* those who are anti-racist also have strong feelings. Socrates asked if something is good because the gods approved it or if the gods approved it because it was good. For us the answer is the second choice.

There is one more way in which citation of factual support for a normative claim can be inadequate. It is possible to cite both true and relevant information that is nevertheless *not conclusive* in deciding the issue at hand, though it is taken to be so. Thus, for example, in the debate over euthanasia it might be suggested that it would be emotionally very difficult and stressful for physicians if they regularly had to inform patients of the availability of euthanasia procedures. While this may well be true, and while it is fairly clear that suffering emotional stress on the part of one of the parties involved is a relevant consideration, it would be a mistake to take this factual information alone as decisive in the matter. Surely there are other matters to be put in the balance, including the value of each human life and the prospects of suffering for the one for whom euthanasia might be an option.

3.10 The Universalizability Criterion

One of the key requirements for sound reasoning in ethics is the universalizability requirement. Suppose I claimed it is justifiable for me to park in a handicapped parking zone whenever I am in a hurry, even though I am not legally entitled to park there, but that it is wrong for anyone else, not entitled to do so, to park in a handicapped zone when they are in a hurry. Intuitively you would find my claim unacceptable. What makes me so special you might ask? And if I could not find some relevant difference between myself and anyone else who might be in a hurry, you would reject my claim as unreasonable. Universalizability—the demand for consistency in the reasons people give in order to justify their normative claims—is recognized as a criterion which moral reasoning must satisfy. It can be stated in more precise terms as follows:

(UR) If *R* counts as a reason in favor of person *A*'s doing *X* in situation *S*, then *R* also counts as a reason for a similar person to perform a similar act in similar circumstances.

To take a different case, suppose Mrs. Jones breaks the speed laws in order to drive her injured child to the hospital. Suppose, further, that she gives as her reason that she was obligated by parental duty and her own love to see to it that her injured child received swift attention. Her reason would satisfy the universalizability requirement (UR) only if it counted as a reason for something like this: Mr. Smith fails to come to a complete stop at stop signs in order to rush his injured child to the doctor's office.

We do not mean to suggest that universalizability is the only criterion moral reasoning must satisfy, nor that it is easy to apply this principle. On the contrary, applying UR is notoriously tough. To give some help with this you should note that UR requires that reasons be generalizable in three ways: they must apply to *similar agents;* they must apply to *performing similar acts;* and these acts and agents must be found to be in *similar circumstances.* Judging the agents, acts and circumstances to be sufficiently similar (dissimilar) to warrant the application (non-application) of the same ethical judgment is a matter of noting true and relevant facts and also a matter of making wise and judicious comparisons and contrasts. In the case sketched above Mrs. Jones' reason applies to Mr. Smith because all three of the similarities are present. However, her reason would not apply to any of these:

1. A nine-year-old child's driving the family car to take an injured brother or sister to the hospital.
2. Mrs. Jones' leaving her other preschool children in dangerous circumstances in order to drive her injured child to the hospital.
3. Mrs. Jones' breaking the speed laws in order to drive her well child to the doctor for a routine examination.

In **1.** the *agent* is changed from an adult who presumably knows how to drive and is licensed to a child who does not know how to operate a car. In **2.** the *act* was changed from the violation of traffic laws to a case of dangerous parental neglect. In **3.** the *circumstances* were changed: the child was not in need of swift emergency treatment.

We began this chapter by noting that reasoning in ethics must be objective, fair-minded, and rational. Even with relevant factual information, a sound understanding of ethical principles, the tools of logic and the universalizability criteria, we still find ourselves needing a measure of thoughtful wisdom and prudent judgment to interpret and assess normative claims.

EXERCISES

1. Explain the difference between giving a justification and each of the following. (3.2–3.7)
   (a) Offering an excuse
   (b) Rationalizing one's activities
   (c) Appealing to emotions in order to influence behavior
   (d) Stating one's motivations
   (e) Citing the sources of one's normative views

2. Suppose Mrs. Karloski drove from Madison, Wisconsin, to Milwaukee, regularly exceeding the speed limit by 10 miles per hour. Give two examples of each of the following: (3.2–3.7)
   (a) Offering an excuse for her speeding
   (b) Rationalizing her speeding
   (c) Stating her motivations for speeding
   (d) Citing where she got the idea she could drive that fast

3. Suppose Mrs. Borbonne wanted to persuade her husband to punish their son for lying to her. Give two examples of each of the following: (3.4, 3.9, 3.10)
   (a) Appealing to her husband's emotions to get him to punish their son
   (b) Stating false information to manipulate him into punishing their son
   (c) Appealing to universalizable principles to justify the punishment

4. The citizens of your home town are debating whether to double the size of their recreational lands. Describe how justification might fail because of each of the following: (3.9)
   (a) No factual support is marshaled
   (b) False statements are offered
   (c) Irrelevant truths are presented
   (d) Inconclusive truths are presented

DISCUSSION QUESTIONS

1. Does the fact that I think it is right for me to use my income to send my child to college mean that you should use your income to send my child to college? How does universalizability apply in a case like this? Does using tax money to support public higher education and fund student loans violate the idea that no one is obligated to pay for the college of anyone else's children? Are other universalizable principles operating in this case?

2. We said we thought the gods approved of things because they were good, rather than the other way around. Do you agree or not? Why? What does that imply for trying to ground all of one's ethical principles in one's religion?

3. Some people find the law to be the source of their views regarding what is right and wrong. If sources are not justifications, then can the fact that something is the law be, in itself, a justification for saying that it is the right thing to do? Should laws be based

on ethical principles? We have laws against fraud, murder, rape, theft, pornography, child abuse and all sorts of things. Does this amount to legislating morality? In a pluralistic culture such as ours, where people derive their ethical opinions from such a variety of conflicting sources, should we or should we not legislate morality?

ANSWERS TO SELECTED EXERCISES

2. Possible answers:
   (a) "I thought the speed limit was 65, not 55."
   "My cruise-control is stuck at 65, I couldn't slow down."
   (b) "More cars passed me than I passed.
   "I got there safely, so there couldn't have been anything too wrong in my speed."
   (c) "I get very bored on long drives.
   "I was excited about getting home for the reunion.

3. Possible answers:
   (a) "Aren't you ashamed to have a liar for a son?"
   "You don't want your son embarrassing his mother, do you?"
   (b) "Do something about your son! He struck me in the face today, then he laughed and shouted obscenities at me."
   (c) "Lying should never go unpunished."
   "A child ought to follow the rules of his parents' house."

4. (a) If the debate disintegrated to repeated insistence that the recreational area should or should not be acquired, factual support would be missing.
   (c) Most facts about your town's climate and the education and religion of its citizens, for example, would be irrelevant to the question at issue, although they all might be relevant to the kind of recreational land appropriate for the town.
   (d) Any of the following *by itself* would be inconclusive, but each might have some relevance: population size, population growth, present park locations, who now uses parks, who would use expanded areas, costs of area development and maintenance, and who would pay the costs.

2 | SOCIAL UTILITY

Count all equally, but choose the good of the many over the good of the few.

Zio Vincenzo
Reflections on Cosmic Harmonics

In making decisions about social policy or personal actions, it is highly desirable to take into consideration the likely and foreseeable results of those decisions. Doing what is in the best interests of the greatest number of people is an important responsibility of not just public officials, but all who live in today's complex, inter-connected world-society. The ethical theory which tries to answer the question, "What makes an action or a practice right or wrong?" by examining results is known as *Utilitarianism*. The hope of the classical utilitarians Jeremy Bentham and John Stuart Mill was to provide an objective means for making value judgments. In particular they were concerned about objectively judging alternative social policies and alternative pieces of legislation under consideration in nineteenth-century England. Accordingly, many democratic ideals operative in English political philosophy are assumed in their theories. After reading this chapter you should understand classical utilitarianism and how the concept of utility in the twentieth-century has been translated into economic terms. Section 1 explains how utilitarians would have us evaluate the consequences of what we are considering doing. Section 2 discusses how, on utilitarian theory, we should evaluate the rightness or wrongness of the rules or actions which lead to those consequences. And section 3 examines some complications and objections advanced against their utilitarian theory.

Section 1
THE EVALUATION OF CONSEQUENCES

Utilitarianism is to be understood, in part, as an attempt to find a common ground for agreement about what actions or practices are right or wrong. In this section we shall examine the utilitarians' starting point: that the best means to achieving such agreement is to put aside personal feelings and evaluate the consequences of actions or practices. The utilitarians started here, out of the conviction that consequences could be defined objectively and because, beneficial or harmful, outcomes could be objectively measured and compared. Utilitarians sought to quantify their judgments out of the conviction that people could agree on such judgments. Agreement between persons, which is frequently called *intersubjective agreement*, is obviously a desirable characteristic of evaluations, especially in a democratic society. First we discuss the classical utilitarian view that the consequences for anyone who might be affected by an action or practice are to count as of equal normative significance. Then we introduce the four objective characteristics of these consequent states of affairs that classical utilitarians would have us take into account: intensity, duration, propinquity, and extent. After reading this section, you should he able to:

- Contrast the views of a universalistic utilitarian and those utilitarian views which consider consequences but only for limited ranges of persons.
- Given a possible state of affairs, list considerations relating to the intensity, duration, propinquity, and extent of the consequences of actions or practices relative to that state of affairs.
- Describe the manner in which utilitarians seek to achieve agreement about normative concerns.

THE CASE OF THE DORM THIEF

There had been an alarming number of thefts in the campus dorms over the past several weeks. Computers, watches, money, books, TV sets, even bicycles had been taken. The residents were upset. But the thief was clever. The thefts never occurred on the same floor twice in a row; they happened at different times of the day; and somehow the thief had managed to avoid even being spotted. As a result nobody knew if the thief was male, female, white, black or what. Nobody that is, except the two sophomore roommates: Boroughs and Jackson.

Jackson pushed dirty laundry off the end of his bed and flopped on the blanket. "Campus security is going to interview everybody in the dorm tomorrow. I saw a notice on the elevator. I hate cops. I'm not telling them a thing."

"Look, Jackson, I know your attitude toward cops," said Boroughs. "But we've got no choice. Cooperating with the police is just something you have to do, no matter how much you hate cops. And, no matter how you feel about Christina either. "

Jackson sat up angrily. "That wasn't called for. I don't see what the laws have to do with turning in Christina. Let the cops catch her without my help—if they can. Besides, I thought she was your friend too. Why do you want to cause all kinds of trouble for her?"

Boroughs just shook his head. "But a law is a law! There must be some way we can come to agreement on this."

"I doubt it," snapped Jackson, "Not if it means harming Christina. I couldn't live with myself if I did something like that."

Just then Carlos Wright, who happened to hear Jackson and Boroughs talking, came in. "Hey, what's all the noise? You guys fighting again?"

"Jackson doesn't want to cooperate with the police investigation," said Boroughs. "But the law says he has to."

"You know what you can do with the law," replied Jackson.

"Hold on, you guys," said Wright. "You're never going to settle anything by shouting at each other. Why don't we do what my Economics professor always says, compare the costs and the benefits. I mean, what are all the good things and all the bad things that happen if you do cooperate and if you don't cooperate?"

Boroughs glanced at Jackson, then said, "Go on. I'm listening."

Wright continued, "We're talking about information that will lead to catching the dorm thief. Right? Now if the criminal goes free, he probably will commit more crimes and make lots more people unhappy. You have to think about the emotional and financial hurt he'll cause all those victims. But if he's caught, the people he ripped off might even get some of their things back and that will certainly make them happy."

"But the thief won't be happier, if caught," said Jackson.

"True," said Wright. "So we have to factor that into the equation. But, it still doesn't balance. If you don't cooperate in the investigation, the dorm crimes will continue and more and more people will be hurt. The unhappiness of all those people out-weighs the unhappiness of the thief."

"I don't want to help cops," Jackson protested.

"That's irrelevant. They don't suffer any burdens or benefits either way. They don't live in the dorm, so they won't be victims. And they don't get paid any more money if they catch the thief tomorrow, next month or never. The people you'll be helping are the students whom the thief is victimizing."

"He's not telling you everything," said Boroughs.

"Shut up!" shouted Jackson.

"What if the thief's someone's special friend?" taunted Boroughs.

Wright just laughed. "It doesn't make any difference," he said. "Everybody counts the same in this equation. Friend, enemy or nothing to you at all, it's all the same."

"Why don't you keep your mouth shut," shouted Jackson to Boroughs as he stormed out of the room and slammed the door. Then Jackson opened the door and shouted in at Wright, "I don't see how you measured the thief's intense pain and embarrassment at being caught against the momentary trouble of being ripped off. Sure it's no fun, but they handle it a lot easier than the thief can handle going to jail!" Jackson left without waiting for Wright's reply.

Wright just looked at Boroughs. "What's wrong with him?"

"I can't imagine," said Boroughs.

1.1 The Quest for Common Ground

Utilitarian theory begins by seeking a common ground for agreement, through which it hopes to arrive at a kind of objectivity in normative matters. It looks for this common ground by focusing on the evaluation of the consequences of actions and practices in an attempt to find characteristics of good and bad results that are at least roughly quantifiable. Utilitarian theory plausibly assumes that intersubjective agreement will then be rather easy to achieve.

In the case study Jackson is caught up in his feelings about turning in Christina to the police, whom he apparently despises. Utilitarian theorists argue that feelings and personal sentiments cannot serve as the basis of agreement in normative matters: feelings simply are not always shared. Boroughs, on the other hand, is caught up in an inarticulate respect for law and authority. He believes it is right to cooperate with the law, but he is unable to say exactly why. Wright shifts the focus of the discussion to something he hopes all can agree upon. As a good utilitarian, he asks Jackson and Boroughs to consider the consequences of the action or practice for everyone who might be affected. He suggests that, given the bad consequences of non-cooperation, Jackson's sentiments, at least in this instance, are misplaced. He suggests that the alternative of cooperation reduces the potential for harm by ending the thefts. Wright provides a substantial base for Boroughs' beliefs about the law because the good consequences he cites count as good reasons for cooperation with the law. There are two possible conclusions one can draw from Wright's statements: (a) In this case people should cooperate with the police, and (b) as a general rule people should obey the law. Both are true, say the utilitarians, because both bring about a preponderance of good consequences over bad.

But, as Jackson's reactions indicate, at least two important questions arise concerning the utilitarian focus upon evaluation of the consequences of actions and practices: (1) good or bad consequences for whom? and (2) how are we to calculate the value of these consequences? We shall address those questions in turn.

1.2 Classical Universalistic Utilitarianism

Classical utilitarians hold that one must consider the consequences for *all* who might be affected by the act or practice in question. This is the meaning of their being called *universalistic* utilitarians. The classical utilitarians were also egalitarian. *Egalitarianism* is the view that each person counts equally in one's normative deliberations. Each person counts for one: whenever the decision affects the person making it, that person counts for one, as does each other person affected by that decision.

Jackson's concern not to help the police is motivated by his desire to protect his friend, Christina. Even though he knows she's the thief and even though he may agree that it would help more people if she were apprehended, he cannot bring himself to turn her in. For reasons relating to human psychology, Christina is more important to Jackson than those others. Jackson is not alone in having these kinds of feelings and personal loyalties. We all would find it very hard, if not impossible, to do something that would harm someone whom we know and care deeply about even though we understand intellectually how doing so would benefit many others for whom we had no special feelings. In the *Star Trek* film Captain Kirk rescues Mr. Spock. In the end Captain Kirk explains to Mr. Spock that for him the good of the one, his best friend, takes priority over the good of the many. One of the objections often raised against universalistic utilitarianism is that it does not give due recognition to these relevant facts about human relationships.

The response of the classical universalistic utilitarian would be that Captain Kirk was wrong to do what he did. He should have resisted his human emotions and assumed the attitudes of personal indifference and general benevolence. He should not have endangered others and himself just to save one person. Everyone counts and everyone counts equally, is the position of classical universalistic utilitarianism. Unless there was something about Mr. Spock which made him indispensably useful to the continued survival of the ship and crew, Kirk was morally wrong to have valued his friend's life over those of other people. There are many who find this response callous and insensitive. But the classical utilitarians can respond that these sentimental feelings only get in our way when tough decisions have to be made. A general who is unwilling to sacrifice lives will not win any wars.

A person making a decision on universalistic utilitarian grounds is called upon to assume an *attitude of personal disinterest*. This means that a person is not to judge a situation on the basis of feelings or emotions that arise out of his own involvement or because of the involvement of persons dear to him. Also the person is to assume an *attitude of generalized benevolence*, which means that the interests of all human beings are dear to him or her and count equally for him or her simply because they are the interests of those creatures. Indeed, Jeremy Bentham noted that any animal capable of feeling pain has an interest in avoiding that pain. Accordingly, Bentham (1789) urged that the utilitarian attitude of benevolence is appropriate not only towards all human beings but towards any sentient creature, that is, any creature capable of feeling pain or pleasure.

Notice how the case study illustrates this requirement of universalistic utilitarian theory. In the case study Wright asks the others to consider the consequences of cooperation or non-cooperation for all who might possibly be affected by the decision. The police are thought to be affected very little one way or the other. Although the consequences for the criminal are thought to be bad, since the thief will be deprived of freedom and suffer humiliation, Wright sees this to be outweighed by the good consequences for the past and potential victims. According to the universal utilitarian, cooperation with the police is the best alternative because it produces the greatest balance of good over bad consequences, taking everybody into account equally.

1.3 Egoistic, Altruistic, and Limited Utilitarianism

Universalistic utilitarianism may be contrasted with other, more limited views about who is to be considered in evaluating the consequences of actions and practices. It contrasts with the views that only consequences for identifiable groups should be considered—for example, that (a) the agent and no one else, (b) everyone else excluding the agent, or (c) a select group of persons (including or excluding the agent) should be considered. These contrasting views may be called (a) *egoism*, (b) *altruism*, and (c) *limited utilitarianism.*

Egoistic utilitarianism is the view that in making normative judgments one should evaluate only those consequences that apply to oneself; no other consequences are relevant. We will discuss ethical egoism in Chapter 3. *Altruistic utilitarianism* is the view that one's normative judgments should rest exclusively on those consequences that apply to others but the consequences for oneself should be counted as irrelevant. A universal utilitarianism differs from an altruistic utilitarianism in that the *universal utilitarian* insists that the agent is to be considered as equal in importance with each of the others who might be affected by an action or practice. A *limited utilitarian* is one who advocates assessing the consequences, but only for the members of a certain group. Limited utilitarianism appeals to those who believe it important to be impartially concerned for others, but not all others. Like egoistic and altruistic utilitarianisms, limited utilitarianism is a species of relativism, since its judgments about what is right or wrong are relative to the membership of the group to which the speaker belongs or for whom the speaker advocates. (See Chapter 1, for a discussion of ethical relativism.)

Anyone who believes one should be concerned only about the well-being of one's family, team, corporation, social group, age group, gender, race, or nation, may be a limited utilitarian. A person who says that the only reason to obey the traffic laws is because it makes travel safer for himself and those in his own car is a limited utilitarian who is not taking into consideration the benefits to other drivers.

In the case study Jackson seems to be discounting the victims and limiting his focus only to Christina and maybe himself. In foreign policy, one would be a limited utilitarian if one held that the United States government should concern itself solely with what is good for America and never consider seriously the impact of American policy on the lives of citizens of other nations.

A good example of limited utilitarianism at work is in the accounting practices typical of business. In keeping the business's accounts, one records the assets and the liabilities of that business. One looks at the consequences of actions not for everybody, but for one entity, the business. Similarly, if one keeps a budget for one's household, one considers the consequences of actions for one's own household. Keeping track of income and expenses is a way of measuring the good and bad consequences of one's decisions. In the case of the household budget the welfare of everyone in the household is at stake, but not necessarily anyone else. Here the comparative analysis of costs and benefits is a kind of limited utilitarianism.

There are serious problems with limited utilitarianism, not the least of which were raised originally by the classical universalistic utilitarians. They prefer their universalistic position because of their belief that the well-being of each person is of equal moral concern. Thinking about one's own circle of associates is understandable, but being moral requires more. It requires that one take into account the effect of one's actions or practices upon those who happen not to be members of the select group one favors. Moreover, the classical utilitarians find great practical difficulty in (a) selecting from among the several groups to which one might belong, which one should be the preferred group and (b) deciding what one ought to do when alternative choices would benefit different groups of which one is a member. Suppose a certain neighborhood will suffer if a certain store closes, but the business will benefit if it relocates. Suppose the owner of the business also lives in the neighborhood. Under limited utilitarianism, should she make her decision as a business person or as a resident? Universal utilitarians urge that, because one has no rational way of deciding between such limited alternatives, one should adopt their universalistic viewpoint.

Universalistic utilitarianism, then, is like limited utilitarianism in that both seek the greatest good—that is, the best balance of good compared to bad consequences. But whereas limited utilitarianism seeks the greatest good of a limited group of people, universalistic utilitarianism seeks the greatest good of the greatest number considering all who are affected, with each counting equally.

1.4 Evaluating Consequences: Intensity

Having discussed the first question, whose interests should be taken into consideration, let's return to universalistic utilitarianism and take up our second question, how ought the value of the consequent states of affairs be evaluated? Utilitarians propose consideration of four objective characteristics of states of affairs that, taken together, count toward making a situation more or less desirable. These characteristics are the intensity, duration, propinquity, and extent of the good or bad involved.

Jackson's last remark in the case study indicates that Christina's suffering will be more severe as compared to the happiness produced for the potential victims, who may never even know that they would have been the targets of her crimes. This matter, the intensity of the good or bad that results, is the first characteristic to take into account. Remember, we are looking at the good and bad in those states of affairs which result from a given action or practice. In estimating *intensity* we are seeking to determine *how much good or bad exists for every affected person*. In the case study Jackson significantly underestimates how angry and financially harmed a college student could be if the student is victimized by the thief, Christina. Some victims have already been affected greatly by the thief's actions, and they may well be affected greatly again by cooperation, for they may be able to recover what they lost. Future victims may or may not be spared psychological and financial suffering as a function of the decision. Others who may never be the actual victims of such crime may nevertheless enjoy the less intense benefit of living more securely in the dorm just knowing that the thief has been stopped.

Some judgments of intensity seem intuitively clear. But critics have argued that such judgments, even if intuitive, are not obviously objective and quantifiable in a straightforward way. One approach to quantifying them is to equate intensity with dollars. The greater the financial value of the asset the more intense the good; the larger the cost of the liability, the more intense the bad. By simple accounting one can measure one against the other and find out, quantitatively in dollars, whether one is in the black or in the red and how much. That may work for tangible, physical assets and liabilities, but what about less tangible assets, like experience, or non-physical products, like services? Or, consider how difficult it is for insurance companies to agree on fair compensation for pain and suffering when these subjective experiences are being translated into insurance settlement dollars. Or, to take a case where self-interest plays a lesser role, consider by what means a jury would decide on the dollar value of pain and suffering if the issue were brought to court. Objectivity in cases like this, therefore, has seemed to some critics of utilitarianism to rest on such *subjective* judgments as that physical suffering and property loss are worse evils than mental anxiety. So a person might be compensated more for losing a finger in a sporting accident than for the anxiety experienced whenever the idea of playing that sport is even mentioned.

1.5 Evaluating Consequences: Duration

Utilitarian theory also looks to the duration of the good or bad as an important consideration in evaluating the desirability of resulting states of affairs. The concern here is whether the good or bad in question is short-lived or long-lasting. A piece of machinery has a dollar value, but in time the machine wears out, ages or is less effective than a technologically superior, newer model. The duration of the asset is taken into account by depreciating its value; that means regarding it as of lesser dollar value each year of its predicted useful life. Duration can be a factor not only in considering the value of machines, but also in considering the value of human beings. To the owners of the team an older professional athlete is often regarded as of lesser value than one of equal talent who is younger. The difference comes in the probable duration of their careers. The younger one is predicted to be able to play more years for the team, and hence to produce beneficial consequences to the team for a greater duration.

Or, to take another example, the use of radioactive materials in our society has given rise to the problem of the disposal of nuclear wastes. Improperly disposed of, nuclear wastes could have very bad consequences for human health and, indeed, the well-being of ecosystems. Many people are concerned about nuclear power and the use of radioactive materials precisely because of the duration of the bad consequences that can result. If the half life of plutonium is twenty thousand years, then even after those years humans will still need to be concerned about emission at half of their present rate. In contrast, one might say, half the atmospheric pollution of burning high sulfur coal falls out within thirty days, a much shorter duration.

1.6 Evaluating Consequences: Propinquity

The third consideration involved in evaluating consequences, on the classical utilitarian view, is the *propinquity* of the results of the action or practice. The question here is how near to the present are the various good or bad results? How long is the interval between the present and the good or bad that comes about? When a person is diagnosed as having the HIV virus, the question may arise about how long it may be before AIDS becomes active within the person. Notice that this is different from the question of duration. Duration is the question of how long a consequence will exist. For example, if a person with HIV develops AIDS, how long can the person expect to live with AIDS? Propinquity is the question of how soon before the consequence will come to exist. A person may not develop an active case of AIDS for years after contracting the HIV virus.

There has been much debate about whether nearness makes a good better or an evil worse. Many philosophers have felt that propinquity is irrelevant, but others deem it not only relevant but important. From the business perspective, propinquity is a significant factor in managing resources, particularly cash flow. If settling a liability can be deferred for several months, the dollars used to settle that liability can be invested for profit in the meantime. This profit, plus the effects of inflation, mean that the actual negative effect of settling the liability several months in the future will be less than the negative effect of settling it immediately. One way to reduce costs, in business, is to defer payments as long as possible. To compensate for the effects of this propinquity consideration, creditors assess penalties, in the form of interest and late charges, thus making it a disadvantage to defer payments too long.

1.7 Evaluating Consequences: Extent

The fourth consideration used in classical utilitarian theory is the *extent* of the good or bad consequences. Extent relates to *how many persons* are affected one way or another and to a greater or lesser degree by the decision. During the Reagan administration the Federal government adopted the policy that all new regulations had to be justified on a cost–benefit basis. Suppose, for example, a proposal emerged from some agency that baby toys not have buttons because a baby might pull them off and swallow them, leading to choking and maybe death. Suppose it was decided that it would cost the Federal government $750,000 to promulgate and enforce this regulation and also cost toy manufacturers $12,500,000 in lost revenue to destroy unsold products that did not comply. Thus the costs total to $13,250,000. And suppose that it could be shown that passing this regulation would prevent 25 youngsters from choking and save up to 5 lives throughout the entire country. If the lives are valued at $1,000,000 each and the chokings, figuring doctor bills, insurance settlements and all the rest, are valued at $250,000 each, then the benefits total to $11,250,000. The net result is a cost of $2,000,000 and the regulation would not be cost-effective, hence it would not be approved. The extent of those benefited in this case was primarily the 30 children and their families. The extent of those harmed included primarily the businesses affected (and their stockholders) and the taxpayers who would have to cover the government's costs.

The case study illustrates that the extent of a decision can be surprisingly great. Not only are the police, and those who do or do not cooperate with them, involved and affected, but at least the criminal, the past victims, the future victims, and everyone who lives in the dorms are affected. Maybe friends and family members of those people are also affected—if John's computer is stolen and John's parents lend him the money to replace it, then they are affected too. And, so are John's siblings if his parents had intended to use that money for some other need of theirs. Potential victims of the thief's future crimes are affected also, though it may be impossible to specify the particular individuals. And, maybe if the youthful thief is not apprehended and rehabilitated, the number of people affected could mushroom to include her other victims and potential victims for years to come. Obviously, Jackson's decision to cooperate or not may affect or extend to a very large number of people. It is not unreasonable to wonder how anyone is supposed to be able to make an objective, quantifiable assessment and comparison of the intensity, duration and propinquity of the bad and good consequences for all of them. Indeed, this is a frequently voiced objection to universalistic utilitarianism, namely that actually considering the consequences for everyone affected is not possible.

EXERCISES

1. Write true statements, one each, about the intensity, duration, propinquity, and extent of each of the following. (1.3–1.7)

(a) population's being immunized against a disease.

(b) city's collecting garbage once a month.

(c) tornado's hitting a town without warning.

(d) tornado's hitting a town after two hours of well-publicized warning.

2. (a) Suppose Jackson, not Christina was the criminal. Explain how his deliberations would be different if he were an egoistic utilitarian. (1.3)

(b) Define in general terms the difference between a limited and a universalistic utilitarian. (1.3)

(c) Assume someone tells the police about Christina. Assume the dorm is dominated by a ring of thieves who know that only Jackson, Boroughs or Wright could have provided the police with the information they obviously used to catch Christina. How could Jackson use this assumption and the distinction between a limited and a universal utilitarian to criticize Wright's viewpoint?

(d) What grounds can you think of to argue in favor of universalistic, rather than limited, utilitarianism?

3. In each of the following sets of comments, only one expresses a universalistic utilitarian stance. Identify it. Then explain how each of the others fails to qualify. (1.3)

(a) 1. "Do whatever you want. If you feel like it now, do it."

2. "The fair is likely to be more exciting than the mismatched game. You ought not go to the game."

3. "You can't go to the game; that would involve breaking your promise."

(b) 1. "Not returning money when you know who lost it is really stealing; that's wrong."

2. "If you don't return the money, someone will probably find out and punish you."

3. "Even if someone finds out, you can't worry about some old man's losing his money." ·

(c) 1. "Since traffic is heavier on Main than on Claremont, the light should be green longer for Main to promote traffic flow."

2. "Everyone should have an equal chance to go, so the lights should be green equally long each way."

3. "Mostly college kids drive up and down Claremont, while the townspeople use Main. So Main should be green longer."

4. Explain the involvement of each of the following in utilitarian theory:

(a) State of affairs

(b) The future in contrast to the past

(c) The quantifiable

DISCUSSION QUESTIONS

1. Imagine the following conversation between a limited utilitarian and a universal utilitarian. Limited: "Your position is really no better than mine, for you limit yourself to people living today." Universal: "A mere omission. From now on, I'll take unborn future generations of people into account too." Limited: "But which future

people will you take into account? You don't even know which future people will exist! So you're really playing favorites, just like you say I am." How would you answer for the universal utilitarian? And then for the limited utilitarian? Tie this discussion into a practical problem, like the world wide loss of forest lands to the agricultural and developmental uses and the effect this has and will have on the standard of living of the people affected in the present and future.

2. In 1.2 we mentioned that the pain and pleasure of every animal which could sense them might have to be taken into account. In view of this, how would you evaluate the utility of animal experimentation and of non-vegetarian dietary habits.

3. The relationship of cost/benefit analysis and the four features—intensity, duration, propinquity and extent—was sketched by means of the examples in 1.4 through 1.7. If cost/benefit analysis is the twentieth-century embodiment of utilitarianism, how does it respond to the criticisms of utilitarianism we have already seen: (1) that it is insensitive and fails to account for special relationships; (2) that it is not clear exactly whose interests one ought to consider; (3) that its calculations are not always as objective, intuitive and quantified as they should be.

4. Do you think a human life should be valued at $1,000,000? If not, how much? It must be worth something to you. How much would you give to save the life of an arbitrarily selected person from another country? How much life insurance do you carry? Did you spend the money to install airbags in your car? Can you afford purified drinking water? How much ransom would you approve our government paying for the release of terrorist held hostages?

ANSWERS TO SELECTED EXERCISES

1. (a) Here are some possible answers: *Intensity*: The pain of the immunization is much less than the pain of the disease. *Duration*: Immunization will typically last 14 months. *Propinquity*: The population being immunized within six months will save more lives than if the immunization is further delayed. *Extent*: Twenty million people are likely to require immunization.

2. (c) Jackson might argue that the thieves might do physical harm to all three of the people who could have told the police. He might use the *intensity* of that consequence to argue that only the consequences for that group of three people should be considered in making a decision. By focusing on that group Jackson would urge a limited utilitarianism, which provides less common ground for decision making than the universal utilitarianism Wright sought.

(d) "All people ought to be respected," or, "Everyone has equal rights to live and to do as he wants," you might plausibly say. *Note*: One point of this question is to show that the obvious ways in which to defend universalistic, rather than limited, utilitarianism are not themselves utilitarian ways. The arguments seem to say that respecting persons and their rights is intrinsically right. This is not to say that utilitarianism is proved indefensible at this point; it is only to present a difficulty to which utilitarians must respond. For instance, a utilitarian might say that everyone will be happier if secure in the assurance that his rights will be respected. Or they might say that the concept of a right really is a way of saying that generally acting as if a person has that right produces, as a rule, a greater preponderance of good over bad results. In this way talk of rights can be grounded in utilitarian concerns about consequences.

3. (a) 1. Not utilitarian because it urges lack of concern with *consequences* of an action.
2. Universalistic utilitarian.
3. This response seems to say that breaking promises is wrong regardless of consequences, a non-utilitarian view.
(b) 1. This statement suggests that stealing is intrinsically wrong; there is no concern here to evaluate consequences.
2. Universalistic utilitarian.
3. Apparently a limited utilitarian view ignoring consequences for old people.
(c) 1. Universalistic utilitarian.
2. No concern for consequences shown.
3. Perhaps a limited utilitarian view excluding college students from the considered group.

4. Your explanation should indicate at least that to evaluate the morality of a given action utilitarians look to its future consequences. (They do not look to past precedents, intentions, motives, or other elements of past behavior.) The consequences are states of affairs the action will bring about. Certain aspects of these states of affairs are thought to be quantifiable and, so, measurable and open to objective evaluation.

Section 2
UTILITARIANISM—THE RIGHT AND THE GOOD

The fundamental utilitarian thesis is that a general rule or specific action is right or wrong precisely because of the consequent state of affairs, good or bad, that it brings about. In this section we complete the account of the way utilitarian theory would require that rules or actions should be evaluated. We shall introduce three final factors to consider—purity, fecundity, and certainty. We shall then look at the diversity of views held by utilitarians concerning what kinds of things are intrinsically good (or bad). These are the things utilitarians would have us strive to maximize (or minimize) as we decide what to do. After studying this section you should be able to:

- Distinguish and present examples of the factors of purity, fecundity, and certainty as these apply to evaluating actions and practices.
- Define *right* and *wrong* in terms of *good* and *bad* as utilitarians would.
- Present a unified statement, with examples, of how utilitarian theory requires that rules or actions be evaluated.
- Distinguish hedonistic utilitarianism from other utilitarian views designed to identify the desirable ends of action and practice.
- Characterize economic cost-benefit analysis as a contemporary species of utilitarian theory.
- Provide examples of cost-benefit analysis employing utilitarian categories.

THE CASE OF THE BAN ON TUNA FISHING

The usual way of catching tuna for commercial use is to search for a school of porpoises and to lay nets for the tuna where the porpoises are heading, since in fact tuna tend to swim with the porpoises. In recent years it has been determined that enough porpoises have become ensnared in tuna nets and have died of suffocation to warrant the United States government's banning this method of catching tuna.

Tuna fishers, asked to evaluate the rightness or wrongness of the government's ruling, tend to point out the following considerations: Every other method of catching tuna is less efficient and more expensive. It would take both time and a lot of capital investment to buy equipment that would make any other method feasible. Whatever methods United States fishers use, foreign fishers, not bound by United States law except in U.S. waters, will continue to use the banned methods and will, therefore, gain an economic advantage over United States fishers. United States tuna fishers conclude from this that the rule is a bad regulation and should be revoked.

2.1 Consequences as Fundamental

The case study exemplifies many of the characteristics of utilitarian thought. Notice that the tuna fishers judge the ban entirely on the basis of its consequences. No method of tuna fishing is viewed as right or wrong in itself. The possible methods are judged right or wrong solely on the basis of the desirability or undesirability of their *consequences*, known as *states of affairs*. Fundamental to the utilitarian tradition is the assumption that *no action or rule of action whatever is intrinsically good or bad. Actions or rules of action are only instrumentally good or bad because of the desirable or undesirable states of affairs they bring about.* For instance, a utilitarian tuna fisher might feel justified in violating the government ban. He might reason that if he violates the ban, he will catch more tuna than otherwise. The chances of getting caught may appear slight and the consequences of being caught—the fine paid as penalty—insignificant, as compared to the profit to be made on the extra tuna. Such reasoning denies that defying the ban is wrong simply because it is the law of the land. The only *wrongness* the utilitarian tuna fisher accepts is the undesirability of consequences.

2.2 States of Affairs and Intrinsic Value

In contrast to practices or actions, utilitarianism readily admits that *some states of affairs are intrinsically good and other states of affairs are intrinsically bad.* Pain, disease, and the loss of liberty might be examples of intrinsically undesirable states of affairs. Similarly, happiness, pleasure, health, and increased freedom might be seen as intrinsically desirable. Accordingly, because the utilitarian denies that rules or actions can be intrinsically right or wrong, the entire utilitarian focus of moral evaluation is on the states of affairs that result from a given action or practice. Since utilitarians maintain that only states of affairs can be intrinsically valuable, the most fundamental normative concepts for the utilitarians relate to the goodness and badness of states of affairs. The rightness and wrongness of actions and practices are derivative concepts in utilitarian theory. This means actions or practices can be defined as good or bad only as instrumentalities leading to the realization of that which has fundamental value, namely intrinsically good or bad states of affairs.

Classical utilitarians argued that judging the value of a given consequent state of affairs should be done, as we indicated in section 1, by looking at its intensity, duration, propinquity, and extent. But, how does one judge between alternative means of achieving a given state of affairs? As we shall see, classical utilitarians addressed that question as well.

2.3 Evaluating Practices and Actions

Utilitarianism is insistent that in judging actions or practices one must look toward the future, toward the consequences of actions and practices. It is forward-looking in its evaluation. Beyond the four characteristics of states of affairs themselves, utilitarians identify three additional factors, features of the alternative actions or practices which one might use to reach those states of affairs, which factors also must be considered in the complete evaluation of actions and practices. These factors have to do with the tendency of the actions and practices to actually result in the desired consequences—that is, utilitarians judge rules or actions in terms of how these contribute or inhibit the actual realization of the desired outcomes. The basic question is predictive—what consequences are most likely to ensue from the various alternative actions and practices open to us?

2.4 Purity of the Actions or Practices

When the tuna fishers of the case study cast their nets, their goal is to catch tuna. They are not seeking to catch porpoises. That there are porpoises caught in their nets is a consequence of their actions, a consequence irrelevant to their goal. In traditional utilitarian language, the trapped porpoises are an impurity of the tuna fishing. In seeking to determine the purity of an action or practice, one is asking whether the consequences the action will actually tend to produce will be purely those (desirable) consequences that are sought, unmixed with unintended undesirable or irrelevant consequences.

Similarly, a fisher might well consider violating the ban in terms of the possible consequences of doing so. She too, contemplates likely impure consequences. To defy the ban is to continue to be competitive with foreign fishers and to catch large numbers of tuna (desirable), but also perhaps to incur a fine (a foreseeable and undesirable result, an *impurity*). To simplify the case, suppose the fine would be $10,000. And suppose the chances of being caught are 5% for each fishing trip she makes. And suppose the increases in profits which result from violating the ban are estimated at $800 per trip. If she makes 20 fishing trips she foresees gaining $16,000. Assume she foresees being caught violating the ban and having to pay the fine at least once in those 20 trips. That impurity will cost her $10,000, leaving her a net balance of pure over impure results of $16,000 less $10,000 or $6,000. In terms of purity, the decision to take the risk and violate the law, say the utilitarians, can be thought of as a matter of looking at the numbers.

The importance of the purity (or impurity) of the consequences arises because of the utilitarian goal to evaluate actions objectively. Utilitarianism requires more than an evaluation of a single proposed action or practice. Rather, it demands evaluation of a range of alternative actions and practices in an effort to determine which among them will produce the best consequences. But to compare the consequences of different actions or practices, we must examine not just the desired consequences. If a paper carrier injured a pedestrian as a result of rushing to deliver the newspapers on time, the timely delivery of the newspapers would have to be balanced against the harm to the pedestrian. Thus, utilitarians would not have us settle for just using any procedure whatsoever which results in a desired end. The concern for purity is the concern that the undesirable, though foreseeable, bad consequences, should be put in the measure along with the good they accompany.

Since we must evaluate alternative ways of realizing consequences and attend to the fact that different alternatives may produce more or less pure results, we can say that utilitarians are concerned that we select those procedures that result not in the *greatest total* good but rather the *greatest net* good when the (impure) bad results are also taken into account. Indeed, it may turn out that in some particularly trying circumstances one confronts only undesirable alternatives, in which case one must endeavor to minimize the bad. For example, when reactor number four in the Chernobyl nuclear facility in Russia melted down in 1986, something had to be done to contain the superheated nuclear reaction so that huge losses of life could be prevented. Fire-fighters were sent in. They did the job, but most of them died of radiation poisoning. These deaths were certainly not desired, but they were foreseeable impurities resulting from using that means of containing the nuclear disaster. As in so many situations, at Chernobyl the ideal of perfect purity was unobtainable. Nevertheless, utilitarians urge that it would be irrational for us not to consider which actions or practices, from among the several alternatives available, are the purest in terms of generating the greatest net good over bad.

2.5 Fecundity of the Actions and Practices

The second factor in evaluating the tendency of general rules of action or specific actions to produce good consequences is the *fecundity* of those rules or actions. To understand fecundity, consider the treatment of bacterial infections by penicillin and its derivatives. This practice for treating bacterial infections has had a genetic consequence: bacterial mutations. The drugs which once were effective against bacterial infections are no longer effective because the bacteria have mutated. As a result of using penicillin new bacteria have come into being which can only be treated by certain newer, broader-spectrum antibiotics. Let's analyze this example. An undesired state of affairs (bacterial infections) existed. An effective means for treating such infections was found (penicillin). The use of that means eventually caused problems (the mutation of infectious bacteria). Thus, at a later time, the original problem (bacterial infections) continued to exist and it was more difficult to treat than originally. A utilitarian would express all this by saying that the original treatment of the bacterial infections by penicillin has turned out to have bad fecundity. *Bad fecundity* means the tendency of nearer consequences to cause, or help to cause, undesirable consequences later on.

Actions and practices need to be evaluated not only for the good and bad they bring about but also for the difficulty of dealing with any subsequent problems they might generate. A cocaine habit has bad fecundity, because the body becomes used to cocaine, and greater doses are required to attain the same effect later. Indeed, cocaine addiction is considered a problem requiring a solution—that is, withdrawal—a problem which becomes more difficult to solve the longer the habit of using the drug continues. What we do now can make it easier to bring about the good later, or it can aggravate the difficulty of relieving the bad later.

Fecundity, of course, can also be good. Piano practice, for instance, has good fecundity, because if you practice now, the problem of learning new pieces in the future is reduced because of the abilities that practice develops. The general rules of building quality products and being honest in all of one's business dealings, while leading to smaller profits in the short run, have good fecundity. As one's reputation for quality and honesty grows, it will attract more business and lead to greater profits in the long run. Contrast this with the bad fecundity of the general practices of building shoddy products and being disreputable. Early gains through the sale of shoddy products will lead to customer dissatisfaction. This, compounded by disreputable dealings with customers and creditors, will lead people in the long run to take their business elsewhere.

The limitation to assessing fecundity arises because of ignorance. To discuss the fecundity of an action or practice, we must consider what goal is being pursued now and whether the means of achieving that goal now will make that same goal harder or easier to achieve later on. Although our intuitions give us some indications, as with the piano and business examples, often there are simply too many unknowns for us to make precise, sophisticated, quantifiable judgments. In the business example, how shoddy is shoddy? In other words, how many corners can the business cut before the inferior quality of its products starts to harm its reputation to an extent represented by a detectable drop in sales. And, at that point, how much will it cost to up-grade the product and reverse that trend? Or will the negative reputation snowball? Or, suppose, for example, that the fishers complied with the ban and developed a crash program for new technology enabling them to catch comparable numbers of fish without comparable loss of porpoises. Might this in the long run give the fishers a competitive advantage over foreign fishers, who might at some future time become subject to a similar ban by their own governments or by international agreement? Or might it make competitive tuna fishing impossible by imposing a cost on United States' fishers that no other fishers would have to share? Such ignorance limits our ability to apply the concept of fecundity with the kind of precision which utilitarianism seems to require.

2.6 Certainty of the Actions and Practices

The fourth factor to be considered when evaluating actions and practices is the *certainty or likelihood* of action or practice to produce the consequences desired. Utilitarians urge that each of the possible consequences of an action can be predicted to occur with differing degrees of probability. Typically, immediate consequences are predicted with the greatest certainty, while remote consequences, where the impact of intervening factors, foreseen and unforeseen, can multiply, are predicted with the least certainty. Utilitarian theory requires that in making evaluations we *assign greater weight to the consequences that are more certain, more likely to occur.* Let's try an example.

Business decisions about whether to invest in various projects are often evaluated in terms of how certain a given alternative is to produce desirable returns. Consider this case: Suppose lost days of work due to poor employee health cost a business $1,830,000 per year. And suppose, as a way of reducing these costs, management considers implementing a comprehensive health program involving physical exercise during work time, along with diagnostic examinations and treatment programs for those found to have dietary or drug abuse problems. Say the package will cost the company $450,000. This looks like a great deal—spend 450k to save 1.83 million! Should management spend the money? The answer is more complicated than simply comparing the two numbers. One question to ask is how likely the new health programs will be in reducing lost days of work due to poor health. Suppose it turns out there is an 80% chance that the lost days of work will be reduced by 30%. Then the calculation goes as follows: 30% times $1,830,000 is $549,000. This is the potential savings. But, according to utilitarian concern for factoring in certainty, this figure should be discounted by our limited certainty (80%). This results in a probable predicted benefit of $429,200. Comparing that to the cost, the probable predicted result is a net operating loss of $38,800. What should management do, turn down the idea? Perhaps.

Or, maybe management should question how that 80% figure was used in the calculations. Saying that an hypothesis is confirmed at the .05 level does not mean it is 95% true. It means that odds in favor of its being true are 95 out of 100. If the hypothesis is true, it is 100% true, not 95% true (whatever that means). If the hypothesis states "There is $10,000 in the vault." Then, if true, one will find the full $10,000, not just $9,500 in the vault. If false, one will not find $10,000 and maybe one will find no money at all in the vault. In other words, the utilitarian proposal that we consider how much confidence we have in our predictions is certainly a wise intuition. But exactly how to factor our levels of confidence into our judgments in any objective and quantifiable way is not clear. Simply multiplying confidence factors without regard for the sophistications of inferential statistics will not work. But, if it takes much more than that, actually applying this utilitarian intuition might turn out to be an impractical demand.

To sum up, different ways of doing things can lead to different results. How should we decide which way to use to achieve what results? Having looked at purity, fecundity and certainty, we can now present a unified account of how utilitarian theory would require that people evaluate the rightness and wrongness of actions and practices. The fundamental thesis is that general rules or specific actions are right or wrong because of their tendency to produce good consequences. Utilitarians then seek objective means of measuring just how good those alternative possible states of affairs, (possible consequences) would be. Classical utilitarians measured the goodness of the consequent states of affairs in terms of the intensity, duration, propinquity, and extent of the goodness involved in these states of affairs. The tendency of alternative actions or practices to produce good consequences is to be determined in terms of the purity, fecundity, and certainty of each alternative relative to its possible consequences.

2.7 Utilitarians on "The Good"

So far we have developed utilitarianism as a theory about objective characteristics that make states of affairs good or bad, and about the rightness or wrongness of rules or actions as a function of their bringing about such states of affairs. For example, someone might decide to stage a performance of a play. We have said that, according to utilitarianism, this decision should be evaluated by its consequences. And we have said that we should consider how many people are effected (extent), how much they are effected (intensity), what unintended results occurred (purity) and so on. The question yet unanswered is: What *exactly* makes a state of affairs good or bad? When we look at the production of the play, and consider how many people are effected, what sort of positive or negative effect are we looking for?

In its reply to this question, utilitarian theory contrasts with ancient theories of what is desirable. The ancient theories assumed that human beings have an essence or basic nature and, in turn, that there is something that is essentially or naturally good for humans to pursue because it entails the development or fulfillment of the potential in our nature. Utilitarianism makes no such an assumption. Rather, it focuses on the individual's own decision concerning what is desirable. In the utilitarian view, the individual knows himself or herself best and is, therefore, the one best able to determine his or her own good. So, utilitarians argue, what the individual desires (provided that it does not harm others) is what she ought to be encouraged to pursue. In this way, classical utilitarianism includes a positive evaluation of liberty and personal autonomy—values we discuss in Chapter 5. Indeed, utilitarians may suggest that knowing oneself and choosing for oneself are themselves conditions of personal happiness.

Jeremy Bentham and John Stuart Mill, the two most prominent classical utilitarian theorists, each developed different specific views about what human beings will choose for themselves. The two classical positions are (a) that pleasure is the only thing of intrinsic value to people and thus worthy of pursuit (advocated by Jeremy Bentham, 1748–1832), and (b) that happiness is the singular intrinsic value worthy of pursuit (advocated by John Stuart Mill, 1806–1873).

In Bentham's view, called *hedonistic utilitarianism, actions and practices are right if they lead to pleasure (or prevent pain) and wrong if they lead to pain (or prevent pleasure).* The method of determining the rightness or wrongness of actions in terms of the variables of intensity, duration, and so on, thus became known as the *hedonic calculus*, a method of calculating pleasure and pain and the likelihood of their occurrence. Bentham himself seems to have been somewhat confused about the relationship of pleasure to pain. Although he spoke of them as opposites, he often thought of pleasure as a generalized feeling state, while he thought of pains as physical phenomena located here or there in the body (Bentham, 1789). It is not very easy to accept that one's only aim should be the avoidance of physical pain and the pursuit of sensual pleasure. Too many other kinds of painful and pleasant experiences are excluded in this view. Thus, one serious sort of objection to hedonistic utilitarianism is removed if the concepts of pain and pleasure are extended to include such pleasures as the anticipation and satisfaction at completing a task, and such pains as frustration and anguish.

Some have held, Mill among them, that *happiness* is the only thing of intrinsic value and, moreover, that happiness is not merely the sum total of pleasures of whatever variety (Mill, 1863). Utilitarianism here assumes the view that *actions and practices are right if they lead to happiness (or prevent unhappiness).* The good, interpreted as happiness, is not merely the sum total of pleasures because there are important qualitative as well as quantitative differences among pleasures. Thus, two lives of equal pleasure, quantitatively, may be of different value because the one includes pleasures of higher quality. Such *higher* pleasure would include those of the intellect, the appreciation of culture, and the general refinement of sensibilities. In this view these more intellectual or spiritual pleasures are preferable to more sensual pleasures, such as eating and sexual gratification. In turn, actions and practices that contribute to the living of a life filled with the *higher* pleasures are deemed preferable in this version of utilitarianism.

2.8 Measuring "The Good" in Dollars

A major problem frequently posed in reflection upon classical utilitarianism centers upon the proposed calculation of either pleasure (pain) or happiness (unhappiness). In our everyday talk it is plausible to speak of greater or lesser pleasures and pains. Likewise, it is plausible to speak of our lives, or periods of our lives, as being extremely happy, very happy, relatively happy, relatively unhappy, very unhappy, or extremely unhappy. This talk reflects a basis in our everyday experience for a rough concept of pleasure (pain) and happiness (unhappiness) as varying in quantity. Yet the utilitarians demand for precise quantifiable calculation, involves the assignment of units of value to pleasure and pain, happiness and unhappiness. This strikes many as a conceptual confusion and a practical impossibility. Thus, the usefulness of utilitarian theory itself is called into question. We might concede to utilitarians that pleasure (pain) and happiness (unhappiness) are normatively important considerations in ethics and social philosophy; that is, utilitarians are theoretically right about the kinds of things that make actions and practices right or wrong. Yet there remains a large stumbling block in the path toward practical application of the theory unless the problems of quantification and measure are solved.

The practice in contemporary economics of cost-benefit analysis can be understood as a partial response to this difficulty of classical utilitarianism. Whereas it is difficult to calculate pleasure (pain) or happiness (unhappiness), it is easy, as many of our examples have shown, to calculate financial gains and losses. Using cost-benefit analysis it seems we can generate and measure objective characterizations of the consequences of actions and policies. Although economists would not pretend that economic profit and loss are the whole story of the goodness and badness of consequences, they are convinced that monetary quantification is at least part of the story. They believe it unlikely that we can develop a single calculation procedure for evaluating all the factors contributing to the goodness or badness of consequences. They believe, however, that we should proceed to use and refine procedures, such as cost-benefit analysis, that yield objective results pertaining to at least some of those contributing factors. Thus cost-benefit analysis is one way utilitarian ideas have been translated into twentieth-century practice. How well it works in capturing the full force of the classical utilitarian position, as others of our examples suggest, is open to question. And even if it worked very well, whether one can capture intrinsic value in terms of dollars is a question yet to be resolved.

2.9 Difficult Questions for Utilitarians

Utilitarianism is seriously challenged by the variety of answers utilitarians have given to the question, "In virtue of exactly what are states of affairs good? Is it the pleasure involved, the happiness, the money or something else?" Suppose the play we previously imagined is a musical with many lovely songs and colorful production numbers. Because of these facts, a hedonistic utilitarian might give the production a very favorable evaluation for the pleasure produced by the songs and enjoyable dances. But another observer might think that a play is trivial and boring unless the script makes a significant social commentary which produces the happiness of a greater understanding of society. Someone who held this Millian view might place a low estimate on the play. And someone else, say the production's business manager, might only be thinking about ticket sales and production costs. For the business manager the play might be good or bad depending on nothing more than the color (black or red) of the ledger sheet's bottom line. Such a variety of evaluations is embarrassing because it casts serious doubt on the idea that people can come to agree on their value judgments by rationally considering the consequences of their actions. Yet remember, such agreement was one of the greatest initial attractions of utilitarianism.

A second embarrassment is also implicit. The utilitarians must say that the seven measured quantities—the intensity, duration, and so on—are quantities of pleasure or of happiness. A hedonistic utilitarian, for example, is committed to saying that the good is the pleasurable and that the pleasurable can be objectively measured. Each of these types of claims has proven controversial. For example, suppose someone said to you that you are not as happy as you think you are. How could you, or that other person, dispute such a claim or even know if the claim about your happiness might not be correct? In your experience, can happiness, or pleasure, be measured objectively? Are there objective ways to compare the happiness or pleasure several different people are experiencing? Granted we can sometimes tell what would make a person happy, but is there an objective way to decide exactly how happy that person is or will become?

EXERCISES

1. (a) The assertion, "Petroleum will be periodically scarce between 1980 and 2010," was much more certain in 1990 than in 1970. What knowledge (data) gained between 1990 and 1970 changed this degree of certainty?
   (b) Give an original example of increased and decreased certainty. (2.6)

2. Describe a problem situation. Then define two alternative responses to it, such that one should have much greater purity than the other. (2.4)

3. (a) Explain the (positive) fecundity of developing in children the habit of walking on the right side of halls and sidewalks.
   (b) Provide original examples of positive and of negative fecundity. (2.5)

4. (a) The Roses have promised their children a chance to work at the county fair. The only other commitment they made for the summer was to let Grandma Rose have the children come for a visit. Now Grandma has written that the children should come the same week the fair is on, because of the special activities in her town that week. As utilitarians, describe the sequence of steps the Roses should take to resolve this conflict.
   (b) How does this sequence bring out the utilitarian idea that actions are intrinsically neither right nor wrong? (2.1—2.6)
   (c) Provide a utilitarian definition of what it means to say an act or practice is right or wrong. "An action (or practice) is right if and only if ....." (2.6)

5. (a) List the steps of utilitarian conflict resolution.
   (b) Provide your own example involving a conflict situation and follow the utilitarian steps. (2.6)

6. Describe cases where:

(a) A hedonistic utilitarian would disagree with another utilitarian who believed in the greatest happiness of the greatest number.

(b) A benevolent utilitarian ruler knowingly rewards an undeserving person and knowingly lies to the population.

7. (a) The following is a cost-benefit exercise. Your instructions are (1) to pick out the cost items and the benefits to the home-buyer, (2) to associate the proportionally correct dollar figures with each cost or benefit, and (3) to identify the quantities in the exercise which measure the factor of propinquity. You need not do a full cost-benefit calculation.

Cost-Benefit Exercise: Home-builders, Inc., has designed two houses that you are considering buying next summer. The houses are identical except for their heating systems. The first has a conventional furnace and electric heat; the second house is designed to use solar power as its main heat source, backed up by a small, conventional furnace with electric heat. The houses, exclusive of heating systems, are designed to sell for $140,000. The furnace for the first house will cost an additional $5,000. The smaller furnace for the second house will cost only $2,000, but the solar collection system will cost $13,000. Electricity to heat the first home will cost $1,750 for the first winter. The electric cost to heat the second home will be 10 percent of the cost to heat the first home in any given year. You must put 20 percent down on either home, and your mortgage payments will be $110 per month higher on the more expensive home. If you were opening a certificate-of-deposit savings account, the bank would be willing to pay you 7 percent on your savings compounded annually. The cost of electricity will rise 20 percent at the end of every third year. Assume you intend to live in the house for 6 years and that you foresee no other costs are associated with heating for that time.

(b) Any process that requires a balanced input and output can be subject to cost-benefit analysis if the inputs and outputs can be quantified. For instance, if the digestive system used more energy digesting food (cost) than the energy released (benefit), then the organism would die. This idea applied to business yields the idea of profit and loss. What is the application of this idea to (1) a hydro-electric power plant? (2) an educational system?

DISCUSSION QUESTIONS

1. Suppose that achieving power was a person's concept of "The Good." How do the seven characteristics—extent, duration, certainty, fecundity, etc.—translate into this? What alternatives to waging a fair campaign in a democratic election might such a person pursue or not pursue and why, on utilitarian grounds?

2. If everyone is allowed to decide for herself or himself what "The Good" is, why do utilitarians rule out harming others as a by-product or even as a means to achieving one's goals? Can you state utilitarian reasons for this restriction?

3. It seems that the ability to foresee results accurately is essential to conducting a utilitarian evaluation. Should people who deliberately fail to do this, thus resulting in harm to themselves or others, be held accountable for this failure. Can you give a

utilitarian reason for holding them accountable or not accountable. Remember, giving a utilitarian reason means considering the consequences.

4. Discuss the issue of abortion from a strictly and exclusively utilitarian perspective. Formulate a sophisticated law regarding abortions, a law that takes into consideration a variety of different kinds of cases. Justify each provision of that law on strictly and exclusively utilitarian grounds.

ANSWERS TO SELECTED EXERCISES

1. (a) 1. Actual scarcities have occurred.
    2. The natural and political causes of these scarcities have become better known.
    3. Environmental laws registered an impact on alternating scarcity.
    4. The Organization of Petroleum Exporting Countries was formed.
    5. Alternative sources of energy have been developed but not quickly.
    6. Consumer demand for petroleum has increased.
    Each of (1)–(6) in some way renders further petroleum scarcities more probable.

2. Remember that impurities tend to enter a situation to the extent that either unpredictable or uncontrollable elements are involved. Thus, for example, an alternative requiring good weather (unpredictable in certain places) or reliance on an untrustworthy person (uncontrollable) might well lead to impurities.

3. (a) Once a person has such a habit, he can do things automatically, without thinking about them. Others can rely on those habits, increasing liberty. This training is easily transferred to later activities, such as bicycle riding and driving motorized vehicles, thereby improving personal and public safety.

4. (a) Here is an outline of the answer (incomplete except for its first step, where the alternatives are filled in):
    1. Define alternative courses of action.
       (i) The children work at the fair and go to Grandma's another week.
       (ii) Send them to Grandma's during fair week, let them work at the fair another year.
       (iii) Work part of the week at the fair, visit Grandma's part of the week.
       (iv) Allow children neither to visit Grandma, nor to work at the fair. (Maybe take them away on vacation.)
    2. Detail the foreseeable consequences of each alternative, including collecting further available data.
    3. Decide whether pleasure or happiness or what will determine the good (and bad).
    4. Specify the intensity, duration, and so on, of each variation of good or bad consequence and ways of achieving them.
    (b) The only elements to calculate in choosing an alternative are the quantities of the pleasure or happiness involved in each alternative's consequence. Thus, actions are viewed as right only instrumentally as they conduce to desirable states of affairs. (See 2.2 and 2.6)

5. The four steps are described in the answer to 4a above. Answer 4a shows how you might answer 5b.

6. (a) Your case should involve more sensual pleasures as one alternative and more intellectual, cultural, or spiritual pleasures as a conflicting alternative.

(b) Rewards are motivators, not just for the people who receive them but for the people who would like to receive them. *Disinformation* may have its utilitarian purposes, too. Deceiving one's own population may be considered justifiable on utilitarian grounds if it can be shown that it brings about consequences that are for the good of the people themselves.

7. (a) 1. The costs of the house without heat and of the alternative heating systems—that is, the costs of the down payments, the costs of the mortgages (principal plus interest), and the costs of heating. In terms of propinquity, if you have the money for the down payment on the more expensive, solar house, you can reap the benefit of interest on a savings account by buying the cheaper house.

2. Cost of the houses $140,000
   Heating systems $5,000 vs. $15,000
   Down payments*   20% of $145,000 or $155,000
   Mortgage payments $110 times 72 months for the solar home.
   Heating $1,750 or $175 per year for three years
                                           $2,100 or $210 per year for years 4–6,
   Savings* $10,000 plus 7 percent interest, compounded
                                           indefinitely, or until withdrawn.

*Indicates propinquity is involved.

(b) 1. Net energy equals energy produced by generating plant minus energy used to produce energy.

2. Net knowledge and abilities equals knowledge and abilities gained by students minus knowledge and abilities of teachers used to teach students. (But given some theories of education the teachers may expend energy, but they gain knowledge and ability through practicing their art. Thus the gross could also be knowledge and abilities gained by students plus knowledge and abilities gained by teachers. If these could be reduced to dollars, we might then get the *net* by subtracting the dollar costs of physical resources, salaries for teachers and staff people, and lost hours of wages for students who are studying rather than working for pay.)

Section 3
COMPLICATIONS OF UTILITARIANISM

The concern to maximize utility is a powerful normative factor in decision making in business and government, as well as in private affairs. In the first two sections we outlined the basic concepts and recommendations of utilitarian normative theory. In so doing we encountered such problems as the insensitivity of utilitarianism to different human relationships, its embarrassment over differing interpretations of *The Good*, and the practical and conceptual problems with objectively quantifying intrinsic value and carrying out the required calculations. In this section we will consider further complications in the interpretation and practical application of this theory. First we will consider whether utilitarianism is most plausibly understood as recommending that actions be evaluated in terms of their utility or in terms of their conformity to rules that have utility. We shall discuss whether utilitarianism requires that agents be held responsible for the actual or merely the foreseeable consequences of their actions. And we will consider how utilitarians might respond to the objections that their approach can do violence to justice, rights and respect for persons. After studying this section you should be able to:

- Distinguish the act and the rule interpretations of utilitarian theory.
- Provide both act and rule utilitarian justifications of actions.
- State the importance of the difference between actual and foreseeable consequences in estimating the responsibility of agents according to utilitarianism.

THE CASE OF THE FUGITIVE SLAVES

The scene is Fostoria, Ohio, along the famous Underground Railroad, which successfully smuggled many fugitive slaves to freedom in mid-nineteenth-century America. A father is explaining to his son why he may have to lie to slave hunters if they should make direct inquiries as to the whereabouts of the fugitives.

"Son, now you listen close. If ever anyone asks you about the slaves we're hiding in the old shed, you tell 'em you don't know what they're talking about. You hear me? You tell 'em you don't know nothing."

"But, Dad, that's lying. Straight out lying! You told me never to do such a terrible thing."

"That's right, son. It's a lie. But if you tell the truth, they'll capture those slaves, maybe kill 'em or else take 'em back to nothing but a lifetime of sweat, shackles and suffering. And your daddy might get into a whole lot of trouble, too."

"But what about those times when you told me that people shouldn't lie to each other so as they can get along better and be able to trust each other?"

"Well, generally that's true, son. But sometimes a rule has to be put aside. And this is one of those few times. Not lying is a good rule, but in this case it has to be broken or something even worse is going to happen."

3.1 Act and Rule Utilitarianism

We have explained how utilitarian theory focuses on the evaluation of actions and practices by looking at their consequences. But we have not distinguished specific acts from general practices. The case study deals with whether a given act would be right or wrong, namely: this boy's lying to slave hunters if they happen to ask him a direct question about where certain fugitive slaves are hidden. The boy, remembering that the rule prohibiting lying generally produces a preponderance of good consequences, wonders why the rule should not be applied here. The father, emphasizing that this particular lie would produce good consequences, says the boy should think of this situation as an exception to the general rule against lying. Both persons are concerned about the place of moral rules in governing conduct. Their two views are those held by what have come to be called *rule utilitarian* and *act utilitarian* theorists.

Fundamentally, both the act and rule theorists are utilitarians for they agree that the ultimate measure of the rightness or wrongness of human conduct is the tendency of that conduct to result in good consequences. But the crucial question is this: Do we apply this ultimate measure to individual actions, or to general practices described by the rules that govern them? *Act utilitarianism is the view that an action is right or wrong as a function of the specific consequences of that particular action. Rule utilitarianism is the view that the evaluation of the rightness or wrongness of an action is a three-step process.* First, one must *state the alternative actions* that could have been taken in a given situation. Second, one must *define the rules* under which one would be acting in taking each of the possible actions. Third, and ultimately, one must *determine the comparative acceptability of the rules* in question by evaluating the utility of the practices implied by each of the rules. For the act utilitarian, the utility of the act is primary. The rule utilitarian gives primacy to the utility of the rule.

In the case study the son is puzzled about the status of the general rule that one should not lie. Apparently in the past his father has given him a rule utilitarian justification of the practice of never lying. The justification points to the good consequences of everyone's following the rule—namely, promoting those desirable states of affairs characterized by harmony and trust among people. In this view, the right thing is always to tell the truth, owing to the general utility of the rule that requires it. Yet the father is now suggesting that the general utility of such a practice should be subordinated to consideration of the consequences of a particular act of lying. The father provides an act utilitarian justification of the lie by pointing out the likely bad consequences for the fugitives and himself if the truth is told. Either the father has changed his mind, or the boy misinterpreted his father's intended meaning in originally justifying the rule against lying. It was only apparently, but not actually, a rule utilitarian defense of the practice of telling the truth. *A rule utilitarian would hold that there can be no exceptions to the rules once they have been shown to be useful.* Rules that have good utility should be followed, always.

There are many benefits produced by the general practice of following rules. Things are easier to decide and we can trust what others are going to do. For example, the traffic rules can be shown to have great utility in terms of saving lives and money. For a rule utilitarian, this having been shown, these laws should be followed. And consider the benefits to all of us if they are, or rather the disastrous chaos that would ensue if they were not. Driving the freeways would be suicidal if people opportunistically disobeyed all the rules. Also, considering the pace at which things happen and the congestion already evident, we would simply not have the time to calculate the utility of each and every particular act we do while driving. It's better for all concerned that there are rules and that they are always followed.

An act utilitarian need not dismiss talk of moral rules as altogether pointless. Rather, in the act utilitarian view, moral rules can be understood as having a place in morality, but as handy guidelines or general recommendations, not as laws which admit of no exceptions. The act utilitarian sees moral rules as aids to decision making, when one is in circumstances that greatly resemble earlier ones where similar decisions were made. However, all rules are subject to suspension, especially when circumstances arise unlike those to which the rule ordinarily has been applied. In the case study the father wants the ordinarily reliable and useful rule against lying suspended, and the focus is upon the utility of the particular act of lying in the unique circumstances that the son might confront—namely, talking to slave hunters.

In summary, then, the usefulness of performing *particular* actions is quite distinct from the usefulness of functioning with a set of moral rules that require or prohibit specified *kinds* of action. It is on this point that the distinction between act utilitarianism and rule utilitarianism turns. It is quite possible that they could require different actions, as illustrated in the case study, where rule utilitarianism requires telling the slave hunters the truth but act utilitarianism dictates the lie.

3.2 Objections to Act and Rule Utilitarianism

Critics who have looked closely at both the rule and act interpretations of utilitarian theory have detected difficulties in determining which view is most plausible. The difficulty with act utilitarianism is that the wrongness of breaking promises, killing, and the like turns out to be nothing more than a matter of statistical generalization, which is false in given cases. That is, for act utilitarians, moral rules are not really binding upon human conduct. Even though generally, murder produces a preponderance of bad consequences, a given act of murder might be justifiable depending on its consequences. For example, a police officer unjustly killing a known drug-dealing, child-molesting, rapist might be justifiable in terms of the good consequences that death produces as measured in saving taxpayers the money for court costs in a capital case and in preventing harm to future victims whose lives might have been ruined, and also maybe in saving the rapist from the misery of life on death row. That would mean, for the act utilitarian, that in this case the murder would be justifiable—a conclusion ethicists find unacceptable on the grounds of justice and the violation of rights. If act utilitarianism can lead to such injustices, maybe it should be carefully reconsidered.

Also the act utilitarian would say that this case counts as evidence against the general rule that prohibits murder. Rules are at best only a form of practical shorthand in decision making; but in no way are they morally authoritative. This also strikes many ethicists as an entirely implausible interpretation of the place of rules in normative theory and practice. If act utilitarianism leads to the view that moral rules are only rough generalizations based on the inconsistent evidence of thousands of individual actions, then act utilitarianism must be mistaken someplace, because that is not what moral rules are.

Seeing the problems with act utilitarianism, other utilitarian thinkers have advocated that the place of moral rules must be given more prominence in their theory. These rules are not to be taken lightly. They are normative principles, not crude empirical generalizations. Actions should be judged in terms of how they conform to rules. And the rules themselves should be justified in terms of their social utility. But on rule utilitarian view it turns out that at times it is actually right to do things that can be known in advance not to have the best possible consequences. This is very puzzling and inconsistent with the stated goals of utilitarianism. How could a theory that would judge human conduct in terms of its conducing to good consequences ever sanction doing things that are known not to maximize the good?

The case study illustrates both of these difficulties. The son experiences difficulty in understanding the place of rules in morality when his father suggests that a moral rule can readily be set aside in particular circumstances, where following the rule would not maximize the good. A rule utilitarian would disagree and say that the boy should not lie. But there is genuine implausibility in supposing that the rule against lying, however useful the general practice of telling the truth might be, should be observed in this case. Even if one were not a utilitarian, in weighing telling the truth against saving a human life one would be hard pressed not to find the lie justifiable. All the more for a utilitarian; a violation of the rule would, in the case at hand, prevent significantly bad consequences. How could a utilitarian require that one tell the truth when lying to the slave hunter was known to result in far better consequences?

3.3 Foreseeable and Unforeseeable Consequences

Further complications in the interpretation of utilitarian theory arise over whether utilitarians would hold people responsible for the actual or merely the foreseeable consequences of their conduct. As any coach knows, there are plenty of ways to lose games; none are intended, but some are foreseeable while some cannot be foreseen. And when the season is finished there is that win-loss record, big as life. Fair or unfair, coaches are often judged in the results-oriented world of sports by the W's and the L's—that is, by what they produced. The issue of fairness aside, how reasonable is it to hold people responsible for things they could not have foreseen and do not intend?

In one view, what has been called one's *objective duty is to perform those actions or adopt those practices that actually turn out to produce the best possible balance of good compared to bad.* In this view, all the foreseeable and unforeseeable consequences of actions and practices are to be taken into account in the ultimate retrospective evaluation of their rightness and wrongness. So the coach is responsible, in terms of her utilitarian objective duty, for all the W's and all the

L's, no matter what factors contributed to achieving them. The point made by the concept of objective duty is that, at least in the utilitarian view, what makes an action right is its actual consequences, regardless of whether they are foreseen.

Since, however, many future circumstances cannot be foreseen, one may clearly fail to do one's objective duty—yet it would not seem reasonable to count such a failure as one warranting blame. How could the agent be blamed, the argument goes, for what could not be foreseen? If the coach had foreseen that the bus would break down, then she may have planned some other way to get the team to the game and the loss due to forfeit would not have gone on her coaching record. But it seems unreasonable to have expected that she could foresee the bus breakdown. Out of the acceptance of this argument has grown the concept of one's *subjective duty*. By definition, one's *subjective duty is to perform those actions, or adopt those practices, that are likely to produce the best balance of good compared to bad foreseeable future consequences.* In this view, people are to be praised or blamed on the basis of the rational quality of their planning and their decisions, not on the basis of unforeseeable but actual results. If it turns out that, owing to unforeseeable turns of events, one's best calculations are mistaken, one is not to blame for any undesirable unforeseen consequences, even if one fails to live up to one's objective duty.

To fail at the time of deliberation to take into account those foreseeable consequences which are likely to result in a failure to perform one's objective duty is, itself, a failure to do one's subjective duty, and such failure would warrant censure on utilitarian grounds. In other words, the coach is responsible for considering all the things that are likely to affect winning and losing. Not doing this is a failure to do her subjective duty. And, moreover, this failure will probably lead to more losses, a failure in objective duty. It is reasonable to criticize the coach if she fails to take the obvious things into consideration. That is, it is reasonable to hold people accountable for doing their subjective duty.

In the case study the consequences discussed are foreseeable. It is possible to predict that the fugitives will get away and the family will be spared future trouble if the lie is told. It is also possible to predict that the fugitives will be captured and maybe killed for bounty (or held against their will as slaves) and the family endangered if the truth is told. The father, then, is doing his subjective duty in taking into account the foreseeable and likely consequences of the alternatives involved. It may turn out, however, that each of the fugitives on reaching freedom will become a murderous criminal who commits a series of heinous crimes. If so, then aiding them in their escape will turn out to have worse consequences than turning them over to the slave hunters, so that protecting the slaves turns out to be contrary to objective duty. However, such consequences are unforeseeable and not likely enough to be of the sort the father or the son should reasonably be held responsible to foresee. In failing to take into account unlikely and unforeseeable consequences there is no failure of subjective duty.

This distinction between objective and subjective duty is important to utilitarianism because it aims at evaluating every action by appeal to actual consequences. Thus utilitarians are forced to say that a person does wrong whenever he or she fails to do his or her objective duty. The coach did wrong by losing when the bus broke down and the team had to forfeit. But if the bad consequences are unforeseeable, utilitarians can agree with many others that a person should not be held responsible, praised or blamed, for what he or she could not foresee and, thus, could not rationally intend or avoid. Other ethicists question the idea that failing to do one's objective duty is necessarily wrong. Why should the coach be said to have done wrong in any sense (objective or subjective) when the forfeit was caused entirely by the bus breakdown and was not by any kind of failure on the coach's part?

3.4 Social Utility vs. Justice, Rights, or Respect for Persons

There is no doubt that social utility is a value. It is desirable, all things being equal, to evaluate one's policy options or choices in terms of which would be the most likely to bring about the greatest net balance of positive over negative results for the greatest number of persons. But social utility, whether conceived in terms of dollars or happiness, is not, many would say, the last word on any issue. And the "all things being equal" clause simply hides too much that should be brought to light and ethically discussed.

Take, for example, the controversy over the legalization of abortion. From before Roe vs. Wade to the 1989 Supreme Court ruling and beyond, this social, legal and ethical question has commanded serious, if not fierce, attention. In an exercise in section 2 we asked that you try to consider the abortion issue exclusively from the utilitarian perspective. What made that exercise difficult is that there are many more dimensions to the abortion issue than simply the consequent states of affairs, good or bad, produced by a particular act of abortion or produced by a general rule legalizing or prohibiting abortions. The abortion issue involves questions of rights. It involves respect for persons, either from the perspective of autonomous adults or from the perspective of their being in the earliest stage of development, or from both those perspectives. The abortion issue also involves, for many people, deep-felt religious or political convictions, as well as high levels of emotional investment in being able to say to themselves that they are conducting their lives in a forthright and ethical way. In addition, since the time when states enacted statutes on this and courts began to rule on it, the law was involved. Hence, this introduces matters of legal rights, the interests of the state, and matters of justice, not the least of which is the distribution of the costs of legal abortions to taxpayers or persons who have the same medical insurance carrier as the person having the abortion. In short, the abortion issue illustrates the point that the consideration of consequences, while important, is not the only important thing. Justice, law, rights, autonomy, respect for persons, even one's own emotional well-being, are also part of the moral picture. A serious shortcoming of utilitarianism is that in its effort to prescribe how we can reach accord on controversial issues, it recommends a way which neglects to take into consideration many of the aspects of vital importance in those issues.

A second concern raised by persons who are outside the utilitarian camp is that cases can arise where fairness, justice or rights conflict with the strictly utilitarian analysis. Another section 2 exercise illustrated the conflict between justice and utility when it asked you to describe a case where an undeserving person is given an award in order to bring about some socially useful results. Awards are hardly as big a problem as punishments. But the case could easily have been put this way: Imagine how a corrupt government official might decide to put to death unjustly an innocent person whom the public wrongly believes is guilty in order to bring about such socially useful consequences as the official's own continuation in office and an easing of the public's clamor for swift action. More than a few dramatic films were made around such a plot.

Or, to take an example where utility conflicts with rights, suppose you sign a lease for an apartment and discover that the lease binds you to a monthly payment which is far higher than you can afford. You thought you would be able to make the payments when you signed, but it turns out you cannot. You ask to be let out of the lease. You argue on good utilitarian grounds that the harm to you outweighs the harm to the landlord who can afford to let you out of the lease and who also can easily rent the apartment to someone else right away. But the landlord, exercising his rights, politely refuses. As much as we might sympathize with your plight, we find it difficult to see the landlord as immoral for having refused. You did sign the agreement and he has the right to insist that you honor it. Suppose, however, you stop payments, pack up and move away. But the police find you and the landlord takes you to court. You give your utilitarian arguments to the judge, who then rules in favor of the landlord. Why? Now you've violated the law which is designed to enforce binding contracts and also you've violated the landlord's legal rights to the lease money. Here too, it is difficult to say that you did the right thing when you skipped out, in spite of the understandable utilitarian reasons for your wanting to be released from the rental contract.

The issue is not closed with our noting that utility can conflict with justice, rights, freedom, law or respect for person. Utilitarian theorists can argue that some, if not all, of these values can themselves be justified on utilitarian grounds. There are utilitarian arguments for ascribing rights to people and for not violating those rights. There are utilitarian reasons for insisting that people are treated with justice and respect, and for ascribing to persons a large number of individual freedoms. But that there are utilitarian justifications for these things does not mean that we value these things for those reasons. Many people would say that those reasons are interesting, but beside the point. We value justice, freedom, honesty, and the like because these things are intrinsically desirable, not because valuing them is conducive to good consequences. And these things retain their intrinsic value for use even in cases where they are not conducive to good consequences. So, that human rights or respect for persons can be justified on utilitarian grounds does not, of itself, establish that we ought to justify them that way or that there is any reason to consider looking to social utility as a basis for justifying them at all.

EXERCISES

1. To say that a person owns some property is not merely to say that it is his or her possession, but that he or she is entitled to it. The owner of property is generally entitled to use his or her property as he or she sees fit. In our society people own houses, cars, boats, pets, and clothes. They buy food and fuel.
   (a) What usefulness does our society's practice of allowing private ownership of property have?
   (b) Can you define stealing in relation to a person's right to own?
   (c) How would a rule utilitarian explain the wrongness of stealing?
   (d) Describe a case in which stealing might seem right despite the rule utilitarian argument against it.
   (e) How would an act utilitarian explain the wrongness of stealing?
   (f) Why is the act utilitarian view of the wrongness of stealing implausible?
   (g) Describe a case where a person's legal property rights conflict with the good of the society in general such that the public good ought to take priority.
   (h) Describe a case where a person's legal property rights conflict with the good of the public such that the property rights take priority.
2. (a) Why would a utilitarian probably say that a person scarcely ever does the right thing? (3.3)
   (b) In light of this, how does the concept of subjective duty allow the utilitarian to avoid blaming people for continually acting wrongly?
   (c) Describe a case in which a person's objective and subjective duty diverge.
   (d) On strictly utilitarian grounds, should a person be held accountable for foreseeable but unforeseen duties?
   (e) On strictly utilitarian grounds, does the fact that certain foreseen consequences were unintended make any difference in terms of one's objective or subjective responsibility?

DISCUSSION QUESTIONS

1. We sketched the case of the police officer who kills the known criminal in order to save the taxpayers tons of money and bring about other desirable results. Apart from act utilitarian considerations, would a police officer be morally justified or not in doing something like that? Does the fact that it could be done without ever being detected make any moral difference in this case? How are considerations of law, justice, and respect for persons relevant, in your view, to a case like this?
2. How does the act utilitarian vs. rule utilitarian distinction play out in conducting a cost-benefit analysis? How do the objections raised against utilitarianism apply to its

contemporary manifestation which is the application of cost-benefit techniques to policy decisions in government, the professions and in business life?

ANSWERS TO SELECTED EXERCISES

1. (a) Property provides *security* by assuring persons that they will have what they have expected to have and have legitimately acquired.

   (b) Stealing is violating a property right by exercising control over something that another person has the right to control.

   (c) Stealing is wrong, the rule utilitarian would say, because it disrupts the security maintained in (a). This security is important in society, for example, so that Person X can rely on Person Y when Y wants to use his property as collateral in obtaining a loan or securing a contract. Without security, trust is difficult; without trust, cooperation is difficult; without cooperation, life is difficult or impossible.

   (e) The act utilitarian would say stealing is wrong because the penalty for the thief, if caught, and the owner's loss of the property, together are usually worse than the good the thief gains from the stolen item.

2. (a) Almost all actions have unforeseeable consequences, some of which are bad. Usually, the utilitarian would argue, some adjustment in any act you actually did would have produced a better balance of good over bad consequences.

   (c) Such a case is, essentially, one in which the act with the best balance of foreseeable consequences differs from the one with the best balance of actual consequences.

   (e) No. Intentions are relevant in assessing a person's character and attitude toward what happened, but the agent's intentions are not part of the consequent states of affairs and hence not, strictly speaking, part of the utilitarian analysis of good and bad. This is another thing people find counter-intuitive about utilitarianism. We generally think that a person's intentions are extremely important in deciding whether a person acted ethically or not.

3 ETHICAL EGOISM

Can people ever act out of motives other than those of self-interest? If they cannot, does that make the recommendation that we should act only out of self-interest a pointless piece of advice? Even if people can act on the basis of other motives, should they not consider self-interest, or would that be foolish? What reasons could there be for being moral, if *being moral* means something different than always acting in one's own interest?

These questions regarding human motivation and conduct focus on facts, on ethical theory and on the validity of normative theorizing itself. Addressing these questions are two theories: *Psychological Egoism*, an empirical theory about how humans are actually motivated, and *Ethical Egoism*, a normative theory about how human conduct, if it is moral, *ought to be* motivated.

We begin this chapter by analyzing the concept of acting out of one's own self-interest. Our aim is to separate the factual, conceptual, and normative issues involved. We will also explore the variety of motives out of which persons may act. In particular we will contrast the pursuit of one's own self-interest with pursuing the interests of others. We are then in a position to distinguish between psychological and ethical egoism as these two theories relate to the pursuit of self-interest. We will look at the facts and the value issues involved, ultimately taking up the central question of ethical egoism: "Should people act exclusively out of self-interest?" The educational goal of this chapter is for you to understand and be able to apply the views of psychological and ethical egoists regarding human motivation and conduct.

Section 1
PURSUING ONE'S OWN SELF-INTEREST

Egoistic theories focus upon the pursuit of self-interest in human conduct. In this section we clarify the concept of *acting self-interestedly* by considering: (a) the contrast between unenlightened and enlightened self-interested conduct, (b) the varieties of things it might be in one's interest to pursue, (c) the compatibility of cooperation and the pursuit of one's own interest, and (d) the differences between "acting self-interestedly," "acting in one's own interest," and "doing as one pleases." After you study this section you should be able to:

- Characterize unenlightened and enlightened pursuit of self-interest.
- Contrast self-interested and non-self-interested reasons for cooperation.
- Distinguish between the subject and the object of interest.
- Explain the importance of the subject/object distinction for the analysis of "acting self-interestedly."

THE CASE OF THE DEFERENTIAL LOVER, PART I

"Look, Michele," said Heather, "Kathleen's coming and she really looks glum today! I wonder if she's got Andy-troubles again."

Michele picked at her lunch salad and said, "I think we should mind our own business. Kathleen's problems are her own."

Kathleen sat down beside her friends and reached for a packet of artificial sweetener. She dumped its contents into her paper cup and stirred her coffee with the thin plastic straw. After sipping the hot brew she said, "Why is it the same old story with every guy I meet? No matter what I do for Andy its never enough! I shop, cook and do all the cleaning. We both work full-time, so why should I do everything? And the slob doesn't even say thanks!"

Heather listened impatiently to Kathleen's familiar complaints. When she finished Heather said, "There's got to be more to it than that. Think! What can *you* get out of all of your effort? You should please yourself sometimes. Why not make your relationship with Andy work for you?"

"Heather, I'm not like that. I couldn't. It's so selfish, so shortsighted! I mean, Andy's got his problems too. He works hard all day. When he gets to the apartment he doesn't need to find it all messy. And, well, I care for him. I'm not an island. I couldn't live with myself if..."

"Kathleen, you missed my point," interrupted Heather. "I didn't say that you should move out of the apartment and live like you're the only person in the world. I meant that people live together because of what it offers. Face facts, you moved in with Andy because *you* wanted to be with him. You did it for yourself, in other words. Andy represents something to you. Security, affection, attention, whatever. I hate to disillusion you, but we all act that way. Even Andy does. Don't be ashamed of what's natural. Use your relationship to your advantage."

"Oh, do tell me how I can, honey," hissed Kathleen.

"That wasn't called for," said Heather. "I'm not patronizing you, I'm just being realistic. There are lots of little tricks you can use to get Andy to do things for you. That's how I keep John interested in me. And he never even suspects. Why just yesterday I bought a little surprise to wear tonight when he gets home from work. I'll bet it earns me a night of fun, and maybe even that vacation to Sun Valley I've been working on. If you don't see me tomorrow, well you can just draw your own conclusions."

Kathleen just shook her head. "Heather, keeping Andy sexually interested is the least of my problems. Besides, all that manipulation doesn't seem right. It's not how I want to relate to Andy."

"I don't understand," said Heather.

Michele said, "I think she means it would be like lying to trick Andy the way you suggested. It's dishonest, insincere. Where's your self-respect, anyway, Heather?"

"You're right, Michele. I don't want to be devious and selfish."

"Hey, you two, have a little mercy. I'm only offering advice. You can take it or leave it. It's all the same to me."

"Heather," said Michele, "These little tricks of yours can ruin a relationship. Take Bill and I, for example. We have something special. I would feel I had lost my self-respect if I resorted to lies and tricks just to gratify myself. Don't you think it's possible? I mean, don't you think one person can care for another for the sake of that other person rather than simply as a tool to be used to satisfy his or her own desires? I do."

"I do too, Michele," said Kathleen. "And more than that, Heather, I feel it's part of my duty as a woman to care for others and put aside my desires."

"Really now! I can't believe you said that, Kathleen," said Heather. "Don't you see how unhappy you are? It's because you are always putting others first. People do what they want to do. They always serve old 'number one' first. Didn't you ever ask Andy why he hasn't married you? Who do you think he's trying to please? You can bet it's not you, sweetie. Look, you'll never be happy until you realize that you are just like everyone else. You have always been pursuing your own interests. I believe that nobody can want others to be happy at their own expense. You can't and you shouldn't try to. It's self-defeating. Besides, who deserves to have their desires met more than you? All I'm saying is put yourself first, Kathleen, or else you'll suffer right to the end."

"Heather, you confuse me," said Michele. "Do you want Kathleen to improve her own life or do you just want her to do what she wants to do? I can't tell which it is."

"I'm confused too, Heather. I care for Andy no matter what you think."

"Kathleen, I didn't mean to upset you. I was only trying to explain your problem..."

Michele interrupted. "Yes we know, but she doesn't have to swing all the way over from total self-sacrifice to using other people only to serve her personal interests. Why can't she stop in the middle? Why can't she be an equal with Andy? She cares for him. So, she shouldn't lose her own self-respect in an effort to please him. But neither should she neglect Andy just to please herself."

Kathleen finished her coffee and stood up. "Look, while you two analyze my love life, I've got to go to the store. Andy ran out of beer last night and he asked me to pick some up during my lunch hour."

"I've got to run too, said Michele. I've got a client to meet in twenty minutes."

"Well, have fun you two, I'm off to use some of John's wonderful money on wine for him—and for me! You know what I mean?"

1.1 Unenlightened and Enlightened Self-Interest

The case study focuses on whether Kathleen is or ought to be *selfish*. Selfishness, however, has many distinct meanings. Throughout this section our discussion of self-interest is meant to clarify these distinct meanings. Let us first distinguish between what has come to be called *unenlightened* and *enlightened* self-interest. Traditionally this difference has been characterized in terms of shortsighted and farsighted planning for one's own benefit. An unenlightened view of self-interest would mean acting on the basis of present feelings and impulses with no thought for the long-term consequences of one's actions. In contrast, the enlightened pursuit of self-interest is more subtle, restrained, refined and farsighted. For example, even if another strawberry margarita or two were appealing, an enlightened egoist would consider the extra danger to himself while driving home, the increased possibility of a hefty fine and time in jail for driving under the influence, and the pain of a nasty hangover as well.

Similarly, an enlightened egoist would recognize that blatantly self-interested behavior, especially behavior that obviously harms or endangers others, will likely bring more grief than reward to himself in the long run. The enlightened egoist recognizes that it cannot be in one's self-interest to live in such a way as to miss out on possible future happiness that could be one's own with a little restraint.

In the case study, Kathleen expresses initial skepticism about Heather's recommendation that she think of her own interests more. Part of her skepticism arises out of her belief that pursuit of self-interest requires one to be obviously selfish and possibly even obnoxious. This strikes her as shortsighted, and she worries about the possible long-range consequences of losing Andy. Heather, enlightened as she is, immediately reassures Kathleen that pursuit of self-interest can be both farsighted and subtle. She plans, through using her little tricks, as she calls them, to keep her relationship with John interesting and fulfilling for a long long time.

Heather stresses creature comfort and material goods, as for example the vacation to Sun Valley, as worthy of pursuit. Michele, by contrast, points to one's self-interest in pursuing such goods as self-respect, integrity, and a trusting relationship with another person. Notice that these are not materialistic goods, nor does one have to be competitively oriented as one pursues them. In other words, the contrast between unenlightened and enlightened pursuit of self-interest need not be characterized solely in terms of being shortsighted or farsighted. One can also be relatively enlightened about the kinds of things one pursues as well as how one goes about pursuing these things.

1.2 Cooperation and Self-Interest

In the case study, Heather maintains that people live together and marry only to more effectively pursue their self-interest. In her view the cooperation that marriage entails is worth the trouble in the long run. Andy is obviously reaping the rewards of Kathleen's undying devotion and attention to his needs. Heather is simply suggesting to Kathleen that she must realize this and that she should see to it that she gets her share of the rewards the relationship with Andy has to offer. Indeed, in Heather's view it is quite appropriate for Kathleen to continue to serve Andy's interests although those interests are not to be taken as intrinsically valuable. Heather is convinced that playing such an apparently self-sacrificing role only makes sense if in doing so one can effectively pursue *one's own* interest.

It is a mistake to think that cooperation with others and pursuit of self-interest are mutually exclusive. One person's interests need not necessarily conflict with those of another. The success of many large businesses is built on the fact that the interests of several people can be better achieved by mutual cooperation and team work. If our interests always conflicted, we would all probably live more isolated, lonely, competitive, if not combative lives. However, the reality of human interaction is that avoiding the tensions and insecurities that would result from isolated living is itself in the self-interest of each individual. Moreover, there are abundant examples of situations where individuals hope to benefit in the long run by helping others. A crude example of such self-interested helping would be a person's bringing hot meals to a rich but bedridden widow with the end in view of being written into her will.

There are also cases where individuals involved in cooperative endeavors stand to gain personally from the effort in ways that would be impossible without the cooperation. Think of a small business partnership for example. It can be conceived as grounded in the pursuit of self-interest by each of the partners. They pool their resources and use the common means of their investment in achieving the distinct ends of the personal profit and well-being of each. It is also possible to conceive of the establishment of government as rooted in each citizen's recognizing the long-term benefits of mutual security and the protection of property that can be afforded only by community strength. Each citizen cooperates to insure the functioning of the state, not directly for the sake of the harmony which cooperation brings, but rather for the sake of the more effective pursuit of each one's self-interest.

1.3 Self-Interest and Doing What One Wants

When a person undergoes medical or psychological treatment, they expect the physician or psychologist to act in the interest of the patient or client. Should a person indicate he intends to inflict harm on himself, the psychologist would not be acting in the client's interest to permit the person to do that harm. There is an important difference, in other words, between *one's self-interest* and *doing what one wants*. To examine this distinction, let's begin by separating *who has the interest* (the *subject* of the interest), from *what is wanted or desired* (the *object* of the interest). Saying "People always do what they want to do" can be true in a trivial way if it only means "All subjects act upon those desires which they have." That is one (quite unimportant) sense of the expression "acting in one's own interest." However, that is not the same as saying that the principal *object* of those interests is the well-being of the person who has the interests. The idea that I want to give you a million dollars is clearly distinct from the idea that it is to my financial advantage for me to part with the money.

For our purposes the crucial sense of "acting in one's own interest" is the one that means "acting in the interest of furthering one's own well-being." What makes a given object of my desire one of self-interest is not simply that I desire it, but rather that my principle goal, which is to benefit myself, can be achieved by the fulfillment of that desire. It is because of this crucial difference that the psychologist can be said to be acting in the interest of the client by preventing the client from doing what he wants. In the same way, a physician can be acting in the interest of a patient, say a child, by providing a treatment which the child may say, very sincerely, that it does not want.

As Heather points out in the case study, people who pursue their own interest, or do what they want, in the crucial self-interested sense noted above, act neither out of a sense of duty nor out of a sense of the value of serving the interests of others for the others' sake. Rather, they act with the ultimate objective of improving their own lot in life. Thus, to say that people are acting self-interestedly is not simply to say that they are acting on interests or wants which they happen to have, such as Kathleen's desire to please Andy. But rather *acting self-interestedly* means that from among the many possible objects of interest or desire, these people have *assigned first priority to their own welfare*. Hence Heather recommends that Kathleen should try to get something *for herself* out of her relationship with Andy.

Since *doing what one wants* and *acting self-interestedly* are quite distinct from a conceptual point of view, an important empirical question arises: Are people ever, in fact, motivated by anything other than self-interested goals?" Judging from what Kathleen says about herself in the case study, the answer is yes. Although Heather counters that by speculating that Andy, for example, is acting out of his self-interest by not marrying Kathleen. Heather goes on to say that Kathleen should acknowledge that she, just like everyone else, is really concerned primarily with her own welfare, though she has been very unwise in pursuing it. At this point Michele observes that Heather is guilty of the very confusion that our conceptual analysis discloses. Michele recognizes that Kathleen is the *subject* of an interest (Kathleen desires Andy's welfare) however continuing to pursue the *object* (Andy's welfare) apparently is not in Kathleen's own self-interest.

EXERCISES

1. Below is a list of characteristics. If any is essential to both the enlightened and unenlightened pursuit of self-interest, mark it *B*; if it fits only the enlightened pursuit of self-interest, mark it *E*; if it fits only the pursuit of unenlightened self-interest, mark it *U*; if it fits neither, mark it *N*. (1.1).

    (a) Always being keenly aware of my own interests and desires

    (b) Always trying to determine the likely consequences for myself of any possible action I might have open to me

    (c) Always doing what the majority wants

    (d) Always seeking the approval of upper management

    (e) Always doing what I feel like doing at a given moment

    (f) Always following my immediate supervisor's direct orders

    (g) Always cooperating with the expressed desires of my clients

    (h) Always acting in accord with the principle of respect for others

    (i) Never frustrating others by my actions if the likely consequence of such frustration is that I shall, over the course of time, be less able to gain my desires

    (j) Always trying to develop my business, social, intellectual, artistic and physical capacities to the greatest possible extent

    (k) Gaining the greatest possible wealth for myself

    (l) Helping the homeless and the hungry in our nation

    (m) Giving business opportunities to others only when such cooperation satisfies my interests more than any other line of action seems to satisfy them

    (n) Always cooperating with fellow workers out of a sense of duty and for the overall benefit of the whole corporation

2. Below is a set of reasons for acting cooperatively. Some are self-interested reasons, some are non-self-interested. Mark the self-interested reasons *S* and the non-self-interested reasons *N*. (1.2 and 1.3)

    (a) If I cooperate with her, we will accomplish what I want.

    (b) If I cooperate with her, she will succeed in her desires.

    (c) If I cooperate with her, many people will get what they want.

(d) If I cooperate with her, she will give me what I want.

(e) If I cooperate with her, the greatest percentage of people will be satisfied.

(f) If I cooperate with her, she will be very receptive to my future requests.

(g) If I am to avoid being frustrated, I must cooperate with her.

(h) If I cooperate with her, I will be keeping my promise to help her.

(i) If I cooperate with her, others will benefit me because of the favor with which they view my cooperation.

3. Below is a series of statements. Some treat Marcia as the subject of a given interest, want, or desire; mark those *S*. Others treat her or her desires and interests as the object of someone else's wants or desires; mark those *O*. (1.3)

(a) The only one who wants us to work on the report over the weekend is Marcia.

(b) However, Marcia would be very displeased if we did a poor job.

(c) Everybody wants to help Marcia finish the report.

(d) Helping her do that report will interfere with our entire weekend.

(e) Although he won't like it, Marcia will want Rick to help out.

(f) Rick always wants to please Marcia.

(g) Marcia created this problem because she enjoys all this attention.

(h) Marcia wants to do have the report out so she can impress her boss.

(i) Everybody around here would be better off if Marcia's report were finished on time.

SELF-EXAMINATION QUESTIONS

4. Check your responses for Exercises 2 and 3 against the answers. Be sure you understand the correct answers before proceeding. Now test your understanding by stating the characteristics of self-interested reasons that distinguish them from reasons not based on self-interest. How should the pursuit of self-interest be described? What does it involve, and what does it exclude? Identify at least two ways the enlightened pursuit of self-interest can be distinguished from its unenlightened pursuit.

5. Review the work you have done in Exercises 1–4. Together they should clarify for you what it means to say that a person acts in his own enlightened self-interest. To test your understanding further, define as precisely as possible the concept of a person's acting in his own enlightened self-interest. Your definition should clarify three things: (a) the concept of the *object* of interest (Exercise 3), (b) how cooperation is possible, provided that it is self-interested (Exercise 2), and (c) what makes the pursuit of self-interest enlightened, rather than unenlightened (Exercise 1).

6. By examining your own circumstances, come up with three examples of how "doing what you want" and "pursuing your own enlightened self-interest" are divergent goals.

ANSWERS TO SELECTED EXERCISES

1. (a) *B* (b) *E* (c) *N* (d) *U* (e) *U*

(f) *N:* According to the egoist my actions are concerned only with my self-interest. So whether an action has been dictated by an authority matters only if *my interest* is necessarily enhanced or frustrated by its being dictated.   Neither obeying nor disobeying is conceptually related to self-interest.

(g) *N:* Cooperation fits only if it is in my interest.

(h) *N*

(i) *E:* Notice that as long as the ultimate concern of action is with the consequence for one's self, the action is self-interested.

(j) *N:* The analysis of pursuing one's self-interest involves no statement about whether it is, or is not, essentially in one's self-interest to develop one's many capacities.

(k) *N:* Here too, the analysis of acting in one's own self-interest does not involve essentially any statement about wealth or pleasure.

(l) *N* (m) *E* (n) *N*

2. (a) *S* (b) *N* (c) *N* (d) *S* (e) *N* (f) *S* (g) *S* (h) *N* (i) *S*

3. (a) *S* (b) *S* (c) *O* (d) *O* (e) *S* (f) *O* (g) *S* (h) *S* (i) *O*

4. Being motivated by reasons of self-interest means having as one's basic concern one's own interest and the extent to which that interest is accomplished or frustrated by any given action. Any means, including cooperation, that is compatible with and effective in achieving my self-interest is acceptable. If one's stated reasons or ultimate concern includes mention of the interests of any person other than one's self, then one's reasons and ultimate concern are not appropriately self-interested. Moreover, if one's stated reasons or ultimate concern do not mention the interests of any parties (one's self or others), but speak instead in terms of finding favor with someone, developing specific capacities or potentials for their own value, exercising certain virtues, or doing one's duty, then these are not reasons of interest at all, either self-interested or in the interest of others.   The enlightened pursuit of self-interest stresses long-term as opposed to short term goods. These goods need not be materialistic. The achievement of these goods might be accomplished without necessarily involving one in competition with others.

5. Your definition should look like the summary statements for each of the sub-sections of this part of the chapter.

Section 2
ETHICAL EGOISM AND PSYCHOLOGICAL EGOISM

In this section we will examine two closely related theories. *Ethical Egoism* is the normative or ethical theory that says human conduct *should* be based exclusively on self-interest. As a normative theory, ethical egoism *prescribes* how decisions *ought* to be made. We will contrast this normative theory with two alternative views regarding the relative importance that ought to be assigned to one's own interests and the interests of others—namely, altruism and egalitarianism.

Psychological Egoism is the empirical or scientific theory that human conduct is motivated exclusively by self-interest. To show that this theory is true a person would have to carefully gather scientific evidence. We will examine a common argument in favor of psychological egoism which is based on an analysis of the origins of socially useful desires in presocial selfishness. It will turn out that this argument suffers from several problems: it is not entirely consistent with the anthropological facts; it relies on a questionable assumption that human nature is fixed and unchangeable; and it commits the logical mistake of assuming that a reference to the historical origin of a thing is itself sufficient to explain the later events and actions. This logical mistake is named the *genetic fallacy*. After studying this section you should be able to:

- Compare and contrast psychological egoism and ethical egoism, giving examples of how each theory either explains or would direct conduct.
- Compare and contrast ethical egoism with altruism and with egalitarianism, giving examples of how each would direct conduct.
- Characterize the genetic fallacy.
- Present the case for psychological egoism based on a theory of the origins of socially useful desires in presocial selfishness.
- Describe how the above cited case for psychological egoism commits the genetic fallacy.

THE CASE OF THE DEFERENTIAL LOVER, PART II

Heather pulled a fresh piece of hotel stationery from the vanity drawer and began a letter:

Dear Michele,

Well I finally got John to take me to Sun Valley. It's beautiful here and we're having a super time. Too bad you and Bill couldn't have joined us. Oh well, maybe next time.

I've been thinking a lot about what you were saying. You remember? When Kathleen, you and I met for lunch a few weeks ago. You were talking about how Kathleen should not go from one extreme to the other, how she should respect both herself and Andy to the same degree. Treat everyone like an equal. Well, I've had some time to think about that and, frankly, I'm not persuaded. The way I see it, when you get right down to it everyone is selfish.

What I can't understand is how people ever got together to form communities or whole nations in the first place. It must be because they thought that in the long run they would be better off if they could avoid the daily worry of being stabbed in the back by their neighbor. Sure, people cooperate. They even get married and try to live—or survive—together. But let me tell you, honey, the beginning of all that cooperation is good old self-interest. It's really the only thing that keeps people together. Take children, for example—first they have to learn that they'll be punished for not being cooperative. Only then will they start to behave. Or, if you prefer, they find positive reinforcements in cooperating and hence that behavior is repeated—because it satisfies their interest in continuing to receive whatever positive reinforcements they received before.

Oh, I know you, Michele, you are probably already thinking about how I'm being illogical. You always accuse me of that, don't you? Well, I don't much care. Even if you can't say how people end up thinking about cooperation by looking at how they started out, I still will go on knowing that people are, at bottom, motivated by self-interest. That will never change because that's just how people are.

Well, John is taking me out to dinner, so I've got to run. I only meant to say hello. Guess I got carried away. Well, I won't let this little disagreement spoil my vacation or my friendship. You know my motto: "Keep number one, number one!" I really do wish you and Bill could drive up and join us for the weekend. I would so enjoy your company. Keep in touch.

Love,

Heather

Heather was about to lick the envelope when the idea crossed her mind that Michele might think she was a terrible person for sending such a letter. Without hesitation Heather tore it up and tossed the scraps in the garbage can. Heather figured it wasn't in her interest to upset Michele.

2.1 Psychological Egoism and Ethical Egoism

In the first part of the "Case of the Deferential Lover" Heather speculated on the reasons why Andy does not marry Kathleen, on why Kathleen entered into such a relationship in the first place, and why people in general do what they do. Invariably, Heather's speculations ended with the people acting on what she takes to be their self-interested motivation. In "Part II" of the case, Heather reveals herself as a convinced psychological egoist who subscribes to the factual belief that people do what they do to improve their own well-being.

Psychological Egoism is the view that people cannot act except out of self-interest. It is a theory about what people can and cannot do. As such, it is a factual or empirical claim about the invariable presence of a single ultimate motivation behind every decision that anyone makes. As a scientific or empirical theory it implies no value judgment. It is simply a claim regarding the facts of the situation—specifically about human motives. This claim extends to all human beings and to all human actions without exception. The view is that although some actions may not appear to be self-interested—for example, actions that involve helping or cooperating with others—all actions really are self-interested on close inspection of the ultimate motives and reasons involved. In other words, the psychological egoist believes that all people are motivated in all they do by the concern to give priority to their own well-being, and that nobody can act out of the motivation of giving priority to anything or anyone else.

Heather's motto is "Keep number one, number one." Heather is recommending that people should always put themselves first. She is making the claim of ethical egoism. Even if Andy, Kathleen, Michele or anyone else could be motivated by concerns other than self-interest, Heather would recommend that they never act on those motives. She holds to the normative view that right action consists of pursuing self-interest. Earlier she recommended Kathleen follow her example and trick Andy into paying more attention to her. She wanted Kathleen to be wiser in pursuing her self-interest and she believed it was right for Kathleen to do precisely that.

Ethical Egoism is the normative view that people should act only out of self-interest. It is considered a *normative* claim because it prescribes or proposes the best way to lead a life. As such it is a claim about what makes human actions right or wrong. The ethical egoist believes that the right (ethical, moral) thing to do is always to pursue self-interest. Although it may be possible, contrary to what the psychological egoists would say, to act out of concern for something other than self-interest, ethical egoists would argue that to do so would be wrong. People should help or cooperate with others only when it is reasonable to expect that their self-interest will be best served by doing so.

2.2 Whose Interests Take Priority

In the first part of the case study, Michele, not being a psychological egoist, had credited Kathleen with genuine concern for Andy's well-being. Michele did not want Heather to misconstrue that concern as the pursuit of self-interest. Moreover, Michele suggested that if Kathleen wished to be less compromised in effectively serving Andy's needs, she might consider her own interest and Andy's interests as being equal in their relationships. Michele defended mutual concern and respect as a viable alternative to both self-effacing deference and egoistic selfishness.

Several views are possible on the relative importance of one's own well-being and that of others. It is important to recognize this in order not to be taken in by a possible argument in defense of ethical egoism. An ethical egoist might try to argue that even if a person could pursue the interests of others for their own sake, surely none is more deserving than the one's self when it comes to having their interests pursued. From this the ethical egoist might wish us to conclude that, therefore, one should not pursue the interests of others but should rather pursue one's own self-interest. Even if the premise of this argument is conceded—that others are not more deserving than one's self—its conclusion does not follow. An underlying presupposition is that one must always choose between putting self-interest first, the egoist's position, and putting the interests of others first, a position known as *ethical altruism*. This presupposition is faulty, however, for there is at least one other possibility. One can hold that the interests of every person should be equally deserving of attention. This position has been called *egalitarianism*. If there is some mistake in the view that one should always be self-sacrificing, that does not immediately imply that one should always be self-interested. As Michele pointed out to Heather, there are three alternatives here: egoism, altruism, and *egalitarianism.*

2.3 Psychological Egoism and the Origins of Social Concern

What evidence can be offered in support of the psychological theory of egoism? One traditional defense of psychological egoism begins with the claim that in the history of human society, and also in the personal histories of individuals, social concern originates out of motives of self-interest. Only out of self-interest did people band together to form communities and societies in the first place; and only out of self-interest can children be motivated to interact as social beings. The view is that presocial (or precivilized) persons are motivated exclusively by self-interest. From this premise it is argued that any new behaviors which persons develop as members of social groups must fundamentally be explained as arising out of those same presocial and egoistic impulses. The argument comes to this: What originated in selfishness must itself be and remain selfish. Heather relies on this argument in her letter to Michele when she says, "The beginning of all that cooperation is good old self-interest."

To evaluate an argument such as this, it is necessary both to examine the plausibility of its premises and to determine whether its conclusion follows from those premises. First look at the plausibility of the premise that presocial behavior is self-interested. Let's divide the case. As to "presocial" behavior of primitive groups, anthropologists tell us that there is more evidence of a communal orientation and greater priority given to the well-being of the tribe as a whole than we find evident in our own "more advanced" civilization. If it is the "presocial" behavior of children which is being pointed to, then psychological theories of moral development indicate that we all begin at a stage where we make decisions so as to avoid what we take to be the immediate negative consequences to ourselves. Children in this stage of development make decisions "Because teacher was watching" or "Because Daddy would spank me if I did that." Even children in the second stage of moral development make decisions for reasons relating to themselves regardless of the consequences their actions might have for others. "I took Tommy's toy because I wanted it." So, the premise may be correct about the personal histories of individuals and wrong about the history of civilization or society as a whole.

But the above result leaves the argument in rough shape. For the same theories which support the idea that children *begin* their moral development by considering self-interest also tell us that people, as they mature, move through one or more stages of moral development that go beyond self-interest. Moreover, even if self-interest can be established as one possible motive for the individual and group decisions, it still remains to be established that self-interest is the *only* motive. Conceptually it is quite possible that social behavior of adults, as individuals or in groups, is motivated in part from non-self-interested concerns. Therefore more facts must be examined before we can accept the premises of this argument as a full statement on human motivation.

2.4 The Genetic Fallacy

Turning to how logical the argument is, we find a serious flaw. Even if it were established beyond dispute that all social concern originates in self-interest, it simply does not follow that all social concern *must remain* self-interested forever. As any butterfly will attest, it is not generally logical to move from premises about how something originates to beliefs about how it must remain in all of its subsequent metamorphoses. Physically, chemically, and biologically, things may be found originally in one state and then later in another. Things, including societies, change. They do not retain for their entire existence all of the properties they had in their original states. Development brings changes in kind as well as changes in degree. As examples, consider the differences between water and ice; between hydrogen, sulfur, and oxygen separately and H_2SO_4 (sulfuric acid); and between tadpoles and frogs.

A defender of psychological egoism might reply that these observations miss the mark, since she is, after all, talking about a psychological phenomenon, and not simply a physical, chemical, or biological matter. But, given all the evidence of change we see, the burden of proof would be with the psychological egoist, who would have to establish that psychological transformations never occur. Surely it is an empirical and not merely a conceptual matter whether the change from self-interest to another motivation is possible. Is it true, for example, that whatever one's motives are in entering a conversation, they remain constant as the conversation progresses? Perhaps you enter a conversation for the fun of some good-natured teasing. But if you perceive the depth of the other's feelings, you may abandon this motivation entirely and switch to making comments that soothe the hurt you unintentionally brought about.

Similarly, it is fallacious to assume that all events and actions are adequately explained by simply describing their original states or situations. This fallacy, commonly called the *genetic fallacy* rests on the dubious assumptions: (a) that references to historical origins are *by themselves* adequate to explain later events and actions, and (b) that intervening transformations never make those origins irrelevant to the explanations of later events and actions. If the opposite were true, then every adequate explanation of a current event in the United States would have to begin with a full discussion of the Revolutionary War, if not the coming of European settlers to the North American continent. But are adult motivations uniformly childlike appearances to the contrary? Or, to put the question more directly, is there something about the self-interested origins of our childhood moral development that makes all our adult decisions motivated by self-interest? It is not logically necessary that this be so, and that is all that is needed to show the psychological egoist's argument to be seriously faulty in terms of its logic.

2.5 Factual Evidence and Assumptions about Human Nature

If it is to be established that all adult motives are self-interested, this must be done scientifically by gathering evidence regarding the motives operative in adult living, not by using a fallacious argument based on what might have been a child's initial motives. And when the evidence is gathered we tend to find adult motivations ranging through several stages, such as: (1) a concern to be accepted and approved ("I knew it was dangerous, but all my friends were doing it."), (2) a concern for law and social duty for its own sake, ("A rule's a rule whether you like it or not."), (3) a concern for the social standards and values behind the rules and laws of one's own society, ("We should change that housing ordinance because it's unfairly discriminatory."), and (4) a profound concern for life and respect for all persons, ("Love your neighbor as yourself.")

The theory of moral development, sketched so briefly above, is based on the work of the psychologist Lawrence Kohlberg. Even if inaccurate in its details, it exposes the seriously problematic character of the theory of human nature underlying the psychological egoist's argument. The idea that because social behavior originates in self-interest, it must remain self-interested throughout its history presumes that human nature is fixed and unchanging. Although we cannot settle this issue here, it is fair to say that this presumption is widely disputed by contemporary thinkers. Philosophers whose thinking otherwise differs greatly, such as the existentialist Jean Paul Sartre and behaviorist B. F. Skinner, agree that there is no such thing as a fixed, stable, and determined human nature. Thus the psychological egoist's contention that human personality could never admit of motives that would lead people to act out of concern for approval, duty, respect for law, friendship, social harmony, the love of another, or concern for others for their own sake, needs a great deal of independent factual support if the argument about the origins of social concern is to be salvaged.

EXERCISES

1. (a) Describe a case in which some person acts in a self-interested way.
   (b) Would the psychological, or the ethical, egoist tend to regard the action in the case you just described as predictable? Explain why.
   (c) How would a psychological egoist explain an action that did not appear to serve the agent's own welfare or interest?
   (d) If an ethical egoist knew of the case you described, what would his moral judgment be regarding the morality of the action and what would the ethical egoist's attitude be toward its agent?
   (e) If psychological egoism were true, what sense could be attached to the advice, "Always maximize your own interest"? (2.1 and 2.2)

2. Describe a fictitious case in which one person may act either egoistically (as an ethical egoist) or altruistically in relation to another. (2.2)

3. Describe a second fictitious situation in which a person may act either egoistically or egalitarianistically on behalf of a group to which she or he belongs. (2.2)

4. (a) Characterize the genetic fallacy by providing an example not drawn from psychological egoism and explaining why the example represents a mistaken reasoning. (2.4)

(b) State the grounds on which a typical psychological egoist might defend that view. (2.3)

(c) State the conclusion the psychological egoist then draws in regard to adult human motivations. (2.3)

(d) Show how the psychological egoist commits the genetic fallacy when arguing based on the supposed presocial selfishness of human motivation. (2.4)

DISCUSSION QUESTIONS

1. In terms of the free-enterprise economic system, what psychological theory or theories of human motivation are presumed to be operative as individuals make decisions regarding the use of their financial resources? Give an example. What psychological theory or theories are presumed to be operating as corporations make decisions with regard to the expenditure of their resources? Give an example. Do scientific facts support those economic assumptions?

2. Not having read the next section, how might a psychological egoist analyze cases of apparent self-sacrifice or even of civic-minded service to the community when the agent honestly denies having acted on the basis of any self-interested motive?

3. Suppose that a person feels guilty and remorseful about having put his or her own interests above someone else's, for example, a spouse has been unfaithful. Do such feelings of guilt or remorse disprove psychological egoism? How would a defender of psychological egoism handle this kind of case?

4. On being discovered, a person feels guilt and shame because what appeared to be an other-interested action was really done out of self-interest, for example, his charitable contribution of money and time was really done to secure a large tax break and win election to public office. Does revealing such a thing about an apparently other-interested act prove that psychological egoism is really true? Would a true psychological egoist feel guilt at being discovered doing such a thing?

ANSWERS TO SELECTED EXERCISES

1. (b) The psychological egoist would tend to regard the action as predictable. People always act so as to pursue what they think is in their own best interest.

(c) According to the psychological egoist, a person's action might fail to be in his own best interest only if the person made some kind of mistake as he attempted to assess his own best interest.

(d) The ethical egoist would *approve* the action and would *commend* its agent. Ethical egoists do not assume people always try to act in their best interest. They might both attempt and succeed in doing something contrary to their own best interests. Hence, approval and commendation for doing the right thing are both warranted.

(e) If psychological egoism were true, everyone would always try to follow his own best interest, so the advice is superfluous. The only sense the advice could have would be to encourage people to be careful not to make mistakes in calculating what action would best serve their own interests.

2. A correctly stated situation will include statements of what is in the first person's interest and what is in the second person's interest. Moreover, somehow the first person's interest should be contrary to, or at least clearly distinct from, the second person's so that actions pursuing the one will differ from those used in pursuing the other. Check your description for each of these characteristics.

3. You should be able to infer the characteristics of a correct answer to this question from those of a correct answer to Exercise 2. Look at each characteristic stated there and infer the corresponding one that should be included here; then check to see that you have included it.

4. (a) The genetic fallacy is a form of argument. Its premise is that in its origins or in its initial form something is characterized by certain properties. The conclusion is that the thing thereafter remains characterized by those same properties.

(b) Two sorts of grounds are given: (1) the presocial behavior of each human child is entirely selfish, and (2) historically the presocial or pre-civilized behavior of human beings is entirely selfish.

(c) From these grounds the psychological egoist concludes: all human behavior is selfish.

(d) Both the individual (1) and human history (2) are considered. In each case the (supposedly) earliest form of behavior is characterized (as selfish). The conclusion is then drawn that all human behavior must, therefore, retain that characteristic.

Section 3
ETHICAL EGOISM AND THE GOOD LIFE

We begin this section by exploring the conceptual relationship of psychological egoism to ethical egoism. How does the truth or falsity of the empirical theory relate to the plausibility of the normative theory about how people ought to live their lives? Then we address directly the basic question of ethical egoism: Should people act exclusively out of self-interest? In so doing we suggest three possible responses to the question "Why should I be moral?" We close with a brief look at those character traits which could contribute most to leading what might be called a life of virtue or the *Good Life*. After studying this section you should be able to:

- Explain the meaning of "*Ought* implies *can.*"
- Discuss the conceptual relation of psychological egoism to ethical egoism in terms of "Ought implies can."
- Show how psychological egoism's being false entails that the ethical egoist should advise people not to act on some of their concerns.

- Contrast the potential meaningfulness of egoistic and non-egoistic living in different kinds of societies and in the light of human mortality.
- State the advice an ethical egoist would give in regard to the *Good Life*.
- Show how the falsity of psychological egoism and considerations of human happiness suggest answers to the question, "Why should I be moral?"
- Contrast the ways formal and material virtues aid in achieving the *Good Life*.

THE CASE OF THE DEFERENTIAL LOVER, PART III

"Here comes Heather," said Kathleen, "She must be just back from vacation. Look at her tan."

"Skin cancer!" mumbled Michele under her breath. But Kathleen, who was signaling to the waiter to bring more coffee, didn't hear her.

Heather pulled up a chair from a table nearby and joined the two women. "Did I ever miss our little lunchtime chats," she said. "How have you two been, anyway? I loved Sun Valley. Told you looking out for number one pays off."

"I'm pleased you had fun, Heather," said Kathleen. "And what a tan!"

"Like I say, Kathleen, people are selfish, so they might as well act that way."

Michele put down her coffee cup and folded her arms. "That doesn't make sense. How can a person not be selfish if self-interest is always our chief motive? So why bother advising people against acting out of any other motive? According to you, they can't!"

"You're right, Michele," smiled Heather. "It would be silly of me to tell you to act out of duty or out of a concern for others. That's impossible! But telling people to be self-interested is another matter. It's all consciousness raising, honey. And there are lot's of subtle little tricks and tactics that I've mastered, too. Some of them, like smiling so that people act in a friendly way toward me, have become second nature. My life is a lot fuller now that I pay conscious attention to opportunities to advance my own interest."

"Maybe so, Heather," replied Kathleen. "But take Andy for example. I don't believe my concern for him is basically selfish. I love Andy. I really am thrilled and happy for him when he does well or when something I do pleases him. That's how I feel even when I don't see anything in it for me."

"Now, Kathleen, we've been through all that before. You're simply not aware of your real motive; or maybe you refuse to admit what it is. That's all. Selfishness is behind everything, whether a person is conscious of it or not."

Michele shook her head skeptically. "Heather, is there absolutely nothing you would be willing to count as counterevidence? And don't just be stubborn. When Kathleen says she loves Andy, that she's moved by his needs, why don't you believe her? Why must you keep trying to explain her love away? Just take her word for it. She's not acting out of self-interest!"

"No, Michele, dear little Kathleen is either confused or dishonest—sorry, Kathleen, honey, but that's life—I didn't mean to hurt your feelings. I just can't imagine any possible case when people don't act out of self-interest, not if they are really being honest about their true motivations."

"Kathleen is your counter-example, Heather. Unless you're willing to say she's been lying to us, she is genuinely concerned for Andy. If that is so, then to put her self-interest first would actually imply that she should stop doing what she most wants to do. She wants to meet his needs even at the expense of her own!"

"You're being the stubborn one, Michele. Look, Kathleen, as a friend I'm telling you, you're wasting your life by pouring yourself out for a man who obviously isn't right for you. You're always saying how he doesn't appreciate you, how he doesn't spend time with you. Well either dump him or change him, honey. Otherwise you're going to go on living one very unhappy life. Believe me, it's true."

As Kathleen listened to Heather she became more and more angry. "Look, Heather, Michele was right. I can't just walk away from Andy. That wouldn't be right. Even though we're not married, I feel we have some kind of obligation to each other. I mean you can't just give up on something because the going gets a little tough. Beside, doing things for him is its own reward. I know what I'm capable of and I know the limitations I'm facing, considering the kind of person Andy is. But, like you say, it's my decision and I accept responsibility for it."

"But, honey, you have so many other potentials. Look at all the things you could do with your life if you got out of this relationship with Andy."

"I've thought about that, too, Heather," replied Kathleen. "But a person can't do everything. No, I'm sticking with Andy. Maybe someday we'll even get married and have children. If we do, I'll want them to grow up in a good family and be happy all their lives, even after I'm dead and gone. I have their future to think about, too, not just my own."

"Sure, whatever you say," smiled Heather. "But children are such a bother you know. Anyway, I've got to run. John's away on business and I'm meeting someone for... ah... lunch. Good-bye, girls. Have fun."

3.1 Conceptual Relations of Psychological and Ethical Egoism

How does the truth or falsity of a theory about how people *do* behave lead directly to any conclusion about how people *ought* to behave? First, if psychological egoism is false, people could still recommend that we act on the basis of ethical egoism. In other words, even if we could act on the basis of motives which were not self-interested, it could be recommended that we ought not do that, but rather that we act only on the basis of self-interested motives. So, the scientific theory could be false, but the normative theory could still be true.

Also, the fact that people do act a certain way does not imply that they are justified or morally correct in acting in that way. That a person cheats on his income tax return does not justify the cheating, nor does it imply that the person ought to cheat. That a person acts out of self-interest does not imply that a person ought to act that way. In other words, evidence that supports the truth of psychological egoism does not necessarily support the normative theory of ethical egoism. By the same token, the fact that a person sacrifices her own welfare for the sake of someone else does not imply that the person was right in making that sacrifice. So, the evidence that might count against psychological egoism as an empirical theory does not necessarily count against ethical egoism as a normative theory. Indeed, there is a real possibility that both theories are false. Cases of self-sacrifice might be telling counter-examples to the psychological theory. And the demands of duty, justice, and respect for the rights of others might take ethical priority over one's own self-interest, thus counting against the truth of ethical egoism.

3.2 Ought Implies Can!

Might both psychological egoism and ethical egoism be true? To answer this conceptual question we first must understand the relationship between *ought* and *can*. Suppose a supervisor tells a sales manager that she ought to increase sales by 150% in the next three weeks, but the facts of her market area are that this is simply not a physical possibility. If these facts were known, then obviously the supervisor's demands would be pointless (if not malicious). We can generalize this insight by saying: *If a person ought to do something, then doing it must be within the person's power.* This is part of what it means to say *"Ought* implies *can."* You can't demand that someone ought to dunk a basketball if he is not physically able to. You can't demand that a person not act out of self-interest if there is no possibility that they can act with any other motive. In other words, if psychological egoism were true, any normative demand to the contrary (such as, "no matter what your interest is, you ought not interfere with another's right to free expression") would be pointless.

However, if psychological egoism is true, does ethical egoism even make sense? This is the question Michele raised in the case study when she asked Heather why she bothered to recommend that Heather act in her own self-interest if there was no way that she could do otherwise. Michele is aware that the pithy expression, *"Ought* implies *can,"* also means that saying a person ought to do a thing implies that *the person is capable of not doing or failing to do that thing.* Telling a person he has a duty (that there is something he ought to do) makes sense only when it is possible for the person not to do as he ought. To tell a person, for example, that she must refrain from exhausting the entire inventory before the next shipment arrives only makes sense if the person (a) has the ability to do that and (b) also has the ability to refrain from doing that.

The idea of a normative theory is to provide reasoning in favor of one course of action where several alternatives are available. Thus, if psychological egoism were true, and people could not help but act in ultimately self-interested ways, then ethical egoism would be pointless! It would make about as much sense to go about recommending that people act out of self-interest as it would to go about urging that people obey the law of gravity. What other alternatives could there be? Not only would ethical egoism, as a normative theory, be ridiculously superfluous, all other normative theories regarding how people ought to act (such as to maximize social utility or to insure justice, or to promote respect for persons) would be superfluous as well. In other words, if psychological egoism were true, then not only would ethical egoism not make sense, the entire ethical enterprise would be highly questionable.

Michele is wise to challenge Heather, an avowed psychological egoist, when she recommends ethical egoism. Heather's reply is interesting, for she realizes that there is only one reasonable way for her to get around the argument in the preceding paragraph. Heather maintains that there is some point to recommending that people become ethical egoists, even if psychological egoism is true and they cannot help but act that way no matter what. The point is to make people more careful. Like anything else, people can do a better or worse job of identifying their self-interest and pursuing it. So urging ethical egoism on people can be understood as a sensible thing to do if there is a range of alternative ways of pursuing self-interest more or less successfully. Following the ethical egoist's recommendation, then, would involve a significant change in one's life to the extent that it involved a person's becoming *more enlightened* in the pursuit of self-interest.

3.3 Psychological Egoism: Empirical Theory or Article of Faith?

Given the conceptual relationships described in 3.1 and 3.2, the issue of the truth or falsity of psychological egoism looms as very significant. In 2.3 and 2.4 we showed that one traditional argument for psychological egoism was open to many serious objections, and other empirical theories maintain that a focus chiefly on self-interest was only one (rather immature) stage people go through on their way to more fully developing their moral decision making. Yet, the question can be asked, even if people claim to be motivated by more "developed or mature" concerns, is psychological egoism still not the most scientifically accurate description and explanation of human behavior and its "real" motivation?

Obviously some decisions are motivated by self-interest. But what about the many apparently non-self-interested things we do—things such as: going to work each day because there's a job there that needs to be done and people depend on us; doing a favor for a friend; letting someone into our lane on the freeway; giving gifts; or contributing time and money to a worthy cause? And what about more heroic things, such as self-sacrifice, or risking our own welfare to help someone else? What might psychological egoists say about these kinds of things? Would they be able to *scientifically detect* self-interested motivations in all such cases?

Although defenders of psychological egoism may succeed in showing that some apparently unselfish acts are selfishly motivated, they must, if the theory is to be established, objectively demonstrate that *all such acts* are. But even the most convinced psychological egoist concedes that there are cases where the supposed self-interested motive is not empirically detectable. In such cases these theorists resort to the contention that the actions in question are instances of self-deception (persons are deceived in not recognizing that they are acting out of self-interest) and that there are unconscious self-interested motivations at work. In fact, the defender of this ostensibly scientific theory can now be accused of trying to maintain that the theory is true not *because* of the evidence, but *in spite* of it.

Has the psychological egoist abandoned the empirical evidence? Has this supposedly scientific theory of human motivation become a non-empirical, or *a priori*, theory, to be maintained in spite of evidence to the contrary? It appears so. While there may be some genuine cases, perhaps all too frequent, where one's self-interest is an unconscious motivating factor or where a person is the victim of self-deception, the would-be defender of psychological egoism as an empirical theory would have to demonstrate (not just assert) that *all* cases of apparently non-self-interested behavior were masked in one of those two ways. Otherwise recourse to claims about self-deception or unconscious self-interest may say more about a person's underlying faith in psychological egoism (as an *a priori* theory) than about the facts of the matter.

When confronted with Kathleen's apparent self-sacrificing behavior, Heather remains adamant that there must be self-interested motivation at its base even though she can offer no evidence to support her claim. If Kathleen is ultimately deceiving herself, Heather has not demonstrated it. Heather has become an advocate of an a priori version of psychological egoism which she will hold to no matter what apparently disconfirming observations anyone might try to present. In cases like Heather's, psychological egoism shifts from being a scientific *hypothesis* (to be confirmed or disconfirmed on the basis of evidence) to being an *a priori postulate* (or article of faith) about human behavior. When the advocate of the theory admits, as Heather did, that no human action could ever convince her that non-self-interested behavior is possible, the shift is complete. Michele detects this shift in Heather's views. However, until there is some factual reason not to, Michele continues to accept Kathleen's statements about her own motivation at face value.

3.4 Ethical Egoism and Pursuit of One's Own Interests

Assuming we have alternatives, the principal normative question is: "Should persons act exclusively out of self-interest?" Since there is very good reason to doubt psychological egoism, it is plausible that human interests can include many other things beside one's self-interest. Apparently many of us are both capable of and interested in behaving in non-egoistic ways. The ethical egoist would recommend, however, that no matter what else might occur as a result of our decisions, we should act ultimately only so as to promote our own welfare. Is this an ethically reasonable recommendation?

Michele responds to Heather's ethical egoism by saying that, given Kathleen's genuine concern for Andy, Kathleen would not be happier if she stopped acting out that concern. In other words, if Kathleen accepted ethical egoism, her life would be diminished to the extent that she no longer would derive any satisfaction from pleasing Andy unless she came to view pleasing him as a way of serving her own interest. In Michele's response some see an important challenge to ethical egoism. People are generally happiest when they do what they want to do, and their happiness is diminished when they are prevented from acting in the ways they want to act. Recall that in 1.3 we pointed out there was a clear difference between "acting in one's own self-interest" and "doing what one wants." Often people want to do things that may not be in their self-interest, or, even if they are, this is not their motive for doing them. For example, (assuming of course that psychological egoism as an empirical hypothesis has been debunked), at times people act out of a concern for duty, for friendship, for the general welfare of society, for justice, for the sake of some worthwhile purpose, or simply to promote the well-being of someone else. However, ethical egoism would recommend that people not act out of any of these motives. So ethical egoism recommends that people sometimes not do what they want to do! For some people, this would mean diminished happiness because they would be ethically wrong in doing what they most wanted to do. One could argue that any recommendation which diminishes happiness without due compensation is unreasonable and should be rejected.

In effect, the above line of reasoning is our first response to the question, "Why should I be moral?" One possible reading of this question is, "Why ought I base my behavior on a concern for anything or anyone other than myself?" Here being moral is contrasted to being prudent about one's self-interests, as an enlightened egoist might be. If human motivation extends beyond the limits described by psychological egoism, then persons already have among their concerns such things as respecting the dignity of other persons, obeying legitimate authority, fulfilling their responsibilities, promoting justice, harmony and freedom, working for the greatest good of the greatest number, and respecting the rights of others. Why should people base their behavior upon such concerns? Simply because they have the concerns. It is not as if they were being asked to introduce moral concern into their lives where such concern was foreign to them and obviously odious. If one has these interests already, then *there already is concern to be moral*. In effect, one reason to be moral is because you already want to be—being moral involves having and acting on such interests and concerns as mentioned above.

3.5 Ethical Egoism and Human Happiness

To evaluate the ethical egoist's recommendation that to achieve happiness each one of us should always act so as to maximize his or her own self-interest, imagine two very different kinds of social environments. First, consider the social environment within which enlightened egoism is universally encouraged. (Indeed, some philosophers have recommended that this is exactly how an utopian society should be conceived and that legislators should write laws on the assumption that those governed by the laws will and should behave as enlightened egoists. Others have characterized life in the corporate and business world in precisely this way.) Within such a society, honesty, hard work, cooperation, friendship, respect for legitimate authority, thoughtfulness, fair play, respect for the rights of others, freedom of choice, and equal opportunity would be encouraged and supported *only to the extent each was useful to the pursuit of an individual's own welfare.* But anyone who actually valued such things for their own sake would be frustrated and thought extremely foolish. In such a social environment the convinced ethical egoist might be able to find her greatest happiness. Although, if the argument in 3.4 is correct, she would still be frustrated and unhappy unless she were able to suppress all of her interests or concerns that were not self-interested. The person who was not an ethical egoist would be extremely frustrated by this social environment. With most people regularly pursuing their own self-interest, the non-egoist might well tend to be manipulated, used, and entirely misunderstood. For example, by appearing to follow egalitarian or altruistic motives, others would easily regard her as being dishonest and deceitful. They might become angry that the non-egoist should think they were so gullible as to be taken in! Moreover, besides having others take advantage of her more self-sacrificing ways, the non-egoist might be moved toward despair by the general lack of gratitude and appreciation of non-self-interested pursuits.

On the other hand, imagine a society where cooperation, friendship, trust, honesty, harmony, justice, freedom, duty, the rights of others, legitimate authority, fair play and the like were valued for their own sake. Within such a society an ethical egoist (even an enlightened one), who openly and honestly professed his egoism might well experience frustration and even be ostracized. It would clearly be in the interest of the egoist to live hypocritically. To avoid this, he would always be at risk of being exposed as a fraud, and would have to expend much energy upon deception and manipulation. In such an environment the life of an ethical egoist would not likely be very happy.

In these considerations about social environment we find the second, although most ambiguous, answer to the question, "Why should I be moral?" The suggestion is that while a life of self-interested prudence is likely to yield more happiness and less frustration in a society oriented toward pursuit of self-interest, being moral (understood as having and acting on a wider range of concerns and interests exemplified above) would yield more satisfaction within a society of egalitarian and altruistic persons.

3.6 Ethical Egoism and the Good Life

Given the types of social environments described above, which do you live and work in? Which kind would you prefer to live and work in? The sort of life that will provide a person the greatest happiness varies not only with the environment in which she must live but also with the kind of person she is and the values she holds dear. We are all familiar with the Hollywood image of the good life, the life of over-abundance, self-indulgence and the where-with-all to do just as one pleases. But even that image does not tell us specifically what one should do to achieve happiness. Turning from the superficial Hollywood analysis of the good life we find other models to consider. For example, some people find their happiness and fulfillment in the belief that they are leading lives of lasting value or that they will leave a mark or make a positive difference after they have died. Many find happiness in putting their time and energy into things which are more enduring, or significant in their own right.

Even if we were to agree that leading *The Good Life* means finding happiness, this could still not be given a specific content which would be the same for everyone. For one person it may mean retiring at age 30 or driving a Porche or living in a mountain hide-a-way. For others it might mean raising children, curing the sick, writing an entertaining novel, serving on the city council, or finding a better way to grow wheat. In the case study Kathleen responds to Heather in these terms. Kathleen sees value in making a significant contribution to the lives of those for whom she cares, specifically Andy's. And she anticipates finding happiness and meaning in helping her future children be happy throughout their lives, even though she expects not to live long enough to be with them for their entire lifetimes.

When human beings contemplate the realities of their own finite existences, and specifically consider their own mortality, they often yearn to live in such a way as to make a difference, or a positive contribution, to something of greater permanence and significance than their own lives. Thus many people are concerned with influencing and contributing to the lives of others who may live on after them. Some attempt to do this by building and sustaining friendships and family relations. On a broader scale, many people feel their lives to be happier and more meaningful to the extent that they perceive themselves as making some contribution, however small or great, to the sciences, the arts, or human culture and civilized traditions. By comparison, people often perceive the pursuit of individual self-interest to be a shallow thing, less capable of sustaining a sense that one is leading a happy and meaningful life. Indeed the meaning of a life dominated by the pursuit of self-interest can be perceived as less substantial to the extent that it is tied to the individual's still being alive to experience and value it. If a person's concerns and interests range beyond his own welfare, then following the ethical egoist's recommendation can be perceived as leading one away from what makes one happiest, and hence away from the *Good Life.*

Implicit here is yet a third possible response to the question, "Why should I be moral?" If a person wishes to lead a happy, meaningful life, and if he or she believes that meaning in life can and does in part depend upon making significant contributions to the lives of others, then being moral can be understood as an integral part of leading that more meaningful life. Thus, valuing the well-being of others and acting out of a sense of responsibility to them may be understood as more meaningful than leading a life devoted chiefly to pursuit of self-interest.

3.7 Virtues Conducive to the Good Life

Think of *virtues* as character traits that contribute to a specific goal. Thus, the military virtues are not the same as the artistic virtues. Virtues are inner motivators; they represent the disciplined tendency of persons to decide to act in ways that are consistent with and conducive to a given goal, without recourse to external positive or negative sanctions. But a character trait that might be a virtue relative to one goal could be a vice (liability) relative to another. For example, always being fair-minded and truthful may make a person a better teacher but may make it tougher for the same person to be successful as a real estate salesperson. Also a specific character trait (virtue) might not be morally good. For example, always attempting to physically intimidate the opposition is an athletic or military virtue that many would consider ethically undesirable.

It is helpful to think of virtues as being of two different levels. At one level, which we can call the *material level*, different philosophers might put different lists of virtues arguing that their list is morally superior to any other. Honesty, purity, truthfulness, cooperativeness, thoughtfulness, loyalty, bravery, cleanliness, self-reliance, modesty, thrift, charity, inquisitiveness, optimism, and so forth might be found on various lists at the material level. Which of these, or other candidates, are the best material level virtues to cultivate depends on each person's own goals in life and on what they believe will make their life happy and meaningful.

Kathleen knows that she could do many different things with her life, and that she has many potentials which will be only partially or incompletely realized, given that she has made the decision to work on improving her relationship with Andy. In this Kathleen is defining her goals and acknowledging her limitations. Some people, by contrast, seem unable to do either of these things. In effect, these people have not developed a series of important character traits that operate at a different level than the material level. This higher (or different) level is called the *formal level*. The formal virtues are applicable no matter which virtues and goals one pursues at the material level. Formal virtues help a person think about his life and organize his activity.

Central to the formal virtues is one we shall call *integrity*. *Integrity*, from the verb *to integrate*, refers to the capacity of a person to integrate decisions and actions with her interests and capabilities meaningfully and thoughtfully, given the limitations and potentialities of life. In this sense, integrity means living a life of balance and internal harmony. (Note that the word *integrity* as used here does not refer to the material virtue of honesty.) There are other *formal virtues* beyond integrity. Some worth cultivating (because they are useful in achieving any particular material level conceptualization of the good life) are the following:

- *Wisdom*—knowing and appreciating the finitude of one's existence and how that finitude impacts on efforts to lead an integrated life;
- *Humility*—having an accurate sense of one's abilities and limitations, and being able to accept that assessment;

- *Temperance*—moderating one's desires and deeds because of an awareness of the dangers associated with extremes of behavior and desire;
- *Responsibility*—accepting authority and accountability for making decisions and commitments affecting one's self and others, within the limits of what can be known and achieved;
- *Perseverance*—remaining constant in one's efforts to achieve an integrated life, given the uncertainty, adversity, and limitations of one's existence;
- *Aspiration*—striving to realize one's fullest potential, within the bounds of leading an integrated, balanced life, and, in so doing, striving to overcome, to the extent possible, the limitations and uncertainties of life.

EXERCISES

1. (a) Some ethical theorists argue that part of the meaning of "Ought implies can" is that persons cannot be held morally responsible for things they cannot do or control. Suppose, for the sake of argument, that some mission absolutely vital to our national defense could be completed only if the one person with the ability to execute that mission would work round the clock without nourishment or a moment's rest for eight days and nights straight. What implications would follow concerning this person's responsibility for completing that vital mission on time? Could the person be held morally responsible for failing?

   (b) How does this illustrate the implications of "Ought implies can"?

   (c) Describe two further examples in which the impossibility of doing something would show a person's not being responsible for doing it.

   (d) In the light of (b) what is problematic about the assertion, "Psychological egoism is true, but people ought to be egalitarian"? (3.1, 3.2)

2. (a) Describe three situations in which a person acts, perhaps, virtuously or dutifully, but under some constraint or coercive force such that he had no choice but to act as he did.

   (b) What would be problematic about asserting that any person who gets into such a situation *ought* to act in the ways you have just described?

   (c) How does this illustrate an implication of "Ought implies can"?

   (d) In the light of (c) what is problematic about the assertion, "Psychological egoism is true, and people ought to be egoistic in their actions"? (3.1, 3.2)

3. (a) What kinds of human motivations exist if psychological egoism is false? (2.2)

   (b) What is the motivation upon which ethical egoism exhorts people to act? (2.2)

   (c) If we assume that people tend to be happiest when they do what they want to do, explain how the ethical egoist may be advocating a view that does not maximize human happiness, (assuming psychological egoism is false). (3.4)

   (d) What connection does the text draw between the falsity of psychological egoism and the tendency to be moral? (3.4)

4. (a) State the frustrations of an ethical egoist in a society in which non-egoistic behavior is the expected rule. (3.5)

(b) State the frustrations of an altruist or an egalitarian in a society in which egoistic behavior is the expected rule. (3.5)

(c) State the satisfactions of an ethical egoist in a society in which egoistic behavior is the expected rule. (3.5)

(d) State the satisfactions of an altruist or an egalitarian in a society in which non-egoistic behavior is the expected rule. (3.5)

5. Begin with the premise: "What is fleeting is less valuable than what is permanent; and what is longer lasting is, in that regard and to that extent, more valuable than what passes more quickly." Use it to construct an argument that ethical egoism is false. (3.6)

SELF-EXAMINATION QUESTION

Consider your goals in life with a view toward the impact of the formal virtues of integrity, wisdom, humility, temperance, responsibility, perseverance and aspiration on each goal. How are you progressing in your own efforts to lead the good life, as you understand it? (3.7)

ANSWERS TO SELECTED EXERCISES

1. (a) It would be unreasonable for the person to think she ought to complete the mission, and it would be unreasonable to hold her morally responsible for failing.

(b) If *ought* implies *can*, then if it is false that someone can do a thing, it is also false that the person ought to do it.

(d) If psychological egoism is true, then people cannot pursue egalitarian interests. Accordingly, if they cannot be egalitarian, then it would be wrong to say they ought to pursue such interests.

2. (a) If a person is pushed in such a way that he or she falls, helplessly, down a flight of stairs, then even if he or she was not hurt, it would be wrong to assert that the person ought to have fallen down in that way.

(b) It would be wrong to assert that another person in such circumstances ought to fall that way, because this would imply that the first person could control how he or she fell, whereas we began by assuming that the original person fell helplessly.

(c) This illustrates the point that saying a person ought to do a certain action assumes that not doing it is within his or her power.

(d) If psychological egoism is true, then the assertion, "People ought to be egoistic in their actions," involves the false assumption that people could try to act other than egoistically. (Note, however, that they could still fail to act egoistically, because they could fail in what they tried to do.)

3. (a) Some human motivations must exist that are non-self-interested. They might, for example, be altruistic or egalitarian.

(b) Ethical egoism exhorts people to act on self-interested motivations.

(c) If psychological egoism is false, people have non-self-interested motivations. If people tend to be happiest when they act on their own motivations, then people will tend to be happiest if they sometimes act on non-self-interested motivations. Since ethical egoism exhorts people not to act on non-self-interested motives, people will tend, on the above assumptions, to be less happy following the ethical egoist's advice.

(d) The falsity of psychological egoism entails that people do already have non-egoistic interests, desires and concerns.

4. (a) The ethical egoist will be suspected and distrusted by his fellows, and their distrust will constrain him from successfully pursuing his self-interest. On the other hand, if his egoism is not known to others, he will be constrained from the direct pursuit of other interests by his instrumental interest, in such a society, in keeping concealed his egoism in order to prevent distrust.

(b) The ethical altruist or egalitarian will either be suspected of deceit or she will be taken as sincere. If she is suspected of deceit, she will be rebuffed and will not gain the cooperation and friendship of others. If taken as sincere, then others will systematically use her to their own ends, ignoring any consideration for her own good.

5. Your argument might go like this: "What is fleeting is less valuable than what is permanent; and what is longer lasting is, in that regard and to that extent, more valuable than what passes more quickly. Nothing is in a person's interest after he or she is dead. Hence to act for the sake of advancing one's own interest is to act for the sake of something without permanent worth. The interests of one's descendants and of society are more lasting than those of the self. Therefore, ethical egoism is false (or unwise), since one ought to pursue the more lasting interests of one's descendants and one's society, rather than one's own more fleeting interests."

4 | RIGHTS AND DUTIES

*...endowed by their Creator with certain inalienable rights, among them life,
liberty and the pursuit of happiness...*

The Declaration of Independence

In contrast to those ethical theories like utilitarianism (Chapter 2) and ethical egoism (Chapter 3) which would have us focus only on the consequences of our actions
in deciding what is right and wrong, other ethical theories insist that, given the
proper intention, the actions themselves can be intrinsically, not just instrumentally
valuable. Such a theory might insist that because persons have certain rights, others
have duties which are based on respecting those rights. To act with the purpose of
respecting the rights of others is an example of something one ought to do. Such
action is intrinsically, not just instrumentally, desirable.

Normative statements about what people or societies ought, or ought not, to
do often refer to the supposed rights or duties of the parties involved. In order to
evaluate these statements, we will need a firm conceptual grasp of the nature of the
rights and duties under discussion. We must also understand the justifications that
may be offered in support of the views that such rights or duties are important
normative considerations. Section 1 outlines a wide variety of claims about rights,
both conventional and moral, that have been recognized by normative theorists.
That section also clarifies the relations of the concepts of rights to other normative
concepts, especially that of duty. Section 2 introduces the concepts of *indefeasible*
and *inalienable* rights and the associated categorical duty to honor such rights. It
also presents Kant's ethical theory, which holds that some actions are intrinsically
right or intrinsically wrong. Section 3 gives one possible justification of claims that

indefeasible and inalienable rights and categorical duties exist. That justification is developed in terms of the concepts of respect for persons and integrity.

Section 1
CONCEPTS OF RIGHTS

To claim that a person has a right is to claim that he is entitled to behave in certain ways in certain circumstances. Typically, it also is to define expectations concerning the behavior of other people relative to the possessor of the right. This section conceptually analyzes major types of rights by relying on distinctions among (a) the circumstances within which assertions about rights arise, (b) the things possessors of the right are entitled to do, and (c) the behaviors expected of others toward the possessors of the rights. How does the concept of a right relate to such other concepts as duty, liberty, scarcity and abundance of resources, opportunity, legality and morality, liability and immunity? How do the eighteenth-century and twentieth-century concepts of moral rights differ in regard to what persons who have those rights can expect of others? After studying this section you should be able to:

- Distinguish and explain the distinction between moral rights and conventional rights.
- Distinguish and explain the distinction between rights that imply correlative duties of non-interference and those that do not.
- Distinguish moral rights from legal powers.
- Compare and contrast legal powers, liabilities, and immunities.
- Distinguish and explain the distinction between eighteenth-century and twentieth-century concepts of moral rights.

THE CASE OF DIAMOND AIR SHUTTLE INC.

The mediator, March, leaned back in his chair and rubbed his bloodshot eyes. He reached for his coffee and slugged down the last cold mouthful. "It's 2:45 A.M. and your deadline is only thirty minutes from now New York time. If you two don't cut the nonsense and hammer something out on this drug testing thing, I'm going to impose a settlement. Neither of you want that."

Simpson, the union's toughest negotiator, was tired too. She rolled her head from side to side and stretched her aching jaw. Then she folded her arms and looked squarely at March. "You have no right to..."

"Save it, Simpson," said Brogan, the negotiator for management. "Your union and my bosses gave him that right when they agreed to bring him in as mediator." Brogan shuffled through a stack of folders, opened one and waved a familiar piece of paper at Simpson. "It's here, in the memorandum of understanding the lawyers drew up. You signed it and so did I, so..."

"Put it away," snapped Simpson. "The workers will never stand for random substance abuse testing. Performance evaluations are one thing, but violating our basic human rights is another. We have the right to our own privacy."

"We have a duty to the public, Simpson. Our shuttles must be safe. Beside, Diamond Inc. would be negligent if our pilots and crew members took off drunk or high or buzzed or spaced or whatever you call it these days. Our liabilities would be astronomical if there was an accident. Imagine the headline: '700 die in shuttle crash, drugs suspected.'"

"When they buy a ticket they sign away their right to sue you, and you know it. It says so on the back of the ticket."

"That's not binding, Simpson" interjected March. "That's one right you can't sign away."

"Brogan, I'm tired of your garbage. Last year the U.S. government granted Diamond Inc. immunity from punitive civil litigation. Diamond's liability is limited to actual damages, nothing more. And Diamond has accident insurance to cover that."

"True," said Brogan. "But the government still has the legal right, if not a public duty, to prosecute us in criminal court for reckless conduct."

"We're not getting anywhere, people," said March.

"Look," said Brogan taking off his glasses and loosening his tie, "Diamond has to expand. We need to qualify for a license to fly between Toronto and Tokyo. To do that we must comply with Canadian and Japanese laws. Both countries require random drug testing."

"Sorry, Brogan," said Simpson. "I guess Diamond won't be able to qualify for that license."

Brogan sighed and opened another folder. He ran his finger down a column of data, then said, "I know drug testing bothers you, Simpson. But maybe, just maybe, we can work a deal," said Brogan.

"Finally!" sighed March. "Whatever you have, put it on the table."

"How about any worker who tests positive has the right to be in a rehabilitation program at company expense and on company time?"

"Nobody gets fired," demanded Simpson.

"Not the first time," countered Brogan.

"Okay, four positives and he's out," offered Simpson. "And, he gets six months severance pay and nothing goes in his employment record," she added.

"He's out the front gate on second positive, no severance pay," said Brogan, "but Diamond keeps his record confidential."

"He's gone on the third time, but gets one month's pay, and I'll take the package to my people," said Simpson. She stood up and extended her hand to the other negotiator.

Brogan shook his head, but accepted Simpson's outstretched hand.

"Good job, people," said March. "And you had four whole minutes left."

1.1 Rights as Entitlements and Justifications

In asserting that a person has a right, we are saying that the person is entitled to do or to not do something. Another way to put it is to say that having a right gives one the ethical or conventional prerogative to act or not act in a certain way. Rights claims can form the basis for justifications. We appeal to our rights to justify doing something or to justify censuring someone who offends one of those rights. For example, in the case study, the key issue is whether Diamond Shuttle will have the right to impose a drug testing program on its employees. If the contract which has been negotiated is ratified by labor and approved by management, then that entity, the corporation, will be entitled to implement that program. Simpson also claims that the workers have a pre-existing right not to have their privacy invaded by the drug testing program. Mention is made of the government's right to bring criminal charges against Diamond Shuttle. Also the rights of accident victims to bring a civil case against the company are asserted and then denied. Each such entitlement claim is an assertion that the holder of the right is *justified in exercising that right* (Diamond wants to be justified in implementing a drug testing program) or the holder of the right is *justified in censuring those who would violate that right* (the union, representing workers, is justified in censuring Diamond if it tries to violate the workers' right to privacy).

1.2 Rights vs. the Right Thing to Do

Before going further, let's clear up an ambiguity in the word *right*. The question, "Does person A have the right to do X?" is not to be confused with the question, "What is the right thing for person A to do?" The first question inquires into A's entitlement or prerogative to do X, if so desires. The person may or may not do X, it is the person's choice and she would be permitted and justified in doing X, if X is her right, although she would not be remiss in not doing X, for, as a right, X is not mandatory. The second question is a broader one. It inquires into what A ought to do. *Right* in this sense means *correct*. To justify the claim that X is the right thing to do one must first decide what kind of issue is being discussed. The question might be about ethics, or about something else, say farming techniques. The answer might be, "X is the right (ethically correct) thing to do because X brings about the greatest balance of good over bad for the greatest number of persons." Or, the answer might be, "X is the right (procedurally correct) thing to do because X is the next instruction listed the in users manual."

In ethics, statements such as "It would be right for A to do X" may be supported by claims about A's rights or the rights of others, but other support also may be offered.   Among other factors which may be considered include considerations of self-interest, the interests of others, or the moral standards of one's society.   Thus, it may well be right for a person to act out of benevolence toward another, although it is implausible to suggest that anyone is entitled to (or has a right to expect) such benevolence.

1.3 Rights of Persons and the Duty of Non-Interference

If you have a right to educate your children as you please, then others in society have the duty not to interfere with how you educate your children. Indeed, if two parents have that right, then *everybody* else has the duty not to interfere with the way they educate their own children. Similarly, if you have the right to sell your house, then everyone else has the duty not to prevent you from selling your house. Likewise, if you have the right to medical care, then everyone else has the duty not to prevent you from obtaining that medical care. Notice the general relationship between rights and duties in these statements.   There is a large group of rights such that, part of what it means to say that *one* person has a certain *right* is that *every other* person has the *correlative duty not to interfere with* that person's proper exercise of that right. In the case study, when Diamond Inc. is given the right to implement a drug testing program, the workers will have the correlative duty not to interfere with (either by sabotage or non-compliance) that program. Similarly, a worker who tests positive for the first time will have the right to go into a rehabilitation program and the right to retain his job. Thus, Diamond Shuttle will have the correlative duty not to interfere with those rights—Diamond would not be justified in prohibiting the worker from attending the rehabilitation program nor in dismissing the worker on the grounds of that first positive drug test.

1.4 Conventional Rights

Most of our examples of rights so far are *entitlements claimed by virtue of the circumstances or relationships within which people find themselves*. Your right regarding deciding how certain children are educated arises out of your parental relationship to those children. If you were not their parents, you would not have that right. Simpson and Brogan, as they negotiate the labor contract, are, in effect, creating rights which will be held by various persons by virtue of their particular circumstances, either as management or labor. These entitlements will accrue to those persons, or more specifically, to persons as long as they are acting in those capacities, only after the new contract has been ratified and put into force. When the contract is no longer in force, those rights will no longer exist.

Other examples of *conventional rights* are the right to enter into contracts, the right to make a will, the right to buy and sell property, the right to operate a car, or to borrow money, and the like.   Corresponding to these examples are duties of non-interference in their exercise.   In a society such as ours, the actions that count as official acts of exercising these rights are specified by convention.   For example, to make a will you must be of sound mind, write down your wishes, and have the document witnessed.   Once this is accomplished, it becomes everyone's duty to honor that will.   As long as you fulfill certain requirements, such as being of sound mind, not agreeing to any contract provision which is contrary to law, or being of an age recognized by law as old enough to enter into binding contracts, you can, under the conventions (customs and laws) of our society, make a binding contract and create rights and obligations for yourself.   If you meet the requirements and wish to enter into a contact—for example, you want to buy a car—others in society are obligated not to interfere with your efforts to do so.   Of course, friends and family members might advise you not to do it, but giving advice is not the same as interfering.   Although they have the right to give the advice, you are not obligated to follow their advice, nor does friendly advice prevent you from entering into the contract, if you still wish to do so.

1.5 Moral Rights

Rights can also be claimed for persons *just because they are persons*.   Your right to life is conceived of as such a right.   It is yours because you are a person, not because of customs, laws or social conventions which put you into certain relationships or circumstances.   The framers of the Bill of Rights conceived of the rights they listed in the U.S. Constitution as basic human rights—what we are calling *moral rights*. They thought of rights, such as those of free speech and a free press, as being possessed by persons independent of circumstances and prior to any mutual agreement or legally binding contract.   The framers of the Bill of Rights regarded any arm of government that failed to acknowledge these entitlements as violating the rights of persons as human beings.   Thus, they did not think that the Constitution itself created the rights or that people were justified in claiming the rights because they were granted in the Bill of Rights.   Rather, they thought of the Bill of Rights as providing a guarantee that in the United States those preexisting human rights would be acknowledged and supported, and not violated, by the power of the government.   In their view the duty not to interfere in the exercise of these human rights existed independently of the Constitution and was simply being acknowledged in the Bill of Rights as a duty of government.

Conventional rights are entitlements that come into existence within conventional structures, such as the customs and laws of a given society or culture, whereas moral rights are entitlements of human beings which are thought to exist independent of and regardless of those structures.   Conventional rights can be vested in human beings or in legal entities, such as corporations, trusteeships, foundations, or governmental offices.   Under the rules of society, for example, the

President has the right to veto a bill passed by Congress. This is a right of the Presidency. Over the last two hundred years the exercise of that right has passed from one human being to another, but not because they were human beings *per se*, rather because for a time they held that governmental office. Moral rights, by contrast, are entitlements of persons only, not legal entities. If the U.S. Constitution were amended next month and the Presidency were abolished, we could not argue that the Presidency has a moral right to continue to exist independently of the Constitution. The person who held that office, however, has that moral right, the office does not.

1.6 Duties Beyond Non-Interference

We have emphasized the correlative duty of non-interference which attaches to many of our moral and conventional rights. But the exercise of our rights can create duties (for ourselves and others) or can put us (or others) in the position to have additional duties which go well beyond simple non-interference. For example, entering into contracts, deeds, promises, wills, and the like may create new rights and new duties for the parties involved. A person may acquire the right to a piece of property (a car) and, by virtue of that same contract, also acquire the duty to pay for that car, along with the duty, imposed by the government on everyone who owns a car, to carry a certain amount of accident insurance. Should the person also wish to exercise the conventional right to operate that car on the public roads, then the person would have the duty to operate that car in accord with all the applicable traffic laws.

A person may have a right to have another person do something for her because the other person contracted (under the contracting conventions operative within the particular social or legal context) to do that thing. Diamond Shuttle Inc.'s contract with the labor union gave the corporation the right to receive a certain amount of the labor activity (perhaps ten hours per day, four days per week) of the people represented by that union. In return Diamond Shuttle has the obligation to pay those people a certain wage (whatever wage was agreed to in the contract). In the negotiations Diamond Shuttle asserts its duty to see to the safety of those who use its services, and hence, wants to implement a drug testing program and dismiss employees who test positive. Simpson, in ultimately accepting the testing program, imposes on Diamond the duty to provide a rehabilitation program and to give dismissed workers severance pay.

1.7 Rights as Liabilities and Immunities

Within the framework defined by specifically *legal* conventions, there are legal entitlements, or rights, that may be understood in terms of *liabilities* of persons (or legal entities). Let us suppose that the legal powers discussed above are exercised. In some cases the legal rights of one person imply liabilities for others. If a person has a right to make a will, then another person (a despicable relative, for example) is liable to be excluded from that will. If a person has a right to bring suit for damages sustained on another's property, then the other is liable to be sued for the damages. In the case study, if an employee of Diamond Shuttle causes an accident which harms passengers, then the corporation is liable. It is obligated to make reparations for any damages in terms of loss of life or property. Diamond also has the legal liability of being sued by the government for criminal neglect. And if it could be shown that the corporation knew about certain risks and chose not to take steps to eliminate them, then the corporation might be found guilty of such neglect.

The intersection of rights and duties relating to product liability is of great concern to consumers and to business. Consumers, exercising their conventional right to bring suit for damages in civil court, or government, responding to its duty to the public by bringing suits in criminal court, can impose serious financial hardships on business. Even if the business is ultimately exonerated or found not guilty, responding to the suit is costly. The business has the duty to respond. Thus, it must incur the expenses associated with fighting or settling the suit. On the other hand, the consumer's right not to be injured due to a preventable accident or malicious neglect is something which a business must honor, particularly if its products or services are of a kind such that its consumers could not reasonably be expected to have protected themselves from that harm when using the product or service in the manner in which it is intended to be used and when exercising due and reasonable caution in its use. If, in the ordinary course of operating your computer, you strike a certain combination of keys and it blows up and blinds you, then you have the conventional right to seek compensation from its manufacturer. The manufacturer is at risk for being sued in such a case.

Diamond Inc.'s civil liability has been limited by government action, which means that the passengers who are harmed do not have the conventional right to sue for punitive damages; they can only recover their losses. Diamond Inc.'s right, in this case, is an entitlement to *immunity* from a certain kind of legal action. Persons who work for the diplomatic service of a foreign nation are immune from having to obey traffic summonses and having to pay traffic fines; that is, they have the right to ignore those items. This is an example of an immunity enjoyed by a specific group of people. To say that persons have such a right is to say that they are *immune* from prosecution for such action. In the case study, Simpson wants Diamond Inc. to give its workers immunity from being dismissed if they test positive. Brogan does not agree, but is willing to give them *limited immunity*—they will not be dismissed the first or second time. But after that their immunity has been exhausted and they are at risk (have the liability) of being dismissed if they test positive again.

There are also cases where everyone enjoys an immunity from prosecution for actions which are normally subject to legal challenge. For instance, people can be sued for slander. People who make false accusations about others in such a way as to damage them emotionally or financially are liable to having a suit brought against them. But if the person talked about is a public figure and if the talk was not intended maliciously, then the speaker is immune from being sued, even if what he or she said was false. All of us enjoy this immunity by virtue of our current laws and court rulings. Or, to take another example, once a legally specified amount of time has passed, persons who commit certain crimes may be immune from prosecution. Murders are not immune from prosecution because that crime has no statute of limitations, but after seven years those who knowingly file a false income tax return are immune from prosecution for filing that fraudulent return.

1.8 Rights as Licenses to Compete

There is a type of right that all may not be able to exercise successfully, owing to a scarcity of resources. In such circumstances it is reasonable to say that persons have a right to compete for a share of the resources. The rights we considered earlier included the corresponding duties not to interfere with the exercise of those rights. But now we are dealing with a different type of right—one that, because of scarcity, involves competition. The nature of this competition itself includes a degree of interference with the others trying to exercise the same right. This limited interference may eventually allow some competitors to win out. For example, it may be that people have a right to drive a car. It may also be that so many people have such a right the highways and freeways simply become too congested to accommodate all those who would like to exercise that right. At this point some regulation of traffic and access to certain roads or certain freeway lanes—some interference in the exercise of the right to drive—becomes necessary.

To see how the type of right that we have called a *license to compete* contrasts with the variety that entails a corresponding duty of non-interference, consider two of the rights guaranteed by the Bill of Rights: the right to free worship and the right to operate a free press. If people worship in ordinary ways, including singing, praying, and meeting together they can worship in different places without having to interfere with each other. It is not that interference is impossible, but rather that non-interference can be carried off pretty well. So far there is no scarcity of meeting places. In contrast, if there were a shortage of paper or competent writers, freedom of the press might well become a competitive thing. When competition for scarce resources is justified, and the resources are indeed scarce, then rights claims of this new variety, rights to compete (for those resources), arise.

Other examples of such rights are the rights to open a business and compete with other businesses in a free market system, or to agitate and lobby for legislative changes. Given that consumer demand is limited, only some who exercise their right to compete in business will be successful. Businesses have the right to compete for customers even though this limits the financial success of the other competing businesses. Given that only some laws can be enacted, and especially given that contradictory proposals for legislation cannot both be adopted, it is clear that agitating for a particular piece of legislation does not entail a corresponding duty of others not to compete or interfere with those efforts. In the case study Diamond Inc. wants the right to fly between Toronto and Tokyo. It is seeking the right to compete with other companies to provide that service and make a profit in doing so. If it is difficult to find qualified pilots and flight crews, then Diamond has the right to compete with other businesses in its efforts to hire qualified personnel.

1.9 Eighteenth- vs. Twentieth-Century Concepts of Moral Rights

There is an important difference between the concept of moral rights commonly espoused in the eighteenth century (out of which our Bill of Rights emerged) and a concept of moral rights that has developed in twentieth-century normative thought. The eighteenth century conceived of *moral rights* as entitlements that hold independently of any governmental structure. Freedom of speech, freedom of worship, freedom of assembly, and freedom of the press were thought of as things to which human beings were entitled by virtue of their being human. The correlative duties attending these moral rights, if there were any, were at most *duties of non-interference.* The duty of other agents—particularly the duty of government—in other words, was not conceived as a duty to act in a certain way, but at most as a duty to refrain from doing anything that would interfere with the exercise of those rights.

In some cases, such as with the eighteenth-century conception of those conventional rights which were licenses to compete, even saying that there was a duty of non-interference would be too much. Classical capitalism as an economic system, if anything, is one which regards totally unregulated economic competition as the ideal. In the eighteenth century it was considered inappropriate for government to regulate (interfere with) private economic competition even if those regulations might protect the moral rights of persons (protect children from illness, exploitation, and possible death from being over-worked in the factories or workhouses).

The twentieth-century concept departs from this *hands-off* notion of rights. The twentieth-century concept is reflected in the 1948 United Nations "Declaration of Human Rights." That document proclaimed that persons have rights to education, a decent standard of living, medical treatment, dignified employment, personal security, privacy, a fair trial, rest, leisure, nationality, political asylum, community participation, and the like. There are two important contrasts between this and the eighteenth-century concept of rights. First, the existence of these rights implies much more than non-interference as a correlative duty. If you have a right to education, then all of the non-interference in the world will not guarantee you that education. A right to work will do no good if there is no job to be done. A right to medical treatment is nothing if there are no medical facilities and health care providers. If there are correlative duties corresponding to such rights, they are duties to take positive steps so that people receive that to which they are entitled. Others have the duty to provide the schools, hospitals, trained personnel, etc. that these rights imply.

Second, serious problems of scarcity arise with regard to rights so conceived. Considerable expenditure of resources would be necessary to guarantee the full exercise of the rights listed by the United Nations Declaration of Human Rights. These resources are very often scarce; they are not abundant or limitless as are resources such as places to exercise the rights of free speech or freedom of worship. It takes money and time to build the medical facilities and to train and employ the health care professionals. The health care budget in most states is second only to the education budget. These represent huge expenditures of tax money in order to ensure the rights of citizens to education and health care. How well these rights are realized depends directly on the resources which are able to be devoted to their realization.

The contrast between eighteenth- and twentieth-century rights can be illustrated with respect to the right to life. On an eighteenth-century interpretation this amounts to the right not to be killed; your right to life is honored so long as no one interferes with your living. On a twentieth-century interpretation, however, mere non-interference does not honor your right to life; you have a right to be kept alive, which may require that food or medical services be provided for you. And, your right to life might even imply, in certain circumstances, that you be provided with shelter and perhaps gainful employment, depending on how broadly one interprets the duties of others to ensure your right to life and whether the resources and economic conditions to provide you with those things exist. But having that right is not just an entitlement. Since everyone has it, it is also a liability. You also have the obligation to assist in providing those same life sustaining resources to others.

1.10 Two Interpretations of Moral Rights in the Twentieth Century

There are two conflicting interpretations of moral rights as conceived in the twentieth century. One school of thought suggests that indeed there are correlative duties, and that a person's having a right to education, for example, implies that someone has a duty to provide that education. Most plausibly it has been suggested that the state, through the agency of government, has the obligation to provide the conditions that will allow persons to fulfill such rights. Some object to this analysis as follows: "If the state has such duties, then surely the state ought to do whatever its duty requires. Yet it seems quite unreasonable to say that any agency, individual, or collective, has an obligation to do something which it cannot do. It may well be beyond the power of the state, or anybody, to do what it is said ought to be done here. Thus, it is unclear whether any sort of duty can be said to be correlated with rights as conceived in the present century." Of course, this objection is quite compatible with maintaining the less stringent view that the state has the duty to see to it that these rights are fulfilled insofar as possible.

An alternative analysis of twentieth-century rights interprets claims about rights as descriptions about the ideal conditions under which human life would be lived. In this view it ought to be a universal goal that conditions conducing to the fulfillment of such rights be brought about. Thus, ideally people would have meaningful work and leisure, ample opportunities for education, quality nutrition and medical care, and so on. But on this analysis it is clear that there is no duty to try to fulfill these rights for persons in circumstances where scarcity of resources renders it impossible. Indeed, on this *rights-as-ideals* analysis these statements assert only what the best state of affairs would be without assigning any particular duties to any party at all, including the state.

EXERCISES

1. Below is a list of rights. Some are conventional moral rights (*CMR*); some are moral rights not based on conventions (*NCMR*). Distinguish each right as one or the other. Where you identify rights as based upon conventions, specify what kind of convention must be operating in societies where people can be meaningfully said to have the rights. (1.1–1.6)

___(a) The right to assembly with other persons
___(b) The right to make a will
___(c) The right to have a job
___(d) The right to run for political office
___(e) The right to sell one's property
___(f) The right to worship as one chooses
___(g) The right to refuse medical aid
___(h) The right to donate one's body to science
___(i) The right not to have others conceal information from one
___(j) The right to have a clean environment

2. Below is a list of rights. Some of these rights involve correlative duties of non-interference (*CD*); some do not (*NCD*). Distinguish each right as one or the other. If there is a correlative duty, specify what is not to be interfered with. If there is no correlative duty, state what rights others have that imply they have no duty of non-interference. (1.3–1.6)

___(a) The right to speak as one chooses
___(b) The right to open a business
___(c) The right to run a successful business
___(d) The right to offer one's property for rent
___(e) The right to have someone buy one's property
___(f) The right to become the renter of any property offered for rent
___(g) The right of a person who is the only one who applies to rent property legally offered for rent
___(h) The right of a landlord not to rent his or her property to any applicant

3. Below is a list including some moral rights and some legal powers. Mark the moral rights *MR* and the legal powers *LP*. (1.4–1.5) A person has a right

___(a) to favor and back a particular candidate for office.
___(b) to initiate the recall of an elected official.
___(c) to have as many children as he or she chooses.
___(d) to make a contract.
___(e) to write a will.
___(f) to choose the town in which he or she wishes to live.
___(g) to have a friend visit in one's home.
___(h) to have one's lawyer move for dismissal of the charges against one.

4. The following narrative contains many statements that assert legal powers, liabilities, or immunities. Mark appropriately: *LP*, *L*, or *I*. (1.7–1.8)

___(a) Lyn Lacer signed a contract with the Shady Shoe Company.

___(b) She agreed to appear in five television commercials for them.

___(c) They agreed to pay her $20,000.

___(d) She agreed to make the commercials at any time during the month following the signing of the contract.

___(e) She gave her lawyer the authority to negotiate a second contract for commercials with Shady.

___(f) Lyn, in the second contract, would not be bound to refuse to work for any other advertising agencies.

___(g) Shady would pay her a greater amount in the second contract.

___(h) Her lawyer would not have to guarantee Lyn's willingness to sign a second contract.

5. Below is a list of rights. Some of these would have been recognized as human rights in accordance with eighteenth-century criteria, others only in accordance with twentieth-century criteria. Mark each right listed below *E* or *T* and explain for each *T* what characteristics disqualified it to be an *E*.

___(a) The right to move oneself from one town to another

___(b) The right to receive an education

___(c) The right to worship whatever deity one chooses

___(d) The right to adequate health care

___(e) The right to do meaningful work

___(f) The right to offer for sale what one produces.

___(g) The right to hold meetings with other people who want to attend them

___(h) The right to have leisure time

DISCUSSION QUESTIONS

1. What some call *human rights* we called *moral rights*. Doing so permits us to raise the question of how far such rights extend. Considering the two ways moral rights can be interpreted in the twentieth century, what are the arguments for and against extending the concept of moral rights to other entities in addition to humans, animals for example? Must these other entities be living, or might they be physical entities (computers) or legal entities (corporations)?

2. Considering the issues associated with product liability, what rights should we ascribe to those who suffer as a result of governmental negligence or liability? Should those in the armed services have the right to sue if they are accidentally injured by a defective piece of machinery which a private company sold to the military? If so, which agency has the liability—the government for accepting the product and putting it into service, or the manufacturer for (perhaps knowingly) delivering a product which could not perform the tasks for which it was intended?

3. Should a person who is awarded a high school diploma have the legal right to sue either the educational institution or its employees if that person has not been educated

to some reasonable level, for example if the person cannot do basic math and cannot read beyond the eighth-grade level?

ANSWERS TO SELECTED EXERCISES

1. (a) *NCMR*
(b) *CMR*: in order for people to make wills, a procedure for making a legal will has to be set up; for example, the will must be witnessed or notarized.
(c) *NCMR*
(d) *CMR*: a person must go through the conventional procedure of filing for office in order to be an official candidate for the office.   There are often other legal requirements as well, such as age.
(e) *CMR*: selling one's property involves the conventional action of making a contract.
(f) *NCMR*
(g) *NCMR*
(h) *CMR*: donating one's body requires a level of convention parallel to the one that allows a person to will his property.
(i) *NCMR*
(j) *NCMR*

2. (a) *CD*: not to interfere with or prevent another person from speaking.
(b) *CD*: not to interfere with or prevent another person from opening the business.
(c) *NCD*: others have the right to open businesses of their own, which may successfully compete with the first party's business, even making it fail.
(d) *CD*: not to interfere with or prevent another person from offering his property for rent.
(e) *NCD*: others have the right to offer their own property for sale, and scarcity of customers may mean that some who want to sell can find no buyers. It is also true that this alleged right is very suspect, because if anybody had the right to have someone buy his property, then someone else would have the corresponding duty to buy the property, which would seem to be an infringement of that person's right to spend money as he chooses.
(f) *NCD*: if all persons have an equal right to rent the property, then there must be legal ways for persons to compete with each other concerning who shall rent a piece of property. Such competition is a form of interference.
(g) *CD*: for no one, including the prospective landlord, to interfere with or prevent the applicant from renting the property.
(h) *CD*: for no one to interfere with or prevent the landlord from deciding that he does not want to rent the property to any applicant. (If it is true that only applicants have the right listed above, then landlords do not have this right. Also, landlords may be prohibited from using race as a criterion in deciding not to rent, yet they may retain this right if it is exercised on the basis of some other criterion; for example, all people who apply have pets, and the landlord refuses to allow pet owners to rent.)

3. (a) *MR* (b) *LP* (c) *MR* (d) *LP* (e) *LP* (f) *MR* (g) *MR* (h) *LP*
In some countries there are legal powers to permit acting on the basis of certain moral rights. In some countries there are laws that abridge some moral rights.

4. (a) *LP*—to enter into a contract

   (b) *L*—to go on television

   (c) *L*—to become liable for payment

   (d) *L*—to become liable to be called to work at a specific time

   (e) *LP*—to authorize her lawyer to act on her behalf

   (f) *I*—she would be immune from having to restrict herself to only one ad agency

   (g) *L*—to pay her more

   (h) *I*—from being bound by what her lawyer negotiated

5. (a) *E*

   (b) *T*: the right to receive an education cannot be satisfied simply by other persons' performing a duty of non-interference. An opportunity, and perhaps teachers, must be provided if the person is to receive the education.

   (c) *E*

   (d) *T*: the right to adequate health care cannot be satisfied simply by other persons performing a duty of non-interference. Persons will receive adequate health care only if medicines, medical equipment, and medical personnel are available or made available to them.

   (e) *T*: the right to do meaningful work will not necessarily be satisfied simply by other persons performing a duty of non-interference. Others may have to cooperate in order to create opportunities for meaningful work.

   (f) *E*

   (g) *E*

   (h) *T*: the right to have leisure time will not necessarily be satisfied simply by other persons performing a duty of non-interference. An elaborate social and technological base may be necessary in order to ensure that persons can survive without working all of their waking hours.

Section 2
CONCEPTS OF DUTY

Some hold that there is a type of right to which persons are entitled without qualification and which they may not, under any conditions, renounce. This is to say that there are moral rights that are indefeasible and inalienable. In this section, after analyzing the concepts of indefeasible rights and inalienable rights, we shall examine Kant's view that there are corresponding duties to respect such rights without exception. The view that there is such a duty is expressed in what Kant calls the *Categorical Imperative*. Three formulations of the Categorical Imperative will be presented and interpreted. The views that there are indefeasible and inalienable rights and a categorical imperative to honor them will be shown to be instances of what is called a *deontological* ethical theory. Such a theory maintains that some actions are intrinsically right. After studying this section you should be able to:

- Characterize indefeasible rights.
- Characterize inalienable rights.

- Distinguish and apply consequential, conventional, and deontological justifications for doing one's duty.
- State three formulations of Kant's categorical imperative.
- Explain why various actions violate the categorical imperative.

THE CASE OF ELROD CLAYMORE

Elrod Claymore was an energetic, vibrant, athletic young man of twenty-five. He thrived on physical activity and was especially satisfied when working with his hands. He had always hoped to work for the National Park Service, enjoying the sensations that nature and hard labor had to offer. Tragically, Elrod was caught in a forest fire in Bluestone National Park, where he had just begun working as a ranger. A rescue squad was able to pull him from the flames and save his life, but not before he suffered severe burns over two-thirds of his body. His limbs and face were burnt worst of all. He would henceforth be blind and unable to walk or use his hands. Moreover, to survive at all, he must undergo years of painful treatment.

Because the wounds and the treatment combined to make Elrod's first few months after the fire hellishly painful, he was treated without his consent, for there was no time when the effects of the pain and medication left him lucid enough to express his own desires. The medical staff worked dedicatedly to bring him back from the brink of death, hoping that he would someday find new reason to live.

During several months of severe agony, fluctuating between wakefulness and nightmare, Elrod gradually recovered his lucidity. After a period when it was hard to tell whether he was rational or was still under the influence of the trauma he was suffering, the time finally arrived when all concerned, including psychiatrists and lawyers, acknowledged that Elrod was able to express his rational wish.

Throughout the early stages of his agony Elrod, on occasion, had managed to cry out that he wished he were dead. Now, obviously self-possessed, he clearly articulated his wish to have treatment discontinued and to be allowed to die.

His reasons were these: He was well aware that the painful treatment was by no means over, and he did not believe future prospects were bright enough to make his continued suffering worthwhile. He saw no good reason for him to wish to live, since he could no longer enjoy any of those things that he had found most meaningful and satisfying. He hinted that he suspected the medical staff were interested in his case more because of what they were learning about burn-treatment techniques than because of a concern for his future well-being. He asserted that he had an absolute right to choose to die. He believed there would not possibly be any overriding concerns of others, or of the state, that could cancel that right or justify his continued suffering. He requested that he be released from the treatment center and be returned to his home to die.

The treatment center staff did not grant Elrod's wish. They were well aware that discontinuing treatment and releasing Elrod at that time would inevitably lead to his contracting a fatal infection. His mother had spoken with Elrod and the staff and begged that he not be released, even if that meant not honoring his wishes. She prayed for a meaningful future for him and for his eventual forgiveness.

2.1 Indefeasible Rights

To say that a person has a right is to say he has an entitlement—your right to worship as you please entitles you to worship as you please. To say that a *right is indefeasible is to say that there can be no circumstances where others can justifiably override that right.* If you have indefeasible rights, others cannot undo, annul, or cancel them for any reason whatever; they may be ignored or violated, but never justifiably so. By contrast, to say that a right is *defeasible* is to allow that (a) while having the right contributes to the justification of action in accord with it and to the justification of the claim that the right should be honored, still (b) in some circumstances a contrary stronger justification may be offered, leading to the conclusion that the right should not be honored. Thus, to talk about whether a right is indefeasible or defeasible is to talk about whether someone else's right or someone else's circumstances might override it. There has been much dispute over whether there are, indeed, any indefeasible rights. Some, that have at times been characterized as indefeasible are the right to life, the right to liberty, the right to free speech, and the right to develop one's talents to the extent that one does not violate the rights of others.

In the case study Elrod maintained that he had a right to die. In claiming that no circumstances were imaginable to him under which he could justifiably be denied the exercise of that right, he was claiming that his right to die was indefeasible. Whether or not his mother and the medical staff believed that he or anyone else had a right to die is unclear. What is clear is that, if they did believe people had such a right, they did not believe the right to be indefeasible. They were acting in accord with a belief that overriding considerations in Elrod's circumstances (indeed, perhaps Elrod's own interests) justified their not honoring his right.

2.2 Inalienable Rights

To say that a *right is inalienable is to say that a person may not renounce it, that the person cannot in any way give up that right.* Contrarily, to say that a right is *alienable* is to say that a person can justifiably renounce her claim to it or transfer it to another. As an illustration, consider two cases of supposed ownership of property. In one case a person who owns things (for example, a car or furniture) enjoys an alienable right of property with regard to them. What makes it alienable is the fact that ownership of the property can be transferred or renounced. If the owner sells the furniture or car, she loses all title to it and is no longer entitled to treat it as she sees fit. By contrast, many believe that no person has a right to sell himself into slavery. In other words, the right not to be a slave is inalienable. If so, then owner-ship of one person by another can never be justified. A person might agree to sub-mit to the bondage of another *as if* he were a piece of property, but his right not to be enslaved would not thereby be renounced; rather, it simply would not be as-serted. Thus, the entitlement to affirm one's personhood would remain throughout the bondage relationship. The fact of the original submission could never count as a cancellation of the inalienable right not to be enslaved.

The Declaration of Independence refers to the rights to life, liberty, and the pursuit of happiness as inalienable. It is possible to think also of many of the rights in the Bill of Rights as inalienable. In the case study, Elrod worries that his case may be of interest to the medical staff primarily because of the knowledge they are gaining about burn therapy; he may thereby be voicing a concern that what he takes to be his inalienable right not to be exploited is being violated. He might also claim that his right to die is inalienable. The non-exercise of the right to die by people who choose to continue living would be quite compatible with continuance of the entitlement on their part. Similarly, a person does not lose the right to sell her property simply because she chooses to retain possession for a time.

2.3 Contrasting Indefeasible and Inalienable Rights

If a right is indefeasible, is it also inalienable? If it is inalienable, is it always inde-feasible? No. The concepts of indefeasibility and inalienability are distinct. To un-derstand them better, let's contrast these two different kinds of rights.

Consider the right to use one's own property as one chooses. The idea of inalienability is that a person cannot renounce a certain right. One does, however, give up rights to use one's property when one rents or sells it. If you had an inalienable right to use your property as you chose, then you would not be able to relinquish that right by renting your property and transferring ownership. Indefeasibility, on the other hand, does not have to do with a person's renouncing or relinquishing his own rights. Rather it involves other persons' conflicting and overriding rights. Some people would say that as long as the property in question is legally yours, no one, under any circumstances, has rights overriding yours. That is, no one can make you use, or himself use, your property except as you see fit. This is the claim that the right to use your own property as you see fit is indefeasible, although we have just seen that it is alienable.

Now consider the right to life. Unlike the right to the use of your property, the right to life has been considered by many as defeasible but inalienable. To say that your right to life is inalienable is to say that you cannot renounce it. It is to claim, for example, that suicide is always wrong for it is the renunciation of an inalienable right. Saying the right to life is inalienable is to claim, for example, that no matter what Elrod says about the right to die or wanting to die, his right to life remains something he cannot surrender and the medical staff must honor that fact. On the other hand, some people who view the right to life as inalienable also support capital punishment. That is, they hold that certain circumstances, namely those of having been convicted of a capital offense, such as first degree murder, give society the overriding right, and perhaps even a duty, to take the life of the criminal. This is the view that the right to life is defeasible—capable of being justifiably overridden by a conflicting right or duty.

2.4 Deontological, Consequentialist and Conventionalist Reasons

The United Nations Declaration of Human Rights, the Declaration of Independence, as well as the Bill of Rights in the U. S. Constitution assert that certain rights exist independent of any governmental structure. We honor these documents and respect the ideals which they embody. We might say that at the very least these rights exist in a practical sense because people and governments respect them and strive to conduct their affairs in accord with them. Governments throughout the world allow themselves to be influenced by these historically significant statements. *We can characterize the assertion that one has a given duty because certain social, cultural or legal conventions, or standards of behavior happen to exist as a conventionalist justification for that assertion.* The force of assertions like "this is how we do things around here," or "in our country we respect a person's right to voice opinions even if we disagree with those opinions" is to suggest conventionalist reasons why persons act in certain ways.

Many thinkers find conventionalist reasons insufficient as a basis for claiming indefeasible and inalienable rights. Indeed, to conceive of such rights in terms of nothing more than the moral standards of one's society seems contradictory. If it became the custom not to honor an indefeasible right would that make the right no longer indefeasible? If *indefeasibility* only meant *currently honored by the moral standards of our society* then saying a right was indefeasible would mean it was not indefeasibility at all—*temporary indefeasibility* is an oxymoron. No. If rights claims like those made in the documents mentioned above are true, then one's ethical duties are grounded in something much less relative and fluid then social conventions.

If indefeasible and inalienable rights exist, then it would be morally right under all conditions to honor them. That is, the corresponding duties to honor such rights would be unconditional. It is a small step from this to the view that performing such duties is intrinsically right. *This view, that some actions are intrinsically right, is the defining characteristic of what has come to be called deontological ethical theory, or deontology.* Deontological theory contrasts with all ethical theories that would define actions as right in terms of their consequences, either for the agent or for others. *Such contrasting theories may be called consequentialist, since they maintain that actions can only be considered as instrumentally (as opposed to intrinsically) right or wrong, to the extent that they conduce to good or bad consequences.* Utilitarianism and Ethical Egoism, which we discussed in Chapters 2 and 3, are consequentialist ethical theories.

2.5 Kant's Ethical Theory

The ethical theory of Immanuel Kant (1724–1804) may readily be interpreted as an instance of *deontological theory*. Kant argues that there are some rights which are both indefeasible and inalienable, and that other people have obligations to honor such rights. These obligations are universal and categorical (Kant, 1785, 1788). *Categorical duties exist under all possible circumstances.* Kant contrasts categorical duties with those that arise only because a person happens to have certain goals or purposes in mind. If, for example, a person wishes to gain physical strength, then the person ought to work out with weights. Working out with weights is certainly not a duty which applies to everyone under all possible circumstances, but it does apply to a person given the hypothesis that the person has the goal of gaining physical strength. Duties a person has as a result of having certain goals or interests are called *hypothetical duties*, meaning that they arise only on the *hypothesis* that it is true that one has such goals. "If you want to gain strength, then you ought to lift weights."

While a person may have many purposes, intentions, and goals, the duties which arise because of having those goals, such as the duty to get up early enough to achieve the goal of going to the gym to workout before breakfast, do not, for Kant, constitute matters of morality. Kant maintains that morality is not a function of any hypothesis that other goals besides duty are to be served. Thus, it is not the case that the only duties one has are hypothetical duties which arise out of one's interest in the pursuit of particular ends, consequences, or benefits. One also has categorical duties. These duties are unconditioned ethical duties. It is intrinsically right to do one's categorical duties.

According to Kant morality is fundamentally a matter of doing one's categorical duties—that is, doing those duties that correspond to the indefeasible and inalienable rights people enjoy regardless of circumstance. Kant would deny that morality is a matter of rationally pursuing one's own self-interest (enlightened egoism). He would deny it is a matter of rationally coordinating the interests of the majority of the people (universal utilitarianism). Nor is morality merely a matter of abiding by the moral standards of one's society, meeting the expectations of one's peers, or fulfilling one's legal obligations because one wishes to conform or be accepted. Morality is not a matter of pursuing any goals or purposes whatsoever, except the goal of doing one's categorical duty. It makes no difference in terms of one's moral duty whether those ends be the production of good consequences or the preservation of arbitrarily constructed conventions.

Of course, particular conventions may well be designed to capture or reflect our categorical duties. For example, the Hippocratic Oath is our society's conventional way for a new doctor to undertake a commitment to human health. But what makes such conformity moral is not the existence of the conventions, but rather the existence of the indefeasible and inalienable rights that inspired and served as justification for the conventions. What justifies the doctors taking oaths committing themselves to human health and life are the rights of persons to health and life and to having commitments to them honored.

We can read the case study as illustrating the contrast between hypothetical and categorical duties. Elrod claims he has an indefeasible and inalienable right to be allowed to die. He believes that for this reason the staff and his mother have a categorical duty to allow him to exercise that right. The duty is not hypothetical, because it is not conditioned by any considerations of any future benefits for Elrod or the others involved, nor by any particular conventions that may govern hospital practice. If Elrod has the right he claims, then he has it even if no official body, be it a hospital governance board or a state legislature, acknowledges its existence. It is his simply by virtue of his being a person.

2.6 The Categorical Imperative—Three Ways of Putting It

We have explained what Kant meant by claiming that moral duty is categorical as opposed to hypothetical. Now let us see what our categorical duty is according to Kant. In an attempt to make himself clear on this point, he offered three distinct formulations of the *Categorical Imperative*. Kant did not see these three formulations as implying three distinct categorical duties. Rather, at bottom, each formulation amounts to an alternate way of specifying the same duty. Thus, each formulation provides but one possible perspective, or insight, into the single categorical duty that for Kant defines morality.

The first formulation of the Categorical Imperative is, "*So act that the maxim of your will could always hold at the same time as a principle establishing universal law*" (Kant, 1785). In this formulation Kant expresses the concept of the universalizability of moral principles discussed in section 3 of Chapter 1. One should act in such a way that the principles governing one's actions are universalizable; no arbitrary distinctions between persons are to be captured in those principles. Of course roles, abilities, and circumstances are relevant to the specification of precisely what actions are being performed. Kant's point is that despite these disclaimers, an action can be morally permissible for one person only if that same action is permissible for any similar agent in the same situation.

Kant's concern for universalizability shows his concern that inequitable or unfair exceptions for particular persons be counted as immoral. Consider first whether breaking a promise for personal convenience could become a universal practice. Kant believes not, for not everyone could indulge in the practice. Although a few could do so, if everyone were to attempt it, then no promises would be taken seriously. Ironically the very act of promising with the end in view of breaking the promise when convenient would become impossible. Or, put another way, suppose everyone made promise-like declarations with the mental qualification, "That is, unless I just don't feel like it." In such a society, no one would accept any of these declarations as ways of unconditionally giving one's word. Similarly, if everybody indiscriminately used resources no matter to whom they belonged, the institution of private property, like the institution of promising, would be impossible.

In the case study, Elrod seems willing to maintain that the maxim (general principle) of the action he requests of his mother and of the medical staff is a universalizable moral principle. His request is that they release him from the hospital in light of his admittedly rational request to be allowed to die. The action could be universalized to the practice of honoring such requests made by patients who are in similar circumstances.

Kant's second formulation of the Categorical Imperative is, "Act so as to treat humanity, whether in your own person or in that of another, always as an end and never as a means only" (Kant, 1785). If the moral law is to apply to all persons, as the first formulation of the Categorical Imperative indicates, then all persons are to count as equally valuable. It cannot be, then, that any person's goals can come to have such value that another person's goals may be subordinated to them to such a degree that the other person is used simply to accomplish those goals. In this view, there is a categorical duty to treat other persons like human beings with indefeasible and inalienable rights, rather than like objects, tools, or machines. It is the having of such rights that distinguishes persons as having intrinsic value from things, the value of which are merely instrumental. This is a claim that to each person is due, minimally, a higher kind of respect, an inviolable dignity, that is incompatible with his being brainwashed, conditioned, made into an instrument for the purposes of others, enslaved, manipulated, exploited, molested, or converted into a domesticated animal. To fail to accord persons this minimal respect is to blur the distinction between persons and things; it is disrespectful of human moral autonomy.

In the case study Elrod is suspicious that the medical staff are interested in gaining knowledge about burn therapy through keeping him alive against his wishes. He is suspicious, then, that he is being exploited, or treated simply as a means rather than as an end. Treating him as an end could well require that his decision to be allowed to die rather than suffer continued agony be honored. Not to do so would be to subordinate the value of his moral autonomy to a supposedly higher value, improved burn therapy.

Notice Kant's exact wording in this second formulation of the Categorical Imperative. He states the imperative as that of treating humanity always as an end and never as a means *only*. Imagine Elrod when he first arrived at the hospital. At that point it was reasonable to presume that Elrod would want to live if it were at all possible. It would certainly have been morally and legally dangerous to presume otherwise. Thus, at that point treating Elrod's burns as effectively as possible was certainly a way of treating Elrod as an end. It might happen, however, that the techniques for best treating Elrod were not yet sufficiently developed and that the medical team would learn something about burn therapy from treating Elrod's case. Under these circumstances, treating Elrod would also be a means to improving medical knowledge of burn therapy. To such treatment, however, Kant would raise no objection. For although Elrod is being used as a means, he is also being treated as an end, and thus not as a means *only*.

Kant's third formulation of the Categorical Imperative is, "Act according to the maxims of a universally legislative member of a merely potential kingdom of ends" (Kant, 1785).   While the language here is complicated, this formulation seems based on the following Kantian reasoning. If individuals are always to be treated as ends and never solely as means, then each person must recognize that all others are morally in an equal position as oneself; they are all moral persons. That is, in effect, to note that all persons belong to the same moral community. Persons who come to this realization recognize two things: (a) they can legitimately pursue those of their goals that do not conflict with the duty to treat others as ends, and (b) they have a duty to facilitate the same possibility for all others. In other words, society should be organized so as to promote each person's freedom and facilitate expressing this freedom within the boundaries of the moral law. Thus, this third formulation of the Categorical Imperative could be read as indicating that persons have a categorical duty to behave in such a way that the principles governing their actions could be adopted by everyone and serve as the basis for a moral community governed by mutual respect.

The case study raises a question whether within a moral community there is a duty to honor serious requests to be allowed to die. Kant did not directly discuss whether there is a right to die. He did sharply oppose suicide. Yet, there is room to ask whether his moral theory, as reflected in the three formulations of the categorical imperative, implies that there is a right to die and a categorical duty to honor it. We leave it to you to consider whether a community where such a right is honored is more or less respectful of persons as morally autonomous ends in themselves than a community where no such right is recognized.

EXERCISES

1. Suppose that a given person has earned a certain amount of money by working for it. In such circumstances it is plausible to assert that the person has a right to all of that money. (2.1–2.3)

   (a) Describe the payroll deduction of income taxes as showing the defeasibility of that right.

   (b) Describe the payroll deduction of a donation to the United Fund (a charity) as showing the alienability of that right.

   (c) In the light of (a), state the characteristics of a defeasible right abstractly, without reference to any particular case of a defeasible right.

   (d) In the light of (b), state the characteristics of an alienable right abstractly.

   (e) In the light of (c) and (d), define the concepts of indefeasible rights and inalienable rights.

2. Below are three reasons for performing each of two alleged duties. Distinguish the reasons as consequentialist *(CQ)*, conventionalist *(CV)*, or deontological *(D)*. (2.4–2.5)

___(a) If you don't give the kids candies on Halloween, they're likely to soap your windows.

___(b) Giving the kids candies is respectful and kind.

___(c) It's traditional to give all the kids candies on Halloween.

___(d) Bakeries have given thirteen cookies when you buy a dozen for so long that now we just call it a baker's dozen.

___(e) Customers are likely to come back to a store where they think they're getting something for nothing.

___(f) A bakery shows its good will towards its customers by making sure that every customer receives a full measure of baked goods for his money.

3. Suppose you have been invited to a party and your host or hostess has asked you to indicate in advance whether you plan to attend. Provide a consequentialist reason, a reason based on convention, and a deontological reason for communicating your plans in advance. (2.4–2.5)

4. State three formulations of Kant's Categorical Imperative. (2.6)

5. Each of the following actions in some way violates the Categorical Imperative. Explain how.

(a) Tom refused to talk to the cab driver, insisting that all he wanted was a ride and that he was doing nothing wrong so long as he paid his fare.

(b) Although supplies were limited and her company had instituted a "one per customer" policy, the checker let her sorority sisters buy two or three.

(c) Mona told her friend, Lisa, that she had broken up with Al because of how badly he had treated her. She went into great detail about his alleged mistreatment, although it was in fact she who had mistreated Al.

(d) Despite his daughter's continued interest and even fascination with woodworking, Harry refused to teach her how to use any of the tools.

(e) When the police officer saw his friends stuck in one of the lines of the traffic jam, he immediately let that line of traffic go until his friends had cleared the area, while all others remained stopped.

(f) Yorba Senior High School's policy forbade boys from enrolling in home economics courses or participating on the school's only volleyball team.

DISCUSSION QUESTIONS

1. Do inalienable or indefeasible rights exist? How do you know?

2. What other categorical duties might there be in addition to that expressed in the Categorical Imperative? Is religion a possible source of categorical duties? According to Chapter 1, naming sources is not the same as giving a justification. How, then, might one justify the claim of any given source that it has properly identified a categorical duty?

3. Consider Kant's claim that all three formulations of the Categorical Imperative really aimed at the same duty although each brought out a different aspect of it. Construct three cases. Make each case such that it satisfies one version of the Categorical Imperative, not the other two.

4. Is the right to life inalienable?

ANSWERS TO SELECTED EXERCISES

1. The right of the government to collect income taxes, or the right of the society to provide for various needs of its citizens, might override the right of the individual to keep all the money he or she has earned, thereby making his right defeasible.

   (b) The individual can renounce his or her right to his or her money by donating that money to some other party, thereby alienating himself or herself from that right.

   (c) An individual's right is defeasible when, even though the individual has the right, some other party has a right, such that there is adequate justification for the other party to act on his or her right to the exclusion of the original individual's being able to exercise his or her right.

   (d) An individual's right is alienable when it is possible for the person to act so as to lose or renounce it.

   (e) An indefeasible right is one such that under no circumstances is there an adequate justification for not allowing the person having it to exercise it. An inalienable right is one such that in no way can a person having it lose or renounce it.

2. (a) *CQ* (b) *D* (c) *CV* (d) *CV* (e) *CQ* (f) *D*

3. *CQ:* If I don't announce my intentions, something undesirable will happen: I won't be invited to another party, my host or hostess might embarrass me at the party, there won't be enough food prepared, or whatever. *CV:* Etiquette and custom say that a person is supposed to announce whether he or she will accept an invitation. *D:* I have a duty to respect people who have been kind enough to invite me to their party. Naturally your reasons may mention different consequences, conventions, or duties from those stated in these sample answers.

5. (a) Tom is treating the cab driver merely as a means to his getting where he wants.

   (b) The checker is treating her sorority sisters in a way that cannot be universalized to all customers.

   (c) Mona is treating Al solely as a means to trying to create an image of herself that she wants Lisa to have.

   (d) Harry is refusing to help others to pursue their goals.

   (e) The police officer is treating his friends in a way in which he cannot treat all the people stuck in the traffic jam.

   (f) The high school is hindering its male students from pursuing goals some of them may have.

Section 3
FOUNDATIONS OF DEONTOLOGY

In Section 1 we analyzed the wide variety of possible rights claims in terms of related concepts, especially that of duty. In Section 2 we examined more extensively the view that there are moral rights that are indefeasible and inalienable. We focused on Kant's theory that there is, correspondingly, a categorical imperative to honor such rights. In this section we will consider how deontological theorists, such as Kant, might offer a justification for their view that some actions are intrinsically right. The guiding questions for this section are these: Why should any rights be taken as indefeasible and inalienable? Why should any duties be taken as categorical? We shall show, then, how the foundations for this deontological theory are imbedded in the concepts of respect, self-respect, and integrity. The concluding section will deal with the Kantian view that acting with the proper intention is what makes actions intrinsically right. After studying this section you should be able to:

- Characterize respect and self-respect.
- Explain why ignoring each of the three formulations of the categorical imperative implies a lack of respect.
- State the conceptual connection between indefeasible rights, respect for persons, and categorical duties.
- Characterize integrity, comparing and contrasting personal and social integrity.
- State Kant's argument that proper intention makes actions intrinsically right.
- Contrast deontological and consequentialist ethical theories.

THE CASE OF THE IMAGINARY SPACE JOURNEY

Come with us on a flight of the good ship Imagination to a planet in a far corner of the universe. Envision a world totally devoid of life. You are not there and never will be. It exists in a solar system millions of light-years distant. You will never have any experience relating to this planet in the remotest way. Not only is there no life whatever on this planet, but it also lacks the kind of atmospheric and terrestrial environment that could ever lead to the development of life. The desert landscape of rolling dunes and large, smooth rocks is disturbed only by hot, dry winds. Forever call this planet Lifeless.

Imagine now a different planet, equally remote from you and from Lifeless. Although again there is no life, conditions may allow life someday to develop there. The proper atmospheric and terrestrial environment, including the right chemical compounds and an abundant water supply, are present. Call this planet Possibility.

Now fly Imagination to a third planet. Here atmospheric and terrestrial conditions enable plant life to grow, nourish, and reproduce itself in abundance, save in a few scattered desert areas or in valleys where poisonous gases lie. It is a planet filled with meadows of tall grasses and wild flowers, forests and jungles, plants of all descriptions. Call this world Flora.

The fourth planet on our journey supports both plant and animal life in advanced forms. Imagine that this is the first of our planets where living things are capable of sensation, awareness of the environment, and movement over the surface of the planet and beneath its waters. Growth, reproduction, and flourishing of animal species are present. The environment is a balanced one, enabling many species to live together. Of course, not all is pleasant. Pain and suffering exist because of the interaction among the species. The law of the survival of the fittest is operative. There are diseases, storms, floods, droughts, and earthquakes. Call this planet Fauna.

Turn Imagination now toward a fifth planet. Here, intelligent creatures called Groms live together with all of the species found on the planet Fauna. Certain geographical areas on the planet offer that narrow range of weather conditions conducive to Grom life. The presence of Groms makes this the first planet harboring more than the plant and animal functions. The capacity for rationality and rational action are present, so that some behaviors are far from instinctual. We can also imagine that some creatures can choose which of their several potentials shall be pursued and developed. Groms are also distinctive in having the capacity to act autonomously. They can also fail to act autonomously. Self-awareness and self-evaluation are additional new possibilities. With these capacities Groms are able to feel emotions about themselves and about their relations with other beings—satisfaction, exhilaration, confidence, care, pride, anguish, frustration, fear, anxiety, shame, and guilt, among others. Feelings of responsibility for themselves and for other Groms are also now possible. Social harmony, mutual respect, cooperation, conflict of interests, war, and exploitation are among the new social potentials found here for the first time. Not only are beings on this planet susceptible to natural catastrophe, but they are threatened as well by environmental abuse. They are capable of destroying the delicate ecological balance vital for the survival of life on the planet. Groms have developed weapons capable of rendering the planet as sterile as the planet Lifeless. Call this planet Precarious.

3.1 Deontology and Intrinsically Right Action

This case study illustrates a variety of values that may be realized or realizable within the corners of the universe we have imagined, or for that matter within our own corner of the universe. The conditions and beings found on various of our five fantasy planets illustrate both instrumental and intrinsic values. On Lifeless, for instance, it seems nothing is good or bad in itself. Nothing seems to be of any particular instrumental value either. Weather has no value, since nothing lives on Lifeless that it can be good for or bad for. The most violent storm or earthquake is no *worse* than the mildest of days. On Possibility, at least instrumental value may be present, because conditions on Possibility are good for the development of life. We could add that the destruction of these conditions would be bad, because it would end the potentiality for the development of life there. But be careful—the assumption operative here is that life itself has some value.

In order to determine the values life involves, consider the other worlds in our imaginary galaxy. Each of the remaining planets introduces new levels of potential for living. On Flora, growth, reproduction, and flourishing of an organism are the new possibilities. On Fauna, typical animal functions and potentials, including sensation, awareness of the environment, and movement, are added. Precarious is the only planet described where the potentials of rationality, autonomy, self-awareness, feelings of satisfaction, responsibility for self and others, feelings of fellowship, social harmony, and mutual respect are present.

It is plausible to suggest that each of the potentials found on the various planets has intrinsic value. Some of them, of course, can also be thought of as having instrumental value, making possible the realization of other potentials. Thus, for example, awareness of the environment may be understood as intrinsically valuable and, at the same time, instrumentally valuable, because it is a condition for Groms to be able to come to respect each other.

If the various life potentials on our fantasy planets are considered to have intrinsic value, then it is reasonable to understand the living conditions there to be instrumentally good when they are conducive to the continued development and realization of those potentials. Planetary conditions are instrumentally bad to the extent that they undermine or make impossible the continued development and realization of the various life potentials. Thus, it seems appropriate to think of the weather and the water supply on Flora as instrumentally good; they contribute to the lush growth. But the poisonous gases are instrumentally bad; they kill plant life. The habitable climate of Precarious is instrumentally good, as it allows advanced life such as Groms to flourish; its natural catastrophes, however, are instrumentally bad, for they can diminish the quality of, or even destroy, such life. Other social conditions on Precarious are instrumentally good or bad to the extent that they render possible, contribute to, undermine, or destroy the human potentials for autonomy, social harmony, and the like that exist there.

3.2 Respect for Persons

In analyzing the case study, we have surveyed some of the capacities that creatures of various kinds enjoy. For these creatures to flourish they must have and exercise these capacities. We have also noted how these creatures can be prevented from flourishing by various planetary and social conditions. This analysis also leads us to a definition of respect. *To respect a creature is to appreciate it for its capacity to flourish; that is, to know and appreciate both its potentials for achievement and its potential ways of suffering.* Showing respect for persons, then, amounts to allowing (not interfering with) and perhaps even facilitating their flourishing, or their exercising their capacities that have intrinsic value.

3.3 The Value of Respect

Respect for persons may be viewed as an *absolute, instrumental value.* The value of respect is absolute because respect is necessary to the intrinsic good of creatures being able to flourish. It is instrumentally good because it is defined as the means to this intrinsically good end. It could also be argued that respect is *intrinsically valuable.* Consider the possibility that some person is not treated with respect. Not only will this course of action probably reduce his ability to flourish, but it is an act of denigrating the person's value. What such an action says to the person is, "You are not really valuable; how you are treated doesn't matter all that much." This is not only instrumentally undesirable for its impact upon the person's conception of self-worth, but it is intrinsically wrong because of the gap between the implicit judgment concerning the person's worth and the facts about the person that render him or her worthy of respect.

Notice the generality involved in this concept of respect. Essentially we are saying that a being has capacities, the development of which define his flourishing. These same beings have limitations, and can, thus, be caused not to be able to nourish. Respect means appreciating both the being's capabilities and the limitations to which it is subject. Respect is broad enough to extend beyond human beings. Animals, for example, clearly have capacities for awareness of the environment, and many are capable of suffering pain. Respect for such beings, then, clearly implies not destroying their capacities for awareness, for example, by blinding them, and not inflicting pain—except for their own good—upon them.

3.4 Respect and Indefeasibility of Rights

Ethical theorists who maintain that people have indefeasible rights by virtue of their being persons, are thinking of rights to exercise the capacities which we imagined for the first time on Precarious. Beings are intrinsically valuable because of having such capacities. This is the ground for the claim noted in Section 2 that to each person there is due, minimally, a higher kind of respect, an inviolable dignity, which is incompatible with her being brainwashed, conditioned, made into a instrument for the purposes of others, enslaved, molested, manipulated, or converted into a domesticated animal. If beings have these indefeasible rights, then there is a corresponding categorical duty to respect these beings, in precisely the sense of *respect* delineated in the preceding paragraphs. If this is so, then we have uncovered one possible ultimate justification for the deontologists' thesis that there are intrinsically right actions. These intrinsically right actions would be those that are respectful of the potentials and capacities that are intrinsically valuable.

3.5 Self-Respect

If it is true that to respect another (person or being) is to permit and even to facilitate flourishing, then self-respect is to do the same for oneself. If we hold that the kinds of attitudes or images a person has concerning himself significantly affect his ability to flourish, then having self-respect will involve having attitudes about oneself that allow oneself to flourish. Self-awareness and self-evaluation first become possible on the planet Precarious. Self-respect also becomes a possibility on that planet.

Self-respect is acknowledging and appreciating one's own capacities and limitations; that is, one's own rights as a person. Surely no sense could be attached to the idea that a self-respecting person might be unappreciative of her own rights as a person. Self-respect will also be a matter of being prudent, of taking care of one's health, of being aware of one's limitations and strengths, and of living within them.   It may also involve endeavoring to maximize the development of one's abilities and talents.

To better understand the connection of self-respect with development of personal potential, we must take a very important fact into account: Human beings have many capacities. It is impossible to develop all of them, for life is too short, and developing some capacities is incompatible with developing others.   For instance, though a person may have the capacities to be both a world class sprinter and a world class swimmer, there is a physical incompatibility between developing both of these capacities. The way one develops muscles and techniques when one is becoming a sprinter makes the body less able to perform as a top-grade swimmer.

Moreover, although it may be possible for many persons to develop various capacities, it may be impossible for all persons to develop the same capacities. We live in a world where specialized labor predominates.   However valuable heart surgery specialists may be, it is impossible that everybody should develop the capacity to be a heart surgeon. If everyone who had the capacity to become a heart surgeon took the time to develop it, there would not be time enough left over for people to develop and utilize the abilities to perform other socially useful tasks, such as feeding the population that might someday be in need of heart surgery. These facts about our world and our society constitute limiting factors that self-respecting persons must take into account as they rationally assess their capacities and choose which of them to try to develop.

3.6 Self-respect and Inalienability

Self-respect is related to indefeasibility in the same way as respect in general is. Whereas defeasible rights can be overridden by the stronger justifications others may have, indefeasible rights cannot be overridden. If one is to be respectful of a person's indefeasible rights, one must honor them. Where indefeasible rights cannot be overridden, inalienable rights cannot be renounced. And just as respect for others minimally involves honoring any indefeasible rights they have, so self-respect minimally involves not denying one's own inalienable rights (the rights one may not renounce). Kant, for example, thought of the development of one's talents as an inalienable right that a self-respecting person would not deny by either ignoring or destroying his or her potentials.

3.7 Personal Integrity

Having looked at the concept of respect on both the personal and social levels, let us analyze a related concept, that of *integrity*, on those two levels. *Integrity is a matter of integrating potentialities.* Personal integrity is based on the elements of self-respect, such as being true to oneself and living responsibly in light of one's limitations.   Self-respect provides the necessary appreciation of what can be self-enhancing and what can be self-defeating. Beyond this, personal integrity demands a decision concerning which to develop from among the large number and variety of one's potentials. Personal integrity involves a decision to develop a set of potentials that are co-possible, or mutually compatible. This is part of the responsibility for oneself that first appears in the case study on the planet Precarious. One measure of the richness or fullness of particular human lives may then be the comparative extent to which, within those lives, there is a development of a diverse set of co-possible potentials.

3.8 Social Integrity

The potentiality for individual persons to develop in a variety of ways raises the question of the degree of integrity those individuals attain. It also suggests the same question for societies, or groups of people. Societies can also develop in various ways. In parallel fashion, decisions must be made about which of the potentials attainable in or by a society are to be cultivated. On our imaginary planet Precarious, social development can take several directions, including those that would promote the continued flourishing of the inhabitants and those that could make levels of flourishing forever impossible through destruction of ecological or social balance and harmony.

Some maintain that the best society is the one that develops the social integrity to allow the greatest amount of personal integrity on the part of its members. This view of societal integrity sees virtue in maximizing each individual person's opportunities to achieve the highest degree of personal integrity. Individuals are thought of as if they were independent atoms, each able to find the greatest possible fullness and richness of personal integrity if left, as much as possible, to themselves. This view of society is called the *atomistic* view.

The atomistic view of society contrasts with what is called the *organic* view. In the organic view, society should aim for social integrity measured in terms of its collective accomplishments. Here, individual lives attain meaning by participation in the activity of the larger whole. To achieve this it may be necessary at times to disparage the autonomy of particular individuals. The individual, in fact, might have little choice but to conform to and work for certain societal goals or to be ostracized. (For a fuller discussion of these two views of society, see Sections 2.3–2.5 of Chapter 7) Given these two possible views of society, and given that integrity has both a personal and a social dimension, one of the most important questions of social philosophy will turn out to be the relationship of the individual to the state.

On Precarious, the feeling of responsibility for others can center upon either of two things. One is each Grom's potential to achieve personal autonomy. This could lead to the development of a society where respect for the indefeasible and inalienable rights of Groms was vitally important. Or the feeling of responsibility for others can center upon each Grom's potential for serving broader social or collective purposes. The same choices are offered on Earth.

3.9 Conscience

It could be argued that respect for persons is a matter of respecting (a) all of the human capacities mentioned in the description of the Groms on planet Precarious, and (b) the integrity of persons. In the view of Immanuel Kant, to be true to one's conscience is to act on the intention of respecting persons and, most importantly, respecting their integrity. Kant points out that no one can foresee perfectly all of the consequences of his action (Kant, 1785). He argues that whether any action is good or bad cannot, therefore, be judged on the basis of something that cannot even be foreseen. However, a person can know the conscience with which she acts. This, then, for Kant becomes the basis for judging the rightness or wrongness of the action. If the person acts in good conscience, attempting to respect persons and their integrity, then her action is intrinsically right. It is right because of the presence of that intention. Kant is saying that to intend to respect persons is to intend to bring about *as best one can foresee* that people are respected in all of the ways we considered in our analysis of respect above. Thus, in Kant's view, it is *the agent's intention that determines whether the action is intrinsically right or wrong*. This is pure deontological moral theory. In contrast, consequentialist theories view the rightness of an action as a function of the consequences it actually produces, such as personal or social benefits.

EXERCISES

1. (a) The beings on Fauna and Precarious have characteristics that no beings on Lifeless or Possibility have. List several typical distinguishing characteristics.

   (b) When you have checked your list of characteristics against 3.1, state more abstractly what it is about characteristics that occur on Fauna or Precarious but not on Lifeless and Possibility that gives rise to the possibility of respect only on the former planets.

   (c) When you have checked your answer against 3.1, state as clearly as you can what respect is, both in terms of the kind of being towards which respect is possible [the answer from (b)] and in terms of the attitude toward such a being that respect involves. (3.2, 3.3)

   (d) What characteristic must a being have in order to have self-respect?

   (e) In light of the answers to (c) and (d), state as clearly as you can what self-respect is. (3.5)

2. (a) Suppose a police officer moves his friends' lane until they all have cleared the area of snarled traffic, in violation of the first formulation of the categorical imperative. (1) State to whom the officer is being disrespectful. (2) Explain what about his action is contrary to the concept of respect. (3) Explain how violation of the first formulation of the categorical imperative involves disrespect. (See 2.6)

   (b) Suppose that Mona lies about Al in order to look good in Lisa's eyes, in violation of the second formulation of the categorical imperative. (1) Explain what about

Mona's action is disrespectful to Al. (2) Explain how violation of the second formulation of the categorical imperative involves disrespect. (See 2.6)

(c) Suppose that Harry refuses to teach his daughter how to use tools, in violation of the third formulation of the categorical imperative. (1) Explain what about Harry's action is disrespectful of his daughter. (2) Explain how violation of the third formulation of the categorical imperative involves a lack of respect. (See 2.6)

3. (a) State abstractly the way in which persons must be treated if they are to be respected. (3.2–3.4)

(b) State the grounds for the view that respectful treatment of persons is intrinsically right. (3.2–3.4)

(c) State the conceptual connection between a person's having an intrinsic right to be treated respectfully and the concept of a categorical duty.

4. (a) Characterize integrity. (3.7)

(b) Define what it means to say that a person has integrity. (3.7)

(c) Define what it means to say that a society has integrity. (3.8)

(d) Compare and contrast accounts of social integrity that view persons individualistically with accounts that view persons as participants in collective social goals. (3.8)

5. (a) State Kant's argument that actions are not right or wrong in virtue of their consequences.

(b) State Kant's argument that actions are intrinsically right in virtue of the intention with which they are done. In your statement include a characterization of the sort of intention that makes an action intrinsically right according to Kant. (3.9)

6. Below is a list of statements. Consequentialist and deontological ethical theories can largely be defined by their agreement or disagreement concerning these statements. In the columns labeled *C* and *D* mark *True* or *False* for each statement, depending on whether it is true or false according to the deontologist and the consequentialist, respectively.

C   D

      (a) Some actions are intrinsically right.

      (b) Some actions are right instrumentally, but not intrinsically.

      (c) Only states of affairs are intrinsically valuable.

      (d) Being respectful of persons is intrinsically right.

      (e) One always ought to strive to be respectful of persons.

      (f) Some states of affairs are intrinsically valuable.

      (g) There are some categorical duties.

      (h) Some actions are instrumentally wrong.

      (i) No rights are indefeasible.

      (j) Being disrespectful of oneself is intrinsically wrong.

DISCUSSION QUESTIONS

1. Obviously the case study was allegorical. In view of the case study and the answers to question 1, which sorts of earthly things satisfy the conditions specified for being worthy of respect and which sorts possess indefeasible and inalienable rights?

2. When a deontologist says that it is a person's intentions which are important in deciding the intrinsic value of an action, consequentialists object that this implies that a person could bring about an intrinsically bad state of affairs but not be called immoral for knowingly doing so. In your view, does having the proper intentions morally justify a person no matter what results are foreseeably brought about by the person's action? If not, construct an example to illustrate your view. How would a defender of deontology respond to your example? Remember to keep in mind the difference between a justification and an excuse as discussed in Chapter 1.

3. How does drug and alcohol abuse relate to self-respect and integrity?

4. In view of such psychological realities as dissassociation, self-deception, and denial, what modifications would you make in the deontologist's claim that the person himself is always in a position to know (or best know) his own intentions.

5. Different businesses operating in the same town, whether in competition with each other or not, can be thought of as economic atoms. The atomistic view of commercial society suggests that each of the businesses, while interacting with each other, should be permitted to realize its potentials to the fullest possible extent. Is "respecting the rights of another business to flourish" inconsistent with economic competition, or should one business be allowed to take over another if it can? If you say that businesses have no such right, explain why not. How does one distinguish, in terms of other persons' duties to respect certain rights, between the rights of a business to flourish and the rights of the owners of that business to flourish?

6. Persons who work for the same corporation can be thought of as cells in the same organism. The differentiation of the duties of different cells and the necessity of sacrificing some cells for the organism as a whole to survive, suggests, if we carry the analogy far enough, that within corporate society workers should not be acknowledged as having indefeasible and inalienable personal rights. That some corporations and societies behave toward their employees and citizens this way seems factually undeniable. If they ought not, then where should we mark their limits? Ethically speaking, if it comes to it, ought a business corporation fail, a government fall, or a society die rather than violate a single individual's indefeasible and inalienable rights?

ANSWERS TO SELECTED EXERCISES

1. (d) Self-awareness is the characteristic it needs.

2. (a) (1) The police officer is disrespectful of the persons in other lanes, whose right to move along their way is equal to the right of the persons in his friends' lane. (2) As the officer focuses on helping out his friends, he is ignoring the capacities of the others, which their circumstances constrain them from using, and he is ignoring the limitations of their time. Appreciating them for their capacities and limitations would imply treating them differently than he is treating them. (3) One is disrespectful when one treats persons as if it were false that they all have general capacities and limitations in common. Yet if one treats some persons in a non-universalizable way, one treats them as if it were false.

(b) (1) Mona is treating Al in such a way as to ignore his capacities and limitations—in this case, his feelings in particular. (2) If one treats a person solely as a means, then one ignores the issue of how one's actions will affect that person's ability to flourish—except to the extent that, if the person does not flourish, he or she may become less useful as one's means,

(c) (1) Harry's action hinders his daughter's development of her potential for using tools. (2) When one does not help and maybe even hinders another development of her potential, one constrains the flourishing of the other.

3. (a) Your answer should take into account that flourishing is related both to capacities and to limitations and that respect is related to all three formulations of the Categorical Imperative.

(c) Something is valuable categorically only if it is valuable regardless of circumstances, what is valuable instrumentally may vary with circumstances, but what is valuable intrinsically is valuable regardless of circumstances.

6. *Consequentialist   Deontologist*

	Consequentialist	*Deontologist*
(a)	*False*	*True*
(b)	*True*	*True*
(c)	*True*	*False*
(d)	*False*	*True*
(e)	*False*	*True*
(f)	*True*	*True*
(g)	*False*	*True*
(h)	*True*	*True*
(i)	*True*	*False*
(j)	*False*	*True*

5 FREEDOM

*Freedom isn't just being left poor and alone to watch your babies die!
Freedom means being able to do what you need to do, it's being able to
learn what you need to know to thrive and flourish!*

Diary of an Urban Freedom Fighter

How curious that some should prize freedom more than life itself, while others should maintain that the concept of freedom is confused and that human freedom might not even be real. As you would expect, freedom is a central concept in normative philosophy, given that it seems unreasonable to hold people responsible for their actions unless they were free to have acted in ways other than how they did act. We begin this chapter by taking up the question of whether or not humans can truly be said to be free. Building on this the chapter explores two main questions: "What is the relationship of freedom to moral responsibility?" and "Exactly what might the nature and limits of human freedom be?"

Human freedom clearly relates to questions of moral responsibility. How can people be held morally responsible for what they do if they are not free to act otherwise? Questions of responsibility depend on how freedom is understood and indeed on whether or not agents can be said to be free. Section 1 responds to these issues by outlining the classic philosophical problem known as *The Dilemma of Determinism*. Section 2 presents the concept of *autonomy* and discusses the conditions under which people can reasonably be said to be autonomous and, so, presumably can be held responsible for what they do. The relationship between personal autonomy and the freedom vs. determinism controversy is spelled out in Section 3.

A second important normative concern related to freedom involves the precise nature and limits of freedom within society. Although freedom is almost universally valued, there are vast differences in what is meant by *being free* and also in the justifications given for limiting a person's freedom.   Section 2 introduces the distinction between positive and negative freedom.   Section 3 explains how prominent theories of praise and punishment relate to the concepts of merit, desert, moral responsibility, and the supposed consequences of institutionalized approval and disapproval.   Section 4 introduces the distinction between formal and effective freedom and explains five proposed justifications for limiting a person's freedom.   The educational goal of this chapter is explain the role of various concepts of freedom in our society's approach to questions about the nature and limits of a person's moral responsibility and social autonomy.

Section 1
THE DILEMMA OF DETERMINISM

Almost everyone agrees it is senseless to hold people morally responsible for what they do unless they can act differently than they do. If they are not free to actually select what they will or will not do, how can they be praised or blamed for what happens?   Yet we frequently hold people responsible for their ac-tions,— we praise and blame them. So, apparently we believe people are free, in some important sense of that word. But wait. Given all we know about he-reditary, environmental, and the psycho-social influences on human behavior, how could we cling to such an archaic belief? None of us is ever really free, say those who hold the view known as *hard determinism*. By contrast those known as philosophical *libertarians* disagree most strenuously, saying humans, unlike other organisms, are characterized in terms of freedom of the will. Meanwhile some, known as *compatibilists*, try to hold the challenging middle position. This section examines the tension between freedom and determinism. It pres-ents the problem and then stakes out the three basic positions named above. After studying Section 1 you should be able to:

- Define and contrast the positions of hard determinism, compatibilism and libertarianism.
- Distinguish the claims that would be made by hard determinists, compatibilists and libertarians.
- Explain how the presupposition of universal causality constitutes a dilemma for freedom and moral responsibility.
- State the major objections raised against hard determinism, compatibilism and libertarianism.
- Given a human action, describe it as it would be seen through the eyes of a hard determinist, a compatibilist, and a libertarian.

THE CASE OF AMY HOLDEN

Judge Bird and the newspaper reporter sat on the old wooden swing that hung by rusty chains from the porch roof of his retirement cottage at Sylvan Lake, Oregon. The reporter snapped on his cassette recorder and asked, "Judge Bird, which case stands out in your mind as the most difficult one you ever tried?"

"That's easy, the case of Amy Holden," replied the judge. He chewed on the stem of his pipe.

"The Green Lake Killer?"

"The same," said the old judge. "But it's not clear that she was really to blame for Thomas Shaw's death."

"Come on, judge. Everyone knows she shot him. She admitted as much at her trial."

"True enough. Her defense attorney never denied that."

"Then what was her defense?"

"Simple. Her attorney argued that Amy could not help herself. The lawyer appealed to Amy's disposition to respond violently when she felt ridiculed. This was compounded by her depression over the loss of her children. Her mind was clouded with feelings of guilt and anger at both herself and Shaw. Her attorney described her as a very unstable woman—fighting a drug problem, too. Amy was a loser in almost every respect. She came from a bad neighborhood, one where you had to be violent just to survive. She had a long police record. She was just a very violent person."

"You mean, your honor, that the defense was that Amy's history, psychology, and character all combined that day and, as a result, killing Shaw that day became an inevitability?"

"That's how I remember it. The defense lawyer said that Amy had to kill Shaw; she could not have done anything else, given everything in her life that led up to that moment."

"What did the prosecutor say?"

"He told how Amy had dated Shaw at various times for over a two year period. At the time of the killing she was pregnant, but it wasn't clear by whom. She tried to force Shaw to marry her. He refused. Then she pulled a gun and threatened suicide. When Shaw laughed and said he wasn't going to be blackmailed, she shot him. Cold-blooded murder is what the prosecutor called it. Amy had plenty of alternatives. She could have sued Shaw, tried to marry someone else, even gone through with the suicide. Lots of options. But the one she chose to exercise, murdering Shaw, was immoral and against the law. She freely chose to kill Shaw and she should be held accountable, said the prosecutor."

"What was the final verdict in Amy's case?"

"Never was one actually," said the judge while he puffed his pipe.

"How so?"

"Amy committed suicide in her cell while the trial was still going on."

"Well, your honor, how do you think the verdict would have gone?"

"I really don't know. Amy dropped out of school in the ninth grade, couldn't get a decent job, and couldn't hold the jobs she did get. Actually, from the way she conducted herself at the trial, I suspect Amy Holden wasn't very intelligent, not even average, I'd say. Probably didn't think too straight. Must have had a hard time of it making good decisions. Then again, juries in a murder trial are notoriously hard to figure. What would you have decided, if you had been on Amy's jury?"

1.1 The Dilemma

A dilemma is a problem such that every apparent alternative is unsatisfactory. The philosophical problem of whether or not people are free, in some morally relevant sense of "free," has traditionally been posed as a dilemma.

PREMISE (a)   Either every event is caused or some human choices are not caused.

PREMISE (b)   If every event has causes, then all human choices, being events, also have causes.

PREMISE (c)   If all human choices are caused, they cannot be other than they are.

PREMISE (d)   If no human choices can, or could, be altered, then people are not free.

PREMISE (e)   But, if human choices are not caused, then, as events in the world, they must be random.

PREMISE (f)   If human choices are random, then people do not have control over their choices.

PREMISE (g)   Either way, if people are not free, or people cannot control their own choices, then it is unreasonable to hold them morally responsible for anything they do.

CONCLUSION: So, it is not reasonable to hold people morally responsible for what they do.

This typical statement of *The Dilemma of Determinism* shows the traditionally expressed connections between believing that events are all caused and believing that people are not free. Similarly, it shows how believing that choices are uncaused leads to the alternative view that they must be random and, so, either way, people cannot be held morally accountable for their actions.

1.2 Illogical or Untrue?

The only ways to avoid the conclusion of this dilemma are to claim either that the argument is logically faulty or that at least one of its premises is false. Many thinkers have challenged various of its premises. For example, some philosophers have drawn a distinction between human actions and physical events, thus attacking premise (b), "If every event has causes, then all human choices, being events, also have causes." In this way they try to maintain their scientific belief that all events are caused and also hold that human actions (not being events) are uncaused. A variation on that theme is the view that human actions are self-caused in the sense that humans are self-determining beings, whereas all other beings or events in nature are more or less interconnected causally.

A second challenge to the truth of the premises might focus on premise (e), "But, if human choices are not caused, then, as events in the world, they must be random." By arguing that human choices are neither random events nor uncaused phenomena, this tactic hopes to identify a third alternative. However, it is not immediately clear what that third possibility might be.

Few have attacked the dilemma as illogical. But it may be possible to show that crucial ambiguities in the concepts of *causality*, *event*, *choice*, and, most centrally, *free* actually mislead us into accepting this argument as logical when we should not. If these terms are ambiguous or vague in ways that affect the logic of the argument, then pointing out these conceptual problems could lead to the dissolution of the dilemma. For example, some people maintain that by training and education we are taught to make rational choices, and so, in a sense, we are conditioned or caused to act freely.

On the other hand, if you accept the argument, you may find difficulty in describing exactly what the causal conditions of human choices happen to be. Should one look to heredity, psychology, character, physical environment, social environment, divine intervention, human passions, or what as the causes of human actions? If you do not accept the argument, what is your rejection of it based on?

Historically most of the debate focuses on these three statements:

1. Every event has a cause.
2. At least some human choices are free.
3. If every event has a cause, then no human choices are free.

1.3 Our Belief in Universal Causality

Everyone who accepts the truth of **1.**, "Every event has a cause" is known as a *philosophical determinist*. Philosophical determinism is the thesis that for every event there is some complex set of causal conditions such that, given precisely these conditions, no other event could occur. This thesis is one of the oldest and most forceful in human intellectual history. It led to the growth of science because it was the bedrock upon which the scientific hope of explaining, predicting and controlling natural phenomena was built. It is not the kind of thesis that can be confirmed or disconfirmed by a single set of experiences. Rather, it is a deeply held postulate or presupposition, among the most central organizing principles of human experience. It helps us shape the chaos of reality and it leads us to expect answers to the question: "Why did this event happen as it did?"

To grasp how central this belief is, contrast the following two arguments: (A) People have looked for unicorns for years and have never found any. Therefore, probably there are no unicorns. (B) People have looked for the cause or causes of leukemia for years and have been frustrated in discovering what they might be. Therefore, probably, leukemia is a random, spontaneous illness that has no causes.

Notice that although these arguments are very similar, argument (A) appears quite sensible as compared to (B). Much of the reason is the strength of our belief in universal causality. Some philosophers suggest that the contrast between (A) and (B) shows that "Every event has a cause" is not an assertion capable of being shown false. It is the kind of thesis that may be denied in one form only to be reintroduced and embraced in another. In addition, developments in experimental psychology and in bio-chemistry, particularly as these apply to understanding the workings of the brain, lend support to some version of the deterministic hypothesis as it applies to human behavior.

1.4 Hard Determinism

A person who accepts **1.**, "Every event has a cause" and **3.**, "If every event has a cause, then no human choices are free," is known as a *hard determinist*. From their acceptance of **1.** and **3.** it follows logically that hard determinists believe that no human choices are free. People cannot help but be as they are. As physical objects involved in the space–time causal nexus, humans, like any other animals, act as they do on the basis of those conditions that determine their lives. Whatever those conditions are—physical, social, psychological, or what have you, known or unknown—they totally determine what each human being does.

In the case study the defense argued that Amy could not help herself—killing Shaw was an inevitability. She was disposed to respond violently when she felt ridiculed. She was depressed. She was overcome by emotions of guilt and anger. She was very unstable and had a drug problem. Moreover Amy came from a bad neighborhood. For these kinds of hard determinist reasons Amy was not free, the defense argued, when she shot Shaw. So she should not be held accountable for the killing, and should not be punished for it.

Hard determinists argue that there is no such thing as free choice. Like all determinists they point to science's successes in explaining and predicting human behavior as evidence in support of their position. They maintain that humans should move beyond pre-scientific concepts like freedom and dignity; instead they should talk the language of conditioning and behavior modification. Our concern should not be so much with praise or blame, but with how to shape and control. To accomplish this we can positively reinforce desired behaviors and, where necessary, negatively reinforce undesirable ones, attaching no moral stigma to either. Punishment makes sense to the hard determinist not as something which a person *deserves* but as a means to some desirable goal, for example as negative reinforcement leading to rehabilitation.

One standard objection to hard-determinism is that it fails to critically examine the connection between caused events and human choices which statement **3.** expresses, "If every event has a cause, then no human choices are free." Even if human choices are events, might they not be free in the morally relevant sense? We will have more to say about this view in Section 1.6. A second objection challenges the scientific accuracy of the view of causality which the hard determinists seem to hold. This objection notes that even within science not *every particular* event can be causally explained and predicted, even if groups of events can be. For example, in the decay of radioactive material it is impossible to predict exactly which molecule will change next even though we can predict the half-life of the decaying radioactive material. Notice also the difference between scientifically predicting how a whole population might behave as contrasted with predicting how a specific individual in that population will behave.   For example, we can predict macro-behavior, such as how the housing market will respond to a sharp and sustained drop in the prime interest rate or how New Englanders will vote in a given national election. But we cannot confidently predict at the micro level, such as that a particular person will refinance a house or will vote for a given candidate.

A third objection to hard determinism is that it does not square with the common phenomenon of personal deliberation and choice. Intuitively we describe these experiences as being free or making a free decision. And a fourth objection notes that in spite of how far the behavioral sciences have progressed, particularly in helping us understand deviant and abnormal behavior, we still cannot predict with any scientifically acceptable level of confidence (which means accurate at least 95% of the time) all the things a rational, unconstrained person acting autonomously may decide to do.

1.5 Libertarianism

Some approach the dilemma of determinism from the other direction by taking **2.**, "At least some human choices are free", as their first principle.   Here human choices are seen as uncaused events. These thinkers also accept **3.**, "If every event has a cause, then no human choices are free." So, it follows logically from **2.** and **3.** that they must deny **1.** and say that at least some events (human choices to be specific) have no causes. Those who hold this view are known as philosophical libertarians.

The major support for the libertarian position is drawn from our intuitions about our experiences of free choice. We all experience times of deliberation as we consider alternative courses of action or weigh our options. We weigh our options without knowing exactly what we should or will do in all cases and without fully knowing all the consequences of our choices. Most importantly, we experience the moment of decision. We are aware of choosing an alternative, of selecting an option. Humans, libertarians point out, quite naturally experience freedom and they are correct in describing themselves as free.

In the case study the prosecuting attorney argued that Amy made a number of deliberate choices. She went out with Shaw, she tried to force marriage on him, she even threatened suicide. This was all planned, as evidence by the fact she brought a weapon. When Shaw freely decided not to be blackmailed, Amy made another free choice, she turned the gun on Shaw. She had other options, but she freely chose murder. Hence, argued the prosecutor, Amy should be held morally and legally accountable, which means she should be found guilty and punished for her crime.

Libertarians advance a second argument. They point to our experience of being tempted and of trying to resist temptation, regardless of whether a person successfully resists or eventually gives in, as further examples of our experience of freedom. As the libertarian sees it, the ability to resist temptations shows that human actions are not caused. The libertarian argues that if determinism were right, then the events that are the causes of human actions would be like desirable impulses that tempt us in a certain direction. Therefore, our ability to resist temptation seems, to the libertarian, to be evidence of our ability not to act on what, if anything, could be described by the determinists as the causes of human action.

Behind both libertarian arguments is the idea of a free will. As the libertarian sees it, we experience ourselves, in the moment of decision, as freely willing one course of action over another. We do not experience our wills as compelled or caused. Similarly, in resisting temptation we experience our own uncaused willpower exerting itself against the causal tendencies of habit and impulse. For the libertarian, the similarity between these two experiences is that both point to the freedom of the will, which the libertarian sees as basic to human freedom.

A third argument sometimes advanced by libertarians is related to the concept of punishment. They maintain that at times people act in the knowledge that what they are doing deserves punishment, but they would not deserve punishment unless they acted freely, hence they must be acting freely. Here, too, Amy Holden is a case in point. She knew the consequences she would face for murdering Shaw. Freely deciding to avoid those just deserts is why, a libertarian might argue, she chose suicide.

The standard objection to libertarianism is the same as the one advanced against hard determinism: libertarianism fails to critically examine the connection between caused events and human choices alleged in statement 3., "If every event has a cause, then no human choices are free." We will take up this point in the discussion of compatibilism below. A second objection against the libertarians comes from the hard determinists who point to the successes of science in helping us explain, predict and control much of the behavior which in earlier centuries might have been wrongly described as random, unexplainable, or the product of a mysterious force known as *free will*. And a third objection relates to the entire concept of a free will. What is it? Where is it? And, how does it work? The objection is that the libertarians have not helped us understand what human freedom is, they have only put off the explanation by changing it into a question about the nature of *freedom of the will.*

1.6 Compatibilism

Some people who accept **1.**, "Every event has a cause," nevertheless reject **3.** and, instead, accept **2.**, "At least some human choices are free." Because they accept **1.** they can be called determinists, but to distinguish them from the hard determinists (as described in 1.4), they are sometimes referred to as *soft determinists.* We prefer to call them *compatibilists* because they hold the view that human freedom is somehow compatible with belief in universal causality. That is, they try to develop a middle position that acknowledges the scientific determinism of **1.** and also the moral freedom of **2.**.

Compatibilists must find some reason to reject the statement that expresses the incompatibility of freedom and universal causality. That is, they must find a way to show that statement **3.**, "If every event has a cause, then no human choices are free," is false. Compatibilists argue that when people are able to make a rational choice and also act on that choice, without being compelled or coerced in so doing, then their choice is free, in the morally relevant sense, even though the choice is not without its causes. In other words, the compatibilists maintain that choices are caused, perhaps by our desires or by our character traits or even by our habitual tendencies, but these factors are compatible with describing our choices as *free.*

In the case study the old judge seems to lean in the direction of compatibilism. In describing Amy he says, "Amy dropped out of school in the ninth grade, couldn't get a decent job, and couldn't hold the jobs she did get. Actually, from the way she conducted herself at the trial, I suspect Amy Holden wasn't very intelligent, not even average, I'd say. Probably didn't think too straight. Must have had a hard time of it making good decisions." The judge seems to hold the view that if she had finished her education she might have learned to be more rational and make better choices. To the extent that she failed to develop her capacities for making good judgments, she was less free than she might have been otherwise. It is interesting to consider whose responsibility it is to help a person develop the character traits, tendencies or capacities to make sound, rational decisions. And, failing to achieve this, who should be held accountable for any unwise choices the person might make—parents, teachers, government, or the persons themselves? The judge also makes a general comment about juries, saying that it is often difficult to predict what they will decide. He does not say their decision is inevitable, nor that it is random. What point would there be to arguing the merits of an issue in court, if the decision handed down were either random or inevitable? Presuming the jury deliberates rationally and is not under any coercion or biasing constraint, a compatibilist would describe the jury as *autonomous* and their verdict as *free.*

Some compatibilists would insist that to be called free our choices must be made rationally, with full awareness of what we are doing and with a full and deliberate consideration of the pros and cons of the issue at hand.   Other compatibilists emphasize that to be free, people must not be coerced, that there be no constraining factors, such as overwhelming fear or hallucinatory drugs, that mitigate freedom.   Compatibilists argue that the scientific evidence in favor of determinism in general also supports compatibilism, but that compatibilism is also consistent with our moral practices and our natural intuitions about deliberative choice.

However, strong objections have been voiced against compatibilism.   It would seem that in the compatibilist view a person is both free and yet unable to avoid his choice. The notion of freedom advanced by the compatibilist appears to be unclear. It also appears to be inconsistent with, or irrelevant to, the moral issue at hand. The notion of freedom thought to be relevant to moral question is the idea that a person is free to act differently than she does. For example, suppose you are in insurance and you choose to call on one client rather than another. The morally relevant sense of freedom is that you could have chosen to call on the other. And hence, you can be held accountable for that decision. But under compatibilism it seems we are denied this concept of freedom. Given what the judge said about Amy's not having finished school and not being very intelligent, how would it be possible to say that she was free when she shot Shaw? Could she really have done otherwise? And, if not, what point is there in calling the killing her *free* choice, or in holding her morally accountable for Shaw's death. One common objection against the compatibilists is that theirs is not the notion of free choice we find morally relevant.

EXERCISES

1. Hard determinism, libertarianism, compatibilism are distinguished by their acceptance and rejection of the three assertions below. In the column marked *HD* put a *T* next to each assertion accepted by the hard determinist as true. Put T's in the columns marked *C* and *L* for the assertions believed true by the compatibilists and libertarians. (1.4, 1.5, 1.6)

   HD   C   L

             (a) Every event has a cause.

             (b) Some human actions are free.

             (c) If every event has a cause, no human actions are free.

2. Define hard determinism, compatibilism and libertarianism as positions simply by reference to which of the above assertions each accepts as true and which each rejects as false. (1.4, 1.5, 1.6)

3. Below is the story of a typical human decision, followed by a series of claims which libertarians, hard determinists or compatibilists might want to make in support of their

respective positions. After you read the story, mark each of the claims true or false for each position: *HD, C,* and *L*. (1.4, 1.5, 1.6)

Terri Tamahan struggled with herself. She knew time was short and she would soon need to decide and act. She greatly wanted to go to the concert. Her favorite group was performing and she had a fine appreciation of their music. She had promised, however, to help in the final preparations for homecoming. The concert had been scheduled, unexpectedly, for the night before homecoming. Terri could not possibly help finish the homecoming preparations and also attend the concert. She knew her friends were counting on her and she knew she'd deserve their censure if she disappointed them. Finally Terri decided. Going to the concert was a great temptation, she would certainly enjoy it more than the alternative. But Terri had made a promise, so she summoned up her willpower, resisted the temptation, and, true to her word, she helped prepare for homecoming.

HD   C   L

(a) Terri had apparently been strongly conditioned to do her duty.

(b) Terri freely decided because she carefully and calmly thought her way through to her conclusion.

(c) The ability to resist the temptation to do what would please her most marks Terri's will as free.

(d) The experiences of *deliberation* and *resisting temptation* are simply experiences of tension between two choices that are close to being equally attractive to a person of a given conditioning.

(e) Even if Terri were conditioned, to be rational implies that she can act freely.

(f) The assertion that Terri knew she would be blameworthy if she did not help with homecoming preparations makes sense; it would not unless Terri were free. So indeed she must be free.

4. Given the answers to Exercise 3 and your knowledge of hard determinism, compatibilism and libertarianism, rewrite the Terri Tamahan story three times using the perspectives of each of the three positions and emphasize what each would see as central and crucial.

5. (a) What are the apparent, unhappy consequences with respect to freedom and with respect to moral responsibility, if the principle of universal causality is true, and what are they if it is false? (1.1, 1.2, 1.3)

(b) Use the concept of a dilemma in 1.1 and your answers to (a) to explain why the principle of universal causality constitutes a dilemma for free will and responsibility. (1.1, 1.2)

6. What are some of the objections raised against hard determinism, compatibilism and libertarianism. (1.4, 1.5, 1.6)

DISCUSSION QUESTION

1. Put yourself in the role of an advocate of one of the three positions described in this section. What would your proposals and policy recommendations be in regard to

domestic problems such as drug abuse, homelessness, teen pregnancy, and unemployment? In contrast, how might a "mistaken" advocate of the other positions criticize your proposals.

ANSWERS TO SELECTED EXERCISES

1. *HD*   *C*   *L*

T	T	-	(a) Every event has a cause.
-	T	T	(b) Some human actions are free.
T	-	T	(c) If every event has a cause, no human actions are free.

2. Hard determinism is the view that every event has a cause and that if every event has a cause then no human actions are free. Compatibilism is the view that every event has a cause and that some human actions are free. Libertarianism is the view that some human actions are free and that if every event has a cause then no human actions are free. All three definitions could be expanded by adding that each view denies the claim not marked *T*.

3. A hard determinist would make the first and fourth claims. A compatibilist might agree with the first two and would certainly accept the third and fifth. A libertarian would accept (c) and (f). A compatibilist might also accept (f), but (f) would not help to establish the compatibility of freedom and causality.

5. If universal causality were true it would seem that no human action is free, since, it would seem, no one could ever do other than what he did. If false, it would seem that no action is free, since it would seem, all human behavior would be random, none self-determined. If it is true either that no one could ever do other than what she did or that all human behavior is random, then, it would seem, no one is ever responsible for what she does.

Section 2
THE CONCEPT OF AUTONOMY

As suggested at the end of the section on compatibilism (1.6), we can say a person is *autonomous* if she acts rationally and without constraint. In Section 2 we analyze the two key ideas, *acting rationally* and *acting without constraint*. This will lead to the distinction between *positive freedom* and *negative freedom*. After studying this section you should be able to:

- Describe cases of acting rationally and irrationally.
- Describe cases of acting under various kinds of constraints.
- Define the concept of autonomy.
- Distinguish examples of positive and negative freedom.
- Characterize positive and negative freedom.
- Give examples of autonomous actions and of positive and negative freedom.

THE CASE OF FRANKIE O'TOOLE

"Where are you going, Frankie?" asked his father.

"Out!" The young man took one last bite of meat loaf and pushed himself away from the dinner table.

"Going drinking again! Probably going to come home drunk and flat broke, just like last time. Right?"

"Look, Dad. I'm twenty-one. It's legal for me to drink. Leave me alone."

Mr. O'Toole, never looking up from his evening paper, said, "Don't worry, I know I can't forbid you. You're a man now, son. A real man." He took a sip of coffee.

Frankie sat back down. "Dad. Just say what's on your mind."

"I was only thinking about your welfare. That's all."

"I'll be fine. I can handle booze better than most guys. And I don't believe all that nonsense about drinking causing health problems. That's a worry for old people, not me. Besides, it's my choice isn't it? I'll take my chances. Nobody can legislate what people do with their own health."

"First, the medical findings are not nonsense, and deliberately ignoring them is foolish. Second, there are plenty of laws designed to protect a person from himself. What about seatbelt laws, for instance? We force children to learn about personal hygiene in school. We outlaw the sale of dangerous prescription drugs. Why do you think..."

"Here I'm talking about consciously deciding that I want to drink. It's my choice, isn't it? Just like whether or not you're going to drink coffee is your choice."

His father thought briefly about the addicting character of caffeine and how that related to alcohol addiction, but decided to take a different approach. He picked up a magazine and handed it to his son. "Look at this," he said, pointing to a slick ad on the back cover. A glamorous yet vulnerable woman clung to the leg of a macho cowboy. The cowboy was looking off into the distance and holding a bottle of imported beer positioned to subliminally, but unmistakably, suggest a phallus. The ad read: "For the man who gets what he wants out of life."

Frankie tossed it back. "So what?"

"Did you ever stop to consider how you might be influenced by exploitive advertising like this?"

"It's just an ad. It doesn't force me to do anything."

"I wasn't talking force. I said influence. Or maybe you want to drink just to prove something. Is that it? Is drinking your way of asserting yourself—showing your friends and me that you're a man now?"

Frankie got to his feet. "I wanted to have a rational conversation about this. But all you want to do is impose your will on me. I'm an adult in the eyes of the law and I'll drink if I want to. That's it!"

Mr. O'Toole looked up at his son and shook his head. "I've heard that one before. Problem is I can't tell if it's you talking or the alcohol."

Frankie grunted and scooped up his car keys.

"Please call, if you need a ride home. You don't have to learn all of life's lessons the hard way."

"Dad. Have I ever got in an accident before?"

2.1 The Concept of Autonomy

There are two aspects to being an autonomous individual: (a) exercising one's rationality in making decisions and (b) being free from coercion and constraint both in making decisions and in carrying them out. For our purposes we shall define being autonomous in terms of being rational and being unconstrained. If a person chooses rationally and without constraint and then acts without constraint, then he is acting autonomously. Frankie, in the case study, seems to be capable of acting autonomously. He is old enough to deliberate about his choices and rationally decide between them. He is free from the obvious forms of external constraint such as legal or parental prohibitions. He appears to be free from the undue influence of mind-altering drugs or medications. But assessing autonomy, even autonomy relative to certain questions at certain times, is a complex business. Let us look briefly at the two conditions for autonomous choice.

2.2 Acting Rationally

Being rational about one's decisions involves being able to do at least seven different things:

1. Identifying and expressing one's goals, at least to oneself.
2. Prioritizing those goals for oneself.
3. Finding some means to achieving these goals.
4. Anticipating the possible and probable consequences, both intended and unintended, of employing these means.
5. If the available means are either inadequate or likely to cause undesirable consequences, reassessing the possibilities both of developing further means or abandoning or altering one's goals.
6. Making a choice in light of the above considerations.

7. Later evaluating the effort and learning from any mistakes one might have made.

All these factors must receive their due place if we are to call a decision *rational*. Is Frankie in the case study being rational? He seems to know his options, which are to drink or not; however, he does not make the distinctions he could make concerning how much to drink, where to drink and with whom to drink. He seems unwilling to acknowledge the adverse consequences, either immediate or long range, of drinking. There is some question about what his goals really are. Does he want to drink because he thinks he'll enjoy it, is it a way to find acceptance from his peers, or is he trying to make some kind of statement about his adulthood? Since his goals are not clear, he seems not to have explored other ways to achieve them; nor has he, in what we read, examined the financial commitment necessary to support a drinking habit. We might have to say that, as the term is presented above, Frankie is not acting rationally.

Our primary characterization of rationality is intended to define an ideal of reflective thought and considered choice. Naturally in daily life one often faces choices which do not permit fully realizing this idea. Many important choices are made in a flash, like deciding when to change lanes on the freeway, responding to a friend's hurried question or someone's insulting remark, or knowing which base to throw the ball to in order to start the double-play. Are these quick choices irrational? Hardly. But they are not the products of complex reflective inferences either—at least not each and every time they come up. Imagine a shortstop who had to sort out her options each time before she decided to throw to first base—even the slowest runners would make it safely to first playing against her. One might suggest, however, that the shortstop knows what the rational thing to do is because of her training and practice. She does not need to think out each play from scratch because she has been coached to know what to do ahead of time. Being rational here means reading the situation and reacting the way one prepared one's self to react. Hence another value of those character traits called virtues (discussed in the chapter on egoism). Cultivating virtues, or good habits relative to one's aims or goals, prepares you for acting rationally when the need for a quick decision arises. So, a second and derivative sense of acting rationally is that one acts on the basis of well-conceived and well-practiced character traits, or virtues, aimed at achieving anticipated goals, whether those goals be driving safely, sustaining friendships, avoiding unnecessary confrontations, or starting the double play.

2.3 Factors Which Impede Rationality

Imagine a situation in which a parent is asked to give informed consent for an operation to be performed on his or her child; a rather commonplace situation in which rational decision making is called for. Yet many things can diminish or undermine the effort at rational decision making. For example here are a few:

- Prejudice and bias, ("The physician is a woman!").
- Emotion, ("I'm so frightened, what if something goes wrong?").
- Stubbornness, ("Nobody is going to tell me the kid needs this operation").
- Indecisiveness, ("Well, I don't know, I mean, whatever...").
- Inability to infer implications, ("I wonder if having the operation means we can't go on vacation the next day?").
- Inattentiveness, ("What did you say?").
- Refusal or failure to become informed of available data, ("I just don't want to hear about what the doctor is going to do, it's all so gruesome").

Sometimes these threats to rationality come from the person's own shortcomings, such as possessing underdeveloped logical abilities or allowing oneself to act on biases and unquestioned prejudice. Other threats are external. Too many distractions or too little time can both prevent one from fully examining the consequences of all available options.

Not taking reasonable care to become informed of relevant and available information can lead an otherwise logical person to make decisions which appear quite unreasonable. At times ignorance is outside of one's control, as for example, if the needed information is not known or there is no time to find it. In such cases the rational thing to do is to make the best decisions one can, given what one can know at the time. The ignorance that works against rationality is the kind that reasonable care would have corrected. Not being aware of available facts because of one's own laziness or unwillingness to learn are examples. This kind of ignorance of available facts can result from a denial of the truth, as was the case with Frankie's refusal to take seriously that drinking leads to serious health problems even for young people. Correctable ignorance can also result from being deceived by disinformation or from being cut off from accurate information, as would be the case if the manufacturers of a dangerous product (say a pesticide) knew of the health problems associated with their product but intentionally misled the public, or if health professionals knew the risks associated with an experimental procedure but withheld crucial information regarding these risks. It is interesting to consider how much a person should be held responsible for taking steps to remedy his own correctable ignorance.

Cleverly deceptive and misleading advertising is often aimed at thoughtless, gullible consumers. Why? Because it is well known that incomplete or false information can lead people to make poor choices, even if they are trying to act rationally, given whatever information, however misleading, is available to them. This is true not just in business, but in social and political matters as well. Government propaganda, official disinformation, and censorship have profoundly negative effects on rational decision making. Democracy is predicated upon people's ability to make rational choices. Governmental, institutional or corporate practices which deceive, misinform, or withhold needed information, no matter how noble or important the purposes for which this might be done, diminish the chances of people in that society, or institution, or corporation of making fully informed, rational choices.

The instrumental value of a free press in a democratic society derives from its ability to provide the information people need to make rational choices. Similarly, adequate education to ensure an informed, thoughtful, and literate public is an absolute necessity, if the information available in a free society is to be used to full advantage by voters. For democracy to work, the media should be largely free from constraints so it can provide the information. Also, the public should be constrained or forced to be educated so that it can be taught how to use that information rationally. These normative positions raise questions about whether, indeed, one should ever be "forced to become more rational".

2.4 Being Unconstrained

The concept of rationality sketched in 2.1 and 2.2 carries a requirement that people have as full and accurate an understanding of the situation and its limitations as is possible. But being rational is the first aspect of being autonomous. The second is being unconstrained in one's choice, which means being unconstrained both in making decisions and in implementing those decisions. The concept of a constraint includes conditions that can affect actions at two different times. Some constraining conditions affect the process of decision making. These conditions *prevent a person from finding certain courses of action to be rational*, though the person would otherwise find them so. For example, knowing one does not have the money at the moment to finance a new business venture prevents one from rationally deciding to act on a business opportunity which otherwise seems attractive. Other constraining conditions come into play after the decision is made and *prevent the person from actually doing what she rationally decided to do*. These are often unforeseeable limitations, which cannot, therefore, be taken into account during the deliberative process. For example, after having rationally decided to pursue the business venture, a sudden and unexpected expense is incurred which requires that the capital that one intended to put toward the new venture be redirected to cover the unexpected contingency.

Either during *decision making* or during *decision implementation*, there are at least three different types of constraints which can come into play: First, *insufficiencies of the means* to carry out the actions, which thereby prevent rationally deciding to take that action. You want to accept a new position, yet realize you have no way of getting to and from the new job without encountering unusual additional expenses.

A second type of constraint is the *imposition of coercive force* by others. For example, one may be physically constrained, or one may be coerced by a threat of harm or injury. Such constraints or coercions, to be effective, will involve some sort of power, which may be that of a legitimate authority or may be completely illegitimate and unscrupulous. You may wish to do something but decide not to, either because you have found a law against it or you are threatened with injury by a bully. Or you may decide to do something and then either discover that a new law is passed prohibiting it or discover a threatening note from a suspicious source warning against doing it. Protective tariffs are a form of such constraint which government uses to restrict trade and protect the commercial interests of its citizens. By making foreign products more expensive, tariffs are an added cost of doing business and discourage some competitors from entering the market.

A third type of constraint is *one's own physical, biological, or psychological state*. Such states, or changes in them, can make certain courses of action unreasonable for us or prevent our carrying out rational decisions. A sore knee may prevent you from deciding to jog as a way of keeping your cardiovascular system in shape. Or, as much as you would like to offer your time, chronic allergies may prevent you from serving as a volunteer coach or referee for a youth soccer league.

Consider Frankie's situation in the case study. Is he constrained by factors that fall into any of these three categories? He does not seem to lack the immediate financial resources or the transportation necessary to go drinking. Parental prohibition and legal constraints are explicitly removed. He does not seem to be compelled by an alcohol addiction or by a psychological need to drink, although this is an assumption which is far from clear. Frankie might indeed be an alcoholic. Also, his father seems to be manipulating his emotions a little, but not so much as to lead us to say that he is preventing his son from implementing his decision. Apart from the possibility that he is an alcoholic, Frankie appears to be free from constraint and coercion as he considers his decision. Perhaps, however, there are deeper psychological forces operative in his relationship to his father and in his self-image as a young adult that influence him in ways which are not in the forefront of his consciousness.

2.5 Positive and Negative Freedom

To gain additional perspective on the nature and significance of autonomy, philosophers introduce two important senses of freedom, a positive and a negative sense. *Negative freedom* can be understood as freedom from constraint or coercion. Negative freedoms are often guaranteed in legislation prohibiting people from constraining or interfering with others as they attempt to conduct their private affairs. It violates, for example, one's negative freedom to be forced to undergo something one does not consent to experience (which is part of the reason coercing prisoners to become experimental subjects is regarded as unethical).

In contrast, freedom in the *positive* sense can be equated with rational choice or rational action. This means that one has positive freedom if one is able to engage in the seven steps of rational decision making listed 2.1: (1) set one's own goals, (2) establish one's priorities, (3) identify the means to achieve one's goals, (4) predict the probable consequences of alternative choices, (5) reassess goals and means to goals as necessary, (6) make a choice in the light of the above considerations, and (7) evaluate the effort and learn from any of one's mistakes.

Notice that being free from constraints does not guarantee that one will make a rational decision. There are too many unfortunate examples in life of people who have the opportunity to think something through calmly and rationally, but simply fail to take advantage of that opportunity for positive freedom. Frankie in the case study, for example, may be free from various constraints, as we discussed in 2.4, but he may still be acting irrationally by deliberately and consciously exposing himself to the short-and long-term risks associated with drinking. Positive freedom is not always guaranteed by negative freedom!

2.6 Autonomy and the Two Freedoms

As an example, consider the following fictitious case: Stan Rosen, age 25, lives in Denver. Raised an Orthodox Jew, Stan now wishes to reconsider certain of his religious practices. He wants to decide, for example, whether or not he should eat pork. What factors may limit his negative freedom to do that? He may not be able to acquire pork because it costs too much, it is not available where he shops, the food stores are closed when he is free to go to them, or he might not have any way to roast the pork or fry the bacon even if he should purchase some. Thus the means to implement his goal may not exist. On the other hand, Stan may feel constrained by religious strictures, family traditions, or communal norms not to eat pork; thus authoritative prohibitions and lingering guilt feelings might limit his negative freedom. Or, after he cooks it, he may not be able to eat the pork because he utterly dislikes its smell, because he has allergic reactions to it, or because he has some psychosis about eating pork; thus biological or psychological factors might also limit his negative freedom. Stan may be operating under posthypnotic suggestion not to eat pork; he may have been deliberately misinformed about pork and think that it will make him sick; he may be threatened with loss of his job if he is discovered to have eaten pork. Any of these can operate to manipulate Stan and limit his negative freedom.

Suppose, however, that there are no limits to his negative freedom; does this mean that Stan has the positive freedom to eat pork? No, other factors can limit his positive freedom. Stan may not be able to identify his options; he may, for example, not realize that he can buy pork in any of a variety of convenient quantities and forms ranging from ham, bacon, hot dogs, and sausage to chops, ribs, and roasts. He may not see that one option is to eat a hot dog at the ball park and another is to buy a six-pound roast for a family dinner. He may not be able to predict the possible or probable outcomes of his choice to eat pork. If he brings home a big roast, will that upset his family, considering their religious practices? If he eats a hot dog at the park, will that upset his family? He may not have considered what his goals are. Why does he want to reconsider whether or not to eat pork? What does he hope to gain or prove by such a decision? Is it a matter of trying something new for the experience of it? Is this part of reconsidering his whole religious lifestyle? What are his more important goals? He may not have given adequate thought to his priorities. Another limit to his positive freedom may be his failure to discover where pork can be conveniently purchased in his neighborhood. He may not have located a store that sells pork and is open when he is able to buy. A final possible limit on his positive freedom may be his inability to deliberate about this question in the light of all the information he has gathered. He may simply not be able to organize his thinking well enough to rationally decide what to do. He may find there are too many variables or too many unknowns for him. Any of these factors can act so as to mitigate Stan's positive freedom.

However, if neither his positive nor his negative freedom has been compromised, then we will want to say that Stan thought through his decision rationally and, with no coercion or constraint, freely and autonomously determined to eat pork. To sum up, to have positive freedom is to act rationally or be rational. To have negative freedom is to act without constraint or coercion. Thus characterized, *to have both positive and negative freedom is, by definition, to be an autonomous individual.*

EXERCISES

1. Rational decision making involves (1) knowing one's own goals, (2) prioritizing those goals, (3) identifying means to the goals, (4) anticipating consequences of those means, (5) reassessing one's goals or means when necessary, (6) making one's decision in the light of the above steps, and (7) evaluating the effort so as to learn from any mistakes one might have made. Describe seven cases of persons failing to make rational decisions such that each case exemplifies failing at a different step of the process. (2.1 and 2.2) You might use a rational consent situation as was used in the text, except change the example, say, to making a decision about one's self. Or perhaps you could build your cases around rationally deciding which model car to buy.

2. Autonomy involves freedom from constraint both in decision making and in implementing one's decision. In 2.4 we mentioned three kinds of constraints: insufficiencies in the means, coercive obstacles placed in our paths by others, and physiological or psychological states of one's own being. Describe three cases of persons trying to make and implement decisions such that each of the three kinds of constraints mentioned is illustrated twice, once as a constraint on decision making and once as a constraint on decision implementation.

3. Define autonomous action in terms of rational, unconstrained decision making and decision implementation. (2.1)

4. In each of the following descriptions a person's freedom—positive or negative—is limited or lacking. State which kind of freedom is at issue in each case. Explain your answer by associating limited positive freedom with less than fully rational behavior, and limited negative freedom with constraints upon one's decision making. (2.5 and 2.6)

   (a) After we fight through three hours of freeway traffic there will be no time left to enjoy the beach before it's time to head back home.

   (b) I wanted a black BMW so much that when I heard the Mart had them in stock, I dashed right down and bought one, even though the Mart is kind of expensive by comparison to most other places.

   (c) We registered at the ski lodge and then found we couldn't ski after all, because somebody had stolen our skis off our car while we were registering.

(d) I kept trying to think through what I ought to do, but the party next door was so loud I just could not concentrate.

(e) We started out in the morning with the idea that launching a model rocket might be a pleasant way to spend a spare afternoon. When none of the shops in town had models we liked, we headed for a shop some 25 miles distant. By then it was noon, and they didn't have any either. I guess we knew it would take a couple of hours to build the rocket before we could fly it, but we kept searching. In all we went over 125 miles, driving around looking. We found some rockets, but none really struck our fancy. Eventually we got home late, without supper, exhausted, and without even buying a rocket.

(f) We spent the whole month doing a market survey in LA and New York for our new product line only to find out when we finished that management wanted to market the new line only in small Middle Western towns.

(g) As I crossed the parking lot toward my car, a man emerged from the shadows, pointed a gun at me, and demanded my money.

(h) When I cleaned out my garage, I wanted to set the trash out onto the street immediately, but it wasn't my pickup day, and the city has an ordinance against putting trash on the street before the pickup day.

5. Define positive and negative freedom. (2.5) Now define autonomous action in terms of positive and negative freedom. (2.6)

6. Construct a thorough example of a person acting autonomously.

DISCUSSION QUESTIONS

1. Should a person be forced to be free—is the maximization of positive freedom a justification for compulsory education in a democratic society?

2. When someone describes himself as a *freedom fighter*, does that imply that he is fighting only for negative freedom, or might he be fighting for positive freedom as well. How do these two concepts of freedom differ in terms of the goals a *revolutionary movement* might pursue?

3. How do concepts of one's freedoms relate to concepts of one's rights?

ANSWERS TO SELECTED EXERCISES

3. An action is autonomous when it is implemented unconstrained as the product of deliberation that is itself both rational and unconstrained.

4. (a) Negative freedom; traffic constrains their freedom.
(b) Positive freedom; did not seek alternative (and superior) means most appropriate to achieve the goal.
(c) Negative freedom; lack of skis prevents implementing decision.
(d) Negative freedom; noise constrains me from concentration and decision making.

(e) Positive freedom; did not reassess goal in light of unavailable means. Also negative freedom; lack of means compounded by eventual lack of time and energy to continue search. (Note: Limits on our negative freedom often lead to extra occasions for the exercise of positive freedom, because they place extra demands on our rationality.)
(f) Positive freedom; did not define the goal of action in advance.
(g) Negative freedom; coerced by a threat of physical violence.
(h) Negative freedom; constrained by the city's authority.

5. Besides in the sub-sections mentioned in the text, these terms are also defined in the glossary. These concepts are central to Sections 3 and 4.

Section 3
MORAL RESPONSIBILITY, REWARD AND PUNISHMENT

Under what conditions is an individual to be held morally responsible for his actions? Specifically, given the concept of autonomy developed in Section 2, are people who are acting autonomously to be held morally responsible? The hard determinists, compatibilists and libertarians all propose different answers, as we shall see. Then, since the concept of moral responsibility relates to our ideas of approval and disapproval, we will explore the different theories or justifications for praise and punishment: one based on what people merit or deserve (the retributive approach), and three based on intended consequences. As these apply to punishment they are the deterrent, preventive, and rehabilitative theories. After studying this section you should be able to:

- State and explain the hard determinist, compatibilist and libertarian answer to the question, "Should persons who are acting autonomously be held morally responsible for what they do?"
- State and explain two possible exceptions to the assertion, "Only persons who act autonomously should be considered morally responsible for their action."
- Identity examples of retributive, deterrent, preventive, and rehabilitative justifications of punishment.
- Compare and contrast the retributive, deterrent, preventive, and rehabilitative theories of punishment.

THE CASE OF ROMAN FULTON

Roman Fulton was 33 years old and employed as a computer design engineer at Tempe's huge Vidimine Electronics International when he was charged with twelve counts of violating Arizona's industrial sabotage and espionage laws. He was tried and found guilty of intentionally destroying the entire computer network of Vidimine's chief competitor, Champdeck Corp. Fulton managed to introduce into the Champdeck computer network a secret "computer virus"—a hidden program which furiously replicates itself throughout a computer network and causes all "infected" machines to malfunction. The day Fulton was found guilty, he was fired from Vidimine International. That same day Champdeck sued Vidimine for compensatory and punitive damages totaling 17.5 million dollars. Vidimine ultimately settled its suit with Champdeck Corp. for 4.3 million.

Roman Fulton was sentenced to serve twelve consecutive 20-month prison terms. The judge said that the penalty would not only keep Fulton from repeating his offense for a long time, it would also serve to warn others that Arizona was not going to tolerate these kinds of destructive and unfair business practices. Roman was shocked when he realized that he would be over fifty years old when he completed serving his sentence.

The prospect of being locked up with hardened criminals frightened Fulton. He figured his only hope was early parole for good behavior. So he resolved to cooperate with every prison regulation and try in every way to show that he was ready to return to society. As it turned out he was incarcerated in a minimum security facility which housed other persons found guilty of "victimless" and white collar crimes. He spent several years working in the prison laundry and he also earned an MBA through a college correspondence program. Never wanting to be caught again, he also conceived of new, less risky, ways to make computer systems crash.

At his parole hearing he expressed regret for his crime but maintained that at the time he had not fully understood its wrongness. He also claimed that he had acted with the implicit approval of his supervisors at Vidimine—although at his trial they had denied all knowledge of what Fulton was doing. Fulton also said he felt he deserved his punishment in that he had to pay his debt to society for breaking the law. Prison officials testified that Roman had been a model prisoner and was, in their view, fully rehabilitated. Roman Fulton left prison at age 41, a man with no family, no friends and no job. He has not been arrested or convicted of any crimes in the two years since his parole. He is currently employed as a systems manager in the central business offices of a huge department store chain based in Houston.

3.1 Does Autonomy Imply Responsibility?

If Roman Fulton acted autonomously, then holding him responsible for having violated the law and damaged Champdeck would seem, on the face of things, the reasonable thing to do. This, of course, presumes that the following statement is true:

1. All persons who act autonomously are responsible for what they do.

Since our focus is on the relationship between autonomy and *moral* responsibility, let us begin by distinguishing between being a *responsible person* and being *morally responsible for some specific action.* A responsible person is someone who, generally speaking, fulfills her obligations. Responsibility in a person is thought of, in most cases, as a virtue, or beneficial personality trait, like reliability, loyalty, or honesty. On the other hand, to say that a person is *morally responsible for some action* is to say that she is worthy or deserving of praise or blame for that action. To fix moral responsibility is to assert where approval and disapproval should appropriately be directed. We recognize that it is possible that a responsible or trustworthy person might have no moral responsibility for some particular situation she happened to bring about. (Anne, a safe and conscientious driver, had an accident when the accelerator on her new car stuck.) Similarly, we also recognize that at times an irresponsible person might be morally responsible for a situation which happens because of what she does or does not do. (Anne, who had a few too many at happy hour, did not check her mirror and backed into someone's car in the parking lot.)

In considering the truth or falsity of statement **1.** the compatibilists, hard determinists and libertarians each advance different opinions. The compatibilist's concept of freedom (developed in 1.6) is very close to the concept of autonomy (developed in 2.1). So compatibilists would say that if Roman Fulton made a rational choice to harm Champdeck by sabotaging its computer system and if he made that choice without constraint, then he should be held morally responsible. For the compatibilists statement **1.** is true. If a person chooses rationally and without constraint, then the person is both autonomous and morally responsible for his action.

On the other hand, both the hard determinists and the libertarians would regard statement **1.** as false, but for very different reasons. Hard determinists would argue that no one can be morally responsible for something unless he was free when it was done. But, according to the hard determinist, we are never free in the sense that we could have chosen to act otherwise than we did. (See 1.4.) Since Roman Fulton could not have done otherwise, given the unique set of factors that determined his actions at that time in his life, he cannot be held morally responsible for what he did. Roman was not free, the hard determinists would maintain. This remains so even if Roman might happen to satisfy the conditions for acting autonomously described in Section 2. Statement **1.** is false. The autonomous person is not free in the sense that he could have acted otherwise. Hence autonomous persons cannot be held morally responsible for what they do.

Libertarians agree with the hard determinists that acting autonomously does not guarantee being capable of having acted otherwise. So the libertarians would not think of an autonomous person as being morally responsible. (See 1.5.) But the libertarians would insist that at times people do act freely, in the morally relevant sense of "free to have done otherwise." So, for libertarians, that Fulton acted autonomously is not really the issue. They would say he should be held morally responsible only if *he also acted freely* at the time when he was autonomously choosing to do what he did. Libertarians would not accept that *autonomy*, as defined in Section 2, guarantees the exercise of free will. Hence autonomy alone does not imply moral responsibility. Persons cannot be held morally responsible for unfree autonomous acts, the libertarians would say.

Since the compatibilists would see the phrase "unfree autonomous acts" as a contradiction in terms, they could not agree with the libertarians assessment. For the compatibilists calling a choice free requires nothing beyond the satisfaction of the conditions for autonomous choice, as described in Section 2. As you can see, some of the differences between the three views—hard determinism, libertarianism, and compatibilism—can be traced to subtle but important differences in their definitions of key words, like *free*.

3.2 Does Responsibility Imply Autonomy?

If Roman Fulton was not acting autonomously in introducing the virus into the Champdeck computer system, it would seem, on the face of things, that he should not be held responsible for what happened. This, of course, presumes that the following is true:

2. Only persons who act autonomously are responsible for what they do.

Another way to put statement **2.** is

2′. Persons who do not act autonomously are not morally responsible for what they do.

Most people would be inclined to say that statement 2′. is generally true. They would point out that it seems unreasonable to hold someone morally responsible for an act she performs either under constraint or irrationally. But others want to make distinctions here. Take, for example, the case of someone who, at gunpoint or under great psychological duress, causes damage to be done to someone else's property. Some would say that being under an externally imposed constraint or coercion relieves that person of some or all of the moral responsibility for that action. In contrast, if a person knows that the information he needs is available if he would just take the time to look it up, and if not looking it up causes him to make a poor decision and cause harm to himself or someone else, many would say that he should be held morally responsible for that. In other words, we generally do not allow people who act irrationally or under self-imposed constraints to be so easily relieved of moral responsibility. Failing to deliberate rationally, especially where no external constraint is operative, is a fault for which people can and should be held morally accountable. They squandered the opportunity to act rationally, and, as a result, they brought about unfortunate consequence.

Philosophers have offered three arguments for holding such people responsible: First acting autonomously is a general obligation we have as intelligent human beings. It would not show much self-respect if a person made life decisions, such as deciding which career path to pursue, without making every reasonable effort to identify his goals, sort out his options, look at the consequences of his possible choices, and the rest (as described in Section 2). No matter what happened to him, given that he deliberately chose his career irrationally and without being externally coerced, we would say it was his decision and he should hold himself responsible for it. Second, in specific cases, harmful consequences result directly from the intentional failure to act rationally and without self-imposed constraint when such action is possible. If a parent deliberately refuses to listen to important information regarding her child's educational needs, then, if the child is unsuccessful in school, we would hold that parent at least partially to blame. That is, we would say the parent is morally responsible, perhaps along with others, for making the child's educational problems more severe. Third, not holding people responsible would have the bad social consequence of encouraging others not to take seriously the importance of rational deliberation. If we did not hold lazy employees responsible for the lost revenue, damage, or problems they might cause, then this would encourage others to believe that if they decided to be lazy on the job they too could claim to be excused from culpability.

Notice that the first reason asserts that we have a general obligation or duty to behave in certain ways regardless of the consequences, whereas the second and third reasons point to foreseeable undesirable consequences and argue that it is due to these consequences that deliberately acting irrationally is something for which one can be held morally responsible.

Another argument against the truth of statement 2'. can be mounted by examining the common legal practice of holding someone liable for accidents that occur through negligence or through a failure to take reasonable precautions. In many states it is, or was, the practice that people who *cause* accidents be held legally and financially liable for the damages that may result. If a child falls and gets hurt on your property, if you miss a traffic sign or exceed the speed limit and become involved in an accident, then, in those states, you would be obligated to pay. If, as a health professional, you fail to follow prescribed procedure or standard practice in treating an injured person, you can be held legally liable. If you neglect your duties as a parent, or as the custodian of a financial trust, you can be held legally responsible.

This notion of legal liability does not presuppose autonomy. Actually it is predicated on the falsity of statement 2'., for it does not raise the question of acting autonomously, only of being legally liable and financially responsible. If the issue of autonomy were raised, then accidental damage might be treated more severely, specifically as a malicious and deliberate attempt to cause harm. But the law presumes non-autonomy. For example, parents are held legally liable and financially responsible for damage done by their mischievous children who are minors. But the law does not regard the parents as having acted autonomously. The law would treat them more severely if it were demonstrated in court that the parents did the damage themselves or ordered their children to do it. The operative presumptions are simply that damaged property should be restored and that the minor child (not an autonomous or fiscally responsible agent in the eyes of the law) who caused the damage, or those responsible for that child (its parents) should make the restoration. Why? Because the child is less innocent than either the victim whose property was damaged or any taxpayers in the community, who had no part in the mischief or accident at all. The person who is less innocent should be held fiscally responsible, even though there is no question about whether the child was acting autonomously.

An objection to this appeal to common legal practice is that the concept of legal liability is not exactly the same as the concept of moral responsibility. Therefore, appeal to these practices does not bear on the truth or falsity of statement 2′. The distinction between legal liability and moral responsibility is used by the hard determinist and the libertarian to maintain that Fulton was legally responsible for his crimes, although not morally responsible. However, even if these facts about liability reflect more on fiscal and legal responsibility than on moral responsibility, it is important to be clear about the values reflected in our legal practices. When a person is held liable, even though he has not acted autonomously, it is in effect being judged that it is more important to ensure safety and protect property than to limit a person's liability to autonomous actions.

3.3 Reward, Punishment, and One's Just Deserts

To be morally responsible is to be in a position where praise or blame is appropriate and, some would say, deserved. Not many people ask for justifications for offering praise, and most of us willingly accept it whenever it comes our way. But even praise, or approval, when we think it is undeserved, can be embarrassing and un-comfortable. Let's take a closer look at praise. There are essentially two ap-proaches or justifications for rewarding people. The first, a deontological approach, is basically that people should get what they deserve; so if you merit praise, recog-nition or approval, you should receive it. ("Joan performed admirably in a stressful situation and she deserves our appreciation. Thank you, Joan.") The second justifi-cation for praise has to do with the consequences of receiving it. For example, if re-wards reinforce certain desirable behaviors in you, then you should be rewarded so that you will remember what you did and repeat that behavior. ("The easy way to potty train your child is just to give him a spoon of ice cream if he produces any-thing at all while sitting there." Or, "Great job of selling last month, Bill. Here's two tickets to Hawaii. Hope I have the chance to give you more tickets next month.") Also, if rewarding you will lead others who seek recognition to do what you did, then, on the consequentialist interpretation, you should be rewarded—even if you do not merit it. ("Joan, I realize you feel your contributions are not unique, but headquarters wants to implement a new motivational program for middle man-agers so we've decided to give you a special award at next month's district meet-ing.")

Theories of punishment, like theories of praise, can be divided into two basic groups, deontological and consequentialist. The first group looks at punishment in terms of giving people what they deserve, the second in terms of the desirable consequences of punishing people. The *retributive theory* of punishment is that it is our duty to punish guilty people because they deserve it. Some who hold to a retributive view of punishment think of punishment as a form of *revenge* or *getting even* which exacts the deserved pain or suffering from the guilty party. In the case study the compensatory damages which Champdeck won from Vidimine can be thought of as deserved retribution that Vidimine was forced to pay to make reparations to Champdeck. Also, at his parole hearing Fulton expresses the view that he has "paid his debt" to society, a view which embodies looking at punishment as a kind of retribution. Retribution is difficult to measure, of course. Some wish to equate how much suffering a criminal should endure with the amount of pain or harm the criminal is thought to have caused. The grieving family of the victim of an accidental homicide might not, however, be the most objective persons when it comes to fixing the punishment for the killer. Others try to take a less subjective approach and set in advance the penalties associated with the violation of specific statutes or laws.

In contemporary thinking the argument for the retributive theory is based not on revenge but on a notion of *respect* for persons, involving fair treatment for all. Thus, it is argued that everyone ought to accept and live under the same limitations of freedom. Criminal actions are seen as the criminal's taking unfair advantage of other members of society. The criminal has disrupted the balance of equal limitations, and punishment is seen as an attempt to restore the balance that the criminal has disrupted. In summary, then, this argument says that respect for all those who accept the limitations of life in society demands punishment of criminals who have taken an unfair advantage over others.

The argument from *respect* extends beyond respect to others and includes respect to the criminal. Failure to blame is failure to give a person what he deserves, which amounts to failure to respect the person (just as failure to praise a person who merited it would be failure to show respect for that person). To treat people as responsible is to give them what they deserve, be it rewards or punishments. In this view mercy is not a virtue; it is a vice, for it shows disrespect. To be merciful is to treat a responsible agent as a child; it denies his autonomy and full moral responsibility. On this theory Fulton, in the case study, was treated with appropriate respect when he was put in prison, assuming he was morally responsible for what he did. Taking this approach a step or two further, Fulton's parole raises serious problems, for his parole is a form of mercy. Also, consider the death penalty. How does execution show respect for a person? More generally, even if doing wrong deserves our disapproval and requires restitution in some form, does it deserve physical or psychological punishment?

3.4 Consequentialist Theories of Punishment

Another group of theories focuses on the desirable outcomes of punishment in order to justify it. The consequences usually examined are those for (a) other potential criminals, (b) society in general, and (c) the criminal himself or herself. Whereas the retributive theory merely assumes that those who do wrong deserve punishment, these consequentialist theories look at punishment in terms of its utility. The *preventive theory* maintains that imprisonment serves a socially useful goal of preventing criminals from repeating their crimes and further harming society. As the judge in the case study pointed out, one reason for putting Fulton in jail was to prevent him from committing his destructive crime again. On the preventive theory prisons need be little more than storage houses for criminals. A careful social analysis would measure the cost of housing a criminal in prison against the cost of that person's being free to commit further crimes. Whenever it became economically or politically disadvantageous to allow the criminal his freedom, then he would be put in prison. But, if the cost of prisons, in terms of taxes, were too high, then a certain number of less dangerous criminals would have to be allowed to go free. Economy is not the only factor, however, that influences actual practice. If it were, all persons suspected of being dangerous would be summarily executed, for the crude dollar cost of extermination (without benefit of due process and the extensive system of appeals and legal protections we are blessed with in this country) would be lower than maintaining the potentially dangerous criminals in prisons.

The *deterrent theory*, like the preventive theory, is aimed at holding down the crime rate. But the deterrent theory aims at using punishment as a threat to deter others, specifically potential criminals, from crime. As the judge in Roman Fulton's case said, his punishment would serve as a lesson to others who might be contemplating similar misdeeds. According to the deterrent theory, seeing that first degree murder is punished by death is supposed to make people think twice about murder and be deterred from committing that crime. This immediately raises the scientific question of whether the intended effect is brought about. Is it a proven fact that capital punishment reduces the murder rate? It also raises another question: Is capital punishment the only way to bring that effect about, or could murder be deterred using some other less severe and less expensive penalty?

The deterrent theory assumes that potential criminals make rational choices based on accurate assessments of the potential risks and benefits of crime. Thus, for a deterrent to work, the potential criminal must see it as a greater cost than the likely benefits of whatever crime she is contemplating. People must believe, and be motivated by the belief, that some type of severe punishment will surely be theirs if they perform some criminal act. If the criminal does not expect to be caught, or, if caught, does not expect to be punished, then punishment cannot deter. Likewise, if we do not publicize the type and severity of the punishments associated with specific crimes, then we cannot expect potential criminals, unaware of their likely fate, to be deterred. An important challenge to the deterrent theory relates to the accuracy of its assumptions about criminal behavior. Another challenge is this: why must the one who is punished be a criminal? In fact, if the goal is to deter others from undesirable behavior, then the actual guilt or innocence of the person who is punished is irrelevant, provided that those whom one wishes to deter should believe that the person being punished was guilty.

The *rehabilitative theory* of punishment seeks to serve society and the criminal by restoring the criminal to society as a contributing member, rather than having the criminal remain in custody and be a burden to taxpayers. The question of responsibility does not really enter the picture. Society is served if the criminal is rehabilitated, even if the criminal was not fully responsible or autonomous when he committed the crime. Whether or not our prison system, or our criminal justice system, actually serves the goals of rehabilitation can be settled only by looking at the evidence, which is far from unambiguous. In the case study Roman Fulton intended to appear rehabilitated so that he could get paroled. Now free, he has apparently committed no crimes. But what about his new ideas about how to avoid being caught next time? Much evidence suggests that our prisons do not return better citizens to society; instead they return better criminals. On the other hand, it can be argued that there are several successful rehabilitation programs and that, given adequate support financially and socially, there could be many more. It is impossible to justify capital punishment on the rehabilitation theory.

Whether or not a person such as Fulton was rehabilitated by his prison experience is an open question. Does giving him a routine job in the laundry count as a genuine effort at rehabilitation? What about permitting him to earn his MBA? If he commits no more crimes, most will say he was successfully rehabilitated. If he commits another crime, some will say his rehabilitation failed; others will say society failed to accept his return. Perhaps he was rehabilitated in the sense that he has now seen the light, knows the error of his former ways, and will never again do what he did to Champdeck. Perhaps he has just grown too old and lost interest in committing such crimes, or new computer technology makes his old crime impossible. In other words, the criterion of what is to count as *rehabilitation* is far from clear.

Hard determinists, who are not fond of the concepts of moral responsibility and just deserts anyway, to be consistent must take a consequentialist view of punishment. Many compatibilists in fact tend to look at punishment in terms of the utility of its consequences also. The historical motivation for reconciling determinism and human freedom has been to show that a scientific view of the world is compatible with holding persons accountable for their actions. Accordingly, there is nothing in the compatibilist's position to prevent one from adopting a retributive view of punishment. Libertarians usually emphasize respect for persons as free agents, so they tend to take a retributive view of punishment. Libertarians feel they are showing the criminal respect by holding him responsible and punishing him as he deserves.

EXERCISES

1. (a) Here are three assertions. Each would be accepted by only one of the following theorists: hard determinist, compatibilist, and libertarian. Associate each assertion with the proper position. (3.1)

     Every autonomous action is free.

     No autonomous action is free.

     An autonomous action may be, but need not be, free.

(b) How would each of the three positions argue in defense of the assertion it takes to be correct?

2. (a) Explain how a person's behavior could plausibly be used to argue for the falsity of the assertion, "Only those who act autonomously are responsible for their action."
(b) State, in general terms, what is typically true of a drunken driver in virtue of which it is plausible to assert that she is responsible for her behavior.
(c) Provide another concrete example where these general terms would also apply. (3.2)

3. (a) Of the following four assertions, one each is involved in the retributive, the preventive, the deterrent, and the rehabilitative theories of punishment. Associate each assertion with the proper theory. (1) "At least that terrible criminal can't commit more crimes while he's locked up in jail." (3.4) (2) "The only way to keep some people from committing crimes is to show them very clearly that criminals are regularly severely punished." (3.4) (3) "Criminal behavior is blameworthy. A criminal deserves to be held responsible for her action and be punished because it is blameworthy." (4) "If a prisoner doesn't learn to do something better than commit crimes, then he is going to keep on being a criminal."
(b) Which of these views is consequentialist? Which not? Explain.
(c) Provide the argument that shows why a hard determinist must take a consequentialist view of punishment.

DISCUSSION QUESTIONS

1. Evaluate capital punishment in view of the particulars of the deontological and consequentialist theories of punishment.

2. What justification is their for punishing persons who commit so-called "victimless" crimes? What is being prevented? How is retribution to be measured? Who is being deterred? And, what does rehabilitation amount to in such cases?

ANSWERS TO SELECTED EXERCISES

1. (a) $C, HD, L.$
(b) A person lacks freedom to the extent that he is constrained. No autonomous action is constrained. Any action that is not constrained is free. Hence, every autonomous action is free. *(C)*
Every event has a cause. Whatever is caused to be as it is, is not free. Thus, no action is free. Hence, no autonomous action is free. *(HD)*
In acting autonomously it is possible, and sometimes true, that the agent could or could not have done other than what he did. An action is free if, and only if, its agent could have acted otherwise. Hence, an autonomous action may be, but need not be, free. *(L)*

2. (a) A person knows she is causing a state of affairs in which either she or others will be unable to control undesirable but foreseeable consequences. This knowledge and choice make the person responsible for those consequences.
(b) Typically a drunk driver knew before beginning to drink that she might become drunk, and typically she knew that she would, perhaps of necessity, drive after

becoming drunk. Thus, typically the drunk driver knew in advance that she was making it more difficult or impossible for herself to act responsibly. Therefore, the driver is responsible both for having caused her drunkenness and for the foreseeable, although not necessarily predictable, results of her diminished capacity to drive.

(c) A known epileptic who neglected to take his medicine before driving.

3. (a) Preventive, deterrent, retributive, and rehabilitative.

(b) Only the retributive view is not consequentialist. You should be able to identify the consequence suggested in each of the other three statements.

(c) No human action is free. So, no one is ever responsible for what he does. Thus, no one is deserving of punishment. Hence, punishment should be administered only to the extent that it has useful consequences, such as conditioning people to behave in certain ways and not others.

Section 4
LIMITS OF FREEDOM

In Sections 2 and 3 we questioned the justification for putting constraints on a person's freedom of action by means of imprisonment. But imprisonment, or punishments of whatever kind, are not the only limitations society places on a person's negative freedom. Taxes, compulsory education, military obligations, zoning laws, traffic laws, and other legal prohibitions are just a few of the other constraints or limits imposed by some societies. This section looks at the question of the goals or reasons which are offered to justify putting limitations on negative freedom. Five basic purposes have been proposed: (1) achieving equal treatment under the law, (2) giving everyone in society a fair chance, (3) preventing harm to others, to property, or to one's self, (4) promoting further development of each person's positive freedom, and (5) restricting socially offensive or morally distasteful behavior. After studying Section 4, you should be able to:

- Distinguish legal restrictions aimed at each of the five purposes listed above.
- Explain how each of the five purposes limits negative freedom.
- Give examples of limitations on negative freedom designed to serve each of the five purposes.
- Explain how sample laws would be justified under various of the five purposes.

THE CASE OF JOAN SMITH-MORGAN

My name is Joan Smith-Morgan and I was fired this morning by the president of Vermilion Group. To understand why, you'll need some background. You see, my father was Redford Smith, owner of the famous Smith Schools of Business, the world's biggest college franchise. Smith Schools were opened in every major city in North America. Daddy made lots of money and used it to give my sister and I everything we might ever want. Right after high school, which Daddy called the "the only known time when those who practice ignorance are not naturally selected for non-existence," he enrolled me in the Miami branch of the Smith Schools of Business. As the founder's daughter I naturally received preferential treatment everywhere on campus. The teachers knew Daddy would fire anyone who didn't give me an A. So I graduated with highest honors in just three years.

Obviously that wasn't fair, being singled out like that. When I was young I took advantage of it, but as I grew up it actually became an embarrassment to me. At one point I even came to resent my father and all the power his money represented. So, instead of going to work for my father, I opened up a child care center in the inner city, at my own expense, of course. I watched pre-schoolers and latch-key kids, and taught many of them to read, too. I had two hopes. One was to make it possible for poor mothers to be able to go to work knowing their child was being well cared. My other hope was to give these kids a little educational help. I wanted to let them have an equal chance to make it in society, rather than falling back into the cycle of poverty. It was certainly contrary to the dog eat dog philosophy my father's business schools preached, but I thought of myself as a kind of inner city freedom fighter. And I was proud of what I was doing.

It was a struggle, but for many years I was able to keep the center open without asking my father for help. But one time I had to. You see, there was this trouble with a local gang. They tried to force me to stop taking the children who were relatives of members of a rival gang. They said they didn't want those kids to learn to read or to learn anything. "Let them survive on the streets, if they can," was what the gang leader said. Gang members would stand near the door of the center and intimidate people so that they would be afraid to leave their children with me. I called my father who made a phone call to city hall. The next day police protection in the neighborhood tripled. Also five gang members were suddenly jailed on narcotics charges. I guess money has its uses.

My day care center was a great success, and I had to hire several people. Things got very expensive and, after about fifteen years, I eventually sold the business to Daddy's corporation as a tax write off. As part of the deal I was hired to remain at the day care center as its manager. Well four months ago my father died and his holdings were sold to the Vermilion Group, a public corporation. I thought they were going to leave me alone, but three days ago the newspaper ran a nasty story about one of my employees. The paper suggested there were rumors she might be involved in a child pornography ring. I knew the story was a lie planted there by somebody in Vermilion's management—they own the newspaper, you see. But the public didn't realize that. Ever since the pornography story parents have been pulling their kids out of day care. I got a phone call this morning. The president of Vermilion Group was outraged. He said Vermilion's public image was being destroyed by the pornography story and that the price of its stock was falling fast. He told me to fire the employee immediately. Naturally I refused. So he fired me!

———————————————

4.1 Maximizing Freedom

In Section 2.4 we defined *negative freedom* as being free from constraints. It is easy to imagine that the ideal would be a freedom involving absolutely no constraints on a person's actions. By implication, however, absolute negative freedom would be very rare indeed. Suppose that there were just one person, call him our imaginary Emperor of Indiana, who was absolutely free from all constraints. If the Emperor wished to eat your dinner, he could take it from you and have it for himself. If he wished to sleep with your spouse, he would be free to do so. If he wished to behead someone, fine. But notice, the Emperor's exercise of negative freedom implies constraints on everyone else. No one could safely drive on either side of the street if the Emperor were continually free to drive on whichever side of the street he wished. And imagine the problem if the Emperor of Indiana declared that everyone in the state was also to enjoy absolute negative freedom. Time to move!

The traditional response to this problem has been rational and straightforward. Negative freedom simply cannot be absolute for everyone (let alone anyone). In fairness to all, no one should have absolute negative freedom. But if we are going to limit our negative freedom, we must find some reasonable way of deciding how many limitations to put on each other. First, it is silly to restrict ourselves needlessly. We should end up gaining more than we loose. And second, presuming there are no emperors among us, we should begin by thinking of everyone as an equal in this business of accepting limits on our negative freedom. It seems only fair that everyone should be subject to the same set of restraints. So, to *maximize freedom means to impose on everyone equally whatever restrictions are necessary so as to end up gaining in the end more freedom than was lost due to those restrictions.*

Let's dissect the above claim. This traditional response has two parts, the first being *egalitarianism*. According to egalitarian thought, every person ought to count equally and so everyone ought to be restrained equally. If restrictions on negative freedom are the issue, then if anyone is to be restricted in a given circumstance, then every similar agent interested in performing a similar act ought to be restrained similarly in similar circumstances. This egalitarian statement is thought of as following from the *principle of universalizability*. (See Chapter 1, Section 3.10.)

The second part of the traditional answer has been that the justification of any restraint should be that, universally applied, it *tends to maximize, rather than minimize, freedom*. Consider, for instance, the traffic safety policy of having signal lights at busy intersections stay red in both directions for an extra two seconds. In this situation everyone is similarly restricted. But obviously everyone would be similarly restricted if there were no double red, or if the double red lasted for sixty seconds. How long, then, should the double red be? Here we can use the conception of maximizing freedom. Without any double red, several more accidents would occur. Cars would be damaged and people would be injured and killed. This harm to people and property is itself a restriction of freedom. The justification of the double red, then, is that it reduces the number of harmful accidents and thus increases freedom.   If the double red lasted sixty seconds, however, rather than two seconds, the additional freedom gained—in terms of lives saved, injuries avoided, and property damage which did not happen—would probably be no more than what was gained at two seconds.   There would probably be no fewer accidents at the intersection, and on the other hand all the motorists and pedestrians would lose freedom because of the restrictions on their movement.   The net effect on freedom, therefore, going from a two-second to a sixty-second double red would be a decline; accidents would fail to decrease further, but limitations on everyone's time would increase.

It is very important to understand the concept of maximizing freedom abstractly.   Any restriction, even if placed equally on everybody, limits people's freedom.   How can this be justified?   The argument in favor of restrictions on negative freedom requires showing two things: First the restriction must be imposed in an egalitarian fashion, treating everyone equally; and second, more freedom must be gained than is lost.   The idea of maximizing freedom, then, is the idea of fairly achieving the greatest positive balance of freedom over restrictions.

4.2 Limiting Negative Freedom to Increase Formal Freedom

Under the laws of our country Redford Smith was free to start his business school franchise and his daughter was free to open up her day care center.   Equal freedom under the law is called *formal freedom*.   For example, citizens over such and such an age are free to open up a bank account, register to vote, apply for a driver's license, own property, marry, start a business, and sign up to serve in the armed forces.   Whatever restrictions apply to these kinds of things, such as the restrictions on how licensed drivers may legally operate their vehicles, apply equally to everyone who enjoys the freedom to apply for such a license.   Based on Section 4.1, the justification for those various restrictions is that they are *egalitarian and result in a net gain of freedom*.   In a free and non-exploitive society everyone, in principle, should enjoy the same legal rights.

Any laws, policies, regulations or rules that restrict or exploit some but not others reduce formal freedom and promote privileged classes.   In our society adults enjoy privileges not extended to children.   Citizens enjoy protections not extended to non-citizens.   At times, those privileges preserved in law allow some people to take advantage of others while remaining immune from legal prosecution by those whom they might harm or exploit.   Considerations of race, wealth, religion, gender, national origin, age, maturity, expertise, aristocratic heritage, occupation, and national security, have been used from time to time to justify, or attempt to justify, non-egalitarian legal systems.   Many regard South African apartheid policies as prime examples of exploitive legislation aimed at limiting formal freedom and preserving special privilege.

At times it is argued that the overall good of society warrants treating people differently in terms of their legal rights or formal freedom.   For example, we supply the President, but not every citizen, with bodyguards.   Few countries apply their laws against murder to their own secret service agents, who may kill in the pursuit of their duty as defined by their government. In the case study, Joan Smith-Morgan, the founder's daughter, was given a privileged status in the business college. This special status gave her several advantages and privileges, putting unequal constraints on the negative freedom of the other students who attended the Miami branch of the Smith School of Business. Egalitarian considerations lead not only to the imposition of restrictions but also to the abolition of special privileges. Promoting formal freedom as a justification for limiting negative freedom does imply restrictions, but restrictions applied equally to all.

4.3 Limiting Negative Freedom to Increase Effective Freedom

A person might be legally free to open a bank account, but unless their was a bank near by and unless she had the funds to deposit, this formal freedom would seem rather shallow indeed. As Joan Smith-Morgan realized when she considered the problems of poverty, applying equal restrictions to everyone under the law by no means guarantees everyone an equal chance in life. Some have superior abilities, some are born into wealthier families, some are hindered by accidents or by illness, and some are given opportunities which are withheld from others. A free and open marketplace does not mean that all the goods are free for the taking nor does it mean that everyone has the means to purchase as much as she wishes. Just as there can be limits to one's financial resources, there may be limits on what is available to be sold. Unfortunately, formal freedom is compatible with poverty, ignorance, and other forms of unequal opportunity.

Effective freedom is the possession of the means and opportunities necessary to accomplish one's aim, whatever it may be. Joan Smith-Morgan, in the case study, sought to increase the effective freedom of the poor mother. To accomplish this she tried to limit their negative freedom by removing constraints, such as having to watch their children instead of being able to go to work. By teaching the children to read Joan was trying to help them get a better education so that they eventually could get better jobs. Earning power translates into effective freedom. If anyone should know this, it would be the daughter of Redford Smith, a man with enough money to get police protection for his daughter with just one phone call to city hall.

Joan's goal of increasing and equalizing effective freedom can also be society's goal. Legislation requiring equal opportunity in employment, public education, minimum health care standards, affirmative action legislation, school desegregation to equal educational opportunity, a graduated income tax system, and special tax deductions for day care, disability, and job training expenses are among the ways a more capitalistic society might use to achieve and equalize effective freedom. One problem this approach encounters is resistance on the part of those who enjoy greater effective freedom in supporting programs aimed at assisting those who have less, particularly if the beneficiaries are thought of as undeserving.

Nationalization of industries, the replacement of private enterprise by government ownership, and centralized economic planning are means used in socialist countries to achieve the same goals. Centralized organization and control of economic resources is intended to assure an equitable distribution of goods and full employment, hence making it possible in theory for people to earn the money to acquire those goods. A problem with centralized approaches currently in place around the globe is that they must find ways to motivate people to turn out more and better products. The thought that through one's own efforts one's lot in life could be improved provides a strong motivational incentive in an individualist (non-collectivist) economic system.

One argument in favor of differential tax systems and the other policies and legislation mentioned above is that governments should limit some of the freedom of their more advantaged citizens in order to guarantee some minimum level of opportunity to all their citizens. This argument does not claim that everyone should be made equal in wealth, skill, health, or the like. Rather, limits are imposed on the negative freedom of the more advantaged only to the extent necessary to achieve a basic minimum level of effective freedom for everyone in society. Of course, once this argument is accepted the key policy question (for both collectivist and non-collectivist systems) becomes exactly what constitutes that "minimum" and to what extent should the negative freedom of the advantaged be limited. In practical terms, this can translate into political questions like: How much of a tax increase should be levied in order to put up decent public shelters for the homeless? And how many shelters is that? And who qualifies to use those shelters?

Some who advance the idea that limiting negative freedom is justified in order to achieve greater effective freedom within a society also maintain that those who already enjoy advantages should never be made to fall below the minimum level in the government's zeal to achieve effective freedom for some other group. In effect they are saying that unnecessary or debilitating limitations on negative freedom should not be permitted. Others urge that at times a government is justified in permitting special advantages beyond formal equality to people who previously have been unfairly disadvantaged. These two ideas combined in an interesting way in 1987 when voluntary programs of reverse discrimination in hiring and promotion were found constitutional by the United States Supreme Court. Reverse discrimination is not required by law. However putting unnecessary limitations on business is also undesirable. The Supreme Court ruled that business in a free market system could, if it wished, voluntarily work for an increase in the effective freedom of women and minorities. In other words, there is no legal limit placed on the negative freedom of a business enterprise to set up its own program of reverse discrimination if that program is aimed at producing a greater net amount of freedom within the total society. However discrimination aimed at preserving the privileged employment status of white males is restricted because it is seen as decreasing the net amount of formal and effective freedom in the society.

Sometimes effective freedom is not governed by specific civil legislation. For example, regulations against cheating and plagiarism, while not necessarily laws of a civil government, are designed to guarantee equal effective freedom to do well on exams and papers. Traditionally in the United States the most prominently emphasized means of securing effective freedom has been by securing equal opportunity, especially equal educational opportunity, for all citizens.   Thus educational policies which limit freedom (restricting cheating) in order to increase freedom (providing everyone the same opportunity to demonstrate their knowledge by earning good grades in a competitive environment) tie in closely with our general societal goal of maximizing freedom.

4.4 The Conflict between Negative and Effective Freedom

Potentially there exists a strong conflict between negative freedom and effective freedom. Whenever goods, resources, or opportunities—such as openings in job training programs—are scarce, these means of effective freedom can be supplied to less advantaged persons only by imposing restrictions upon more advantaged persons. So that one person can be given job training at government expense, others must suffer limitations on their effective freedom by being made to pay the taxes necessary to fund that job training program. Clearly the pursuit of maximal effective freedom, conceived of as the acquisition of wealth in an unregulated, tax-free economic system, clashes sharply with the simple ideal that everyone ought to have the maximum amount of negative freedom compatible with the equal amount of negative freedom for everyone else. For, as we have seen in the early history of the free enterprise system, the unchecked pursuit of individual wealth can lead to many economic and human disasters.

In today's free enterprise system a person is free (formally free) to start a business, if he or she can find the capital (effective freedom) to do so. However, the person's profits from that business will be limited to some extent by the government regulations affecting that business and by whatever taxes are imposed on it. Hence the new business will not enjoy unlimited negative freedom. Consistent with the restrictions put on competitors, the negative freedom enjoyed is intended to be *equal and maximal*. However, as the poor of any nation intuitively know, talk of freedom, such as the freedom to start one's own business, has a hollow sound to persons who lack the funds for a minimally nutritious diet, much less for the luxuries the rich pursue with effective freedom.

4.5 Limiting Negative Freedom to Prevent Harm

We have seen that limits on negative freedom may be used to try to achieve equal treatment before the law (formal freedom) or the means and the equal opportunities for achievement (effective freedom) or both. A third goal, or reason for limiting negative freedom, is to prevent harm to life, liberty, and property. The harm can be directed against particular individuals or against society as a collective group of people. Laws against treason, bribery, sedition, conflict of interest, and tax evasion, as well as governmental regulation of commerce, product liability laws, and land use, are all designed to protect the general public or society as a whole from various kinds of harm.

Laws against battery, murder, child abuse, and rape are designed to protect people from physical and psychological harm. Laws empowering courts to remove children from the custody of their parents are examples of laws intended to be used to prevent harm to children. Laws against kidnaping, detention against one's will, and deprivation of legal opportunities are designed to prevent harm to individual liberty. Laws against theft, fraud, industrial sabotage, and deceptive advertising, as well as laws regulating financial transactions, are all aimed at preventing harm through loss of property.

The justification for limiting actions that cause harm is that people, either individually or collectively, should not be harmed if they do not and would not give their prior consent. The relationship of harm and consent is interesting. Some advocate restricting negative freedom in order to prevent harm even if those restricted do not consent to be protected. Consider, for example, seatbelt laws, motorcycle helmet laws, restrictions on the sale of alcohol and prescription drugs. On the other hand, people are sometimes harmed with their consent. For example, shady business practices designed to induce panic selling can create market conditions where prices fall dramatically. During this panic, refusing to sell one's holdings appears contrary to one's interests, since the value diminishes daily. But consenting to sell is sure to produce a loss. In situations like this one's consent (to sell at a loss) can be described either as voluntary or as the product of duress. If you resign your position because you feel that your work is being de-valued and that you are about to be dismissed soon anyway, you might describe your resignation as your voluntary consent to leave your post and you might also describe it as having been made under duress. Duress limits autonomy and hence, as argued in Section 3, responsibility. Some maintain that there should be laws to protect people from decisions made under duress—for example, the business executive who is "forced out" should have the right to sue.

Laws aimed at preventing people from harming themselves cannot rely on the concept of consent for people can always claim that they should have the negative freedom to harm themselves if they so choose. But laws against self-harm can be justified. A primary justification can be built on the idea that harming one's self actually produces unnecessary and unacceptable costs (financial or psychological) for others. For example, motorcycle helmets must be used because otherwise head injuries to motorcycle riders would create unnecessary and unacceptable financial burdens on taxpayers in terms of hospital care and unemployment compensation. Thus, limiting the negative freedom of motorcyclists increases the effective freedom of taxpayers. A second justification often associated with laws against self-harm is more directly related to preventing the harm. It is argued that people do not really understand where their own best interest lies. For example, there are laws allowing parents or guardians to decide for children or for the legally incompetent what is in their best interest. These laws are designed to prevent the child or the incompetent adult from harming himself. Prohibitions against the purchase of dangerous prescription drugs, also come under this justification. Most of us, not having the needed medical expertise, might only harm ourselves if we tried to diagnose and treat our own maladies. Restrictions on the use of fire crackers, smoking in public places, and the sale of alcohol to adults between the ages of 18 and 21 might be defended partly in terms of protecting people from themselves and partly in terms of protecting others from harm.

There are two kinds of objections to such laws. One is that in general negative freedom is to be maximized and specifically it should be maximized when no harm *to others* is involved. The second is that no governmental body is better able to perceive the best interests of individuals then they are themselves. So, governmental efforts to protect people *from themselves* may well work out to harming the person after all. When no harm to others, including taxpayers, is involved, it is difficult to argue solely on the basis of a superior assessment of another person's self-interest without opening the door to a governmental big-brotherism.

4.6 Limiting Negative Freedom to Increase Positive Freedom

The fourth reason offered for limiting negative freedom is that certain limitations can work to increase a person's positive freedom. In Section 2 we used the example of compulsory education to illustrate this goal of increasing a person's positive freedom. Laws designed to help people decide and act more rationally can be directed against the person's own negative freedom or against the negative freedom of other people. For example, laws concerning informed consent, truth-in-lending, and unit-pricing can be seen as designed to increase the opportunity to exercise positive freedom. The goal of increasing positive freedom is closely related to the goal of preventing people from harming themselves and others. The operative assumption is that, given relevant information presented in clear and usable ways, people can make more rational decisions and better avoid harming themselves. Laws against the use of narcotics can be viewed as aiming in part at helping people avoid any potentially harmful situations that might arise when their rationality is impaired by drugs.

The laws cited above support the ideal of positive freedom only to the extent that they ensure the opportunity to make a decision based on fuller information. A more direct approach would go beyond laws attempting to ensure the opportunity to be rational and would prohibit people from being irrational in various ways. Laws warning people about the danger of smoking, for example, do no more than present information for grounding a rational decision. They do not attempt to enforce rationality by prohibiting persons who profess to value their life from smoking. Other laws tend to be more forceful in promoting positive freedom. For example under certain circumstances it is legally possible to have a person committed to a mental institution against his will, even though he has not harmed anyone and there is no clear or present danger that he will do so. Such laws attempt to enforce positive freedom by permitting the detention of a person judged of unsound mind, depriving him of liberty, and thereby constraining him from engaging in his esoteric practices. But if this justification is acceptable, it is only acceptable if it is aimed at rehabilitating the person. Under this justification he can be detained only until he is able to more rationally come to realize that he does not really want to engage in those irrational things after all.

4.7 Limiting Negative Freedom to Prevent Offensive Behavior

A final reason offered for limiting negative freedom is to prevent behavior that, while not essentially harmful, offends the norms and values of society. Socially distasteful or offensive behavior is prohibited in order to prevent anxiety, frustration, mental anguish, and social disturbance. Laws against prostitution, polygamy, sodomy, incest, homosexuality, and pornography are sometimes defended in terms of attempts to prevent behavior that some, or many, in a society find offensive. These laws often arouse strong feelings, because many view them as unfair attempts to legislate morality and encroach on personal liberties, while others view them as necessary to maintain the moral fiber of society and prevent people from antagonizing and annoying others by their distasteful behavior.

A pluralistic society with its confluence of different cultural traditions, diverse religions and different sexual codes of behavior can expect the problem of trying to prevent offensiveness to be extremely difficult. The behaviors and mores of any group can be viewed with outrage by another, which in turn may practice something thought utterly distasteful or offensive by still another group. Experiencing cultural differences can also lead in the other direction, away from prejudice and ethnocentrism toward increased tolerance and even personal enrichment. The experience of diversity can be a liberating and rewarding one: it need not be threatening or upsetting.

Should there be restrictions placed on the vocabulary people can use in public places or over the TV and radio? Should there be restrictions on who can view sexually explicit films? And what about laws restricting the production of dramas which are offensive on religious or political grounds because they depict ideas which some find irreverent or contrary to orthodoxy? Laws aimed at preventing offensiveness certainly conflict with the ideal of maximal negative freedom, since a majority may readily find a behavior offensive even though it does not harm others. Most persons, realizing that everybody has such harmless quirks and manners, may agree that it would be better if people could simply enjoy the wider negative freedom conferred by greater tolerance of individual idiosyncrasies. It is at least fair to note, however, the extremely strong feelings people have about some behaviors they find offensive. Grave-robbing, necrophilia and mutilation of corpses are simply disgusting to most people. The mutilation, however, harms neither the corpse nor the bereaved. And, how should we handle animal experimentation, which some find offensive and others claim is vital? What about hate crimes?

EXERCISES

1. (a) Below you will find descriptions of the purposes served by 16 real and possible laws. Distinguish the general ways in which each imposes a limit upon negative freedom of the individual. Laws marked with an asterisk (*) serve more than one purpose. Next to each description mark the purpose or purposes served by that law. The five general purposes for which laws limit negative freedom are to:

Treat everyone equally under the law [FF—Formal Freedom (4.2)],

Provide the means or opportunity for persons to achieve their aims, [EF—Effective Freedom (4.3)],

Prevent harm to persons and property (PH) (4.5),

Promote further development of everyone's positive freedom (PF) (4.6),

Prevent offensive behavior (OB) (4.7).

    1. No person should be required to witness against himself.

    2. Extortion should be illegal.

    3. Broadcasters should be required to present some public service advertising free of charge.

    4. A person's ethnic background should not prevent him from securing housing.

    5. Sexual intercourse with farm animals should not be legal.

    6.* Teachers should have to pass a state test of competence.

    7.* Persons convicted of drunken driving should be imprisoned for three years.

    8.* Grass on a person's property should not be allowed to grow over six inches long.

    9.* All beer bottles should have a warning about the dangers of drinking printed on them.

    10. Gender should not be a consideration in employment or promotion.

    11. Physical assault should not be permitted.

    12. There ought to be a ban on the sale of pornographic materials.

    13. Foul and irreverent language ought not be permitted in public.

    14. Arson should be illegal.

    15. Those accused of a crime should have the right to confront their accusers in court, even if the accuser is a minor.

    16. All retail stores should be closed during the hours of religious services.

(b) Whenever regulations achieve any of these purposes, someone's negative freedom is limited. Take the first five regulations listed above. Identify some person whose negative freedom would be limited by each regulation.

(c) When you are sure you have made a correct identification, state how that person's negative freedom would be limited by the regulation.

2. (a) Either by reference to real regulations or by making them up yourself, provide five examples of regulations, each designed to serve one of the five aims listed above.

(b) Identify in each case the person or persons whose negative freedom would be limited.

(c) State how that person's negative freedom would be limited by the regulations.

DISCUSSION QUESTIONS

1. In view of the justifications for limiting negative freedom, should public education be required of all persons under the age of eighteen? Notice that this question has several

parts such as public vs. private education, and the various ages of the persons who would receive it.

2. Since one way to conceive of public education is as a means to provide the person with sufficient knowledge and ability to function as a free member of a free society, should a person who is granted a high school diploma but who cannot read above a fourth grade level have the legal right to sue the school district which awarded her that worthless and misleading credential?

3. Consider legislation aimed at protecting persons from harm, restrictions on the use of dangerous pesticides, prohibitions against open fires during dry seasons, the minimum highway speed limit, prohibitions against the sale of alcohol to persons under 21, refusals by the Food and Drug Administration to license medications unless they are demonstrably safe and effective, etc. In terms of specific cases and the maximization of freedom for all, what are the reasonable limits of the government's authority to promulgate such laws?

4. In this chapter we have defined four concepts of freedom: Positive, negative, formal and effective. Looking back over the examples used, particularly in Section 4, discuss how various kinds of freedom relate to the concept of a person's legal rights?

ANSWERS TO SELECTED EXERCISES

1. (a) 1. *FF:* provides every accused person with equal treatment.   2. *PH.*   3. *PF:* increases information upon which to base decisions.   4. *EF:* prohibiting such discrimination increases opportunities of finding certain levels of housing for those who desire and can afford it.   5. *OB.*   6. *H, PF:* assuring teacher competence increases educational effectiveness and, in turn, produces more chances for rational decision making in the society.   7. *H, FF:* provides equal treatment for all convicted of that crime.   8. *OB:* prevents offense where tall, weedy grass is considered to be offensive and unaesthetic.   *H:* controls rodents and insects while also maintaining higher property values.   9. *H, PF.*   10. *EF:* prohibiting gender discrimination increases the chances of persons who seek certain kinds of employment or levels of promotion to achieve their aims.   11. *H.*   12. *OB.*   13. *OB.*   14. *H.*   15. *FF*   16. *OB.*

(b) 1. Prosecutors and those allegedly harmed by the person required to witness.   2. The would-be extortionist.   3. The broadcasters.   4. The realtor and the seller or landlord of the house.   5. Persons desiring sexual intercourse with corpses.

(c) 1. The prosecutor would be prevented from forcing the person to testify and the person harmed might be prevented from gaining a desired restoration or retribution through the law.   2. The extortionist is threatened with imprisonment for the extortion.   3. The broadcasters are prevented from accepting profitable commercial advertising in those places designated for free public service announcements.   4. The realtor and seller or landlord are all prevented from making ethnic background a criterion for selecting a buyer or renter for the house.   5. Persons desiring sexual intercourse with corpses are threatened with punishment for such behavior.

6 JUSTICE

Being fair means if folks are alike, then you oughta treat 'em alike, but if they're different, well then that's how different you oughta treat 'em.

Koby's Reflections on Justice

Questions of the rightness or wrongness of particular actions or policies often turn on whether or not they promote justice. Hence, examination of the concept of justice is an integral part of both ethics and social philosophy. In Section 1 we discuss the varieties of circumstances within which questions of justice arise. We introduce the distinctions among distributive, compensatory, and retributive justice. In Section 2 we analyze what has come to be known as the *formal principle of justice*, which is often expressed this way: "Treat persons alike who are alike in morally relevant respects; treat persons proportionately differently to the extent that they differ in morally relevant respects." In Section 2 we examine the relation of the formal principle of justice to the concept of equality. In Section 3 we face the crucial question, "What constitutes morally relevant differences among persons?" The chapter's goal is to enable you to rationally evaluate claims that justice is or is not being done.

Section 1
TYPES OF JUSTICE

In this section we shall examine the variety of circumstances within which questions of justice arise. We shall identify the conditions that must be met if a just result is to be attained in such circumstances. In so doing, we shall consider the significance of issues such as scarcity of resources, conflict of interest, and universalizability as they give rise to and contribute to the satisfactory resolution of problems of justice. We shall then focus on the distinction among questions of distributive, compensatory, and retributive justice, paying special attention to the relation of compensation and retribution to moral responsibility. After studying this section you should be able to:

- Distinguish cases in which a question of justice arises from cases in which none is involved.
- Explain this distinction by reference to the cases.
- Define arbitrarily unjust judgments in terms of morally irrelevant characteristics.
- Distinguish cases of compensatory and retributive justice from each other and from cases of distributive justice raised without specific reference to compensation or retribution.

THE CASE OF THE JOBLESS STUDENTS

Mr. Sands, the high school guidance counselor, smiled as he entered the auditorium of Jane Pitman High. "I've got good news. We were given a special government grant for our Summer Jobs Program. We now have job openings for 50 people. How many of you are interested in applying for a job through our program?"

His heart fell as he saw scores of hands go up. "That must be nearly 150 of you!" he said. "I don't know what we're going to do about this problem. We can't satisfy all of you. I'll take it up with Mrs. Ketting this afternoon. She will make an announcement tomorrow setting the ground rules for who will be eligible to apply."

Later that afternoon Mr. Sands met with the principal, Mrs. Ketting. "What are we going to do? One hundred fifty kids want jobs. We can take the applications on a first-come-first-served basis, I suppose."

"That may not be fair, because the seniors are in class for two hours after my announcement time, but the juniors are on free time. The juniors will have the advantage of being able to apply first," said Mrs. Ketting.

"Maybe we can set quotas. Let's reserve 30 jobs for seniors and 20 for juniors. The sophomores and freshmen will just have to wait till next year."

"No, Mr. Sands. Let's set it at 10 for sophomores, 20 for juniors, and 20 for seniors, and let's say that half of the jobs go to women and the other half to men, depending on which of our young men and women apply first."

"That sounds okay. Will you make the announcement then? Tell them I'll receive applicants in my office."

"Fine. ...No, wait a minute, Mr. Sands. Last year we had some trouble with this program. Your predecessor, Bixby, was fired because he altered the numbers on the applications. He made it look like some who really applied late had applied early. He was always playing favorites with the students, and this time he was caught at it. We should make sure that those students who got jobs unfairly last year do not get them this year. We should also make sure that the ones who missed out on jobs because of Bixby's little tricks get jobs this year."

"Yes, I agree, but only up to a point. I agree that we should not mess with the order of the applicants. I also agree that we should first give jobs to those who missed out last year because of Bixby's foul play. But I don't think we should hold it against the kids whom Bixby helped. After all, they didn't ask for favors; and they didn't learn about the matter till well after they were in their new jobs. It wasn't their doing, but Bixby's!"

"Yes," said Mrs. Ketting, "I see your point. We will not hold it against them; except for three of them. You remember, don't you? Armstrong, Tjin, and LaStrada all got jobs by falsifying their applications. This year they should not be eligible."

"I agree."

"Okay. I'll make the announcement. Thank you, Mr. Sands."

1.1 The Concern for Justice

Questions of justice arise whenever there is concern about apportioning benefits and burdens fairly. Such things as appointive offices, welfare assistance, taxes, jobs, military conscription, natural resources, food, economic and educational opportunities, incomes, punishments, and rewards may be apportioned justly or unjustly. In the case study Sands and Ketting are concerned about justice; they are concerned about how to distribute job opportunities among the students at Jane Pitman High.

Let us examine two circumstances which must exist before such questions of justice arise—scarcity of resources and conflicting interests regarding accesses to those scarce resources. Let us also examine one of the conditions necessary for the satisfactory resolution of such questions—namely, the universalizability of the resolution.

1.2 The Scarcity Requirement

If there was no real *scarcity* of desired materials, resources, opportunities, etc., then questions of justice would not arise. If there were an abundance of available materials, resources, opportunities, and so on, and if there were no way in which others could interfere with a person's taking advantage of that abundance, then the person would have no interest in justice. Thus, for example, it is the scarcity of affordable rental apartments that raises the question of the fairness of practices such as excluding certain groups of financially qualified renters from access to some of those apartments on such grounds as that some would-be renters might keep pets, have children, be married, be students, or be unemployed or on the grounds that they might not be of a certain race, political party, ethnicity, gender, religion, or age group.

Of course it is unrealistic to think of there being an abundance of all of the things in which people can take interest. The finite character of both life and the world's resources precludes it. The case study presents an all-too-familiar instance of scarcity: more students desire jobs than there are jobs available under the government grant to the high school. If there were more jobs than applicants, then there would be no question of the fairness of the procedures for selecting those to get jobs from among job applicants.

1.3 The Conflicting Interests Requirement

Another condition necessary for there being a concern about justice is that *persons must have conflicting interests* in having that which is scarce. That is, given the potential for real scarcity, sufficient numbers of people must be interested in having what is scarce so that not all can be fully satisfied. For example, there must be more qualified people wanting to rent apartments than there are apartments to be rented. In such cases it becomes reasonable to be concerned about how to justly allocate the short supply. To see that this condition is an addition to the condition that there must be scarcity, imagine a case of something's being very rare, say iguanas or space shuttle launches. Suppose that all who seek iguanas for pets or all businesses which wish to put a payload into space using the space shuttle are able to have their wishes fulfilled. In these examples, the scarcity of iguanas or space shuttle launches does not suffice to raise a question of justice; there are no conflicting interests.

In the case study there are conflicting interests among the students who want jobs. Assume that all of the jobs are equivalent, in the sense that none is especially interesting or exciting. The fact that there are only fifty jobs for students at an average-sized high school—the fact that the jobs are *absolutely* scarce—would not in itself give rise to any question of justice. If only ten students raised their hands, there would be no problem. It is the *relative* scarcity (that is, the absolute scarcity in combination with the fact that interested students outnumber job vacancies) that creates a competition of interests. The relative scarcity leads to a need to develop a fair procedure for trying to satisfy the students' interests.

It might be useful to note that *people with conflicting interests* means something different than *person with a conflict of interests*. A person who has a conflict of interests is a person with two or more potentially incompatible interests. For example, a government official who knows that by his voting for or against a certain regulation he could harm or benefit himself financially is said to be in a *conflict of interest* situation because his personal financial interest is potentially in conflict with the public good—that interest he is responsible for serving by virtue of being a government official. We are not speaking of that kind of situation, however, when we talk about *people with conflicting interests*. We are talking about several persons who have the same interest; they all want the same thing, but those interests conflict because not all of them can have their interests satisfied.

1.4 Universalizable Resolutions

Questions of justice arise under conditions of scarcity where conflicts of interest are present. Just resolutions of such conflicts must be *universalizable* resolutions. A just, or fair, solution to the types of problems we have discussed requires that the persons be respected as persons. Therefore, whatever rules apply to questions of justice must apply indiscriminately to any person. No arbitrary discriminations and exceptions are to be made in favor of, or against, individuals on the basis of morally irrelevant considerations. This universalizability condition should be familiar from Chapter 1, Section 3. The point here is that it applies centrally to matters of justice.

As an example, consider the problem of justly distributing scarce organs when they are needed for transplants in order to save lives. Universalizable rules governing the distribution would apply morally relevant criteria in all cases, for example, considerations of the desperate circumstances of the potential recipients, suitable tissue match between donor and recipient, the possibility of rejection, the likelihood of positive result following the transplantation, and the like. No rules which arbitrarily preferred recipients because of such considerations as relationship to the medical staff, wealth, race, gender, city of birth, or the like would be universalizable.

In the case study Mr. Sands and Mrs. Ketting are struggling to discover a universalizable set of rules for proceeding. They do not want to repeat the playing of favorites in which Bixby had indulged the previous year, for Bixby clearly made arbitrary discriminations. They are seeking procedures that can be used indiscriminately in all cases. Where they do see a need to make exceptions to the rules, they endeavor to specify morally relevant differences. When they do make exceptions based on morally relevant differences, they are willing to extend those exceptions to any person who also has the relevant differentiating characteristic. Thus, it is not simply because Armstrong, Tjin, and LaStrada are who they are that Sands and Ketting want to exclude them from the pool of applicants. Rather, Sands and Ketting identify what they take to be a morally relevant difference in their case: their past cheating on job applications. They exclude them on that basis. It is reasonable to suppose that they would be willing to universalize this procedure and to exclude anyone else whom they later discover to have cheated.

1.5 Justice and Deserts

Questions of justice are questions about what people deserve. They are questions of giving people what is due them under the conditions and in the manner specified in the preceding sub-section. They are, then, in most general terms, questions of the distribution of benefits and burdens. Two special types of cases where distribution comes into question deserve our special attention: (1) cases where persons have been denied deserved benefits or have suffered undeserved hardship, and (2) cases where persons have enjoyed undeserved benefits or have undeservedly avoided their share of a burden. In these special types of cases, questions of just compensation or punishment arise together with questions of responsibility. In what follows we will, therefore, distinguish between the general issue of distributive justice and the more specific issues of corrective justice, compensation, and retribution.

1.6 Distributive Justice

The most general question of *distributive justice* is how to weigh conflicting interests in deciding how to allocate benefits and burdens. It is a problem of comparing the merits of conflicting claims. It is also a problem of devising criteria for making universalizable comparisons. The problem of allocation may (but need not) come into dispute independent of anyone's ever having been undeservedly burdened or benefited in the past. Thus, questions of compensation or retribution for such undeserved burden or benefit are really species of the more general problem of distributive justice.

For example, as medicine progresses, new life-saving technologies are regularly developed. In the early stages of such development, the technologies are scarce, that is, they cannot be made available to all who need them. At this stage, the question of how to allocate them, given that not all can be saved, is a question of distributive justice. Medical practitioners and institutions confront the question of "Who is to be saved when not all can be?" The merits of conflicting claims to the benefits of the new technologies must be weighed in non-arbitrary ways which apply universalizable criteria for making the necessary comparative judgments. Typically, such judgments are currently made either on the basis of "first come, first served" or on the basis of randomizing procedures which allow each potential beneficiary an equal opportunity to be treated. Only rarely, if ever, would considerations of compensation or retribution come into play in making such judgments.

In the case study Mr. Sands and Mrs. Ketting confront a question of distributive justice. They must decide how to give out jobs to the students fairly in light of relevant considerations of what the students deserve. Ketting and Sands compare the merits of the conflicting claims to the jobs and decide upon appropriate general procedures that take into account the students' deserts. If all had an equal claim to the jobs, then a simple first-come-first-served procedure would give all a fair opportunity to apply. The situation is complicated, however, by the fact that some students would be able to come to Sands' office sooner than others and that people from the upper classes seem deserving of a greater portion of the jobs. Thus, a quota system is devised to take these factors into account. The quota system, you should note, is addressed to the general question of distribution. Unfortunately, factors of past favoritism and past cheating must also be taken into account. They raise the more specific questions of compensation and retribution.

1.7 Compensatory Justice

Questions of *compensatory justice* arise in circumstances where there has apparently been undeserved denial of benefit or undeserved suffering or hardship in past distributions of benefits and burdens. The questions have to do with compensations to correct for those misfortunes. In some cases compensation may take the form of restoration of something that a misfortune has cost a person. Thus, if a baseball is stolen, just compensation would seem to be restoration of the baseball or one similar to it. In other cases, however, such restoration may be impossible, so that any compensation must take some other form. For example, if a leg is lost in an accident, there is no possibility of restoring it with a new leg (given the current state of the surgical arts). Instead, compensation must take some other form, such as the gift of an artificial limb, financial compensation, or both.

In the case study a question of compensatory justice is raised. The preceding year Sands' predecessor, Bixby, had played favorites in allocating a similar set of jobs. As a result, some students were moved down the list of applicants unfairly and did not get jobs. This constitutes an undeserved denial of a benefit that they deserved by virtue of their being on the original list. Sands and Ketting believe those students are now deserving of some compensation. The current procedure is, therefore, modified in order to ensure that they get jobs this year. In accordance with the ideal of justice, a job this year is seen as at least a rough equivalent of a job last year.

We have developed, within our legal system, a way of handling, to some extent, some questions of compensatory justice. If persons believe they have been wronged and are aggrieved, they can seek compensation in the civil courts. For example, if you are injured by accidentally stepping on a sprinkler head while playing soccer, you can bring a civil suit against the owners of the field on which you were playing. Your suit would assert their liability (see Chapter 4, Section 1). If you won your suit, the owners would be obligated to compensate you for the pain and injury you sustained. Legal claims alleging harm are called *tort claims*. In a tort claim one private party (or legal entity) sues another private party (or legal entity) or sues a public agency seeking compensation for that harm. Tort claims are a major part of our justice system. They should be distinguished from criminal cases where the people collectively, through the agency of government, prosecute individuals for having broken a law.

1.8 Retributive Justice

Questions of *retributive justice* arise in circumstances where there has apparently been undeserved benefit, undeserved avoidance of burden, or an undeserved infliction of hardship by one person upon another. The questions have to do with what *corrective action* is appropriate to offset any undeserved advantages that might have arisen, or what *punitive action* is appropriate as a burden to the one who inflicted undeserved hardship. Broadly speaking, then, questions of the fairness of punishment are questions of what retribution is due. Given that someone has undeservedly acted at another's expense, what is to be done?

The case study also illustrates questions of retributive justice. Mrs. Ketting first suggests that students who were given jobs unfairly by Bixby the preceding year should be denied jobs this year. This amounts to a suggestion that they benefited unfairly and that proper correction requires that they be denied jobs this year. Mr. Sands counters by suggesting that their benefiting the previous year was none of their doing and that they do not, therefore, deserve to be punished this year. The offense was Bixby's, and he has been punished with loss of his job. However, Armstrong, Tjin, and LaStrada cheated to gain unfair advantage the preceding year, and Sands and Ketting agree that they deserve to be denied jobs this year.

Going back to your soccer injury for a moment, in your suit you can ask for more than compensatory justice, you can ask for retributive justice as well. If it can be established that your accident would have been preventable had it not been for negligence on the part of the owners of the soccer field, then the court might award you *punitive* damages as well as compensation for your actual pain and injury. These additional damages are intended to punish the owners for not having taken reasonable precautions to prevent injuries such as the one with which you are undeservingly burdened. Should the matter also involve the violation of a law, for example if the owners knowingly installed the wrong sprinklers with the malicious intention of hurting someone, then we, the people, through the agency of our government, namely the office of the prosecuting attorney, might bring criminal charges against the owners. If they are found guilty, then there could be additional punishments imposed for having violated the law.

1.9 Compensation, Retribution, and Responsibility

The case study reflects not only concern with questions of compensation and retribution, but also an important connection between these questions and those of responsibility. In considering whether retribution is appropriate, much seems to turn on whether the person in question is morally responsible for his unfair advantage or the infliction of hardship on others. It seems appropriate to punish persons only for things for which they bear responsibility. Thus, it seems inappropriate to punish the students who unfairly got jobs last year if they got them because of a factor for which they were not responsible and of which they were ignorant. Similarly, it would seem in principle unjust to visit hardship upon people, as surely punishment does, for such things as their race, their height, their sex, their having been born poor, and the like, where it is clear they bear no responsibility for such matters.

On the other hand, the case of compensation raises a major question for those concerned with justice: Who is to bear the burden of providing the compensation? Where persons can be readily identified as responsible for others' having been unfairly disadvantaged, the answer seems fairly clear. Those who have unfairly benefited should supply the compensation, even though doing so may be burdensome. However, there may be cases where it is reasonable to say that some persons are undeservedly disadvantaged, being neither responsible for their own hardship nor deserving of it; and yet no other persons can be identified as responsible. In such cases is compensation still due such persons? Who shall be asked to provide it? For example, is compensation due to American Indians? If so, who should provide it? Is compensation due to the victims of violent crime, or of accidents caused by uninsured motorists? If so, who should assume the responsibility of providing it?

EXERCISES

1. Below is a list of statements describing different situations. In some of them a question of justice is raised. Mark each such statement *QJ*; then state what the question is. In some no question of justice is raised. Mark each such statement *NQJ*; then state which factor necessary for questions of justice to arise is missing. (1.2–1.3)
   ___(a) So far 27 persons have applied for the 35 openings we have in our management training program.
   ___(b) At least 15 more persons are planning to apply tomorrow for the remaining positions.
   ___(c) There's only one piece of pie left, but nobody seems to want it.
   ___(d) If all the new tax money goes into teacher salaries, nothing will be left to improve the quality of the textbooks the children use.
   ___(e) Everybody agrees that Toby should keep the abandoned kittens he found.
   ___(f) With the decline in student enrollments, no student will have to share textbooks this year.
   ___(g) Both firms want to have the advantage of making the final bid for the contract.
   ___(h) Should Kelly be given the lead for her years of faithfulness to Play People, or should Lori get it for the financial contributions she has collected?
   ___(i) Dolores got the job because she was the only one who wanted it.
   ___(j) During the next two years, if there is no drought, there will be enough food for everyone to eat as much as they wish and can afford.

2. Define arbitrarily unjust actions in terms of morally irrelevant characteristics. (1.3)

3. Below is a list of statements and questions about situations in which a question of justice is raised. If the issue is one of compensatory justice, mark it *QCJ*. If it is one of retributive justice, mark it *QRJ*. If the issue is one of distributive justice raised without specific reference to compensation or retribution, mark it *QDJ*. (1.6–1.8)
   ___(a) Martha was never paid in any way for the days she took off work while she was having her baby, even though all employees are entitled to sick days with pay.
   ___(b) How much money should each employee be asked to contribute to the flower fund for sick colleagues?
   ___(c) What could be fairer than "first come, first served" in allocating organs for transplantation?

___(d) Who should have to pay for town-organized recreational programs?

___(e) The people who play should be the people who pay.

___(f) People who abuse the equipment and damage or destroy it should pay to put it back into good shape.

___(g) Rich people should have to pay more because they can afford more.

___(h) Since people only get rich by taking unfair advantage of others, the rich should always pay more taxes to make up to the poor people what they have been cheated out of.

___(i) The reason the rich people should pay is because they cheated the poor people in the first place. They shouldn't retain an unfairly gained advantage.

___(j) Since Martha missed a chance to apply for promotion while she was out having her baby, should she be given a special opportunity to apply now?

___(k) If we could prove that Charles Mailer Prig moved up the dates for applying for promotion so that Martha would miss them, then we should fire him.

DISCUSSION QUESTIONS

1. Is compensation due to American Indians? If so, who should provide it? How much should be distributed and to whom should it be distributed?

2. Is compensation due to the victims of violent crime, such as assault, rape, robbery, or murder? What form should it take, financial, psychological or what? Who should be responsible for providing (paying for) it?

3. Is compensation due to the victims of non-criminal acts, such as auto accidents caused by uninsured motorists? If so, who should assume the responsibility of providing it?

4. Smith must distribute salary changes to six employees: A, B, C, D, E, and F. The first three are "senior specialists" and the second three are "associate specialists." The six currently make the following annual salaries: 80K, 78K, 71K, 47K, 42K and 34K respectively. All are males except C and F. Inflation last year was 7%. Smith has 10% of the sum of their current salaries to distribute. On a ten point scale, with 10 as the top, their work performance last year was evaluated as follows: 8, 8, 6, 2, 4, and 9 respectively. Their years of service with Smith's company are: 22, 21, 25, 9, 7, and 12 respectively. A, B, and D are married and have large families. A, C and E have spouses who work, but B's and F's spouses are not employed. D has spent the last several months going through a very messy divorce. If you were Smith, what distributions of salary changes would you make taking into consideration the concepts of justice discussed above.

ANSWERS TO SELECTED EXERCISES

1. (a) *NQJ:* no scarcity

(b) *QJ:* Of the 42 applicants children wanting to begin the management training program, which 35 should be admitted to the program?

(c) *NQJ:* No conflict of interest—in fact, no interest.

(d) *QJ:* How should the funds from the new tax be distributed in the school budget?

(e) *NQJ:* no conflict of interest

(f) *NQJ:* no scarcity

(g) *QJ:* Which, if any, firm should enjoy the final bid advantage?

(h) *QJ:* Who should be given the lead in the play?

(i) *NQJ:* no conflict of interest

(j) *NQJ:* no scarcity

2. Actions are arbitrarily unjust when distributions they involve are based on morally irrelevant features. (See 1.3)

3. (a) *QCJ* (b) *QDJ* (c) *QDJ* (d) *QDJ* (e) *QDJ* (f) *QRJ* (g) *QDJ* (h) *QCJ* (i) *QRJ* (j) *QCJ* (k) *QRJ*

Section 2
JUSTICE AND EQUALITY

Our basic sense of justice is disturbed if we discover that, as benefits and burdens are distributed, two apparently similar persons are treated quite differently. Our sense of justice is satisfied only when we are presented with reasons explaining how the persons differ in some morally relevant respect. The basic principle underlying this sense of justice has come to be called the *formal principle of justice.* It requires that persons who are alike in morally relevant respects ought to be treated alike, and that persons who differ in morally relevant respects ought to be treated differently in proportion to the differences between them. In this section we will analyze this most fundamental principle of justice. We will learn why it is considered to be a *formal* principle and distinguish its *formality* from the *materiality* of other principles. We will also analyze an ambiguity in the notion that justice requires equality of treatment, showing that on the one hand equality of treatment may be identified with the formal principle of justice itself, and on the other hand it may be taken as an implausible material principle of justice. We will then examine two presumptions for justice that derive from the formal principle, contrasting the implications of each. After studying Section 2 you should be able to:

- Distinguish formal from material considerations of justice.
- Distinguish different meanings that "equality" may have, explaining why, on each meaning, equality is either a formal or a material principle of justice.
- Distinguish formal and material principles of justice from the presumptions of justice.
- Explain the conceptual connection between the presumptions of justice and human ignorance.

THE CASE OF THE JOB VACANCY NOTICE

"Hey, Olsen, come in here. Would you?"

"Yes, Mr. Kargenian. What is it?"

"I'm trying to write a job vacancy notice for the position of office secretary. How does this sound to you?" Kargenian read from his yellow pad. "Wanted: capable and experienced woman, age 25 to 35, for full-time clerical position. Pay rate: $9.50 per hour. Job entails typing, filing, word-processing, use of standard office machines, handling crates up to 30 lb., composing business letters and office memoranda."

"I wouldn't specify the age and the gender in the job description. Besides, why not consider a male for the position?"

"Come on, Olsen. I don't want an administrative assistant who gets $14.00 an hour. I want a young, good-looking secretary. A new girl can make things a lot more fun around here."

"Oh, you want a playmate, not a secretary."

"Maybe, but you'll never hear me say that on the record," laughed Kargenian.

Olsen, however, was serious. "Look," he said, "administrative assistants and secretaries do just about the same work around this place. For you to specify age and gender is unfair to many people who are able to do the work you want done. What happened to giving everyone an equal chance? You have to treat people equally unless you can find some reason why they are different."

"That's silly, Olsen. I treat people who seem different as if they are different unless I find a reason to treat them equally."

"Come on, Kargenian, discrimination on the basis of gender is way out of step with the times."

"Look, Olsen, would you quit with this gender talk. What's wrong with the word 'sex'? Or, don't you ever discriminate between boys and girls. Well, to me a healthy young woman is a whole lot more attractive than any man I know!"

"Kargenian, what's with you? We're talking about job opportunities, not sex partners."

"Fine, then. So let's talk jobs. Women aren't as strong or as smart as men, so they don't deserve the same jobs or the same pay."

"What scientific basis is there for saying they're not as smart? That's plain nonsense! And besides good looks aren't important given what you put in the job description. Now, if you were hiring a model...."

"Looks count with me, Buster. And what about the differences in physical strength?"

"Kargenian, what rock have you been living under? What difference does physical strength make on this job. Anyone who can lift 30 pounds is strong enough. The union agreement requires we call in the movers for anything heavier. Any woman who can lift a four-year-old child can handle your physical strength requirement. The job is really no different than the administrative assistant's job that pays $14.00."

"Fine, you win, Olsen. I'm scratching the business about age and sex out of the vacancy notice. But I can't be held responsible for what special factors I might consider as I review applications or conduct interviews."

"You can try to zero in on the relevant factors if you put your mind to it, Kargenian. But if you have trouble, why don't you let me interview the candidates with you?"

2.1 Formal vs. Material Principles of Justice

The ultimate or first principle of distributive justice is the formal principle: *treat relevantly similar cases similarly and treat relevantly different cases differently in proportion to the difference(s) between them*. This principle entails that injustice is done when similar persons are treated differently or when persons who are different are treated similarly. It is called a *formal* principle *because it does not specify what respects are to be counted as relevant similarities or differences* among persons. No two cases or persons will ever have absolutely all characteristics in common, but that does not answer the question of whether they are the same or different with respect to their morally relevant characteristics. In turn, *material* principles of justice are precisely those principles which *do specify which are to count as the morally relevant similarities or differences* among persons.

For example, it is just to give students the same grade unless they deserve different grades and different grades unless they deserve the same grade. That expresses the formal principle of justice. But, what differences are materially relevant to deciding what treatment they deserve? One we can readily accept is that the quality of their work is materially relevant. If two students do the same quality of work, they should get the same grade, and if one does much better work than the other, then she should get a much better grade than the other. It seems intuitive from a formal point of view, that different grades should be given only where there are relevant differences between the two students. And, it is most plausible to suggest that material differences in the quality of the work should weigh most heavily in determining differences in the grades. It is also plausible that other differences between students should not be counted as relevant. For example, eye color, family income, gender, popularity, physical attractiveness, number of siblings, shoe size, and many other differences are not materially relevant when it comes to distributing grades justly.

2.2 Differences One Cannot Control

The formal principle of justice suggests that some characteristics are not relevant differences among persons whereas others are. Many have suggested that characteristics for which no one can bear any responsibility and over which one has little or no control, such as eye color, race, gender, native ability, and the like, are not to be counted as relevant similarities or differences when justice is being considered. As an example, consider a legislative proposal which would restrict child care income tax benefits only to expenses for the care of one's first child. Considerations of the kind now under discussion suggest that such a proposal might be unjust on the grounds that there is no relevant material difference between the first child's need for care and the needs of subsequent children for care while the parent is at work. None of the children are responsible for being first, second, third, or later. And each child needs care. In effect the argument is, then, that the only material difference that generally exists between such a first child and later children is one for which these children are not responsible and could not possibly have controlled. Therefore, this difference cannot be counted as a relevant one in their treatment.

We are not saying that something must be in one's control to be a material principle of justice. Nor are we saying that it is unjust to discriminate between persons on the basis of anything but those characteristics over which they have control. There are circumstances in which we can make discriminatory judgments on the basis of factors over which persons have no control. And, we do justifiably make such judgments. For example, in deciding which persons one might want to have on an athletic team, or in a drama company, one would be foolish not to consider native talents and raw abilities over which the person could be said to have little, if any control and for which the person is not responsible. Certainly other factors over which one has some control are also relevant; for example making the most of one's native talent is another factor, as is attitude and work ethic. But native talents one is born with are factors over which a person has no control and yet on the basis of which, in some kinds of cases, it would be reasonable to discriminate.

The entire discussion in the case study is based upon what appears to be the shared acceptance of the formal principle of justice by both Olsen and Kargenian. They are both concerned about whether there are relevant material differences in the potential male and female job applicants. Kargenian seems uncertain about what the relevant differences and similarities might be in assessing applicants for the job, but he and Olsen never waver from the view that the relevant characteristics should be identified, so that any difference in treatment can be based on differences with respect to those characteristics. Olsen presses Kargenian to be specific, and Kargenian somewhat begrudgingly acknowledges that it is important to address

Olsen's questions. Another question raised in the case study, but never handled thoroughly, concerns the justice of the differences in salary between (female) secretaries and (male) administrative assistants—two apparently identical jobs. If you experience a lingering concern about this, it indicates that you, too, accept the formal principle of justice and feel a need to specify *relevant material differences* where persons are treated differently.

2.3 Proportional Treatment

Besides highlighting the importance of identifying some relevant similarities and differences among persons, the formal principle of justice requires that any differences in treatment be directly *proportional* to the relevant material differences. If the quality of one student's work was only slightly better than another's, then the one deserves only a slightly better grade. By contrast a third student whose work is markedly inferior to that of the other two deserves a markedly lower grade. If one person were slightly more deserving, given slight differences in relevant characteristics, it would be an injustice to treat that person much differently from the others with whom he is compared. Likewise, slight difference in treatment is unjust if there is a great difference in desert.

Consider the issue of justly proportioning punishment to offenses. Those who commit crimes differ materially from those who do not. It is commonly believed that we should relate the severity of the punishments to the seriousness of crimes. We also believe that some forms of punishment should be rejected as cruel and unusual. It used to be that pickpockets were publicly hanged. That practice appears unjust in terms of the requirement that differences in treatment be directly proportionate to differences in desert. While pickpockets may well deserve different treatment, it seems implausible that their relatively slight offense justifies so great a penalty. On the other hand, many today suggest that white collar crime and crimes committed by privileged classes are among the most serious of offenses, greatly affecting many lives. Some argue that there is a real injustice in allowing such criminals to be punished only slightly if at all. [Note that throughout this discussion no specific (material) criteria have been specified for determining what makes crimes minor or serious; the discussion has remained formal.]G

The case study poses a question of the justice of a major salary difference between secretaries and administrative assistants, when there is no discernible difference in the jobs. If there is a difference in the jobs, is it so great as to justify an hourly wage difference of over 40%?

2.4 Correlation of Distributions with Deserts

While the formal principle of justice does not tell us what material characteristics make a person *deserving* or what sort of *proportional distribution* she ought to receive for that desert, it does suggest the relationship of the desert to the distribution. To see this relationship, imagine an absurd practice in which it would be violated.

Imagine that persons who worked hard and were very productive were therefore penalized. The harder they worked and the more they produced, the more severe their punishments. Similarly imagine that people who caused other persons trouble, pain, hardship, and suffering were rewarded, with the greatest rewards going to those causing the most damage and pain. Should we call these arrangements just? Direct proportionality is maintained here—but rewards are directly proportioned to the creation of burdens, and punishments to the creation of benefits. These practices, even though they maintain proportionality, run contrary to the concept of justice. Why? Because the concept of justice involves distinguishing between benefits and burdens, rewards and punishments, so that rewards go to those who create benefits (things of positive value) and punishments to those who create burdens (things of negative value). To conceive of the treatments in our imagined cases as just would require imagining that pain has a positive value and productive work a negative value.

2.5 Equality and Formal Justice

Often the concern for justice is identified with the concern for equality. For example, a supervisor who favors his friends when deciding shift times can be accused of not treating everyone "equally." That would be the same as accusing the supervisor of using an irrelevant factor, personal friendship, as a material principle of justice in the case of distributing the benefits of good shifts and burdens of undesirable shifts. In other words, the supervisor should be reminded that formal justice requires that he ought to have a materially relevant basis for treating people dissimilarly and personal friendship is not such a basis. But great care must be taken whenever talking about justice in using the word *equality*. Talk of equality is often confused, and it is important to discern what is meant when people invoke the term *equality*.

At least three things can be meant by the claim "Everyone should be treated equally." On the first interpretation, the concern for *equality* is identical with the concern for justice as captured in the formal principle of justice. Here, "Everyone should be treated equally," simply understates the full meaning of the formal principle. Indeed, another way of phrasing the formal principle is to say that those who are equal in relevant respects are to be treated equally and those who are unequal in relevant respects are to be treated unequally in proportion to the relevant inequality. The concern for equality can remain quite formal, inasmuch as none of the important respects in which persons may be equal or unequal is specified. In this sense of equality the discussion in the case study is focused as much upon equality as upon justice.

2.6 Equality and Material Justice

In a second and non-formal interpretation, *equality* becomes a disguise for a material principle of justice (that is, one that specifies some characteristic to be morally relevant for deciding that people are to be treated similarly or differently). Unfortunately, using the term *equality* in this way often is confusing and misleading. To see how this can happen, consider a possible discussion about treating wage earners *equally*. Suppose we have two families of different sizes with one wage earner each. Someone might maintain that treating equals equally means that since each worker is one worker and each does one job, then each should be given an equal salary. Someone else, however, might note that the first worker is working to support eight people and the second to support two people. This person might argue that treating equals equally and unequals unequally here requires that the one worker receive four times the salary of the other, since this is the proportion of the inequality of need between them.

Can you see how, by referencing equality, the two opinions about allocating salaries justly invoke more than a formal conception of justice? The evaluators are implicitly invoking their views on the *material respects in which equality is to count*. What are the relevant respects, in other words, for two parties to count as equals? One invokes the material principle that salary is to be proportioned to work done, and the other that salary is to be proportioned to the need as measured by the number of people to be supported. It would be better in such discussions if talk proceeded explicitly in terms of the material principles of work or need and their relative merits, rather than in a confusing and misleading manner where both speak of *equality* but each means something different by it.

In the case study the issue of equal pay for equal work is implicitly raised when it becomes clear that men are paid more than women for a job involving virtually the same work. You can probably pick out the material elements in this practice, if you recall that the formal assertion of equality would not go beyond the idea that persons who are equally deserving should receive equal distributions. Material elements enter the picture when we say that equality in work makes persons equally deserving, and equality in pay means that they have been equally rewarded.

2.7 Strict Equalitarianism

A third and also non-formal and material interpretation construes *equality* in the strict "one person one share" sense. When the concern for equality is invoked in either of the manners discussed above, it is about what has come to be called *proportional equality*—that persons are to be treated differently only *in proportion* to their inequality. Advocates of *strict equality*, however, are interested in having equality itself accepted as a *material* principle of justice. *Strict equalitarianism would require that all benefits and burdens be distributed equally to all persons, with each person receiving an equal share.* Typically strict equalitarianism is based on the belief in the equal humanity of all persons, regardless of other differences among them which might exist. While it is often maintained and acknowledged that such an equal humanity secures to all persons certain moral rights (see Chapter 5, Section 3), it is quite different to claim that being human qualifies a person for an equal share in the distribution of all of the benefits and burdens individuals or societies can bestow.

Many find the strict equalitarian principle, if taken literally, absurd. They argue that in addition to whatever common humanity people enjoy it is clear that they differ in important respects. It would be utter folly, for example, and surely an injustice, to subject all persons to open-heart surgery when only a few need it, or to demand that everyone pay for a freeway that only a few could ever possibly use. The absurdity of such cases may lead a strict equalitarian to argue that he has been misunderstood; what he advocates is each person's being given an equal share of society's resources in order that the differing needs of each may be met. Similarly, all persons are to carry equal burdens or responsibilities. Opponents reply that even this version overlooks the obvious fact that some needs of some people (such as the need for open-heart surgery) are far more expensive than others, and strict apportionment of wealth would make meeting those vital needs impossible. Similarly, since some people are much more able than others, equal burdens might well imply burdening the less able with *responsibilities* beyond their capacities. If the equalitarian replies that benefits ought to be distributed in proportion to need, or burdens proportioned to abilities, then strict equality has been abandoned and a concern for equality proportioned to need or ability has taken its place. However, the equalitarian might propose that whatever our needs, we will all be given an equal share of resources with which to respond to them—similar to the practice of some health insurance companies which limit their coverage to $1,000,000 regardless of what kinds of health services are being paid for. But how might the strict equalitarian respond in the case of distributing responsibilities?

2.8 Presumptions of Equality and Inequality

Let us go back to the first understanding of concern for equality as presented in 2.6, the one that identifies concern for equality with concern for justice as specified in the formal principle of justice. Even when it is agreed that equality is to be understood formally, a problem arises, because often we must make decisions of justice in a state of at least partial ignorance where time does not allow us to overcome that ignorance. We may be uncertain whether people are alike or different in morally relevant respects. *Rules stating how we are to proceed in circumstances where we are ignorant yet we must decide due to time constraints are called presumptions.* Many who value equal treatment of all persons think that justice requires, given such uncertainty, that persons should be presumed to be equal and, thus, treated equally, until it is shown that they differ in morally relevant respects and are, therefore, deserving of different treatments. They acknowledge that people are not strictly equal in all respects but suggest that the *burden of proof* falls upon those who would treat people differently to provide an account of their reasons for doing so. In this view, only exceptions to equal treatment require justification.

Yet, the formal principle of justice would seem to indicate that a second presumption is also possible and sometimes reasonable: that *where people are seemingly different, they should be treated differently until it is shown that they are alike in morally relevant respects.* Once their likeness is demonstrated, they can be treated equally. In this view, some exceptions to unequal treatment require justification.

The question of which presumption is to be operative in a given set of circumstances depends upon what is believed or known about the respects in which the persons involved are alike or different. Thus, if persons are believed to be alike in some relevant respects, then the first *presumption of equality* would seem to apply: the burden of proof or justification would fall upon those who wish to treat the persons differently. On the other hand, if persons are believed to be different in some relevant respects, then the second *presumption of inequality* would seem to apply: the burden of proof or justification would fall upon those who wish to treat the persons alike.

As illustration of both of these presumptions in operation, consider two pairs of managers who have completed an important assignment. The first pair has come to the assignment with similar abilities, and the quality of their work is equally high. Given what is known in this case, it is safe to presume that each will be given the same salary bonus. If it turns out that one receives a bonus and the other is fired, the burden of proof would seem to fall on their supervisor to justify the difference in treatment. Consider now the second pair of managers. They are known to differ greatly in ability, and their work more than reflects that difference. One has done an extremely good job, the other is a disaster who only makes problems and never solves any. The work of the first reflects her care and effort, the work of the second shows that she has no apparent concern to do the assignment well. Given what is known in this case, it is reasonable to presume that different actions will be taken in their two cases. If it turns out that both managers are fired, or both are given bonuses, or even if both continue to draw their salaries without ever a word being spoken in praise of the one and criticism of the other, then the burden of proof would seem to fall on the supervisor to justify the equality of treatment of two such different managers.

In the case study Olsen and Kargenian confess that they are operating on these two different presumptions of equality and inequality. Olsen says, "You have to treat people equally unless you can find some reason why they are different." Kargenian calls Olsen's presumption silly, saying, "I treat people who seem different as if they are different unless I find reason to treat them equally." In this particular case, Olsen's presumption is more appropriate, given what we know about how strength and good looks are rarely relevant respects for distinguishing men and women as applicants for this job and especially what we know about their irrelevance for distinguishing between secretaries and administrative assistants. But if we did not happen to know these things, if the facts were quite different, if we knew that strength and good looks were often extremely relevant and indeed crucial in distinguishing between secretaries and administrative assistants, the way they are relevant in distinguishing between body-builders or professional dancers, then the opposite presumption, the presumption of inequality, would be the appropriate one.

2.9 Culturally Relative Presumptions

You should be very careful here about whether presumptions of inequality or of equality are culturally relative. If you will reflect a moment about part of the history of women in our culture, you will get a clearer view of this question of relativity. There was a time when (a) many secretaries were required to lift up to 100 pounds or more, and (b) women were widely believed to be substantially less smart than men. Given that, for whatever reason, most women were then unable to lift 100 pounds, and assuming that believing women intellectually inferior to men was at least plausible—given that women were denied access to many educational opportunities— it would be reasonable for any person, on these bases, to presume that women are relevantly different from men with respect to a job requiring significant strength and intelligence. However, when the job changes so that lifting no more than 30 pounds is required, then, objectively, the strength to lift 100 pounds simply becomes irrelevant to the job. And when the empirical evidence that women are certainly not the intellectual inferiors of men has already become quite clear, it is objectively no longer reasonable to presume women relevantly different from men with respect to this job; contrarily, it is reasonable to presume them relevantly similar.

2.10 Presumptions of Innocence or Guilt

Let us look at two spheres where the presumptive principles of justice operate in our everyday thinking about what is fair, and where the presumptions do seem to make a difference. Consider first the presumption in our American judicial system that all who are charged with crimes are innocent until proven guilty. This may be taken as an instance of the first principle: people should be presumed equal until it is established that they are not so. In this case it is presumed that all are alike in being innocent, and the burden of proof falls on prosecutors to establish guilt beyond a reasonable doubt. It is obvious that the presence of this presumption as an *operating procedure* makes our judicial process quite different from other possible systems where no such presumption of innocence is operative. The contrast is even greater if a system is imagined to hold the opposite presumption—where persons charged with crimes are presumed to be guilty until they are able to prove themselves innocent.

By contrast consider a case where the presumption of inequality is operative. In our society parents treat their own children differently than they treat the children of others. Parents make differential distributions of the benefits they have at their disposal. It would not seem odd at all if parents invested in piano lessons for all of their children and did not send their neighbors' children to take similar lessons. Here parents presume that their children are unequal to their neighborhood peers, in that the parents are related in an especially important way to their own children. It would seem odd, and even unfair, if parents denied their children piano lessons that they could well afford because they could not provide lessons for children not their own.

EXERCISES

1. Below is a list of statements which indicate that some treatment is for some reason either just or unjust. Distinguish those statements invoking formal principles of justice (*FPJ*) from those invoking material principles (*MPJ*). When a formal principle is invoked, also distinguish whether it is that of treating similar cases similarly (*SS*) or of treating dissimilar cases dissimilarly in proportion to the differences between them (*DD*). (2.1–2.4)

___(a) Since both men worked equally hard, they earned the same money.

___(b) They were treated the same because there was no difference between them.

___(c) Mary and Alice should not have been assigned such different jobs, since there's only a small difference between them.

___(d) Mark and Bill need the same money for food, since their appetites are equally large.

___(e) Sally should have been the more highly praised, since she tried the hardest.

___(f) Merideth deserved the raise, because Alison plagiarized her report to impress those at the meeting.

___(g) A merit raise policy that makes no distinctions between very unlike persons cannot be just.

___(h) Greater privileges should normally be given to senior children.

___(i) People shouldn't make distinctions in how they treat people, unless those treated differently are really different.

___(j) The darker a person's skin, the better he should be treated.

2. (a) Below is a list of statements that employ some concept or another of equality. Distinguish the use of a formal principle of proportional equality (*FPPE*) from the use of a material principle of proportional equality (*MPPE*) and from the use of a material principle of strict equality (MPSE). (2.5–2.7)

___1. If Jonas and Zeb are going to be treated equally, then Jonas should be given the greater reward, because he did more work.

___2. Since these entering freshmen are all equal, one no different from another, they should all take the same courses.

___3. When two groups are equal, they ought to be treated equally; that's only fair.

___4. If the Abbotts and the Babbitts are only a bit unequal, while the Abbotts and the Cabots are very unequal, then the differences between the treatments of the Abbotts and the Cabots should be greater than the differences between the treatments of the Abbotts and the Babbitts.

___5. Dorothy's pay should not be equal to Kevin's, because he has his whole family to support whereas Dorothy is only supplementing her husband's income.

(b) State what distinguishes a principle as formal in contrast to material.

3. Below is a list of statements. Some state a principle of justice, either formal or material. Mark those either *FPJ* or *MPJ*. Some state a presumption of justice, either a presumption of similarity (*PS*) or a presumption of dissimilarity (*PD*). (2.8–2.10)

___(a) In general, persons' backgrounds should be considered similar until proved dissimilar.

___(b) Persons known to have passed organic chemistry, however, should be considered different unless known to be similar.

___(c) Equals should always be treated equally.

___(d) You can't assume that a person should be licensed as a doctor until she's proved qualified.

___(e) We assume that our customers in good standing can meet their debts until experience shows that they cannot.

___(f) Larger contributions should be expected from persons of greater abilities.

___(g) More help should be available to persons with greater needs.

___(h) The difference in treatment between two persons should be proportioned to differences between the persons.

___(i) Whites should be assumed to be as intelligent as blacks until proven otherwise.

___(j) Persons from similar backgrounds should be given similar opportunities.

4. Abstractly state the circumstances in which no presumptions concerning similarities or dissimilarities would be appropriate.

DISCUSSION QUESTIONS

1. Suppose you must specify the admission requirements for a highly competitive medical school. Your duty is to be just and to specify the material considerations which are relevant for admission. In addition to distributing the benefits of admission fairly, you also may consider compensatory and retributive factors, not only with regard to the characteristics of applicants but with regard to the characteristics of the sub-groups in the population whom these applicants, once trained and licensed, will very likely serve.

2. Consider the distribution of fringe benefits on the basis of need, for example, giving some employees child care at company expense, or granting maternity leaves with pay. To justify this, which side of the debate has the burden of proof?

3. Recall the example of the income tax break for child care in 2.2. It might be argued that the proposal is not unjust. Such an argument would focus not on how the children are treated but on how the taxpayer is treated. Having children is something thought to be in the control of the working parent. Hence discriminating between those who decide to limit their family to one child and those who decide to have more than one might be a materially relevant basis. What do you think? Is the proposal just or unjust?

4. The United States Supreme Court has ruled that voluntary programs of affirmative action in the case of hiring and promotion are legal. Such programs give advantage to members of under-represented groups on the basis of criteria over which those persons have no control, such as gender and race. Evaluate the material principles of justice used in such cases.

ANSWERS TO SELECTED EXERCISES

1. (a) *MPJ*

   (b) *FPJ, SS*

   (c) *FPJ, DD* (problem is one of proportionality).

   (d) *MPJ*

(e) *MPJ*

(f) *MPJ*

(g) *FPJ, DD*

(h) *MPJ*

(i) *FPJ, SS*

2. (a) 1. *MPPE* 2. *MPSE* 3. *FPPE* 4. *FPPE* 5. *MPPE*

(b) In a formal principle the similarity or dissimilarity of treatment is related merely to similarity or dissimilarity of the people treated, without specifying the respects in which the people are similar or dissimilar because of which they deserve to be treated similarly or dissimilarly, respectively. A material principle, in contrast, includes a specification of the characteristics of people in virtue of which they ought to be treated similarly or dissimilarly.

3. (a) *PS*

(b) *PD*

(c) *FPJ*

(d) *PS*: persons should be presumed to be unfit to be licensed as doctors until proved otherwise.

(e) *PS*

(f) *MPJ*

(g) *MPJ*

(h) *FPJ*

(i) *PS*

(j) *MPJ*

4. If, with respect to each of the characteristics that were relevant to how people ought to be treated, one knew which characteristics each person had, then one would know whether the people were similar or different in each of the relevant respects. Under that condition, there would be no need at all for presumptions of similarity or dissimilarity. Thus, human ignorance about which of the relevant characteristics each person has is a necessary condition for its being appropriate to make presumptions of similarity or dissimilarity.

Section 3
CRITERIA OF MATERIAL JUSTICE

The formal principle of justice does not tell us which characteristics of people are morally relevant in deciding how to treat people. Proposals suggesting which factors should be relevant are called *material principles of justice*. In this section we examine various material principles of justice. We shall consider the range of criteria proposed as marking significant differences among persons. The principal criteria to be examined in some detail are related to work and to need. We shall examine circumstances where it is plausible to suppose that these criteria apply and others where it is implausible. After studying Section 3, you should be able to:

- Distinguish ability, productivity, effort, and need as standards of material justice.

- Match the justifications traditionally provided for each of these standards of material justice with the standard it attempts to justify.
- Match possible social circumstances with the standard of material justice each tends to make appropriate.
- Compare and contrast circumstances of overabundance and extreme scarcity as they bear on the virtue of justice.

THE CASE OF THE SENATOR AND THE SOCIAL WORKER

"The Senate Committee on Labor and Welfare special hearings on welfare reform are now in session. Please be seated." The chairperson's familiar words rang through the crowded hearing room. "The chair recognizes Senator Judith Dexter for the purpose of questioning Mr. Lestroff, the special witness representing the Social Workers for Reform Association. Senator Dexter."

"Thank you.   Now, Mr. Lestroff, you testified yesterday concerning three programs: The Food for Children Program, which assists with hot lunches in schools and day care centers; the Job Retraining Program, which prepares middle-aged people for mid-life career changes; and the Unemployment Compensation Program, which is basically a government hand-out for those too lazy to go out and find work. I can support the first two programs; but I strongly object to the third. There's no reason to pay these people. Work is available in this country. They're able to work, aren't they? The work pays well enough. So, it is my judgment that those who are unwilling to use their talents to take these jobs are at fault. They don't have any handouts coming to them, especially when the money comes from the pockets of hard-working taxpayers. If they fail to find the work that is out there to be done, or if they fail to perform satisfactorily at jobs they are qualified for, then that's their problem—not the government's. Their needs could be met by their own honest effort, and we should not step into the picture. Don't you agree, sir?"

Lestroff had known of the Senator's long-standing objections and had done his best to prepare.   Although he felt strongly about the issue, he checked his emotions. These people needed this program. And he was not going to mess things up by being irrational at these crucial hearings. "I might agree, Senator, except for four serious problems: First, in some areas of the nation there is not enough work; or if there are jobs, they are jobs for which the people in this program are not qualified. You cannot turn an out-of-work engineer into a health-care professional overnight. Even given that some of these people can be retrained in time to take advantage of job opportunities, there are others who simply lack the mental or physical skills to hold the more demanding jobs required by our technological society. These untrainable persons also need support. That they do not fit a job slot in our society is no fault of their own. Second, there are some jobs, especially for unskilled workers, that just do not pay enough to support an individual. Some jobs are seasonal, others are only part-time, some just pay too little and are useful only as second-income jobs. A high school kid might be able to get along working at a fast food outlet and living off his parents, but some of the people this program is helping are middle-aged folks with kids of their own to support.   Third, given the government's unwillingness or inability to move unemployment below the 5 percent level, there always will be people who need this program. Fourth, some people are in need of this program because they cannot work owing to disabilities or to their responsibilities to care for small children or sick and aging parents. Until we adequately fund day care centers, there will remain a large number of persons who are physically able and willing to take a job, but who could do so only by neglecting others. No, Senator, on balance I cannot agree with your assessment. There is a need for this program."

3.1 Material Principles of Justice

Finding adequate material principles of justice is crucial if the formal principle of justice is to be fleshed out and made fully usable. Without material principles there would be no specification of which characteristics of persons are to count as morally relevant in making decisions about the distribution of benefits and burdens. The formal principle of justice does not tell us which factors ought to be considered relevant; it tells us how to proceed once we have decided what those relevant factors are.

Factors over which persons have little or no control can be considered materially relevant in certain circumstances.   For example, natural talent, intelligence, sensitivity, temperament, attitude, judgment, or strength of character, can be, in specified contexts, relevant bases for discriminating between persons in terms of how they are treated. Although one can endeavor to develop one's native talents, to refine one's judgment or to increase one's sensitivity, there are limits to how far self-improvement programs in these areas can go. Given persons with equal ability, experience and potential, the decision as to which will be selected to receive some benefit, such as a promotion, along with all the burdens and responsibilities it entails, is a decision reasonably made on the basis of characteristics such as those listed above, even though they are characteristics over which the person has little or no control.

On the other hand, other characteristics over which people have little or no control are widely regarded as unacceptable criteria for determining desert. Thus, it is clearly possible, and too often true, that in housing, employment practices, and the distribution of a community's services, persons may be treated differently because of their caste, ethnicity, religion, class, race, gender, or age. Yet it is widely recognized that practices such as elitism, classism, racism, sexism, and ageism amount to arbitrary and unjustifiable discrimination and constitute some of the most blatant cases of injustice known.

By contrast to such things as race, gender and ethnicity, both the work and the need criterion—the two prime candidates for material principles of justice—may be understood as having a greater initial plausibility as criteria for making justifiable discriminations between persons. In the case of the work criteria, it is reasonable to suppose that people are being held responsible for something over which they can exercise some control, namely their own labor. In most cases persons can be held responsible for the development of their abilities, the quality of the work they do, or the amount of effort they put into their work.

In the case of the need criterion, it is reasonable to suggest that persons are on roughly equal footing as persons. That is, they all have some very basic human needs, such as nourishment, shelter, and the like. On this criterion people are equally deserving of having these needs met. They are easily met in an affluent society. Though it is not reasonable to suppose that people are responsible for their having such needs, neither is it reasonable to suppose that whether a person's needs are met is morally neutral. Moreover, people can, typically, do something about seeing to it that their needs are satisfied, whereas nothing can he done, with rare exceptions, about one's caste, class, race, sex, or age.

3.2 The Work Criterion—Ability

One of the two principal contenders as a material principle of justice is the work criterion. Many have argued that it is reasonable to distinguish among persons in the distribution of benefits and burdens in terms of equality or inequality of their work. You should notice, however, that this is really no simple criterion but rather a cluster of criteria, all somehow being work-related characteristics of persons. Thus, in order to treat the subject responsibly, we need to break it down into at least three sub-criteria relating to: (1) ability to work, (2) productivity in work, or (3) effort invested in work.

Consider first the work criterion relating to *ability*. This criterion gains its plausibility from the obvious differences in the abilities required to perform various tasks, the importance we attach to what can be done with some abilities, and the relative rarity of the development of those abilities. Thus, if there is a rationale for the high earnings of doctors or judges, it seems not to be a function of either their higher productivity or effort, although it is recognized that both must invest much effort in cultivating their special abilities. It would seem, rather, to be much more a function of the importance we attach to their abilities and to health or satisfactory resolutions of legal problems. Similarly, sanitation workers and day laborers tend to receive a low salary, again because of the value we place on the service they provide and because the ability needed in their work is not very specialized, sophisticated, or scarce. In the case study this difference in rewards for jobs as a function of the skills required to do them is mentioned by Mr. Lestroff. The legitimacy of assigning salaries in accord with such considerations is never questioned by either the social worker or the senator. Should it be?

Some question the ability criterion, holding that it is most important that persons be treated differently only when they can reasonably be held responsible for the differences between them. While one can be said to be responsible for how well one develops the abilities one has, people do not have much control over the native abilities they have to begin with. This has been taken as arguing against distributing benefits on the basis of abilities. There is another side to the question of distribution, however, the issue of the distribution of burdens. Where this is the primary concern, few have taken exception to the notion that it is reasonable to hold persons responsible for developing and performing to the best of their abilities. Those who work to less than their full potential have been thought less deserving than those who work as best they can. Some people argue that it is only fair that those with rare and useful abilities be asked to develop them.

3.3 The Work Criterion—Productivity

Many view the second work criterion, *productivity* or contribution, as more satisfactory. It seems that people can more easily be held accountable for the amount of work they do. Thus, many think it is fair to pay fully productive persons, or persons who make significant contributions in their field, more than relatively unproductive or lazy persons, who make little if any significant contribution. In cases where piecework is being done, it is clearest that payment is being made in a manner strictly proportional to the productivity of the workers. Hourly wages and distinctions between salaries for part-time and full-time work may reflect differences in productivity over differing periods of time. One possible reading of the senator's concern in the case study is to take it as a concern that the Unemployment Compensation Program unfairly rewards nonproductive workers who could be productive if they would simply go out and do the work that, in the senator's view, is waiting to be done. In her view unemployed persons not only are unproductive but are responsible for not doing productive work.

It becomes difficult to measure productivity or contribution when we go from thinking about the kind of work done on assembly lines or by manual laborers in other fields to thinking about the kind of work done by teachers, nurses, administrators, executives, scientists, artists, entertainers, athletes, diplomats, ministers, lawyers, and a number of other professions. Just how is productivity in such fields to be conceptualized? How are contributions of persons in such fields, including some of the greatest achievements in history, to be compared with and rewarded proportionately to the productivity of the average laborer who puts in a full day in an auto assembly plant? Moreover, there seems to be a connection between making contributions in such fields and having the abilities to make such contributions. Besides, it is also true that at times good fortune or unusual developments beyond one's control play a big part in making such contributions or achievements possible. Given these facts, some argue that not everyone has an equal opportunity to make these contributions. They argue that people are not accountable for these differences of opportunity between them and that, therefore, differential treatment on this basis is not just.

3.4 The Work Criterion—Effort

One work-related matter where there does seem to be equal opportunity and where it is, therefore, more plausible to hold people responsible is the *effort* that people invest in whatever work they do. It is because of this advantage over the ability and productivity criteria that some have defended effort as a standard of material justice. On this criterion, hard-working manual laborers, health-care professionals, executives, ministers, and artists all would be compensated equally for their efforts, and less hard-working people in whatever field would be compensated to a proportionately lesser degree. Thus, a lazy doctor or judge would be paid less than a hard-working garbage collector. Another reading of the senator's concern in the case study is to take it as a concern about the difference in the efforts of those who work regularly and those who are unemployed and served by the Unemployment Compensation Program. She mentions that it is unfair to treat "lazy" non-workers as deserving of the same rewards as hard-working taxpayers who are making genuine efforts to meet their own needs.

While effort is in some ways the strongest of the work criteria of material justice, it also has weaknesses. The clear but unhappy possibility is that, through lack of ability or knowledge, the productivity of a person may be very low even though his or her effort is great. According to the effort criterion, such a person's efforts would yield great rewards. Yet such rewards seem problematic in two ways. First, from whose labors are these great rewards to come? Clearly, the more productive workers will have to prop up these hard-working, but less productive workers. The intuitiveness of the productivity criterion argues against this solution.

The second problem is more abstract. You will recall that questions of justice arise because of conditions of scarcity. If benefits become too scarce, however, no just distribution will be possible, for there will be little or nothing to distribute. Here some thinkers invoke the value judgment that it is better for conditions to remain such that just distributions are possible than for conditions to become so bad that questions of justice become irrelevant in a sea of misfortune. Their point is that using the effort criterion of material justice is in tension with securing the conditions under which justice remains a virtue. The more resources are expended on persons whose efforts are insufficient to meet their own needs, the less resources can be reserved to protect against catastrophe.

3.5 The Need Criterion

In the case study, while the senator focuses on the work criterion, the social worker's position is based on a very different set of considerations. Mr. Lestroff, the social worker, is much more concerned about the need criterion. He is especially concerned about the needs of untrainable or disabled persons as well as persons who, in his view, are locked out of the sophisticated economy where they could earn sufficiently to meet their needs. Their needs, as he sees them, remain deserving of serious attention.

The need criterion is the principal alternative to work as a proposed material principle of justice. In this view it is thought just to treat people differently in proportion to their needs. Indeed, many think it part of the concept of respect for persons that their particular needs be understood and appreciated. (For a discussion of this concept, see Chapter 5, Section 3.) The concept of human need is a complicated one, however, and it is important for us to analyze it. Let us say that a person needs something if he would suffer without it. Some needs may be called *survival needs*; they are so basic that without them a person's survival would be threatened. The needs for such things as food, water, shelter, health care, and the like are generally recognized as falling into this category and as being needs that all have equally, by virtue of their being persons.

As society becomes more complex, it may well be that other things are needed in this most basic sense, such as transportation (so that one can get to work) or education (so that one can manage one's life in a sophisticated and rapidly changing social environment). In the case of other needs, even though survival would not be threatened, the quality of people's lives would be compromised significantly if what they needed were not available to them. Thus, various things are necessary for the accomplishment of particular goals or purposes that people come to believe to be important to give meaning to their lives. Failure to meet such needs can make people very unhappy.

3.6 Earned vs. Deserved

It is important to note in discussing both the work and the need criteria of material justice that there is a distinction to be drawn between what a person has *earned* and what a person *deserves*. In all foregoing discussion we have focused primarily on what a person deserves. This leaves open the question as to whether his deserts depend on what he has earned. The most fundamental question of material justice is why persons *deserve* anything, or, put another way, "What is the basis for their deserving whatever they do deserve?"

One of the several most frequent answers to this question is that they deserve what they earn. It is obvious that those who defend work criteria, especially the productivity and effort criteria, are concerned that persons must earn their deserts. Yet, it is equally clear that need is a strong contender as a possible standard of material justice and that, however deserving a needy person may be, persons do not, in any sense, earn their needs. As an example, consider educational opportunities. People generally believe that children deserve these opportunities. It is plausible to say that a person needs and deserves a high school education. It is also plausible to say that through success in college a person has earned the opportunity to attend professional school or graduate school. Note, however, that having earned this opportunity, deciding whether the student is to be admitted, given a relative scarcity of places in the entering class, is a matter of desert.

3.7 Work, Need, and Social Circumstances

Work and need have been shown to be standards of material justice with a great deal of plausibility. The work criterion derives its plausibility at least in part from the idea that persons deserve what they earn. On the other hand, the need criterion gains its plausibility from the idea that there are some basic needs that all persons have in common by virtue of their being persons. These needs are deserving of attention if we are to remain respectful of human beings. Let us now consider how differences of social circumstance may be understood as influencing the applicability of these criteria.

First, consider social circumstances where all of the following conditions are met: (a) there is sufficient work so that there are jobs for all who need them, (b) the jobs available to each person include jobs that the person has the abilities to perform, and (c) the jobs pay well enough so that whenever a person takes one, it will enable her to earn enough so that her needs are met. Many would argue that in circumstances such as these, people have a responsibility to do the work. They hold that people are at fault if they do not work and, therefore, do not earn enough to meet their needs. In circumstances such as these the work criterion in some version appears completely applicable, and there is nothing unjust about not meeting the needs of persons who are capable of meeting their own needs but simply choose not to do so.

As the social worker in the case study argued, social circumstances can differ by not meeting the conditions specified above. (a) It may be that there are fewer jobs than there are people who need them. (b) Persons may be unable to perform the jobs that are available owing to simple lack of ability, impairment, or other obligations, such as the obligation to care for a child or a parent. The lack of ability may be socially dependent in the sense that skills that people do have can become outmoded and no longer needed in a rapidly changing and technologically progressive society. Or it may be that in a nation as a whole there are sufficient jobs to match the abilities of the people, but the people with the abilities are not located where the jobs are, and inadequate provision is made for getting the people and the jobs together. It could also be that some are denied opportunities to do the work for which they are qualified owing to various forms of job discrimination. (c) It may be that the jobs for which some people qualify, or that they are able to handle given their other responsibilities, simply do not pay well enough to meet their needs. The wages may be extremely low, or the work may be part-time or seasonal. It is plausible to suggest that the greater the extent to which the conditions specified in the preceding paragraph are compromised, the more reasonable the application of the need criterion becomes.

In any of the varieties of circumstances just described it is difficult to fault a person for being unable to meet his own needs. If the proposition is accepted that there are basic needs that all persons, as persons, deserve to have met, then justice requires that those needs be met where persons cannot meet them for themselves.

It is precisely the applicability of the work vs. the need criterion that is at issue between the senator and the social worker in the case study. There are two ways of understanding their dispute, one more charitable to the senator than the other. On one reading, the less flattering, the senator is simply unwilling to accept the principles that underlie our present discussion. That is, she can be understood as holding that only persons who earn their own way are deserving of having their needs met. "If people are not capable of earning their own way, then let them perish," is an implication of this way of thinking. On the second reading, the senator accepts the principles that underlie our discussion but disputes the social worker's account of the social circumstances that exist in the nation. That is, she may be willing to admit that persons who are unable to earn their own way are deserving of having their needs met; she may simply disagree that there is inevitable unemployment in the economic system as presently constituted, or that some are truly unable to work, or that some jobs do not pay sufficiently well.

It is clear that the social worker accepts the underlying principles in our discussion and holds that social circumstances are such that the work criterion is not always strictly applicable. He believes there is a real need for the Unemployment Compensation Program for this very reason.

3.8 Extreme or Sudden Scarcity

One kind of circumstance, which we have not yet considered, makes it clear that not all cases of failure to meet basic human needs are cases of injustice. That circumstance is one of *extreme* or *sudden scarcity*. If there simply are not sufficient resources available to meet such basic needs for all people, then it is impossible to do what justice requires. It may be better to say that the principles of justice cannot be applied, since the judgment that justice was not done presupposes that it could have been done. Justice is a virtue that can only exist in circumstances where benefits exist to be distributed and the burdens are not simply overwhelming. If crops fail because of drought that irrigation cannot overcome and food becomes extremely scarce, it is certainly a misfortune that some starve. But the simple fact that some starve does not by itself constitute an injustice. The human capacity to provide alternative deserts, which might then be weighed as more or less just, was lacking in those circumstances where food was not available to be distributed to the population.

Conditions of relative scarcity can lead to some very difficult questions. Suppose there is not enough food to feed everyone, but there is enough to feed some. At this point questions such as these might arise: Should we feed only those whom we select to contribute labor towards securing more food? Should we feed only those who are closest to death or otherwise in greatest immediate danger of starvation? Should we feed only those who have large numbers of dependents? Should we feed only those who are young and strong enough to be able to survive the present disaster? Since we cannot feed everyone, we cannot meet the need criterion for the whole community. Since there are more who can work than we can feed, we cannot meet the work criterion for the whole community. However, once we decide which group to try to feed, whether that turns out to be everyone or only a subgroup of people, we can then apply one of the two material principles to that subgroup.

EXERCISES

1. Below is a list of statements employing different principles of material justice. Mark those employing an ability principle *A*, those employing a productivity principle *P*, those using an effort principle *E*, and those using a need principle *N*. (3.2–3.5)

___(a) Anybody with the hands and mind to be a great surgeon should be led into a career in surgery.

___(b) Let's give a big cheer for Buddy and the long, hard hours he worked to make homecoming a success.

___(c) A child shouldn't have bad teeth because his parents can't afford a dentist.

___(d) We are gathered here tonight to honor Mickey Spillane as the greatest of mystery writers, for he has published more mystery stories than any other writer.

___(e) You will be paid 20 cents for every quart of strawberries you pick.

___(f) It's only fair to let the fastest swimmers swim in the meets.

___(g) Any kid who works out faithfully at every practice should be included in the meets.

___(h) If a man needs twice as much money to support his large family, then he should work twice as much and earn the money.

___(i) There ought to be special classes for any kid with potential like Wanda's.

___(j) In respect for the community leadership they have provided and the fine parents they have been, senior citizens should pay less for hospitalization than those who have yet to prove themselves.

2. Below is a list of eight arguments, each of which attempts to justify or discredit the use of a particular principle of material justice. Use *A, P, E* and *N* to designate arguments concerning the ability, productivity, effort, and need principles, respectively. Then use *J* or *D*, depending on whether the argument attempts to justify or discredit the use of the principle you have designated. (3.2–3.7)

___(a) A child deserves the opportunity for substantial education, for without it he will suffer misfortune for which he cannot be held responsible.

___(b) Of the great, great things must be asked. Society, after all, could not survive without their great contributions.

___(c) The cost of hospital care for the elderly must be higher than for younger people, because the elderly require more hospital services.

___(d) Wanda didn't do anything to deserve to be so bright. Benefits should not be based on mere good fortune.

___(e) John tried as hard as Mary, so how can you give him less credit? All you can really ask a person to do is to try.

___(f) If John didn't do as well as Mary, that's because he's not as experienced as she is. But John can't help that. So, it's not fair to judge him on his relative lack of success.

___(g) If you don't finish the design specifications, I can't sell them and make money. If I don't make the money, how am I supposed to pay you? Don't tell me you worked hard.

___(h) Everybody has the same needs. So when resources are inadequate to meet everyone's needs, then some other way must be found to determine who is deserving.

3. Below is a list of four sets of social circumstances. Each tends to justify one of the principles of material justice to the exclusion of the others. Mark each set of circumstances *A, P, E* or *N* depending upon which principle it tends to justify.

___(a) In this desperate society the labor of productive workers is sufficient to meet only their own needs.

___(b) The society as a whole and the variety of kinds of people within it can enjoy a higher standard of living if everyone does work that utilizes his or her talents and capacities than if some or all persons work using less than their scarcest talents.

___(c) Although some persons' best efforts are insufficient to meet their needs, the ability to meet the needs of all is amply met within the society as a whole.

___(d) The society as a whole and the variety of kinds of people within it can enjoy a higher standard of living if everyone works as hard as she can than if some or all persons make only lesser efforts.

4. Compare and contrast circumstances of overabundance and extreme scarcity as they bear on the virtue of justice. (3.2, 3.8)

DISCUSSION QUESTIONS

1. As with the 1964 Civil Rights Act, in 3.1 we included religion in our list of factors over which one ought not discriminate in matters of employment and housing. The list of factors is generally conceived as a list of things for which persons are not responsible or over which persons have no control, such as race, ethnicity, gender and age. Beyond the superficial consideration of being able to join or not join a given congregation, to what extent does a person have responsibility for being religious or have control over his religion? What about sexual orientation, specifically homosexuality? Is that within a person's control or not? What influence should the answer to that question have on housing and employment discrimination for or against homosexuals? In a just society, should discrimination on the basis of sexual-orientation be prohibited?

2. In 3.6 we distinguished what a person deserves from what the person has earned. Consider a college education. Is that something a person deserves or has earned? Who should bear the burden of providing that benefit, the person or the society? How do social circumstances, as mentioned in 3.7, affect this?

3. Governments often form partnerships with large corporations, which are private profit-making enterprises. In doing so governments have been known to give those private enterprises significant tax breaks, major grants for job training, parcels of real estate at prices below the market value, and other incentives as well, all ultimately paid for by taxpayers. In terms of justice, are such benefits deserved? Do taxpayers deserve the burdens of paying for such benefits? Some government programs provide seed money to help persons start businesses. How do issues of work, need, and desert affect the justice of doing this?

4. To what extent might a person's professional promise or work potential be considered a material principle of justice, perhaps a fourth version of the work criterion? What are some arguments—pro and con—for such a proposal?

ANSWERS TO SELECTED EXERCISES

1. (a) *A*
   (b) *E*
   (c) *N*
   (d) *P*
   (e) *P*
   (f) *A*: The swimmer's ability is the basis for including him or her, although it may be assumed that performance can be predicted on the basis of ability.
   (g) *E*
   (h) *P*
   (i) *A*
   (j) *P*

2. (a) *N, J*
   (b) *A, J*
   (c) *P: The argument is that the elderly should pay more because the medical staff must produce more in order to keep the elderly healthy.*
   (d) *A, D*
   (e) *E, J*
   (f) *P, D*: John's inexperience is used as the basis for discrediting considering his productivity.
   (g) *E, D*
   (h) *N, D*

3. (a) *P*: The society will not survive if the needs of the unproductive are met.
   (b) *A*: Each using his or her abilities, benefits each and benefits all.
   (c) *N*: The society can meet the needs of all its members, and those unable to meet their own needs are presumably not responsible for being unable.
   (d) *E*: Each making his or her best efforts benefits each and benefits all.

7 SOCIETY

We, the People,...

United States Constitution

What is a society? When is a society a state? What are the legitimate purposes of government? Where does the ultimate authority over actions reside? What are the limits of governmental authority? Should the state serve the interests of the people or should the people serve the interests of the state? What should a group of people do if they want to rationally establish a governmental organization? These questions, and others like them, have been the focus of intense philosophical concern from Plato's time until our own. The various answers given have been used to sponsor tyrants, and spawn revolutions, served as the justifications for all manner of governmental institutions from totalitarianism to democracy, from fascism to socialism to classical liberalism, and some have even argued for anarchism. The educational goal of this chapter is that you examine the range of possible answers to the questions raised above. Section 1 defines basic terminology and raises the question of sovereignty: "Who should have the ultimate authority over actions?" Section 2 contrasts two opposing views of the state, one seeing the state as an atomistic collection of individuals, the other as an organic whole, in some sense more than the sum of its individual parts. Section 3 raises the question of the legitimate purposes of government, contrasting divergent theories of government's rightful role in a society.

Section 1
ULTIMATE AUTHORITY AND THE RIGHT TO RULE

We begin this section by defining key terms such as *society, state* and *authority*. To understand precisely what different theories and positions propose, it will be important to take note of these early definitions. That accomplished, we will be able to focus on a central issue, namely the question of sovereignty: "Does any person or group in a society have the authority or moral right to demand and secure the co-operation of others in attempting to attain fundamental shared human purposes?" This complex question will demand careful analysis and thoughtful response. We will explore the three major responses philosophers have offered: the theories of *dictatorial sovereignty, popular sovereignty,* and *individual sovereignty.* After studying Section 1 you should be able to:

- Characterize what a society is and explain what a state, as a kind of society, is.
- List some of the purposes that people might view as being among those common fundamental human purposes which define a state.
- Distinguish between authority and power, and between derived and underived authority.
- Compare and contrast the theories of dictatorial sovereignty, popular sovereignty, and individual sovereignty.
- Explain how the question of sovereignty can be answered in part by appeal to different domains of concern.

THE CASE OF LAMBDA SEVEN, PART I

Lambda Seven was one of 15 exploratory space vehicles sent to various sectors of the universe to search for inhabitable planets. When the spacecraft crashed on an uncharted planet it was destroyed, and only a little of its life-support equipment could be salvaged. Many of the 500 people aboard the Lambda Seven died during the crash or from injuries and strange diseases encountered in the alien environment. All hope of rescue and return home being abandoned, the 120 Lambda Seven survivors finally met to discuss their common future. The first question they faced was who should have ultimate authority over their group.

Subcommander George Gonzales, a veteran of many space flights, spoke first. "I will take on the duties of leader and judge. In accord with the Intergalactic Association's military regulations, after Captain Stamp, who died this morning from her unfortunate injuries, I am next in command.

And, since I control our security forces here, I think it is only right that I assume the burdens of leadership."

"Now hold on there, Gonzales," said the director of the research team, Martha Ramford. "My research people are the only ones with the know how to make a go of this thing. We should take charge. We'll select a subcommittee of scientists to establish a list of needs, identify priorities, and handle policy decisions. The rest of my research people can head up various community projects and supervise survival operations. Let's see, we'll need shelter, food, security..."

From the rear of the assembly came the angry voice of Alice Wilson, "There are only 120 of us left! We're all in this together, so we should all have a say in decisions. The military rules apply only in the space craft itself, which is nothing more than a twisted heap of plasteel right now. So, Gonzales, if you want to be in charge of something, the wreck can be your territory. What we're talking about is carving a home for ourselves out of this strange, hostile new planet. As for you and your experts, Ramford, we need your knowledge, but that doesn't give you the right to make up laws and dictate policy. No, the people should rule. We'll just have to find a way to share the chores of government. That's the only right way to do it."

"A fine speech, Wilson, but not too practical," came the reply of Tom Walsh, the only nurse-practitioner who had survived. "Nobody is going to tell me what to do, not Ramford, not Gonzales, not you, Wilson, not even the whole 120 of you. No individual, and no bunch of you either, has the right to force me to do anything against my better judgment. If I don't like what's happening, I'm not going to cooperate. That's my prerogative. And, don't forget, I'm the only medical specialist around."

1.1 Society and Community

For our purposes we will understand the word *society* to refer to *any group of people who engage in cooperative behavior for the sake of a common goal.* Given this very broad understanding of *society* we can say that there are many examples of societies in our culture: bands, teams, clubs, policy committees, crews, research groups, social groups, service organizations, office staffs, armies, departments, partnerships, chambers of commerce, corporations, charitable organizations, political parties, guilds, unions, boards, councils, professional associations, street gangs, political action committees, and more.

At times a society will maintain a place of common residence, a meeting hall, or a headquarters. Churches, fire brigades, labor union locals, and country clubs usually establish permanent facilities of this sort for their own use and some societies rent their facilities for use by other societies. We will say that when the members of a society regularly reside and take meals together, the society can be called a *community*. Greek houses on college campuses, military companies, religious orders, and the experimental communes of the sixties, are just some examples of societies which can be called *communities* in this sense of the term.

1.2 Factors Affecting a Society's Survival

In order to exist with some understanding of their reason for being, societies make various kinds of efforts to consciously identify and maintain focus on their shared goals. Bands practice their music, businesses hold planning meetings, and clubs evaluate potential new members in terms of how they might contribute to the goals of the club. A second thing societies do is set up their own rules and procedures for governing themselves. Corporations, both for-profit and not-for-profit, adopt by-laws and formally empower governing bodies to make policy decisions in the interest of the corporation. National and international societies (in our sense of the word) such as, for example, The Girl Scouts, Little League Baseball, The National Organization of Women, Rotary International, and The Red Cross, also have formal internal by-laws and elaborate governing structures which link local clubs throughout the country and the world.

However, not all societies engage in formally adopting laws and empowering governing boards or rulers. A family, for example, is a society. Although many families have their own rules, a family can exist without negotiating a written concord embodying its internal set of laws. It would be a mistake to characterize the cooperative behavior based on mutual expectations and understandings as being random or unorganized simply because there is no written document being followed. On the contrary, from their very earliest days societies fall into, assent to, or more consciously accept, sets of behaviors which determine mutual roles and expectations. These can be called the *customs* or *norms* of that society, and can be a way of talking, dressing, acknowledging leadership, or cooperating on achieving some shared interest. For example, though it is not written down as a formal rule, each week when a local Rotary club meets, its members try to greet every other club member present, start the meeting with the Pledge of Allegiance, rib the club president as he or she reports news regarding the club's charitable or fund-raising projects, have lunch, hold a raffle, and listen to a guest speaker. Individual roles and responsibilities for making all this happen each week are accepted ahead of time. One person may see to food arrangements, another conduct the raffle, a third provide the guest speaker and so on. If each member does his or her part, the meeting will come off smoothly. But if roles go unfulfilled, expectations become frustrations and the purposes of the society are thwarted. Naturally, when this happens, a society is in trouble.

Group customs and norms (as well as more formal laws, regulations and job descriptions) are sufficient to establish *divisions of labor* and to create *mutual expectations*, *roles* and *responsibilities* within any society. The creation of these expectations and responsibilities aim at bringing about the more or less adequate achievement of the purposes of the society. This is why a measure of individual dedication and a willingness to contribute one's time and effort are essential, along with an acceptance of the customs and norms of the group, if a society hopes to succeed. Yet even with (1) an understanding of its goals, (2) internal rules and structures, and (3) the involvement of its members, societies may still be frustrated.

Why? Because environmental factors play a major role in determining whether and to what extent a given society will flourish. Many of these factors may be beyond the control of the society itself. Without the needed financial, physical, and technological resources no society could sustain itself. A band cannot practice without instruments, swim teams need access to water, a business needs a market, and a service club needs persons who need its services. The list of things external to the society itself which can limit or prevent the society from being successful are many and varied. As the Lambda Seven survivors look around at their new planet they are beginning to see a number of things, such as unfamiliar hazards and strange diseases, which pose more or less immediate threats to their survival as individuals and, should they decide to band together, as a society.

1.3 The State

Historically there have been many conceptions of the state. It has been thought of as an organism of which we are all cells, as a legal or contractual entity to which we are all parties, as an association to which we voluntarily or involuntarily belong, and as a particular kind of society which attempts to meet human needs. It is this latter idea which we will build upon. Think of the *state* as a certain kind of society, specifically *that society which directs its cooperative norm-bound behavior toward those shared purposes which are the fundamental shared purposes of human beings.*

First, let's look at what makes a particular human purpose *fundamental*. Otherwise we might take the word *fundamental* to express only the intensity of a person's emotion about a certain purpose, without objectively characterizing that purpose in any particular way. What makes a purpose fundamental? One fairly clear meaning is that it is a purpose whose achievement is *necessary* to the achievement of other purposes. Then the most fundamental purposes of human life will be those such that, without achieving them, life itself would not be possible. Thus, *survival* and *safety* could be listed as two fundamental human purposes. Some thinkers would limit the idea of the fundamental purposes of human life to those *without which survival and safety are threatened or made impossible*. Others contend that the idea should be broader, that the state should be organized around those human purposes *without which human life would not flourish or would not be worth living*. This notion has proved very difficult to define in any clearly objective manner, though the clearest attempt is made by those who advance the *organic* theory of the state. (See Section 2.)

1.4 Sovereignty and Authority

Beyond controversies over what the state is and what the fundamental purposes of human life might be, there lies a more basic and ultimately more crucial question. It is the question of sovereignty: "Which members of the state, if any, should have the authority or the right to require and secure the cooperation needed to pursue and attain those shared, fundamental, human purposes for which the state exists?" This is precisely the question being argued by the Lambda Seven group in the case study. There are some important distinctions this question utilizes. First is the distinction between the *power or ability to control* and the *right or moral entitlement to control*. A homeowner, for example, has the right to control who comes into her home. A thief may have the ability to gain entrance, though obviously the thief lacks the right. In the context of achieving the purposes of the state, *power* can be defined as the ability to lead or control the state, in contrast to *authority*, defined as the right to lead or control. In the case study, Gonzales, the military subcommander, has the power to seize and hold control of the Lambda Seven group, but the challenge raised by Ramford is that Gonzales does not have the authority.

There are two kinds of authority to be distinguished. Authority can be either a derived or an underived right. That is, authority might be given or delegated from one person in authority to another, as when the president delegates authority to administrators, agencies, and governmental operatives. Instances of delegated authority are very frequent in our culture. Corporations delegate authority to their boards of directors. Boards delegate to corporate presidents, who in turn delegate authority to vice presidents, managers, executives, directors, and so on, depending on the hierarchy within the particular business. Taking another look at what Gonzales is saying in the case study, one might interpret his claim as being that authority has been passed to him by virtue of the Intergalactic Association's military rules and the unfortunate death of his superior. In other words, he might not be claiming absolute authority, for his appeal to military rules would limit what he might try to do, and he might not be claiming underived authority, for his argument is that these rules in effect delegate leadership to him.

However the philosophical question of sovereignty does not concern delegated authority. Rather, it is "Who should have *un*derived or *un*delegated authority?" Once lawful authority has been established, it can be delegated; our concern is not with delegation. We want to ask, "Who has the underived moral right to establish all subsequent authority?" There have been a number of answers to this. They can be classified into roughly three theories: (a) dictatorial sovereignty, (b) individual sovereignty, and (c) popular sovereignty. Let us look at each of these in turn.

1.5 Dictatorial Sovereignty

The theory of *dictatorial sovereignty* holds that some identifiable subgroup in the state, perhaps one person, has the underived authority to rule the state. This authority is often regarded as complete and absolute, although it need not be viewed as absolute. Saying authority is *complete* means that it extends to every aspect of the life of society and the lives of its members. Saying authority is *absolute* means that no act based on that authority can legitimately be challenged by any other person or agency in the state.

Dictatorial sovereignty is usually argued for by appeal to one of three basic theories. The first is that the dictatorial ruling class, or oligarchy, has the right to rule because *those whom the gods ordain to rule should rule*. This is often called the theory of the *divine right of kings*. Gonzales, in the case study, appeals to military regulations in a way that is at least reminiscent of how a would-be king might appeal to a divinely inspired document as the source of his authority. The important question of how we know that this particular person or group has been divinely selected to rule is not answered by this theory. There are two traditional responses to this question, however. The will of the gods is thought to be manifest either in the assumption of power of a particular dynasty or through the approval of the state's religious institution. Whatever the answer offered, the question of how people know the will of the gods is crucial to the success of the divine right theory. Anyone can claim the divine right to rule. Only a clear procedure for finding out whose claim is legitimate can save the divinely based dictatorship from the political turmoil and civil war that result from conflicting claims of would-be rulers.

In the case study Gonzales does not explicitly claim that the gods have anointed him to be the ruler. But he does suggest that since he is the military commander, he could easily seize control. If he did, he would be described as one who holds an alternative theory, namely that dictatorial authority belongs to any person or group with the power to seize it. This is the theory that *might makes right*. If someone is able to put together the military power, political support, and popular appeal, then the person can take over control of the state. It often happens in human history that such a person gains control of the government and, after a time, is recognized or acknowledged to be the official ruler. An important problem is associated with this theory, however. The theory that might makes right does not explain why the person who has seized power *ought* to be acknowledged as the rightful authority. There are practical reasons, such as the fact that resisting could bring severe punishment. But the difference between power and authority raises the question of the *right* of the person to rule. Historically this question has led rulers deposed by dictatorial powers and their followers to go into exile still claiming the rightful authority to govern. It has led them to seek to regain the control of the state by encouraging war and popular rebellion against the dictator who has seized rule by force. It has also led those who have seized power to seek ways to ratify that power, through national elections or by receiving acceptance and recognition of other legitimate authorities.

Ramford's views are not objections to dictatorial sovereignty, but to Gonzales' version of that position. Ramford actually holds to a third theory in support of dictatorial sovereignty, namely that those who have the knowledge or expertise should rule. Ramford argues for a dictatorial oligarchy of experts. Her appeal is that the scientific knowledge of the research team best qualifies them to lead. This can be called the *technocrats rule* theory. It is based on the view that experts, who are the only ones who can see what is really in the state's best interest, should have the authority to move the state in that direction, even if the remaining members of the state do not agree with their analysis of what is needed and what is to be done. Knowledge, according to many thinkers, uniquely qualifies a person for the role of ruler. In our society people appointed to various agencies and government posts are often selected on the basis of the knowledge or special expertise which qualifies them for such positions. This theory is, like the others, also open to question. How shall we determine who is the most expert among us? What is the relationship between knowledge, technical expertise, and the ability to rule effectively? And should knowledge *alone* qualify one for leadership, or are there other important factors to consider?

1.6 Individual Sovereignty

In the case study, Nurse Tom Walsh takes the radical position of refusing to cooperate or be dictated to by any person or group of persons, including the entire 120, even if they should speak with one voice. In so doing Walsh is advancing a version of the theory of individual sovereignty. The theory of *individual sovereignty* maintains that each and every person is sovereign over himself. Each person, in other words, has the underived authority to act as he chooses. No one else has a right to interfere. The theory is typically supported by persons who give priority to individual self-determination. In this theory Tom, or any other individual, would be entitled to be free to make his own life, to choose his own values, to follow the dictates of his own conscience, and to adopt his own lifestyle.

Defenders of individual sovereignty argue that this entitlement is a right which no one has the authority to supersede and which no one can morally surrender. In other words, taking personal responsibility for decisions is central to this approach. You cannot wash your hands of responsibility by saying that the government decided something for you and you have no choice but to go along with it. One's own ultimate moral responsibility cannot be surrendered to others, whether an individual or a group. Walsh might be willing to listen to what Ramford's experts have to say, he might be willing to form some kind of voluntary cooperative relationship with Gonzales, Wilson and all the others, but he can never surrender his sovereignty to them, nor can he agree with the idea that they have the right to force him to do what they want. Persuasion and voluntary cooperation are compatible with individual sovereignty. But, the use of coercive force to demand compliance is something the sovereign individual cannot accept. Naturally, this theory presents many problems. How is cooperation to be secured if the very existence of the whole society depends on some vital contribution that only one unwilling member can make? How shall criminals and external enemies be handled if one assumes that they too are individually sovereign? How is public safety and the efficient use of scarce resources to be assured, if cooperation depends only on persuasion and never on coercion? What do you do with people who refuse to be persuaded?

1.7 Popular Sovereignty

In the case study, Walsh's position is an extreme response to the dictatorial views of Ramford and Gonzales. It is also a contrast to Alice Wilson's views. Recall that

Wilson also objected to Gonzales and Ramford, but, unlike Walsh, Wilson appealed to the theory of *popular sovereignty*. This theory maintains that the people as a whole—the group of people who together compose the society—collectively, not individually, should have ultimate authority. Under the theory of popular sovereignty, the people of the state are thought of as having the ultimate right to express their collective will, which is itself the ultimate authority. Like the various versions of dictatorial sovereignty, this theory leaves important questions unanswered. How is the collective will of the people to be recognized? How do the people, taken as a group, manifest what they, as a group, desire? How does a group voice its decisions?

Insight concerning both the difficulty of recognizing the will of the people and distinguishing between individual sovereignty and popular sovereignty can be gained by examining something we take so much for granted, the concept of voting. Within the United States, although not only here, the people as a whole are thought of as having the ultimate authority to protect citizens against harm caused by others. Our national, state and local governments make laws against a wide variety of such harms. The lawmakers gain their authority to make such laws by having been elected to represent us. Thus, when a person votes for a legislator, the individual citizen is not understood as delegating to the legislator the *individual's authority*, for no one individual has the authority to make laws or regulations. Instead, the citizen, by voting, is understood as helping to clarify what we, the people, as a total society, want. In elections, the idea of "majority rule" is that the will of the people is shown, or determined as best it can be, by whatever the majority of people vote for. Sovereignty is understood, throughout, as residing with the people taken as a group, but not with the people as taken individually.

Are popular sovereignty and individual sovereignty compatible theories? One could maintain that the collective is sovereign over those purposes that are shared by everyone, but that each individual is sovereign over those purposes that are her own personal concerns. But, as the case study suggests, this division into "collective vs. individual concerns" will not always work. Nurse Walsh may want to maintain his own individual sovereignty, but he is the community's only medical resource. To achieve their shared fundamental human purposes, which include surviving, they require his skill, knowledge and cooperation. If he is individually sovereign, they cannot rightfully claim his cooperation nor could they force him to cooperate. But if they are a sovereign collective, then they can rightfully make that claim, impose on him the obligation to render medical aid when needed, and rightfully coerce him into providing it.

1.8 Domains of Concern

One way to overcome problems like the one cited above is to define domains of concern. A *domain of concern* is a group of purposes. We might conclude that different theories of sovereignty apply to different domains of concerns. Complete sovereignty, in other words, would not be of any one type—dictatorial, popular, or individual. The experts might be sovereign over concerns such as military security or technical management of resources. The population as a whole could be sovereign over concerns such as establishing rules and laws to regulate interpersonal and commercial interaction. Each individual could be sovereign over such concerns as her own optimal health and happiness. This idea holds promise, but serious and very difficult problems remain in determining the exact limits of each of the ranges of concern. Conflicts between what the individual may want and what the group may want are inevitable. Perhaps the chief problem is deciding who has sovereignty, the ultimate authority, over the *life* and *labor* of each member of the state. This question will be brought into sharper focus in Section 2.

EXERCISES

1. Describe two groups of people in such a way that one group clearly is a society and the other is not. Describe two societies such that one is a community and one is not. (1.1, 1.2)

2. Below is a list of purposes, each of which some group of people is cooperating to achieve. If that purpose has traditionally been suggested as characteristic of the state, mark it *S*. If it is not a generally shared or common human purpose, mark it *NC*. If that purpose is not regarded as fundamental, mark it *NF*. Note that some purposes are neither common nor fundamental. (1.2, 1.3)

___(a) To prevent cruelty to animals

___(b) To earn money

___(c) To have sufficient food for every citizen

___(d) To make mobile homes safer from fires

___(e) To minimize the hazards of the natural environment

___(f) To maximize individual freedom

___(g) To provide a sense of dignity and meaning for human life

___(h) To make each individual happy

___(i) To provide educational opportunities

___(j) To find a cure for AIDS

___(k) To defend against possible military attack

___(l) To come to a consensus regarding a new contract offer

3. Below is a list of reasons why a certain something ought to be done. Some of these reasons are appeals to power, mark them *AP*. Others are appeals to authority. If it is an appeal to derived authority, mark it *DA*, mark it *SA* if it is an appeal to sovereignty or underived authority. (1.4)

___(a) Unless you want to work for me tomorrow, finish that project before 5:00 P.M.

___(b) Young man, I outrank you in this army.

___(c) Slave, pull that oar or feel the whip!

___(d) The people of this city have the right to a police force that can protect them from being assaulted in broad daylight.

___(e) By virtue of my position as director of human resources, I am pleased to offer you a job with our firm.

___(f) This is my company, and I can make whatever rules I want.

___(g) This is our club, and we can write any by-laws we want.

___(h) I'm entitled to swim any stroke I please because this race is designated as "free style."

___(i) I'm entitled to swim any stroke I please for my own pleasure.

___(j) I don't see why you were disagreeing with her. She's the expert in these kinds of things.

___(k) The city council just passed an ordinance that all city employees are required to reside within the city limits.

___(l) The city council wants to put a referendum to a vote of all the citizens. The referendum has to do with where city employees must reside.

___(m) John, I'm going out of town for a few days, will you look after things at the office while I'm gone? I told everyone to think of your words as if they were my own.

4. Below is a list of assertions about sovereignty. Different assertions are true for different theories of sovereignty. On the left are columns marked *DS*, *PS*, and *IS*, for dictatorial sovereignty, popular sovereignty, and individual sovereignty, respectively. Mark a *T* or an *F* in each column beside each assertion, depending on whether the given assertion is true or false according to each of the three theories of sovereignty. (1.5, 1.6, 1.7).

D PS IS

(a) Every person is sovereign over her own actions.

(b) When the actions of an individual affect the purposes of the state, the individual is not sovereign.

(c) A person's sovereignty may be based on his knowledge or technological expertise.

(d) A person's authority may be based on his knowledge or technological expertise.

(e) When everybody is affected, or might be affected by an action, the ultimate right to decide rests in the hands of the community.

(f) If an individual has the power to enforce his will, then there may be no higher right to decide.

(g) The circumstances of a person's birth cannot establish her right to rule.

(h) The right to lead can be distinguished from the power to lead.

5. (a) What does it means to say that sovereignty is complete?

(b) Use this concept of completeness in order to characterize a domain.

(c) Describe any two domains in such a way as to support the assertion that one sort of sovereignty holds in one domain and another sort holds in the other domain.

(d) Abstractly state how the concept of domains might be used in order to make the three theories of sovereignty more compatible with each other. (1.8)

DISCUSSION QUESTIONS

1. What authority does the state have in deciding the levels of health care that rightfully should be provided to all citizens? Does the state have the authority to become

involved in health care questions for those persons who would not be competent to exercise individual sovereignty in such matters? What right might persons who are not members of a society (visitors or illegal aliens) have to emergency health care in that society and at whose expense?

2. What are the rightful limits of an employer's authority to impose its will on its employees in terms of duties, wages, working conditions, company plans (such as dropping a product line, layoffs, and unannounced plant closings), and worker housing and living accommodations? Should those limits be protected legally, that is, is it within the scope of the purposes of the state to put such legislation in place or are such matters within the domains of the individual sovereignty of the employer and each employee? What happens if the employees form a union—does that alter their sovereignty over this domain?

ANSWERS TO SELECTED EXERCISES

1. You have correctly described a society if you have clearly stated a purpose that the members of the group share and you have described their acting cooperatively in order to achieve this purpose. Your other group will fail to be a society if it has no common purpose (as, for instance, people listed on the same page of the telephone book seldom share a common purpose simply because they happen to be listed together), or if its members do not cooperate to achieve that purpose (as, for instance, when a crowd is pushing and shoving with everyone trying to get to the same place all at once.)

2. (a) *NC, NF* (b) *NC* (c) *S*
   (d) *NC*: since some people have no involvement with mobile homes. It is a fundamental concern, since it is a concern for survival.
   (e) *S*: this concern is similar to the one above, but it is general enough to be common.
   (f) *S* (g) *S*
   (h) *NF*: although perhaps a state could regard this purpose as fundamental.
   (i) *S*: in the nineteenth and twentieth century.
   (j) *S*: the survival element is clear, but it may not be immediately clear that everyone has an interest here. However, we do. Protecting ourselves from a deadly epidemic need not wait until everyone is infected.
   (k) *S* (l) *NC*, although it may be fundamental to those concerned.

3. (a) *AP* (b) *DA* (c) *AP* (d) *SA* (e) *DA* (f) *SA* (g) *SA* (h) *DA* (i) *SA* (j) *SA*
   (k) *SA*: is claimed—however, one might interpret this *DA*, in the sense that although the city council approved it, their authority is derived or delegated from the electorate.
   (l) *SA*: appealing to the sovereignty of the electorate.
   (m) *DA*

4.
	DS	PS	IS
(a)	F	F	T
(b)	T	T	F
(c)	T	F	F
(d)	T	T	T	(Particular delegated authority.)
(e)	F	T	F

(f) *T   F   F*

(g) *F   T   T* (According to *IS*, it is the fact of one's birth, not its circumstances, that makes one sovereign.)

(h) *T   T   T*

5. (a) To say that sovereignty is complete is to say that it extends to every aspect of every action.

(b) A domain is defined by some sort of action or some aspect of actions. Thus, if sovereignty is confined to a domain, it is not complete.

(c) The domains should not overlap; if they do, conflicting claims to sovereignty will arise. And the domains should be described so that traditional theories of sovereignty make it plausible that each sort of sovereignty holds in one of the domains but not in the other.

(d) Your answer to this should be framed around these two requirements.

Section 2
THEORIES OF THE STATE

Section 2 examines the inevitable conflict between the interests of the individual and those of society. How this conflict is resolved depends on one's view of the state, which, in turn, depends on what one takes to be the fundamental, shared, human purposes for which the state exists. We will examine various theories of the state, defining and distinguishing them in terms of each view as fundamental, shared, human purposes. The theories we will look at are classical liberalism, socialism, and fascism. Finally, we will consider the social contract theory as a normative approach to resolving the problem of the inevitable conflict of interests between individuals and the state. After studying this section you should be able to:

- Describe the conflict that arises between the interests of the state and those of its individual members.
- Compare and contrast atomistic and organic theories of the state.
- Compare and contrast fascism, socialism, and classical liberalism in terms of their views regarding fundamental, shared, human purposes.
- State the elements of the social contract theory.
- Explain the intended normative function of social contract theory.

THE CASE OF LAMBDA SEVEN, PART II

Nurse Tom Walsh's challenge did not go unheeded by the others of the Lambda Seven group. Everyone saw the danger in his threat to withhold his medical expertise if he didn't like the way things were going. An outraged Gonzales hurled his own threats back at the nurse. "What if I were to withdraw my military forces just because I didn't like a particular decision. In that case you and all the others would be totally defenseless. But why should my soldiers risk death to defend you? Why, especially if you claim the liberty to withhold your labor as a nurse anytime you happen to feel like it? Mark my words—individual interests, personal liberties, and special exemptions will destroy our community. The group must take priority. None of us exists except to serve the group! Personal interests which threaten the group cannot be tolerated."

Ramford picked up Gonzales' theme of cooperation. "Look, Tom, what if we all held out, cooperating only when it was to our own selfish interest, then the whole bunch of us could end up quite dead. Nobody has yet proved that the good of each is the same as the good of all. Holding out for one's own interests denies even those who want to cooperate access to the resources and talents they might need to survive. Besides cooperation has its positive points—for one, it's enjoyable. Group spirit is a good thing, you know. After all, we are all in this together. We should begin to centralize planning and make the most of our situation!"

Until this point Sharma, the agriculturalist, had kept his thoughts to himself. But now, in that slow, deep rumble that was uniquely his own, he spoke, "True, Ramford, my friend, the Many is more important then the One, but there are a great number of us. In fact, we have enough people to form three or four small communities. It might be wise to separate into these smaller groups, designing each to be self-sustaining. Certainly the discord we now experience would be minimized because we would not be so conscious of differences in class or occupation. We could all work and share in the production of what our own communities need. Whenever possible we would take turns at various community jobs, more or less equally benefiting from the work."

"Absurd!" burst subcommander Gonzales. "We need centralized leadership. We must remember our mission—why we came here in the first place, what we are all about! We must be willing to make some sacrifices for the sake of that mission and for the sake of the Lambda Seven project. How could a bunch of small, weak communities defend themselves against common enemies? And what if one discovers something very useful; how would that knowledge be shared with the others?"

Sharma turned toward the officer and said, "I did not mean that we would have to be so isolated that we never communicated. What I meant was..."

At this point nurse Walsh broke in again, "One big group, three little groups. I don't want either. I claim there are limits to what can be demanded of any of us. I'm not willing to say that soldiers must fight and die any more than I'm willing to say that I must practice medicine. We're not a community, we're not a colony. We're nothing more than a bunch of unfortunate people thrown together here. That does not give any of us, nor any group of us, the right to demand something of any other person or group. What measure of our personal freedom any of us decides to surrender is entirely up to that individual to determine."

"I, for one, am tired of all the stubborn posturing," said Alice Wilson. "Why don't we sit down and negotiate. Let's see if we can't agree to surrender some of our individual prerogatives in order to form a pact or agreement of some kind. Perhaps by mutual consent we can form a contract, charter, constitution or agreement of some kind which specifies our individual liberties as well as our community obligations. It's worth a try, anyway."

2.1 The State and the Individual

Income is taxed. Soldiers die. Private property is reclaimed by laws of eminent domain. Scarce resources are rationed. Criminals are denied their liberties. Laws regulate the conduct of business and commerce. That the interests of particular individuals are often in conflict with the interests of the state is obvious. The normative question to ask is: "How far can the state rightfully go in this?" To answer this question, we must examine those purposes for which the state exists.

The state, we said in Section 1, is that society which is concerned about achieving fundamental, shared, human purposes. In order, then, to get a clearer idea of what those fundamental, shared, human purposes are, let us begin by distinguishing the *purposes* themselves from the *means* used to achieve them. *Purposes* are goals, such as survival, security, economic wealth, wisdom. *Means* are ways of achieving goals. (A committee on "ways and means" is not intended to establish the purposes of a society but to find the fiscal resources with which the society can achieve those purposes.) Accordingly, when we think of something as a means, we are focusing on its instrumental value. For example, there are several ways to acquire wealth—work, inheritance, theft, or gift. For now, however, our concern is not with particular ways that states might use to achieve their goals—although the ethical character of these ways is of major concern in other contexts—rather, we shall focus on those fundamental, shared purposes themselves.

Second, among purposes or goals having intrinsic value, we should distinguish fundamental goals from derivative or secondary goals. Survival is a fundamental goal. Enjoying a game of volleyball is a secondary or derivative goal, even though it might be argued that the enjoyment of the game is intrinsically valuable. But we must be careful here. The difference between what is fundamental and what is not is a matter of degree. We can recognize examples at both extremes, but there is a gray area in the middle. Some goals, such as having friends, being healthy, and being protected from certain diseases, are difficult to classify. Some theorists would be inclined to call them fundamental; others would not. Some would argue that the state should work to make human relations more harmonious and friendly, to provide programs that improve the health of its citizens, and to seek ways to protect the citizens from dangerous diseases. Others would argue that these goals, while important, are beyond the scope of the state's legitimate concerns. In other words, everyone can agree that purposes that are not necessary for human life are not fundamental, even if the achievement of these purposes is intrinsically valuable. The difficulty for the definition of the state's rightful purposes comes about because people disagree concerning which purposes are necessary.

The contrasts we developed in Section 1 between individual sovereignty, popular sovereignty and dictatorial sovereignty can help us understand disagreements over which human purposes should be regarded as both fundamental and shared and which should not. Keeping those three concepts of sovereignty in mind, we shall look at three theories of the state: Classical Liberalism, Socialism and Fascism. In effect, by examining these theories, we are trying to answer the question, "Which human concerns are shared and fundamental?" These three theories represent three different visions or ideals of the state and what its rightful purposes are. In practice, some nations combine these ideals in various ways at various times in their histories. Also, different ideals may be invoked when considering different domains of concern.

2.2 Classical Liberalism

One way to approach the issue is to define the fundamental purposes of the state as being precisely those of particular individuals. *Classical liberalism* is the theory of the state which focuses on the interests of the individual as opposed to the interests of the collective and which stresses minimal interference and maximal personal liberty. Thus, in saying that survival is a fundamental human purpose, the classical liberal is talking about the *survival of individual people*, not the survival of the community or the state. If Walsh, in the case study, were to agree to any theory of the state, it would be to the theory of classical liberalism. His major theme is that the group does not have the right to interfere with his exercise of his own personal liberty. This is in complete agreement with the classically (eighteenth century) "liberal" view that the state is a tool aimed at guaranteeing that individuals can go about their private business, see to their own concerns, and do so with a minimum of interference either from other individuals or from governments.

The purpose of the state, then, on the view of classical liberalism is to protect individuals from harm while allowing them as much freedom as possible. Individuals are to be left free to pursue their own goals, without being hindered by others. This theory sees people as potential threats to each other. It says that the state exists to protect us from each other but otherwise not to interfere with our personal goals. Our social, economic, religious, educational, moral, artistic, and recreational interests are our own concerns. The state must not, in this theory, interfere with our freedom to dispose of our wealth as we choose. Taxation, as one way of limiting our liberty, is to be tolerated only if the uses to which the taxes are put increase our liberty by further protecting us from the interference of others. But taxation for social programs aimed at benefiting others but not increasing our own liberty would not be acceptable on this view.

Some classical liberals introduce an ethical limitation on this freedom. They say that classical liberalism does not allow complete freedom to do what one wants, but only the legal freedom to do what one is allowed to do. In other words, the fact that private drunkenness cannot be outlawed under this theory does not mean that people are morally free to get drunk. These thinkers distinguish classical liberalism as a theory of state from other normative theories that may specify one's personal morality. Such thinkers typically argue that if behavior does not cause harm to others, it should not be prohibited by the state, even though it may be morally wrong, self-destructive, or foolish.

Many classical liberals hold the theory of individual sovereignty. You will recall that Walsh, in the case study for Section 1, held the theory of individual sovereignty. But some who favor classical liberalism hold the theory of popular sovereignty, which would permit them to hold the view that the people as a group have the right to restrict the liberty of any individual if, in the exercise of that liberty, harm to others would be caused.

2.3 Atomistic Cooperation and the Tragedy of the Commons

Classical liberalism is often called an *atomistic* theory of the state. It sees the state primarily as a collection of individuals. A theater audience, for example, is primarily a collection of individuals. Each is seeking to enjoy the show; they have that purpose in common. They come together for that purpose, but, except for not interfering with each other's enjoyment, they do not cooperate to achieve that purpose. After the show is over, each goes about his or her separate business. The state, in atomistic theories, can be understood by analogy to the audience. In the ideal state each person could freely pursue his or her own interests independent and free from interference.

What happens if the people in the theater determine that they would enjoy the show more if they talked quietly with the person next to them? As the noise level rose it would become more and more difficult to converse and to hear the performance. Even the actors and actresses could be affected by the rumble of constant talking. Their performances would be altered. As people commented to one another, the noise in the theater could rise to a level which ruined everyone's enjoyment of the show. As Ramford said, "Nobody has proved that the good of each is the same as the good of all." Ramford's point is that each person's pursuit of self-interest can work against the interests of the group taken as a whole, and at times make it impossible even to achieve the interests of each individual.

Suppose, for example, that the farmers in an agricultural region all grow the same crop and market it at the same market. Assuming a fairly steady demand, the price for the crop will vary depending on the supply. Specifically, if the farmers as a group market too much of the crop, the price will fall. Realizing this, the farmers form a cartel and agree among themselves how much each of them will market. As long as each holds to the agreement, then the price will stay firm. Now suppose that one farmer realizes that his individual self-interest lies in marketing more than the agreement called for. The price will fall a little, but his own profits will be substantially higher, he reasons. Other farmers, seeing what is happening, quickly recognize that the cartel has been broken and decide to market more crop in order to try to ensure that they will not loose money as a result of the falling price. But as more and more farmers, acting in their own self-interest, market more and more crop, a situation of over-supply exists and the bottom falls out of the market. Desperate to earn what he can, each markets as much as possible, but this only drives the price down further. The good of the group and the good of each member of the group is destroyed, not achieved, as each pursues his or her own self-interest. This kind of example, known as a "tragedy of the commons" situation, is often used as a criticism of any atomistic theory of the state, and specifically as a criticism of classical liberalism.

Eighteenth-century defenders of classical liberalism staunchly maintain that the good of the group as a whole is best achieved by each member pursuing his or her own self-interest. But, as real-life tragedy of the commons examples multiply in our century,—smog, acid rain, the destruction of the ozone layer, polluted beaches, rush hour grid locks—this assumption has come into serious doubt. Consider our natural resources, such as lumber. Over the course of time, lumber can be replaced. So, even though the supply is limited, if it is managed it can be made to last. As some is harvested, new planted forests will come to maturity. But suppose each of us uses just a small bit more than his or her share. We can justify our individual excess because of the importance (to us) of our goals and because we have only used a tiny amount more than is our due. But what happens to our resource? With millions of us over-demanding lumber, the resource is depleted, and all of us are then frustrated in our aims because of its absence. As another example, we all value defense. But in times of hostilities it is not in our interest, as individuals, to join the armed forces, go to war, and risk death; our individual interest dictates that we avoid the risk. But the collective interest in national security will be frustrated if everyone waits for the other person to go out and do the job. Even in our society, which is heavily based upon an atomistic theory of the state, we take a collectivist or group-first approach to defense. We supply many inducements to encourage volunteers. But should there not be enough volunteers forthcoming to defend the nation, we have in the past (and surely would again) imposed a military draft on the civilian population.

2.4 Socialism

That theory of the state which emphasizes the value and importance of *cooperation* is *Socialism*. It emphasizes the importance of collective effort, careful planning for group needs, and cooperative work in securing those needs. As you might suspect, socialism is compatible with the theory of popular sovereignty, which emphasizes that authority rests with the people taken as a whole. Ramford argues for socialism when she says, "Holding out for one's own interests denies even those who want to cooperate access to the resources and talents they might need to survive. Besides cooperation has its positive points—for one, it's enjoyable. Group spirit is a good thing, you know. After all, we are all in this together."

However there are crucial ambiguities in Ramford's emphasis on cooperation. The first ambiguity is whether she is calling for the formation of a single society or many smaller ones. Her call for centralized planning suggests it is the former. But, as Sharma the agriculturalist points out, a socialistic approach does not have to be massively collectivist. A number of smaller, self-sufficient communes might be the way to go, Sharma suggests. Gonzales points out the problems with that approach, urging that it creates difficulties of planning, common defense, and sharing of knowledge and resources. But those can also be seen as creating more possibilities for each individual to become more creative, involved and connected to ensuring the continued life of his or her smaller commune. This, in turn, is viewed as an intrinsic value under socialism.

Another, more fundamental, ambiguity in Ramford's proposal is that her concept of cooperation might be interpreted in either of two very different ways. She might be saying that cooperation is useful so that each of our individual interests can be achieved. Or, Ramford might be saying that the cooperation is valuable in itself. For she does say cooperation is enjoyable and that building group spirit is a good thing. As Ramford's speech emphasizes, cooperation can be understood so as to be compatible with an atomistic understanding of the state, or it can be understood so as to imply an organic understanding of cooperation and the state. Let's look at organic cooperation and contrast it with the atomistic concept.

Suppose we approach the need for cooperation simply from the perspective of the tragedy of the commons. To return to our theater example, probably each group will soon realize that everyone had better be quiet so that all can hear. Any group that is slow in coming to this realization is also likely to be prodded by the shushing that surrounding groups will quickly supply. The outcome is that all groups are likely to become fairly quiet as they watch the play. In an atomistic sense, the members of the audience are cooperating. By that we mean, first, that they are cooperating in having a common goal of wanting to enjoy the play and, second, each is employing the means of keeping quiet (not interfering) in order to achieve their common goal.

In saying that their cooperation is *atomistic* we mean foremost that priority is given to the individual's goals. *Atomistic cooperation* is only a *means* to achieving individual goals. But each member of the audience, (each atom) establishes his or her own goals, which can rightfully be exclusively concerned with his or her own self-interest. A secondary point in saying that the cooperation is atomistic is that there need be no interaction among the members of the audience in order for them to employ their means (each can shut his or her own mouth) and thus achieve their goal. The only "common effort" (if we can use the term in this context at all) is that they not interfere with one another.

2.5 Organic Cooperation

As many coaches will attest, to win a championship a team needs more than players who are individually good. It needs team unity, team spirit, and a sense of cooperation that puts winning ahead of personal statistics, in other words, that puts the good of the team ahead of the good of individual players. And, as the team strives for the championship and wins more and more games, their confidence builds, team spirit grows and the players experience the joy of winning. Moreover, many would argue that an individual player might pursue the development of team spirit not only to help the team win or to enjoy that spirit himself or herself, but also for the non-self-interested reason of helping or allowing other team members do well and enjoy themselves. Similar relationships are likely to exist, for example, in a harmonious family or harmonious office staff. The members of a family can cooperate not just for the atomistic reasons of achieving their own needs, but for the reasons of help-ing the family as a whole achieve its collective purposes and helping other individu-als in the family experience and enjoy that spirit of cooperation. Also, in a family, which is an organic unity, what happens to one individual can profoundly affect the lives of others. A problem like substance abuse is not just one person's problem, it affects everyone in the family. If an employer transfers a spouse to a new work lo-cation, this can affect the career of the other spouse and have a major impact on the children's schooling and everyone's social relationships.

Cooperation within a successful team, a loving family or a productive office is not easily interpreted on a strictly atomistic level. Something more is going on; or, as the saying goes, "The whole is more than the sum of its parts." This phenomenon is sometimes described as *organic* cooperation. Organic cooperation is cooperation not simply to achieve self-interested ends, and not merely to provide the planning necessary to avoid a tragedy of the commons. Organic cooperation is considered *intrinsically valuable*. It is also a means toward *creating and then maintaining a new collective unity*, the team or the family, which has *goals of its own, beyond the original goals of the individuals which compose it*. The productive office staff comes to respect one another, enjoys working together, and may begin to do things on a social as well as a purely business level. The team seeks to develop, to maintain, and to exhibit its spirit, as well to seek the victories and pile up the impressive statistics the individuals might originally have sought. The family seeks harmonious relationships among its members, not merely so that the members are not hampered by their family membership, but also because they find that their relating with each other harmoniously is an intrinsically enjoyable way to live. In an organic community people feel accepted, have a sense of belonging, and feel a sense of purpose.

Where atomistic cooperation is strictly a means to other ends, organic cooperation is seen as intrinsically valuable. Where atomistic cooperation is limited to achieving the goals of individuals, organic cooperation includes efforts to achieve the goals of the group or the collective, and, typically, also includes goals that arise out of the interactions between group members. Organic cooperation can also be aimed at developing a sense of group unity, spirit, harmony and purpose. Atomistic interpretation is more confined and individualistic in its aims.

While cooperation, at least in order to prevent tragedies of the commons, is central to socialism, the nature of that cooperation, as atomistic or organic, is usually not defined in socialist thought. This, as we noted, is true of Ramford's brand of socialism as well. However, this is not necessarily a criticism of socialism.

Rather, socialism can develop within either an atomistic or an organic view of the state. This is what makes socialism such a powerful theory of the state in the twentieth century. There are atomistic socialist countries and collectivist socialist countries. It is interesting to study the actual policies and practices of various countries—apart from their rhetoric—and to classify those policies as being compatible with atomistic socialism or organic socialism.

2.6 Fascism

Fascism is clearly an organic theory of the state. It includes a broader selection of goals as fundamental, shared, human purposes. Fascism is the theory of the state which emphasizes the priority of the state over the individual. Not only would it include the survival and safety of the community, as does socialism, but it would add the pursuit of a sense of the significance and mission of the state and the continuity of civilization. In classical liberalism the goals of the individual took priority; but in fascism the goals of the state take priority. As Gonzales puts it in the case study, "... individual interests, personal liberties, and special exemptions will destroy the community. The group must take priority. None of us exists except to serve the group! Personal interests that threaten the group cannot be tolerated."

Within fascism the individual is viewed as gaining a sense of the meaning of her life by seeing it as part of a whole, a unity. The individual is important only because he is part of a large, important, and continuing purpose—the health and growth of the state. This purpose is included in the concept of fundamental, shared, human purposes because, in the fascist view, the health and growth of the state is necessary for survival—the survival of the state. According to the theory of fascism, to survive, the state needs a sense of mission, scope, grandeur, and importance. From this the people can derive their individual significance. The lives of individuals become meaningful as they come to see how they contribute to the continuing collective organism, the state. Next to this the individual's life is petty and momentary. Accordingly, without the state's having such stature, the individual's life would be meaningless because of its insignificance. Since without meaning life is seen as not worth living, belonging to the state is seen as a fundamental purpose, if not to the survival, at least to the worth, of the individual.

If you are having trouble accepting the idea that such a view of the state can truly captivate the minds, hearts and lives of people, imagine the state by analogy to a major corporation or religious organization. In those societies it is not uncommon to find people who devote their lives to the enterprise, who derive their sense of meaning from serving the ongoing mission of "the company" or "the church." It is not uncommon for people to project the value of the survival and well-being of that society as being of greater importance than the individual interests of themselves or any other members. Under fascism patriotism can take on a religious fervor and furthering the goals of the state can motivate people to fanatic extremes.

In fascist theory the state is a living totality. Divisive special interest groups and claims of personal exemption are not tolerated. Under fascism all social institutions—religion, morality, commerce, law, education, transportation, resource development—and are organized and directed toward fulfilling the long range interests of the people viewed as a whole. Naturally the leaders in the fascist state must claim to have the wisdom and insight to recognize what the long-term good of the total society is, and also the ability to organize and direct an enormously complex effort toward achieving that goal. In support of this effort the fascist state often articulates a "philosophy" which upholds virtues of personal integrity, cooperativeness, self-sacrifice, heroism, loyalty, and patriotism. Convinced that unless everything and everyone is brought into line with its policies the state itself is taking serious and unnecessary risks, the fascist state strives explicitly for a comprehensive totalitarianism, which means, state control over every aspect of each person's life which may have any effect the collective good. It should come as no surprise, given the above, that fascism is most comfortable with the dictatorial theory of sovereignty.

In the case study Gonzales articulates this fascist perspective when he says, "We need centralized leadership. We must remember our mission—why we came here in the first place, what we are all about! We must be willing to make some sacrifices for the sake of that mission and for the sake of the Lambda Seven project." Centralized authority located in an individual, a central committee, or a strong ruling party helps to make possible more complete organization, integration, and cooperation. Fascism, correspondingly, regards pacifism, unwillingness to self-sacrifice, and individualism as vices. Often a measure of austerity, self-denial, and personal discipline is deliberately built into a fascist model of society. Fascist thinkers feel this helps people avoid the laziness and selfishness often associated with lives of pleasure and self-indulgence. In a fascist theory of the state the individual is given no special privileges or exemptions, unless those exemptions serve the collective good. There are in principle no limits to the state's legitimate authority over the labor or life of the individual. The state can ask anything of anybody. Under fascism no individual has the right to refuse; all have the duty to obey. Although fascism has been racist or nationalistic in some of its historically prominent forms, the sketch of fascism presented here shows that it is not an essentially racist or nationalistic theory.

2.7 Contrasting Classical Liberalism, Socialism, and Fascism

The difference between classical liberalism and fascism is the difference between taking an atomistic as opposed to an organic view of fundamental shared human purposes. The atomistic view sees human needs in terms of individual needs. Thus, classical liberalism gives priority to the individual and limits the fundamental human purposes to the safety and survival needs of the individual. On the other hand, the organic view focuses on collectivist human needs. In contrast, fascism gives priority to the group over the individual and defines the fundamental human purposes in very broad terms, being sure to include as a top priority the ongoing survival and flourishing of the state itself. Underlying these contrasting theories of the state are opposing concepts of human survival needs. Classical liberalism thinks of these needs in terms of the individual. Fascism thinks of them in terms of the group goals and purposes.

Socialism differs from classical liberalism in that collective planning is valued highly, at least instrumentally to avoid the tragedy of the commons and thereby ensure the survival of the state, if not intrinsically, as something enjoyable in itself. Socialism differs from fascism in that only under fascism is the life of the individual totally to be focused on the goals of the state, since, according to fascism, only participation in the achievement of those goals is thought to give meaning to the life of the individual. Socialism can be either atomistic or organic in its interpretation of cooperation. Those versions of socialism which are atomistic will tend to give priority to individual over group interests, particularly if no harm to the group or to others is evident in so doing. Those versions of socialism which are organic will tend to give priority to group goals over individual goals, particularly if advancing group purposes can be more easily and efficiently achieved by so doing.

Politically, much is made of the difference between capitalism and communism. Capitalism, in its eighteenth-century *laissez faire* form, tends to be associated with classical liberalism, although in theory capitalism is quite compatible with atomistic socialism. Communism, because of its twentieth-century manifestations, is often associated with totalitarianism, but conceptually the communist economic system fits better within organic socialistic thought. A look beyond the political rhetoric at the actual policies being implemented reveals that today both economic systems are in practice socialistic. Granted today's capitalistic societies are more atomistic and more inclined to grant significance to individual liberties, whereas today's communist societies are more organic and apt to emphasize the significance of society as a whole. Yet the policies of the capitalistic West include such things as social security, government regulation of commerce, Medicare, mandatory education of the young, workers compensation and disability programs, government insured banking, government insured pension programs, and many other programs that go well beyond the limitations classical liberalism would place on the legitimate purposes of the state. In fact, many of the proposals made by Karl Marx (1818–1883) have been put into practice in "capitalistic" countries. Similarly, communist states are realizing the need to use practice to temper theory. "Experiments" with competitive, free-enterprise economic programs, such as private farming and the creation of special incentives for more efficient production, are showing that quality and productivity can be increased in ways that are inconsistent with traditional collectivist economic ideology.

2.8 Social Contract Theory

In order to understand how people, acting rationally, should rightfully decide among alternative theories of sovereignty and among such other notions as classical liberalism, socialism, and fascism, many thinkers have presented versions of the social contract theory. In the case study, for example, Wilson says, "Why don't we sit down and negotiate. Let's see if we can't agree to surrender some of our individual prerogatives in order to form a pact or agreement of some kind. Perhaps by mutual consent we can form a contract that specifies some of our mutual liberties as well as our community obligations." As Wilson rightly senses, the conflicts among liberalism, socialism, and fascism seem very difficult to resolve in theory, because they are based on such different ideas about human needs. Her appeal to the social contract theory, however, suggests a practical solution. She is proposing that people ask themselves, "What individual liberties am I willing to part with in order to be guaranteed that my fundamental human needs will be satisfied?" Following the social contract approach allows individuals to reason together and negotiate about what their fundamental needs are and what sacrifices of personal liberties they are worth.

The social contract theory tells us what rational people ought to do. It proposes that people should negotiate agreements between themselves and the other members of the community. These agreements, or contracts, would call for the surrender of certain individual prerogatives, in return for which the community will address itself to meeting the individual's fundamental human needs, however these needs come to be defined. Social contract theorists need *not* hold that people actually sit down and agree to such contracts as a matter of historical fact. The *social contract theory is best understood not as making assertions about actual human history* at all. Rather, the theory is a *normative* one. It addresses the hypothetical question: "If a rational group of people were going to set up the best social organization and government possible, for any people whatever to live under, no matter what those people's interests or particular psychological characteristics might turn out to be, what would this group of rational people decide?" Reading the case study for Section 3 of Chapter 4 would be beneficial. You should notice how that case study has characteristics in common with social contract theory: (1) your reflection proceeds independent of your self-interest, and (2) the attempt is made to reach a rational conclusion about what ought to be done on the basis of the characteristics of the beings involved.

As a person considers the hypothetical question posed above, (What would a rational group of people do to set up the best possible social organization?), the person should think of the people in the group as beginning this fictitious negotiation with everyone under the "veil of ignorance." That is, initially nobody would be in a position to know where his or her personal self-interest lies. Under the veil of ignorance people take an objective look at their shared needs; nobody is biased by knowing that once the state is formed he or she will or will not have certain economic or political advantages. This starting point for reflection is called *the initial position*. In the case study the people are operating under the veil of ignorance. Nobody knows yet who will rule, who will be called on to make sacrifices, or who will benefit most or least from the state they eventually form. Thus the Lambda Seven group is able to enter into their social contract without concern for unshared interests.

Many social contract theorists move from this stage to the support of one or another of the theories of the state discussed earlier. Many twentieth-century theorists urge that the next step in the reflection should be a conservative one. They argue that since we do not know that people will turn out to be friendly or benevolent, it would be neither rational nor prudent to be too trusting. Our strategy should be to focus chiefly on provisions to prevent ourselves from harming each other. Thus, while cooperation is advantageous, it should take second place to security. On the other hand, if adequate guarantees for personal security can be arrived at, then the advantages of collective defense and centralized economic planning should be pursued. Others suggest that taking such a conservative approach predisposes people to mistrust and unnecessarily thwarts their potential for individual and communal achievement. Since people live up, or down, to the expectations of themselves and others, strategically it would be wiser to try for more than simply a society where everyone leaves everyone else alone. These critics of the conservative strategy urge a bolder, more forthcoming approach, where people willingly risk their very lives and fortunes in the adventure of building a society founded on mutual trust and on the presumption that good, honest folks would willingly put the needs of the group ahead of their own. You might ask yourself how presumptions about the fundamental character of human nature impact on the kind of social contract which ultimately evolves.

The social contract theory begins with the assumption that individuals have personal interests independent of the possible interests of any collective. Social contract theorists also presume that states ought to be conceived of as being generated out of the gathering together of individuals intent on best fulfilling their fundamental human needs. It is not surprising, then, that from the seventeenth-century British philosopher Thomas Hobbes on down to contemporary times, few social contract theorists have been fascist. While seeing clearly the atomistic possibilities for fulfillment in human life, they have been either implicitly or explicitly skeptical of the existence and the absolute value of organic human purposes. Their strongest skepticism, however, has been of the comparative value of organic purposes. Social contract theorists attribute a positive value to an individual's freedom from interference by others (negative freedom) and to setting and pursuing one's own goals (human autonomy). They recognize that these values would surely be sacrificed in a dictatorial, totalitarian state, where it would not be clear that the result of this sacrifice would be anything beyond the fulfillment of the dictator (at the expense of everyone else). Thus, social contract theorists have judged that the values of negative freedom (liberty) and human autonomy should not be sacrificed or even jeopardized for the sake of a possible organic fulfillment, at least not in a fascist regime, and probably not under organic socialism either.

The social contract theory, freed from being viewed as a statement of historical fact, and seen rather as a normative theory, tells us how rational people could and should resolve problems of conflicts of interests. They should resort to contractual agreements, charters, constitutions, or other forms of mutually agreeable, binding accommodations. In the case study Wilson invites the others to be rational about the resolution of their disagreements. Her invitation will not determine which theory of the state they will select; it does not define their fundamental, shared, human purposes. But it does indicate how to begin to identify these purposes and decide what losses of personal liberty or personal freedom they are worth.

EXERCISES

1. (a) State the minimal list of shared, fundamental purposes of all individuals.
   (b) State the minimal interest of the state.
   (c) Describe the kinds of circumstances in which conflict may arise between these two sets of interests. (2.1)

2. (a) State the purpose of the state according to the organic view of the state.
   (b) State the further purposes of persons that the organic view of the state theoretically fulfills.
   (c) Explain the further kind of conflict that would arise between a state that pursued organic purposes and a person who accepted your list in 1.(a) but did not accept your list in 2.(b)
   (d) Explain why according to the organic theory this conflict dissolves. (2.3, 2.5 and 2.6)

3. Below is a list of assertions about what the common, fundamental, human purposes are. Different ones of these assertions are true according to the classical liberal, the socialist, and the fascist. On the right are columns marked CL, S, and F for these three views. Mark a T or an F in each column beside each assertion depending on whether it is true or false according to each of these three views of the common fundamental purposes. (2.2 through 2.7)

   CL   S   F

   (a) Agreements to cooperate should be enforceable.
   (b) Full human dignity must extend the significance of an isolated individual's life.
   (c) Harm caused by others should be avoided.
   (d) Planning should be sufficient to prevent the disruption of the state.
   (e) The rights of individuals not to be interfered with so long as they are, in turn, not interfering with or harming others should be guaranteed.
   (f) The state is justified in pursuing goals other than those of individuals when it is necessary in order to prevent individuals from indirectly harming each other.
   (g) The state is justified in pursuing goals other than those of individuals because the citizen's identity is completed and his life fulfilled only by participating in the achievement of these greater goals.
   (h) The state is justified in pursuing goals other than those of individuals when it is either necessary or helpful in order to provide a dimension of benefits individuals would otherwise lack.

4. (a) State the assumptions of social contract theory about the conditions under which the social contract is best made.
   (b) State the function that the theory is intended to serve.
   (c) State why it is supposed that if the assumptions are true, the function will be fulfilled. (2.8)

DISCUSSION QUESTIONS

1. In 2.1 we distinguished purposes from means. How sharp is that distinction in actual practice? Has national defense, for example, become an end in itself, rather than a means to an end? What about other major government programs and social institutions? Should the perpetuation of those programs and institutions become ends in themselves?

. 2. In 2.2 we described a classical liberal as one who is most concerned with personal liberty and non-interference from others or from the government. Where does that put the classical liberal on today's political spectrum? What is a contemporary liberal in comparison to a classical liberal? In terms of specific policies, where might they agree, and where might they differ?

3. Many see the tax policies of government as aimed specifically at creating incentives and disincentives. Along with the revenue generated, these motivational devices serve to promote certain purposes and thwart others. In view of the tax structure, what is the government's (local, state or national) implicit statement regarding fundamental, shared, human purposes? Is it correct?

4. Are human beings essentially good or essentially bad and what does this imply about our shared, fundamental, human purposes and the three theories of the state discussed?

ANSWERS TO SELECTED EXERCISES

1. (a) The minimal common fundamental purposes are to survive and to ensure continued survival.
   (b) Minimally the state's interest is in surviving and ensuring its survival.
   (c) When the state's survival is in question (because of attack, for example, or because of any factor which threatens the breakdown of society—a food scarcity, rebellion, a catastrophic economic or natural disaster, etc.), sacrificing or endangering the individual's survival may help ensure the survival of the state.

2. (a) According to the organic theory the state should set lofty goals, such as advancing culture or civilization, with which citizens can identify.
   (b) Individuals, divorced from the state, are insignificant and isolated. The goals of the state theoretically provide citizens with significance and meaning for their lives through identification with and participation in the goals of the state, which transcend the limitations of individuals.
   (c) Such individuals would feel constrained, forced against their own will, to accept and pursue goals with which they might not identify nor agree.
   (d) According to organic theory, this conflict dissolves, because persons cannot fulfill themselves as individuals. The greatest satisfaction possible for persons, according to organic theories, is to participate in the development of culture or civilization, the goal of the organic state. Thus, theoretically only uneducated, confused or socially unbalanced persons could experience the conflict at all.

3.   *CL   S   F*
   (a) *T   T   T*
   (b) *F   F   T* (Socialist theorists need not accept this if they take an atomistic approach.)
   (c) *T   T   T*
   (d) *F   T   T*
   (e) *T   F   F* (Such is the importance of group interests, according to the socialist and fascist.)
   (f) *F   T   F* (The classical liberal finds it unjustified; the fascist finds the interference justified but not for the reason given here.)
   (g) *F   F   T* (Although atomistic socialists find this false, organic socialists could accept this.)
   (h) *F   T   T*

4. (a) The condition is hypothetical, not historical. It is assumed that society does not yet exist, that the "original position" obtains. It is also assumed that the *veil of ignorance* is in place and, thus, nobody knows his or her own interests nor anything else that would allow him or her to infer what those particular interests will turn out to be.

   (b) The theory is intended to provide a normative statement about how to go about rationally deciding what sort of society, state, and government would be best for human beings to form.

   (c) It is supposed that if people were to reason about desirable social conditions, they would be able to negotiate and agree with each other regarding sacrifices of some personal liberties in order to obtain guarantees that certain fundamental purposes will be achieved.

Section 3
THE PURPOSES OF GOVERNMENNT

The contrasts among classical liberalism, socialism, and fascism arise out of differences in what each sees as the fundamental human needs. These differences yield very different views of the purposes of the state. The government is the organizational structure charged with carrying out the state's purposes. The government, then, is viewed as having different legitimate purposes depending upon your theory of the state. In this section we will examine the range of government purposes people have thought to be appropriate. First we will clarify what a government is. We will then examine the relationship between the concepts of government and of sovereignty in order to identify the possible purposes of government. After reading Section 3, you should be able to:

- Define "government" and give examples of possible governments for a variety of societies.
- Compare and contrast the theories of anarchism, limited government, and totalitarianism in terms of the purposes of government.

- Describe and identify the difference between participatory democracy and representative democracy.

THE CASE OF LAMBDA SEVEN, PART III

Tom Walsh and Martha Ramford were returning to their quarters after the earlier discussions when Ramford asked, "I didn't understand what you were trying to do back there, what with all that talk about how nobody can force you to cooperate if you don't want to. What exactly do you think a government should try to accomplish?"

"Nothing, frankly! My honest view is that there should be no government. People should act voluntarily without any of the constraints of governmental authority. I don't like majority rule, I don't like being represented by somebody else. I want to speak for myself. Responsibility for what happens to me is not something I wish to give away to some dictator or some almighty committee. And I don't think governments, which are, after all, just groups of people carrying out policy decisions, have any rights which people as individuals don't have. Specifically, I don't like the idea of the government being the only group in a society with a right to coerce someone into doing something."

"Tom, you're taking this too far. Seems to me that some governmental structures are absolutely necessary," responded Ramford. "I can agree that the government's functions should be limited, but surely we need some agency to resolve conflicts of interest between citizens. And we need some agency to provide for the security of the people. It would be an incredible waste of effort, if not entirely impossible, for each of us to try to enforce agreements, provide for our own safety, resolve our conflicts, and still have time left to do the other things we need and want to do."

"Who says we have to act as individuals. I have no objection to voluntary cooperation. But be realistic..."

"You be realistic! What if someone refuses to cooperate. You think all one-hundred-twenty of us are perfectly honest and wonderful people. Not likely, and that's why your purely voluntary system just won't work. To protect ourselves from each other, if for no other reason, we need a government with the power to establish and enforce laws."

Walsh shook his head. "You know, Martha, you have a warped view of human nature. But, besides that, once it starts, it gets away from you. Government power takes on a life of its own. At first government starts out as just a security force, but sooner or later it spreads. It gets involved with such community affairs as resource management, transportation, communications, and the enforcement of contracts. After that comes encroachments into even more private matters, like private business transactions between buyers and sellers or between employees and employers. It soon attempts centralized management of the economy. From there it moves into education, health care, and all sorts of programs to benefit different sub-groups of people, like working mothers, the handicapped, retirees, and so on. It can even get involved with organizing morality, religion, and recreation. No, Ramford. Once you take that first step you start sliding down a slippery slope, and there is no way to stop."

"Wait a minute. I'm not Gonzales. I didn't say that government has the right to stick its nose into everything. What it can rightfully do or not do is an open question. I can imagine situations where a government might have a rightful role to play in some of the things you mentioned. But I would not think it has unlimited authority and I certainly would not claim that it can use any methods it wishes to accomplish its goals."

Tom laughed. "So yes to some things and no to others. Is that it? And I suppose you would have the government itself be responsible for controlling its appetite. That's like dangling raw meat in front of a hungry tiger and asking him to resist the temptation to pounce."

"Ridiculous," said Ramford. "We'll only stand for as much government as it takes to meet our needs. No more, but no less either."

But the skeptical Walsh was undaunted. "Did you ever stop to figure out the percentage of people in government positions on Old Earth. How many days of work last year went to pay your various tax bills? Was it 160 days out of 250? And what about all the corruption, even in the hallowed Intergalactic Association," quipped Tom. "I rest my case."

3.1 "Government" Defined

Any organization of persons vested with the rightful authority to pursue a society's goals can, for our purposes, be called a *government*. This definition applies to any form of society, from a club, to a family, to a corporation, to the state. The task of government is, by definition, to achieve the goals of the society that forms it. The shareholders of a corporation have the common interest of making a profit from their business venture. As a society they form a government, the corporate board of directors, which concerns itself with that common interest, establishing and enforcing policy toward the end of making a profit for the shareholders. Whatever additional purposes the shareholders might agree on will also become purposes which the corporate board should pursue. So, for example, if the shareholders meet and agree that worker safety is also a top priority, a priority so important that they are willing to reduce their profit margin to achieve it, then worker safety becomes a purpose that the board of directors is obligated to pursue.

To achieve the goals of the society which formed it, a government must often work to secure the cooperation of various people. Often these people are the members of the society which the government is attempting to serve. But at times they are not, as the apartheid policies and events in South Africa clearly demonstrate. Also the government must decide on divisions of labor, making sure that all the necessary jobs are being done and the good of the society which it exists to serve is being secured. A manager must decide who in the office is going to do what, what the priorities will be, and what resources will be devoted to each.

Whether this decision is made in a consultative or authoritarian way is, at this point, not the issue. Rather, the manager, as the agent of the governing board, is carrying out the purpose of that government, which is but one piece of the complex process of serving the interests of those who formed that governing board. Notice that under this interpretation of the role of government, the only interests which a government has the duty to pursue are those of the society which formed and sustains it.

In their attempt to direct the behavior of people toward the society's goals, governments establish and attempt to enforce more or less formal policies, regulations, and statements of duties and responsibilities. In the case of the state, these regulations take the form of laws, policy positions, executive orders, or official guidelines. Their aim is to control behavior. The state's government articulates its regulations by means of legislation. Governments of states make laws to regulate the activity of persons within the area of their control—whether or not they are citizens of the society which constitutes that state. The aim of these laws is to prevent people from acting in ways which work against the goals of the state and to compel people to act in ways deemed necessary to the achievement of the goals of the state. For example, to prevent harm to people there are laws against violence, theft, polluting the environment, etc. To achieve the goal of adequate health care, there are laws requiring pre-school inoculations, providing programs of sex education, and requiring people to pay taxes so that emergency services are available to those in need.

3.2 How Much Government?

In the case study Walsh comes out against the whole idea of having a government. In effect Walsh raises the frequently asked question: "Why do we need all these rules, regulations, departments, and people in taxpayer supported government positions?" The theoretical response has already been suggested. In our extremely large, anonymous, pluralistic, and complex society, where people with different customs, mores, traditions, interests and concerns live together in teaming cities which are themselves hundreds and thousands of miles apart, the purposes of the state—those which are shared, fundamental human purposes—would be seriously endangered without some form of government and law. We need the mechanisms of government if we even hope to have these purposes fulfilled. Yet the rules, officers, bureaucracy, fines, and red tape can sometimes become quite an obstacle to seeing the overall necessity of some form of government. As government pursues the goals of the state, it develops agencies, structures, bureaus, departments, and any number of things that seem to make it at times more an obstacle to human goals than a servant.

The problem of the growth and proliferation of government and governmental structures is not too serious in many societies, because most societies are voluntary. People can sell their stock, quit the team, drop out of the club, resign their position, move to a different housing complex, divorce their spouse, and, in general, disassociate themselves from societies if they become convinced that continuing to live as a member of that society would frustrate, rather than fulfill, the purposes for which the society, and their membership in it, exists. Voluntary disassociation, however, is less feasible in the case of the society known as the state. People in self-imposed exile must live somewhere and it is virtually impossible to find anywhere on Earth not governed by some state or other. Immigration laws, financial penalties, cultural ties, kinship and friendship bonds make it extremely difficult to quit a particular state. Another reason why state governments are much more difficult to do without lies in the purposes they serve. Their purposes are the state's purposes—the meeting of people's fundamental human needs. So long as we have these needs and see satisfying them as the reason to form a state, we have reason to accept some state and, if it has such, its government. We can do without some societies, but as humans with shared fundamental needs, we cannot easily do without states.

We are not saying that all governments are necessarily good. At times they can become rather serious threats to the state they have been created to serve. This may occur when a government or individuals in it take on purposes that are not legitimate purposes of the state. Some people point to the U.S. involvement in the Middle East and in Central America as an example of this. Some claim that our government has no business being involved in those places because we, as a state, have no national interests which depend on how the disputes of countries in those regions of the world are resolved. Others say those disputes are elements in the global strategies of states hostile to our own, but that even if they were not, our state has a great interest in the outcome of those disputes. Another situation where government serves purposes other than those of the state occurs when government officials, charged with protecting and working for the common good, use the power of their offices to promote their own personal interests at the expense of the common good. Wide-spread government corruption, misuse and abuse of the power, and the chronic inability of government to police itself, can destroy essential trust and can lead persons in the society to advocate revolutionary means for the purpose of establishing new governmental institutions.

A second kind of situation when a government may not be pursuing its rightful goals is when it seeks its own preservation even to the possible harm of the society that formed it. People often point to the failure of the German Third Reich to negotiate a surrender toward the end of World War II as an example of a conflict between the interests of the Nazi government and those of the German state. This distinction is often echoed as world leaders condemn the actions of foreign governments while simultaneously reaffirming friendship for the people of that state. Another example of the government serving its own interests and not those of the society it is intended to serve can occur when a management group attempts to maintain itself in power (managers protecting their own jobs) contrary to the financial interests of the owners of the corporation (the society for which they work).

3.3 Classical Anarchism

In the case study Ramford articulates the traditional argument as to why states need governments. Her argument comes to this: As humans we have shared fundamental needs. Take personal survival as an example. To meet this need we must ensure our safety from the violence of each other and from the violence of people who are not members of our society. The mechanism to serve even this very limited goal is a government. It serves to organize us in case we must band together for our common defense. It sets up the laws we need to prevent us from doing violence to each other. It enforces these laws and punishes those who break them ensuring that even if violence does occur, it is stopped, peace is restored, and a repeat of the crime by the same criminal is rendered less likely.

As Ramford tells Walsh, if the argument holds, then total individual sovereignty in all domains of concern is not appropriate. Walsh, however, holds out for the theory of anarchism in its classical form. Advocates of *classical anarchism* reject all forms of government since it is wrong to maintain that any group of people can rightfully do what no individual can do (inflict harm on others, for example) and it is foolish to grant any group in a society (the police) the right to exercise a monopoly on the use of coercive force in that society. But, according to the classical anarchist, that is exactly what government is. By controlling the military and para-military one group within a society has been vested with the power to coerce others to do their will. Secondly, the creation of government in any form implies that individual autonomy and individual moral responsibility have been compromised. But no person can surrender his or her moral responsibility, nor can the person hide behind the idea that others (the government) decide for him what to do. A third issue of concern to the anarchist is how advocates of government (in any form) explain how it has become justifiable for a group of people (the government) to rightfully do what no individual or group of individuals in the society can do. For example, why is it right for the government to confine criminals to jail, but if another group in society did the same thing (held someone against their will) it would be illegal? Why can the government seize property but if someone else does it the seizure is called theft? Why are other employers and manufacturers liable for injuries caused in the work place or damages caused by their products, but the government is free to exempt itself from such liabilities?

Nurse Walsh, an avowed anarchist, does not advocate chaos and certainly would not say that anarchism means that people are free to go on a wild rampage of destruction. Rather, he takes the position that voluntary, cooperative, social arrangements, free from any of the authority or constraining forces of government, are reasonable and appropriate ways for persons to handle their mutual concerns. The anarchist view is that people can naturally be fair to each other, keep promises, and work cooperatively. They do not need governments to make and enforce laws. The anarchist typically believes in complete individual sovereignty, and values individual liberty more highly than any of the possible advantages of even limited government. Anarchism has come to be associated with terrorism and, to some extent, with ethical nihilism. But these connections are not part of classical anarchist theory. Some anarchist theories are pacifist, others not. Some anarchists imagine socialistic utopias, others see the ideal as more individualistic. Considering what Walsh said in the earlier case studies, he would probably be best described as an atomistic anarchist.

Of course, as Ramford points out, the anarchist's approach runs up against some formidable problems. What is to be done about external enemies—if cooperation is voluntary, what if people are too slow or unwilling to be persuaded to risk their lives and fortunes in combat against a common foe? What should be done about people who cannot be trusted and refuse to play by the rules (criminals)? To this latter problem some anarchists respond that each individual has the right to protect himself and his property and to enforce any agreements he and another have entered into. But the problems of individual enforcement are many. What if the person lacks the power to enforce? What if the person mistakenly directs his or her power against the wrong person? What if excessive force is used? In all this serious problems about rightful authority, human rights, and justice arise. Images of the potential horrors of individual enforcement lead some to forsake anarchism for some version of limited government.

3.4 Limited Government

In the case study Ramford advocates *limited government*. She begins by saying that government should provide security, prevent harm, and perhaps adjudicate internal conflicts. She does not start out by claiming anything more ambitious, such as that government ought to improve transportation, health care, education, or living standards. Later, Ramford seems to suggest that governmental interests may extend to these other areas, but that she would consider each in turn on its own merits. We cannot tell from this case study, or earlier ones, whether Ramford would want government to establish or enforce standards of morality, regulate artistic and literary activity, or moderate religious practices. All of these are possible purposes of government as is evidenced by some (though not all) of the typical arguments advanced regarding such issues as pornography, prostitution, offensive language used in public (such as on the radio), censorship, the banning of certain films and books, prayer in public schools, and other things.

The argument in favor of limited government can be developed beyond what has been said in 3.3. Considering the complexity of a typical society, governments can serve two further purposes beyond providing security and securing the people's cooperation in pursuit of the fundamental purposes. These two further purposes are securing legal agreements between people and providing for differences in needs and abilities. Let us look at them more closely. First, in a complex society such as our nation we often need to enter into agreements with strangers. We do this whenever we use a credit card, sign a contract, bid on a project, buy a piece of equipment, or get married. We use the government to make these agreements secure. When you get a bank loan, sign a lease, pay tuition, or take your car in for service, you may be entering into contractual agreements with people whom you do not know and whom you have no particular reason to trust or not trust.   The government stands behind these contractual agreements to make sure that all parties live up to their responsibilities.   Laws regulate how contracts are made and what their terms may be.   The government enforces the contract on all parties by its power to penalize any who fail to fulfill their part of the agreement.   Without this guarantee we would be forced, out of practical necessity, to limit our dealings to those whom we knew and personally trusted.   It is not likely that any highly industrialized and complex nation could survive if contractual obligations were not backed up by the power and authority of governmental law.

Second, our complex society leads to high degrees of specialization.   Each of us depends on many others in order to live.   For example, very few of us grow food and almost none of us could say we grow the variety and quantity which would constitute a balanced diet.   But someone grows it for us, others process it, others package it, others deliver it, others sell it on the wholesale market, and still others sell it retail.   And this does not even take into consideration those who manufacture the machinery and chemical products needed for agriculture, those who advertise and market the products, or those who conduct research on superior ways to farm. Other groups are involved in the production and delivery of energy resources or in transportation, communication, health care, defense, social services or education. People argue that we need some governmental mechanisms to regulate and coordinate all of these activities, so that they all come together for the good of the state.

In this argument the distinction between what we need for survival and what we need for our well-being is unclear.   Communication, transportation, health care, and education are all needed for survival in certain ways.   But also they all lead to greater opportunities to be productive and self-sustaining in a complex society. They also hold out the potential for achieving a better quality of life, more opportunity for self-development and recreational outlets, improved health and the chance to pursue diversified interests.   These make life more enjoyable and enhance our well-being.   For example, health care leads not only to survival through cures and healings, but also to a healthier, happier life through preventive medicine and the control of dangerous diseases.

Once it gets going, where does it stop?   Whatever the strength of the arguments for some form of limited government, Walsh's fear in the case study must be addressed.   How will the government itself be controlled?   Often the government is charged with the function of controlling itself.   This crucial self-regulatory function can be accomplished in a variety of ways, such as building checks and balances into the government's power structure; providing for separation of legislative, enforcement, and judicial powers; providing for regular changes of the persons in leadership roles; providing impeachment and recall procedures; allowing for a free press and for academic freedom so that people have the liberty to criticize government activities without fear of reprisals; and limiting government secrecy, executive privilege, and special prerogatives to only those situations necessary for the security of the state. Each of these proposals has its strengths. The skeptical Walsh might reply that all of these are still not adequate. The temptations of power are great, and leaders throughout human history have fallen prey to them. They have found ways to use government to their own personal advantage. There are so many examples of the abuse of governmental power, of favoritism, corruption, collusion, conflict of interest and bribery, that the problem is not one of identifying the limited purposes of government but keeping the government limited to only those purposes.

These problems are not new. Plato (427 B.C.–347 B.C.) suggested one way to resolve problems of corruption and keep reasonable limits on government. His proposal ran something like this: Select potential leaders at a very early age. Separate them from the business and military sectors. Train them to be strong, well-informed, wise, and just. Satisfy all their human needs and finally grant them absolute power (Plato, 473 B.C.). Plato's idea is that although these leaders will have tremendous power, their wisdom and virtue, along with the fact that there is nothing more that they could possibly want, will guide their use of this power so that it serves the good of the state.

3.5 Totalitarianism

Plato developed his ideas not in support of limited government but in the service of *totalitarianism* and the dictatorial concept of government. Gonzales, in the earlier case studies in this chapter, advocated fascism and would push for a totalitarian, dictatorial form of government. Under the totalitarian theory, government could rightfully become involved in every human purpose to *improve* every aspect of society. It could, for example, strive to make communication and transportation more efficient by assuming governmental control over the postal service, the telecommunications industry, and by establishing government operated utility service, a government press, government radio and television networks, government airlines and rail carriers, a government freight system, etc. It could strive to regulate all forms of commerce and manage the production and distribution of essential resources such as gas and electric power, water, food, shelter, welfare, and medical care. It could seek to improve the physical and psychological health of the population by government operated training and fitness centers, by prescribing the curricula and ensuring that the proper civic values are effectively taught. It could work to improve the moral character of citizens by regulating the programs presented in schools, churches, museums, libraries, and the entertainment media. It could seek to protect the people from disruptive social influences by centralizing social planning and controlling the distribution and exercise of economic and political power in the society.

In contrast to the theory of limited government, the concern in totalitarian theory is not with how to limit government authority but with how to acquire, maintain, and strengthen it. Regulating the press and other media, establishing secret security forces, relocating the population into smaller, more rural communities, rewarding loyalty to the government, and imposing mandatory "education" (indoctrination) programs on all citizens have been used along with torture, terror and imprisonment as tools toward this goal. Fascist theorists argue that given their concept of the state and fascist views about the fundamental human purposes, these governmental measures are justifiable—protests regarding the violation of human rights notwithstanding. Given the dictatorial theory of sovereignty, the goals and measures named above could be accommodated. But, using the classical liberal theory of the state and the theory of individual sovereignty, these goals are sorely mistaken and these measures are morally outrageous. Looking at the concept of popular sovereignty and a socialist view of fundamental human purposes, many of the goals listed above are worthy, although some of the measures suggested may be judged too severe or too extreme to be permitted.

3.6 Combinations of Theories In Practice

Although fundamentally organized on the basis of popular sovereignty (or as the Constitution of the United States puts it, "We, the people..."), in practice our nation combines a variety of theories of sovereignty. We allow for individual sovereignty in certain domains of concern, such as morality and religion. We generally advocate popular sovereignty in domains such as the regulation of education, basic health care, and the production and distribution of goods and services, in that all of these are topics about which our legislatures make laws. In normal times popular sovereignty is the order of the day, as even the president's authority over matters of foreign trade, foreign policy, and the use of military force, however absolute or limited, is derived from the electorate. But we also allow for complete dictatorial sovereignty in the event of an emergency. If the president or a governor proclaims a state of emergency, then he or she has the authority to make policy and issue executive orders that can affect all aspects of our social lives. Thus, not only do we allow for different concepts of sovereignty in different domains, but we also allow special circumstances, such as a clear and pressing danger to the state to expand or contract the domains of concern.

3.7 The Will of the People

We have indicated arguments against the individual sovereignty theory and the dictatorial sovereignty theory. The first leads to anarchistic theories of non-government, which appear inadequately to meet our shared, fundamental human needs. The latter leads to totalitarian governments that so threaten individual liberties as to make them unacceptable. An important argument against popular sovereignty is that it demands that the government not only work for the purposes of the people taken as a whole, but also work to discern the will of the people taken as a whole. This creates the problem of how to learn what "the will of the people" is. The problem has two chief aspects: First, is there really a single collective will of the people—or is that just theoretical fiction? And, second, if there is something called "the will of the people," how can the leaders learn what its desires are?

There is also a third problem: What should the government do if it sincerely believes that the will of the people as expressed on a particular issue is in conflict with either the long-range good of the state or with the will of the people as expressed on another issue? As an example, consider the government's dilemma in matters of affirmative action and achieving genuine equality of opportunity. It is considered to be the will of the people that no person should be given any special advantages by virtue of race, religion, ethnic origin, gender, and the like. Acting on this will, the government has legislated against certain kinds of discrimination. But in looking at specific cases, the government has also upheld the rights of employers to undertake voluntary programs of reverse discrimination, noting that it is also the will of the people that the exercise of free trade not be unduly regulated. The will of the people as expressed and understood in one set of circumstances conflicts with the will of the people as expressed and understood in another set! What is the government to do—particularly if it also believes that voluntary programs of reverse discrimination, while viewed by most citizens as unfair, actually are in the best long-term interest of the country? Problems like this are sometimes resolved by assuming that the will to heed is the one which aims at long term social goals (equality and free trade) and the one to disregard is the one which focuses on short-term means (reverse discrimination). But seen as a conflict between equality and free trade, the problem can be viewed as a conflict concerning goals, not goals vs. means. In this case we might resolve the problem by determining which goal is viewed as the more important. This leads us right back to the basic problem of how we are to discover the will of the people in the first place.

3.8 Democracy

Every government, whether it runs a business, a church, a club, or a state, if it is to be responsive to the society it serves, must find ways to know what that society wants. Defenders of the theory of popular sovereignty, and of government based on that theory, suggest two ways. The first is to presume that some person or group of people can be trusted to know and act on the will of the people. The person might be a divinely guided dictator, a popular and charismatic leader, or someone wise enough to know what the people would choose if they were to be able to express their choice in the light of their own long-term interest. The group might be some combination of such people, or it might be selected to represent a particular interest group and express its point of view. Whether it is the tribal council, the elders, the past-presidents board, the central committee, the planner–manager group, the heads of major departments, or whoever, this approach says that government should look to the insights of some presumably experienced and well-informed subgroup (perhaps a group of one) within the society to tell it what the will of the people is. The second way is to provide means for the people to express their own opinions. These means might include letter writing, elections, demonstrations, or town meetings, where the presiding officer tries to express a group's consensus on an issue.

In practice both ways are used in many societies. For example, we try to settle some issues through *participatory democracy* which corresponds to the second approach above. That is, we involve everyone affected by the issue in the decision making process. We put it before the whole club to discuss, we send it out for ratification by the entire union; or we hold a town meeting, call an open hearing, put it to public referendum, call a meeting of everyone in the apartment complex, ask the entire staff what it wants, etc. This method, while open and direct, has many practical drawbacks. For one, getting everyone together is neither speedy nor efficient, but time consuming and cumbersome. How would 40,000,000 Californians meet to discuss and solve the State's water problem? How feasible would it be to call a meeting of the entire membership of the AFL–CIO or the Democratic or Republican Party and decide on priorities for one of those massive organizations? Participatory democracy in many cases seems ineffective, if not counter-productive. What should we do, for example, in cases calling for urgent strategic decisions? To remedy these kinds of problems, states and other societies move toward the use of representative democracy.

Representative democracy provides for people from various interest areas (in our country these are conceived of as different geographic locations, but they could be thought of as different job groups, different socioeconomic statuses, different genders, different races, or whatever) to elect representatives who in turn will speak in councils, legislatures, and congresses on behalf of their constituencies. If the society in question is a state, then representative democracies, where officials are elected by vote and charged with the duty of pursuing the interests of the state are called *republics*. Within any representative democracy a major normative problem for the person who is elected is how best to "represent" the interests of the constituency and also balance those against the interests of the society taken as a whole. Inevitably the elected official acquires a different perspective on problems than the perspectives of those from which she was elected. This increased knowledge and appreciation for the greater complexities of the problems, perhaps along with a fuller appreciation of how different alternative solutions would impact on other interest groups or on the society taken as a whole, often leads the person to experience conflicts with the idea of "speaking on behalf of" the constituency. The person must decide when to exercise her own judgment and when to vote strictly as the people who elected her, in their relative ignorance and self-interest, would want her to vote. The representative must decide if she is primarily a reporter who decides based on public opinion polls, or a leader who helps inform and shape those opinions. In either case, how the representative's action helps to define "the will of the people" remains unclear.

The problems democratic decision making encounters go beyond those mentioned above. The way issues are presented, the number and complexity of the alternatives, and the ways in which background "data" is couched can all but determine the outcome. The presence or absence of relevant information can make a telling difference. The absence of the opportunity to reflect and consider matters can lead to hasty and misguided decisions. The oratorical powers of emotional people might win out over a less eloquent but more rational point of view. The fatigue level or interest level of the group, even the order of the agenda, can lead trivial problems to be examined in excruciating detail while vital issues are dealt with hastily or not at all. Clearly, the problems in this list affect all kinds of decision making, but they are mentioned here because their negative effects on the quality of any decision making process become magnified as more and more people with their own special interests become involved. Thus they pose additional risks for democracies.

There are many problems for democracies as they seek to know and carry out the will of the people. How can we be sure that the individual selected to lead or represent us actually knows our collective will? Is voting the best way of revealing our collective will? What about opinion polls or a method of phoning-in our views? Should we require that all votes be unanimous or that things be done by consensus, instead of majority rule? But consensus is rarely possible. And if we go with something besides majority rule, what percentage should we agree to? Should different percentages be needed for different kinds of issues—say, a plurality to win an election, a two-thirds majority to amend the Constitution? But if we reject unanimity and consensus, because they are rarely possible, how can we claim that the collective will is being expressed? In a recent election a president was selected who received only slightly more than half the popular votes cast. If you totaled the people who voted against that president with the number of eligible people who did not vote at all, then nearly 65 percent of the people had not expressed a desire to have that person be president. Yet, he was elected, by the will of the people.

EXERCISES

1. (a) A club for professional writers and a group of owners of professional teams exemplify two different societies. Either describe the governmental functions that these societies would want because of the kind of societies they are, or begin from your own pair of contrasting examples and describe the governmental functions that those societies would desire. (3.1, 3.2)
(b) Define government, checking to see that your definition fits the governments you have described. 3.1

2. (a) State how anarchists and advocates of limited government agree or disagree about the reasonableness of giving any group in the society an exclusive right to the power to prevent harm caused by others and to ensure maximal individual freedom. (3.3, 3.4)
(b) State the assertions about the value of freedom to which anarchists and advocates of limited government agree. (3.3, 3.4)
(c) Explain why totalitarian government is acceptable and congenial to the organic theory of the state and the dictatorial concept of sovereignty. (3.5)

3. (a) Cite a real example of participatory democracy in some society other than the state. What are the strengths and weaknesses of using that form of democracy in that society?

(b) Cite a real example of representative democracy in some society other than the state. What are the strengths and weaknesses of using that form of democracy in that society?

(c) Characterize participatory democracy by stating (1) the theory of sovereignty under which it operates, (2) what involvement the sovereign has in formulating a rule or law, and (3) whether the authority of those formulating the rule or law is derived or underived. (3.8)

(d) Characterize representative democracy in these same ways. (3.8)

DISCUSSION QUESTIONS

1. Given the definitions of "democracy" and "republic" used in 3.8, which major countries could rightly be classified as democratic republics? On what conceptual grounds did you include or exclude such nations as the USA, Mexico, Canada, Cuba, China, Japan, Russia, Poland, Spain, Iran, Israel, El Salvador, North Korea, South Africa?

2. If, according to 3.8, democracy has so many problems, what better ways might there be to discover the will of the people? Or, given the power of home computers and the prospect of linking all of us in a huge network where instantaneous mass communication was feasible, maybe direct participatory democracy could be more widely used. What would your views be on having the opportunity to vote almost at any hour of any day on the vital issues facing your society? Would we need representatives in such a system, and if we did, how would their duties change if each of us could vote for ourselves on pending legislation?

3. If the USA and Russia both claim to be democratic and both describe themselves as based on the concept of popular sovereignty, then what exactly are the philosophical differences between the two nations?

4. Characterize the government forms, theories of sovereignty, and purposes of those societies known as "the corporation" and "the church."

ANSWERS TO SELECTED EXERCISES

1. (a) The club (provided it is not involved in collective bargaining) may want to limit itself to defining who can become a member, what are the responsibilities of membership, who can become officers, the duties of officers, and who has the rightful authority to take over when an officer is unable or unwilling to fulfill his or her responsibilities. However, enforcement powers and judicial roles may not need to be specified in voluntary societies, especially if there are no strong conflicts of interest. A society such as owners of professional sports teams, however, is very likely to experience conflicts of interest. Therefore, additional regulations granting

enforcement and arbitration powers to league authorities (say, the commissioner) will be appropriate.

(b) A government of a society is any organization that has the authority to pursue the goals of that society.

2. (a) Anarchists find such a practice unreasonable and morally objectionable because they fear that the power granted to prevent harm and ensure freedom will be used to cause harm and restrict freedom, resulting in a net loss to individuals over a situation where no governmental authority existed. Advocates of limited government believe that with a careful system of checks and balances, individuals can experience a net gain in liberty and suffer less harm if government with an enforcement power is formed.

(b) According to both anarchists and advocates of limited government, the freedom of the individual from constraints imposed by the interference of others is desirable and ought to be as great as it possibly can be.

(c) It is not at all surprising, and it may be helpful, to have government involved in all aspects of life (totalitarianism) if the most satisfying life for the individual is one that is totally involved and absorbed in the goals of the state. If the government is backed with dictatorial authority based either on its wisdom or divine right to rule, then much of the turmoil and many of the errors associated with other concepts of sovereignty can be avoided.

3. (c) (1) Popular, (2) Directly formulate rule of law, (3) Underived.

(d) (1) Popular, Elect representatives to formulate rule of law, (3) Derived from those who elected them.

8 | LAW

When did I ever tell you the laws had to be moral? Or just!

Koby's Reflections on Justice

A wide variety of laws regulate many of the most important aspects of our social lives. There are laws concerning social interactions such as entering into contracts, the exchange of property, business dealings, education, government, taxation, safety, land use, and health care, to name just a few. There are also laws regarding more personal things such as sexual practices, the use of dangerous substances, and gambling. These facts raise many questions. What are the advantages of the rule of law for society? What prerequisites make possible the rule of law? Section 1 deals with these two questions. In Section 2 we will analyze the concept of a legal obligation. We will ask how law relates to morality and how it relates to the penalties imposed on those found guilty of breaking the law. We will question what makes such penalties appropriate. The goal of this chapter is for you to understand the potential advantages of the rule of law, the prerequisites needed for the development of the rule of law, and the relationships between the law and morality and between the law and legal penalties.

Section 1
THE RULE OF LAW

Laws regulate conduct by telling us what things we are legally obligated to do or legally prohibited from doing. Although laws do not affect every aspect of our lives, they do exert a major influence over our conduct, especially in some of the more socially important areas. In this section we shall examine the rule of law in order to discover its many advantages over reliance on social mores, customs, and traditions. In our civilization governments make laws, enforce them, and settle disputes concerning them. We can think of the group of laws developed by any given governmental authority as a *legal system*. Several legal systems affect our lives, for governments at all levels—national, regional, state, and local—make laws. In this section we will ask what the prerequisites are for the development of legal systems and the rule of law. The answer will involve a combination of factors: what issues the laws in question cover, how the laws are made and amended, how they are enforced, and how disputes of law are adjudicated. After studying this section you should be able to:

- List the theoretical advantages of the rule of law over the rule of social custom.
- List the four types of prerequisites for the rule of law, and distinguish which specific prerequisites fall under each.
- Given example laws or situations, identify any prerequisites for the rule of law they do not meet, and explain how the example law or situation could be changed to fulfill those prerequisites.
- Supply examples of laws or situations that fail to meet each of the prerequisites of the rule of law, identify the prerequisite they do not meet, and explain how your example law or situation fails to satisfy it.

THE CASE OF PLANGTON HEIGHTS

Judith Franllow, 12-year-old daughter of Vern Franllow, quietly approached the old man who sat in the rocking chair on the wooden porch. He perked up as she climbed the steps. He knew Vern Franllow was the richest and most politically influential of the new group of land developers, real estate people, and industrialists who had caused the population of Plangton Heights to swell to 24,000 in recent years. And he liked talking to young Judy.

"Good morning, Mr. Thorntwister. How you doing today?"

"Fine, Judy. I'm just sitting here remembering."

"Remembering what?" asked the precocious child.

"Oh, what Plangton Heights used to be like before it got to be a big city. That corner where the new library stands used to be the only crossroads for ten miles around. There were only fifteen or so families living around here when my father brought us in. We all were mostly farmers except for the teacher, the shopkeeper, and the blacksmith. Oh, and there was old man Green who lived out in his forest all the time and never socialized much. Most everyone worked all week and went to the crossroads on the weekend. I remember the old general store, the stable, and the school where we held town meetings, and I remember our old church. Did you know everybody in town helped build that church? Everyone except old man Green, that is. We were real proud of that. Why, in those days, Judy, we didn't have no mayor or no sheriff even. Didn't need 'em, you know. If anybody got difficult we just ignored 'em, or my father would ride out and calm 'em down. We all grew up together, you know. Everybody sort of knew what they could and could not do."

"But what about outlaws?"

"Oh, there weren't no outlaws in these parts. We knew everybody for miles around and they all knew us. We just lived our lives and when there was something that needed to be done, like rebuilding the schoolhouse after a tornado knocked 'er down, why we all would just pitch in and do it."

"But who collected taxes? Who built the roads? Who hired the teacher? What if people argued about something, who decided who was right? Like if there was a fight or something."

"Well, first off, we didn't have most of these here complications that you see nowadays. No taxes, 'cause, like I said, if something came up, we all just put in what was needed. Except if we didn't see why, that is. I remember none of us farmers cared about building a road to open up old man Green's forest for logging. As to fences and property lines and such, why there was land all over the place. Mostly it was easy telling yours from mine cause nobody seemed to care. There was more than any of us knew what to do with. My father was sort of the judge till he died, and then Mr. Grownker, the storekeeper, just took over being judge. I remember that 'cause there was no real problems with Mr. Grownker except one time. Who was it? Ah, Barcon, I think her name was, yeah Mrs. Molly Barcon. She felt that Mr. Grownker cheated her on the price of bacon. Or was it flour? Anyway Grownker wouldn't even talk to her about it and nobody else had acted as judge for so many years that we all just let it go. As I recall, Mrs. Barcon left town after that."

"Maybe she was right, but nobody would stick up for her."

"Don't know," said the old man. "But, Judy, it was good in those times, before old man Green sold his forest to the paper company and them strangers and foreigner types started coming in and causing trouble. We had to elect a sheriff to keep the peace. But he wouldn't do nothing till he knew what the laws were. So we had to get together in the town hall to make up laws. The paper company had lots of money and lots of influence in the state capital too. It demanded roads, it put up fences, it built a railroad yard, a paper mill. Then more folks started moving in. Pretty soon we had a factory and we even had our own slum. I remember lots of dissension and bitterness. The paper company said our sheriff was always arresting its workers, but was leaving us farmers alone. It was hard times. Once our old church caught fire. All us farmers came running. But none of them strangers helped fight the fire. I bet one of 'em started it. We called in a federal judge, but we couldn't prove a thing cause nobody was saying nothing."

"Then what happened?"

"Oh, in time we all got over it. But we came out of it with more laws, lawyers, and politicians than I care to count."

"But once everyone knows the laws, then at least they all know where they stand," said the girl.

"Yup. And now we got all sorts of laws telling us what we can do and what we can't do. Now you have to do everything all legal-like. Why, you can't even buy a house no more without exchanging papers, going to the courthouse, and getting two witnesses who ain't even in your own family. When I was a kid my father bought our whole farm just by a handshake. Now you need title searches, registers of deeds, your credit is checked, and their ain't no end to all the things people do 'cause they can't trust each other."

1.1 Advantages of the Rule of Law

When we say that a society is governed by the rule of law, we mean that it has established the governmental authority to (a) make laws, (b) enforce these laws, and (c) resolve disputes over these laws. We can call such governmental authority—the legislative, enforcement, and judicial systems—its *legal institutions*. By saying that a society lives under the rule of law we further mean that the laws are designed to regulate the conduct of all its members by indicating what is permitted, what is forbidden, and what is required in that society.

When we say that a society is governed by social customs, mores, or traditions we mean that only customs, traditions, and generally accepted ways of acting serve to guide conduct. In such a society there may be no governmental authority that is responsible for making, enforcing, or adjudicating laws. Plangton Heights started off that way in the case study. It had no mayor or city council to make laws; it had no sheriff to enforce its laws or even its customs; and it had no officially elected or appointed judge to handle disputes. Plangton Heights ended up under the rule of law. The people elected a sheriff to keep the peace. They had town meetings to agree on laws. They brought in the territorial judge to settle disputes. They did these things in order to establish the rule of law in Plangton Heights. Much of this section is devoted to detailing the specific prerequisites that must be met if the rule of law is to exist.

For Plangton Heights the time of transition from the rule of custom to the rule of law was one of great turmoil and difficulty. Plangton Heights was, in a way, suffering growing pains. For several reasons the growth of Plangton Heights made the rule of law progressively more desirable for its people, while custom, mores, and traditions became increasingly inadequate and ill-suited to govern their society. Let's look at those reasons separately.

1.2 Promotion of Social Stability

One theoretical advantage of the rule of law is that laws promote social stability. Laws tell people what is expected of them and what they can expect of others. Laws create regular methods for handling one's affairs, particularly the ones that are most important from the point of view of the society. Thus, even if you wished to buy a house from someone you did not know, you could rely on the laws to lend a regularity to that business transaction. The laws specify what selling a house requires and what buying a house requires. Thus house selling, like most examples of exchanging property, is a stabilized activity in our society. As our legal system grows, we introduce stability into more and more aspects of life. In the United States we are engaged in stabilizing health care delivery systems, education opportunities, the treatment of persons who apply for jobs, seek housing or want bank loans, the safety of foods and pharmaceuticals, and the location of various kinds of enterprises (commercial, residential, agricultural, or industrial).

1.3 Provision for Cultural Diversity

A second theoretical advantage of the rule of law is that it provides for cultural diversity. Customs may differ from group to group. In the case of groups with different ethnic, racial, economic, or religious backgrounds, the cultural differences could be rather great, indeed even conflicting. In a pluralistic society, to rely only on these customs as a basis for social interaction would be to invite great strife, if not chaos. Laws can cut across these differences in customs and traditions. You may not share the customs or traditions of some other members of our society; nevertheless, you and they are still bound by the law to act or not act in certain ways. In this way the cultural richness of a pluralistic society need not lead to a conflict because of mutually incompatible traditions and social mores. Pluralism is possible because the important social interactions among people of all heritages and backgrounds do not depend on their individual customs but on the rule of law. If you tried to live in Plangton Heights in its early days, you might have faced the problem of either adopting its life style, to the point of even attending "our church," or living in relative isolation like old man Green. He wasn't a farmer, and his neighbors, all farmers, would not pitch in to build a road to allow him to log his forest.

1.4 Provision for Social Complexity

Complexity within a society is also provided for more adequately by the rule of law. Custom and tradition tend to be less adequate as society becomes more complex. New interests arise in society, new goals are developed, and new people with differing backgrounds come on the scene, entering into new relationships with each other. Laws can be made that account for these diversities and social complexities. Consider laws regulating such complex and delicate economic factors as banking, or the investment and exchange of stocks, bonds, and securities. Or, to take a more familiar example, consider the federal income tax law. This massive piece of legislation attempts to account for the wide variety of personal differences in how people acquire and dispose of their income, while at the same time, deriving an equitable tax from each. It also tries to account for differences in people's needs, and in their abilities to pay taxes. In addition, by creating tax incentives for various kinds of activities (e.g. conserving energy, supporting educational or charitable agencies, creating new jobs, investing in research or in capital improvements) it attempts to support the diverse goals of our complex society. It is a complex law, because our economic interrelations are complex. The law, rather than trying to minimize this complexity by neglecting important and relevant differences among people, tries to accommodate this complexity and respond to these differences. Although it may not fully succeed, it does far excel any unwritten traditions or customs concerning what constitutes a fair tax burden for each individual.

1.5 Creation of Opportunities

An important theoretical advantage of the rule of law is that it liberates us and creates new opportunities for us. The law can create opportunities by enfranchising persons with certain legal rights or entitlements, such as the right to an education at public expense, or the right to equal treatment in important matters such as securing housing and being considered for employment.

Another way the law creates opportunities is by making it possible for us to enter into contracts even without knowing or coming to trust those with whom we have dealings. The law relieves us of the burden of having to personally get to know and trust everyone that we depend upon. You probably do not know all the people who grow your food, deliver your fuel and energy, build your homes, educate your children, or operate your transportation and communications systems. You can buy stock in a corporation, realize a dividend, vote on a corporate policy, and sell that stock, all without ever meeting another shareholder or visiting the place of business. Our rule of law makes that possible. This liberates us to do more of what we would like to do; it also provides opportunities for us to do things that otherwise we would not dare to do. The rule of law allows us to live together even if we do not come to trust each other, but it does presume we all more or less trust the law and have confidence that the government can make others live up to it. In a sense, trust has not become irrelevant; it has been changed into a trust in our legal institutions. We must, then, concern ourselves with whether or not they deserve our trust. Without this trust the rule of law could collapse.

1.6 Provision for Orderly Amendment and Transmission

The fact that the law is institutional brings a number of potential *procedural* advantages. There are regular procedures for updating laws and for writing new ones to cover new needs. On the other hand, there are usually no regularized ways to update or expand custom or tradition. Also, laws are usually collected into codes or statute books. Thus they can be more easily made public; they can be transmitted from generation to generation with less chance of being altered by failures of memory; they can offer more specific guidance to police forces in terms of telling them exactly what conduct is not to be tolerated; and they offer a firmer basis for judges to rely on in determining whether or not a crime has been committed and punishment is deserved. These can be called the procedural advantages of laws. A number of procedural prerequisites are necessary to realize these advantages. We will be looking at these prerequisites in a moment.

1.7 Substantive Prerequisites for the Rule of Law

In reviewing its advantages, we have suggested some prerequisites that make the rule of law possible. Let us now develop a more careful list of these prerequisites. Some relate to the issues the law addresses. These are called *substantive* prerequisites. Others, which relate to how the laws are made and how they are adjudicated, are called *procedural* prerequisites. A third group relates to how society responds to the laws and how the laws are enforced, and are called *practical* prerequisites. In part we can evaluate and compare legal institutions and systems by determining how well they meet these three sets of prerequisites. A good part of what makes one law, legal system, or legal institution (legislative, police, or court system) better than another is how well they compare in terms of the prerequisites we are about to list.

At a *substantive* level, people can decide to make laws to regulate almost any aspect of their lives. But if they neglect certain of these aspects, then, many have argued, their society simply will not be able to endure. A superior legal system will ensure society's survival by providing for the peaceful and rational coexistence of its people. When a society grows in such a way that (a) it becomes normal for persons to have dealings with others whom they do not know and cannot personally trust, and (b) subgroups within the society have different and even contrary customs, mores, and traditions for regulating inter-personal dealings, it is plausible that law must (come to) function where custom and the like will no longer be adequate.

Minimally there are three areas where laws are necessary to ensure peaceful, rational coexistence, giving us the three substantive prerequisites for the rule of law:

1. Laws must provide people with security from the violence of others.
2. Laws must provide people with access to and control over the resources necessary to live.
3. Laws must provide enforcement for contractual obligations made between people.

There are reasons for each substantive prerequisite. Physical, economic, or political power gives one person an advantage over another. This could lead to people achieving their goals at the expense of harming other people. In order to prevent the abuse of physical power, laws usually rule out overt violence. Some legal systems also regulate economic and political power in order to minimize their potential for harm. The traditional argument for these regulations is that without them society might become little more than a human jungle, where only the strongest would survive.

Since resources are limited and since people need them to meet their needs and pursue their aims, some form of regulation and control of resources is crucial to society. Laws guaranteeing property rights are an obvious example. But other laws, such as minimum wage laws, agricultural price supports, tariffs and laws regulating commerce with other countries, also serve these goals. Obviously the scarcity of a given resource requires a more systematic regulation of its distribution and use. But, in a delicately balanced economic system, even the overabundance of a resource might warrant regulation for the purpose of protecting those who would be harmed if the market value of that resource fell too far.

The importance of guaranteeing that contracts not be violated arises out of the great utility of entering into binding contracts to achieve one's basic needs and secure one's goals. In contemporary society none of us is self-sufficient. Contractual relationships allow us to survive and flourish in the midst of social complexity. But laws are needed that will guarantee that agreements are kept. Without such laws, business and commerce as we know it would collapse. We would have to resort to the risky and brutal strategy of privately enforcing contracts ourselves. As we said earlier, in our society we often must deal with people whom we do not know and may not fully trust. But without the support of the legal system, such dealings would be extremely difficult and dangerous.

1.8 Procedural Prerequisites: Legislative

Even the best set of laws can be the source of injustice and difficulty if certain procedural requirements are not met. These procedural requirements fall into two groups, those relating to the making of the laws and those relating to the adjudicating of the laws. Let's first look at three *legislative procedural* prerequisites.

4. The laws must be general.
5. The laws must not be retrospective.
6. The laws must be free from contradiction, ambiguity, and vagueness.

That laws should be general means they should apply to groups of persons, or to everyone who meets certain conditions, rather than to specific people by name. This is especially important, for it makes laws universalizable by requiring that the legislation specify the characteristics of those to whom they apply. Further, it would be a violation of justice (see Chapter 6) to make laws that aim to hinder or to advantage a specific individual person (human or legal) without regard for the characteristics of that person by which she or he deserves such treatment. Thus, for example, a state can make a law requiring all who operate motels to install smoke detectors, but it would be unfair if the state made a law requiring one specific motel operator to install smoke detectors while allowing other motel operators the economic advantage of not having to comply with such a law. It would be unfair for the state to require one business to dispose of its toxic wastes in certain ways while not requiring the same of other business (or government agencies) which produce the same toxic wastes.

Retrospective legislation is problematic, because it puts people under obligations to have done something in the past without their having had the knowledge that they were under such an obligation. This would be unfair, because it would not allow them the opportunity to control their conduct in the light of that obligation. Consider the unfairness involved if a state made a law today requiring smoke detectors in motel rooms for the past ten years and then penalized motel operators so many dollars per year per motel room for noncompliance. The rationale for laws not being retrospective also suggests that those who come under obligations by new laws must be given a reasonable time to comply. If regulations for a product's safety are imposed, then providing in the law some amount of time for manufacturers of the product to come into compliance seems only reasonable.

The requirement that the laws be free from contradiction, vagueness, and ambiguity means that they should avoid obscurity and aim for precision. Obviously a law should not contradict itself. But laws do not exist in isolation; they are incorporated into a system of laws. No law in a legal system should contradict any other law in that system. A state law requiring smoke detectors in all rooms of rest homes, for example, might contradict another state law prohibiting the installation of electric devices in rooms equipped with medically required oxygen lines. Depending on how these laws were interpreted, it could easily be impossible to comply with both of them. Similarly, overlapping jurisdictions can lead to contradictory legislation. A city may require a certain method of waste disposal, but the state or federal government may prohibit it.

Ambiguous laws are susceptible to two or more differing interpretations. Many people criticize income tax laws because they find them ambiguous. For example, travel expenses involved in going away from home to earn income are deductible. But there is ambiguity in the concept of *home*. Some view it as the place where a person's family resides. Others interpret it as the place where one lives while one is working. So, if you live with your family in New York and travel to work in Chicago, your travel is a business expense. But, on another interpretation, if while you work in Chicago you live in a motel, then travel to and from New York to see your family is personal recreation and is not deductible. This ambiguity led the federal government to define *tax home* as the place where you live while you earn your income. Such definitions, happily, can overcome the problem of ambiguity, although they add to the difficulty non-experts face in correctly understanding the law.

Vague laws are obscure, because it is not clear that the law applies in a given case or what precisely is required by law. If a state required "that those who operate rest homes install smoke detectors," it would be unclear whether that law applied to those who operate "hospices," "retirement villages," or "nursing homes," which might be distinguished from "rest homes." Further, it would not be clear whether the obligation could be satisfied by installing one smoke detector in each home, one on each floor of each home, one on each wing of each floor, or one in each room. Ambiguity and vagueness lead to obscurities that provide loopholes for the unscrupulous. They leave our legal obligations unclear; thus, we can be victimized by others. Because our obligations are not clear, we also may find it more difficult to plan our lives.

Two other *legislative procedural* prerequisites apply to those who make the laws. These are:

7. The laws must be publicly promulgated.
8. The laws must be easily accessible.

Both of these requirements allow for people to better understand their legal obligations and, in turn, better organize and plan their lives in their light. Further, people need access to the law so that they can know what they can legally expect of others as well as what others expect of them. Without promulgation and accessibility the rule of law tends to break down. The confusion in Plangton Heights was not resolved just by adopting laws; the laws had to be promulgated and made known to the citizens. When laws are not promulgated or easily accessible to the population, it is easy to come to view the government as capricious or arbitrary. People will not know what their duties are, what they can expect from others, or what actions will lead them to be in violation of the law and subject to penalty. Rulers can then use such secret "laws" to victimize enemies.

1.9 Procedural Prerequisites: Judicial

In addition to those procedural prerequisites for the rule of law which apply to the legislative function, there are *judicial procedural* prerequisites as well. When laws are violated or when disputes arise, the judicial system comes into play to determine guilt, apply a penalty, adjudicate disputes, and, at times, issue orders requiring or prohibiting further actions. For the rule of law to be fully in effect a fair and impartial judicial system is necessary. This calls forth the judicial prerequisites for the rule of law.

9. The laws must be adjudicated by persons who have no conflicts of personal interest at issue in that adjudication.
10. The laws must be adjudicated with an unbiased and objective consideration of all relevant matters of fact and law which are presented in evidence.
11. The laws must be adjudicated in ways which allow all the disputing parties to present arguments concerning matters of law and matters of fact.

The reason why a judge must not have a personal interest in the case before her is that it could lead her to be unfair. The judge might be moved to be sympathetic to the side he or she has an interest in. Or the judge might be moved to be overly harsh to that same side in order to ensure himself or herself that impartiality has not been compromised. In the case study the storekeeper–judge, Mr. Grownker, seemed to lose his impartiality when Mrs. Barcon's case against his operation of the store came up.

The requirement that issues be adjudicated objectively and without bias means that judges should not allow prejudices or irrelevant factors to influence their decisions. Suppose that a group of citizens brought suit against an employer for not giving declared homosexuals an equal chance at being hired or promoted. And suppose there was a law prohibiting such a practice. A judge who was prejudiced against homosexuals might be influenced in the direction of that employer because of that prejudice, but the law would not thereby be served.

Injustices can also be done if an unbiased judge hears a case. A judge who refuses to let all parties present their side of the dispute is being unfair. Mr. Grownker tried to cover his conflict of interest by refusing to hear Mrs. Barcon's side of the dispute. There was no rule of law in Plangton Heights at that time, and so there was nothing for Mrs. Barcon to do but accept the injustice or leave town.

1.10 Practical Prerequisites for the Rule of Law

Even given wise laws that satisfy the substantive and procedural prerequisites listed, it is still possible for the rule of law to be subverted or undermined in a given society. To further ensure the rule of law, three more prerequisites must be met. These prerequisites relate to the readiness of people to accept the law and to how the laws are enforced. They are:

12. The laws of a community must generally be obeyed by the members of the community.
13. The enforcement of one law must not require the violation of another.
14. The laws must be regularly enforced without regard for who may be in violation.

Let us look at the reasons for each of these requirements. First, it is financially impossible for the vast majority of societies to employ, train, and equip enough law enforcement officers, judges, and prison guards to enforce the laws, to run the courts, and to operate its legal justice system unless most of the population generally obeys the laws. If most people ignore a law, then, for all practical purposes, it becomes unenforceable. For example, prohibitions against alcohol are thought to have failed largely because the public widely violated them. Moreover, widespread disapproval of specific laws tends to undermine public respect for the rule of law.

If the enforcement of one law means the violation of another, then the police force will be rendered ineffective in that enforcement. Drug laws are hard to enforce because violations tend to occur in private places such as homes. Thus law enforcement officers are hindered from apprehending violators by other laws concerning entering and searching private residences without warrants. Or, if detecting violations of the law requires wiretapping, then this may be a closed option, because in some cases wiretapping violates the right to privacy guaranteed by other laws. Notice that in the cases discussed here, the laws are not themselves in conflict. Everyone can refrain from use of illegal drugs—obeying those laws, that is—while everyone is also respecting others' privacy. The problem is to enforce the drug laws without violating the privacy laws.

The respect for law is quickly undercut if laws are selectively enforced. If the police generally do not arrest their friends, or if they enforce certain laws in the inner city but neglect the violations in the suburbs, respect for law deteriorates. If, for example, the vice squad enforces a city's laws against the sale of semi-automatic weapons, spousal abuse, extortion, gambling, assault, obscenity, or prostitution only when there is a public outcry and political pressure, but otherwise lets these things slide, at least in certain districts of the city, then respect for such laws will quickly evaporate. It seemed that the sheriff in Plangton Heights created discord by showing favoritism to the farmers over the newcomers. The universal scope of the legislated law (see prerequisite 4) is subverted and the legal system is undermined if the law is enforced only selectively.

EXERCISES

1. List the theoretical advantages of the rule of law over the rule of custom. (1.2–1.6)

2. (a) List the four types of prerequisites necessary for the rule of law.
(b) After checking your answer to (a), list each of the following 14 specific prerequisites under its appropriate type: (i) the community must generally obey the laws, (ii) there must be laws providing for security against human violence, (iii) the laws must be free from contradiction, ambiguity, and vagueness, (iv) judges must be free from conflicts of interests in the cases they judge, (v) laws must not be retrospective, (vi) laws must enforce contractual obligations, (vii) judges must be unbiased and objective in considering cases, (viii) laws must be publicly promulgated, (ix) the enforcement of one law must not require violating another, (x) laws must be easily accessible, (xi) judges must allow all disputing parties to speak to all matters of dispute, (xii) the laws must not be selectively enforced against any particular groups, (xiii) the laws must be general, (xiv) there must be laws providing people with access to and control over resources. (1.7–1.10)

3. Below is a list of situations or laws in which some prerequisite for the rule of law is unmet. (We refer here to the numbered listing of prerequisites in the text, not in 2.b above.) For each item on the list, state what prerequisite is unmet. Then modify the item so that the prerequisite is met.
(a) The police officer stops two drivers for going 55 mph in a 45-mph zone. The 35-year-old white female, a mother with her child in her car, is warned but not ticketed. The 19-year-old Hispanic male is both warned and ticketed.

(b) Middleton county's hospital is barred by county regulations from accepting children under the age of three months, while the state requires local government units to provide facilities for all persons with congenital hydrocephalus.

(c) In Whoseincharge, no legal obligations are involved in the signing of agreements between persons about what each will do for the other under various prerequisites.

(d) When the judge assumed the bench, he sold all his Agribusiness stock, but he never wavered in his view that there's no place for the small family farm in modern America.

(e) Most department stores are open on Sundays despite laws to the contrary.

(f) In 1990 Congress enacted a statute requiring that companies now or previously responsible for dumping chemical wastes are financially responsible for bringing any dump sites they ever used into compliance with current Federal standards for waste disposal.

(g) To enforce a law against unnatural sexual acts, a police laboratory developed an infrared video camera and an ultra sensitive microphone such that police could cruise by and direct these devices from the street at people's bedrooms thus determining if any laws were being violated.

4. Supply examples of laws or situations that fail to meet each of the prerequisites of the rule of law, identifying the unmet prerequisite. Use the abstract language of unmet prerequisites to describe how your examples of laws or situations fail to meet each of the prerequisites. Your examples should follow the pattern of those in Exercise 3, and your descriptions should be like those given in the answers to Exercise 3.

DISCUSSION QUESTIONS

1. Should there be laws which permit governments to engage in activities which individuals are prohibited from engaging in? Specifically, consider the enforcement of contracts. Should only governments have the right and the duty to insure that legally binding contracts are enforced? How would various alternative situations impact on the prerequisites for the rule of law?

2. Laws exist within societies other than the state. They might be called the "practices" of a church, the "policies" of a corporation, the "rules" of a club, or the "protocols" of a health care or research institution. In any case, which, if any of the 14 prerequisites for the rule of law would apply to such societies other than the state?

3. Laws arise in response to perceived needs. In a pluralistic society interested in human dignity and respect for persons, it becomes important to consider laws relating to dying. In view of the advantages of the rule of law and the legislative prerequisites, write a law covering doctor participation in euthanasia for terminal patients. Your law should specify the extent to which, and the conditions under which a health professional participates in or contributes to satisfying the rationally and clearly expressed wish of a patient to die.

4. Customs and practices are often the basis for laws. Such is the case with the practice of professional confidentiality. But laws regarding confidentiality, as they apply to the lawyer–client relationship, the physician–patient relationship, or the priest–penitent relationship do not mirror exactly what that custom was or is. Should the laws regarding confidentiality also include limits to its use, specifically, when, if at all, should it be made legal for a legal, medical, or ministerial professional to violate

confidentiality? What would be the advantages or disadvantages to the rule of law if confidentiality were absolute or not?

5. Civil disobedience, as practiced in the civil rights movement, anti-apartheid protests, anti-nuclear protests, and anti-abortion protests, is often justified on the grounds that persons are appealing to ethical principles which go beyond the respect for law and those social standards which the law embodies. Assess non-violent civil-disobedience from the ethical perspective. Does introducing the element of violence alter your assessment? Why?

ANSWERS TO SELECTED EXERCISES

2. (a) Substantive prerequisites, legislative procedural prerequisites, judicial procedural prerequisites, and practical prerequisites.

3. (a) Prerequisite 14, enforcement of the law against all violators equally, would require ticketing all persons going a given speed and ticketing no one for going at lesser speeds.

(b) Prerequisite 6, keeping the law free from contradiction, would involve (a) making an exception in one of the existing laws, or (b) repealing one of those laws.

(c) Prerequisite 3 provides for laws to govern contractual obligations. In Whoseincharge such laws still need to be written.

(d) Prerequisite 10, that the judge should be unbiased and objective, is violated, even though prerequisite 9, that the judge should have no conflict of interest, has been met. At least the judge should be disqualified or disqualify himself from hearing cases involving small family farms or farmers.

(e) Prerequisite 12 is unmet because the laws are widely violated. Only greatly changing citizens' attitudes about the acceptability of stores being open on Sunday will make the laws enforceable.

(f) Prerequisite 5, that laws should not be retroactive, is unmet. However, the reason for this prerequisite is that people should be given fair notice of their duties. But, in the case of toxic waste, it is reasonable to expect that industry- and government-scientific experts *should have known* the dangers. Their duty to society pre-existed. In such a case, a retrospective law may be justifiable.

(g) Prerequisite 13, that the enforcement of one law should not involve violating another, is problematic here, since police officers would presumably lack the legal right to violate the privacy of persons, particularly those not even suspected, in a random sweep to discover possible criminals.

Section 2
LAWS, MORALITY, AND SANCTIONS

Having reviewed the importance of the rule of law and examined the prerequisites needed for its development, we can turn to one of the foremost questions in the philosophy of law, namely how one should interpret a *legal obligation*. Two interpretations dominate much of the contemporary thinking about the law. One sees the law as establishing a set of moral duties or ethical obligations for people to meet. This raises the crucial question of the relationship of law to morality. The second theory sees legal obligations as ways to describe the likely negative consequences which may be imposed on those who violate statutes. These penalties are called legal sanctions. This second interpretation raises the question of why we use legal sanctions. It also suggests the further question of the appropriateness of the use of specific sanctions when one takes into account the society, potential offenders, wrongdoers, and any persons harmed. In this section we will examine these issues. After studying this section you should be able to:

- Distinguish descriptive and normative interpretations of given example laws.
- Given an example law, supply both a descriptive and a normative interpretation of it.
- State the difference between the descriptive and the normative interpretations of the law.
- State the reasons cited to justify the imposition of legal sanctions.
- Distinguish the factors having to do with the potential offender, the actual offender, the person wronged, and society as a whole that influence the appropriateness of the sanction to be applied.

THE CASE OF THE RESUSCITATION EQUIPMENT

Leisure Industries owns and operates a number of nursing homes in several midwestern states. Indiana has passed a law that requires resuscitation equipment in all nursing homes. The corporation's lawyers, Phelps, Ross, and Ramkin, are debating the question of compliance.

Lampson Phelps popped a pumpkin seed into his mouth and began to chew and talk at the same time. "We have to send a memo to the vice-president in charge of operations explaining why we are obligated to comply with the Indiana law. What do these legal obligations really mean for us?"

"That's simple," said Ross. "Just explain that failing to install the equipment in our Indiana facilities will mean fines of $1000 per home, per year. We have seven nursing homes there, so that's $7,000."

"Hold on, Ross," said Lucille Ramkin. "I know that vice-president; she'll toss off $7,000 as trivial, compared to the costs of compliance. She would probably not install the resuscitation equipment because the installation costs are far greater than the penalties for not putting them in. I think we should tell her that the law imposes a moral duty on us. We should comply because it is immoral to neglect one's legal duties unless some other overriding moral principle is being violated by doing that duty. The state has the authority to impose this requirement on us. So, if we want to operate nursing homes, we are morally bound to comply with these regulations."

Ross was about to reply, but Phelps interrupted: "Maybe we should just give her both opinions. Now, let's look at this Indiana statute itself. What precisely does it require? How long do we have to show compliance? How is it going to be enforced? What are the chances a judge will hit us with the full penalties for non-compliance the first year?"

Ramkin said, "There is more to this business of penalties than Ross indicated before. Ross spoke about the possible fines we would have to pay Indiana. But there may be lawsuits brought against us by the families of people who are put in our care. Suppose these homes are not equipped with resuscitation equipment. We could end up being sued for negligence and wrongful death. Civil suits like that can cost us millions. And there is always the possibility of being prosecuted for criminal offenses relating to knowingly ignoring this statute. That could mean jail time. Before she makes any decisions, the vice-president better be informed of the possible consequences she is risking."

Ross broke in, "Look, Ramkin, there are costs no matter what. We have to buy all the resuscitation equipment, we have to find a place to put it and we have to employ specially trained personnel to operate it. None of that is going to be free."

"I'm surprised at you," Ramkin said to her colleague. "Those costs are not penalties for non-compliance, they are expenses we must incur to bring ourselves into compliance. It could happen that we pay penalties for non-compliances, settle our negligence suits, and still have to incur all the new personnel and equipment costs. As I read the costs and benefits here, the smart thing to do is to get on board with this new law right away. At least that way we can hold our costs down to the expenses associated with compliance and not incur any fines or other sanctions."

2.1 The Concept of a Legal Obligation

Groups of people feel certain shared purposes or goals are worthwhile enough to make laws in order to achieve them. That is, people are willing to put themselves and each other under some form of obligation in order to achieve certain purposes. We can express this using the concepts developed in Chapter 7, in this way: If the people as a group are conceived of as having the moral authority to rule, (that is, given a concept of popular sovereignty), one way to understand law is as an expression of the commands of the sovereign which is the people. These commands should not be thought of as mindless nor arbitrary. Through the instrumentality of government, that society known as the state, taking stock of the goals and purposes for which it exists, expresses its firm resolve that certain actions be required and others forbidden. These expressions are known as its *laws*. Also, given the importance of those goals and purposes, the state attaches statements of the penalties, known as *sanctions*, which are to be visited upon those who fail to comply with the law.

Notice that, conceived in this way, the idea of law can be articulated with no reference to morality or to justice. Unless achieving justice and expressing morality are also taken to be among the purposes of a society, there is no conceptual necessity for the laws of that society to take morality or justice into consideration. Or, expressed another way, one's legal obligations, whether they are part of one's moral obligations or not, can be distinguished conceptually from one's moral obligations. No matter how immoral or iniquitous our legal obligations are, they are our legal obligations. This immediately gives rise to the question of how our legal obligations, if distinct from our moral obligations, compare to our moral obligations. It also raises the question of which set of obligations takes priority. As Phelps puts it in the beginning of the case study, what does "being under a legal obligation" really mean?

Conceptual analysis reveals the distinction between legal and moral obligations. It also reveals that a legal obligation is an imposition made by law on conduct. But the law does not physically prevent us from doing something, nor does it make us do something. Thus the law is not a limit in the way that a wall or some other physical or psychological constraint is a limit, preventing us from moving. Nor is the law a stimulus that causes us to react without deliberation. The law is an imposition which tells us what we are obligated to do or not do. Further, it tells us that failure to comply will, in all likelihood, result in some form of penalty. A legally binding contract, for example, creates legal obligations. Certain things are to be expected of a party. Each party has the legal right to expect things of the other. Failure to live up to one's part of the contract will result in some form of punitive action, such as, perhaps, the forfeiture of property.

Thus, our analysis of legal obligation, yields two quite different ideas. First there is the idea of an *obligation or the creation of a duty of some kind.* Second there is the idea of the *penalties or negative consequences to be suffered if the obligation is not fulfilled.* The case study illustrates these two interpretations. We shall call the first one, which focuses on our duty, the *normative* interpretation of law. Ramkin articulates this view when she says that the law imposes a duty that it is immoral to neglect. We shall call the second, which focuses on the probable implications of non-compliance, the *descriptive* interpretation of law. Ross presents this view in the case study when he cites the potential fines for non-compliance. Let us look at each view in more detail.

2.2 The Normative Interpretation of Legal Obligation

Some view the law as creating genuine moral duties for people. There are several arguments for this view. The first points to the sovereign's authority to put individuals under obligations with respect to certain behaviors. If the sovereign has the moral right to make laws, then those governed by that sovereign have the moral duty to obey those laws. Furthermore, the normative interpretation reminds us, there are important similarities between being moral and obeying the law. The law tells us what we ought to do. Furthermore, the connection between law and morality is very close in those cases where people view the law as the embodiment of moral goals, such as respect for persons or justice. Living morally and living by the law are both seen as rule-guided ways of living—that is, using rules or precepts to govern or guide one's conduct. For many people in normal circumstances being moral means, at least in part, living according to the laws. Another important argument for the normative interpretation of legal obligation points to the beneficial consequences of the practice of obeying the law. The utility of the practice of abiding by the law is projected as being a net benefit for the greatest number of persons. Thus, there are strong deontological (see Chapter 4) as well as utilitarian (see Chapter 2) considerations advanced for accepting one's legal obligations as one's moral duty.

2.3 Morality and the Law

Seeing legal obligations as moral duties raises the question of the precise relationship of law to morality. By appealing to the overriding right of the sovereign to legislate, historically some thinkers went so far as to see obedience to law as an overriding moral obligation, one which takes priority over all other moral obligations. Others, citing actual examples such as existing laws against rape, robbery, murder, fraud, breaking contracts, lying under oath, and sexual misconduct, maintain that while the legally derived moral obligations may be conceptually distinct from other moral obligations, for all practical purposes legality and morality are, or should be, one and the same. Thus, for the sake of social stability, and to simplify things so everyone can always know what they ought to do or not do, and also to continue the traditional connection between a community's moral ideals and its laws, it makes sense to make law and morality, for all practical purposes, the same.

The arguments above suggest that it is perfectly reasonable to consider moral obligations—such as advancing justice, respecting persons, insuring autonomy, preventing harm, and bringing about the greatest net good of the greatest number—when considering which legislation to enact. While agreeing with this, we need not agree that all our moral obligations should be made into laws. It is not clear that one friend's moral obligations to be loyal to another friend needs to become a Federal law, a state statute or a city ordinance. Considering that the purpose of law is not to replicate morality but to further the shared goals and purposes of a society, we can identify many ethical responsibilities which should not become codified into law. For example, it does not seem reasonable to make laws requiring people to respect parents, to share equally in routine housekeeping chores, to live in accordance with their conscience, or strive for integrity and sensitivity. Our moral obligations neither begin nor end with our legal obligations.

Further, saying that we are morally obligated to obey the laws need not imply that there are no moral considerations which might override such an obligation. The twentieth century has given us too many strong counter-examples. There are many cases where governments have enacted laws which were immoral or unjust. Consider the laws of Nazi Germany requiring religious and racial discrimination and persecution, for example. Or consider America's segregation laws, or South Africa's apartheid laws. That such legally enacted statutes patently violate universal ethical principles shows that our moral obligations as human beings and our moral obligations arising from the general duty to obey the law can conflict. While prima facie it is our ethical duty to obey the law, another more fundamental ethical duty, such as to respect persons, can override that obligation. In such a case, following the law just because it is the law would be an immoral thing to do.

We can measure the justice of a system of laws only if we view morality as a conceptually independent standard. Only when morality is distinct from law can we criticize law and seek to make our laws more just or more respectful of human rights. The appeal to universal ethical principles, such as respect for persons or justice, must take practical as well as conceptual priority over the law or else there would be no way to improve laws. The ethical appeals for legal reform made by Martin Luther King, Jr., Mohandas Gandhi, or Steven Biko made sense only because some moral principles are more fundamental and take ethical priority over the moral principle that the laws ought to be obeyed.

Consider also how people generally respond in situations where enforcement powers break down, as in cases of continued mass rioting, catastrophic natural disaster, or war. These are seen as situations where there is, in effect, no law. In such cases of lawlessness morality can remain. Morality here is not the unenforced law; rather it is a less well-articulated set of values, principles, and personal moral codes. Even if all of the entire legal system should, for some reason, break down, people would not be morally adrift. There are still universal ethical principles, such as justice, social utility, respect for persons and their moral rights, respect for individual autonomy, an appreciation of the value of cooperative effort, and fundamental honesty in one's dealings with others.

2.4 The Descriptive Interpretation of Legal Obligation

Another way to understand what it means to assert that something is the law is to describe the consequences likely to be visited on those who do not abide by that law. If a person acts in some way contrary to the dictates of the law, then that person will, in all probability, suffer certain penalties, if the legal system operates as it is intended. The fact that people often view the breakdown of law enforcement as an occasion when there is no law suggests that a very practical interpretation of the law, at least for those people, is that one's legal obligations, in the absence of the enforcement powers of the state, are nil.

This interpretation of legal obligations sees them in terms of penalties that will result if these obligations are not met. Thus, the descriptive analysis focuses on something that almost everyone views as an important practical consideration: How much, if at all, will I suffer if I am detected disobeying this law? The descriptive interpretation often results in a calculated analysis of the costs and benefits involved in compliance and non-compliance, taking into account how one can maximize one's chances for gain while also minimizing one's exposure to loss. In the case study Ramkin undertakes to identify some of the risks associated with non-compliance, such as exposure to expensive liability law suits, and also lists the expenses associated with compliance.

Advocates of the descriptive view of the law say that it frees us from the vagaries and difficulties associated with trying to make moral judgments, for it sees legal obligations as nothing but factual descriptions of the probable consequences of a given course of action. But divorcing the concept of legal obligations from some sense of duty can also be seen as a serious error in conceptual analysis. It misses the normative punch of calling something a legal *obligation*. Whatever it is, an *obligation* is more than merely a sort of inadequate way of talking about what is probably going to happen if a person decides to behave in a given way. Saying that a person is probably going to catch cold if she goes outside on a wintry day with her hair wet is not conceptually the same as saying that she is obligated by such an action to catch a cold.

The descriptive view is also criticized for being too broad. There are many circumstances in which we can predict harm for non-compliance, yet the items to be complied with are not laws. The child can predict discipline for not being obedient, yet many of the procedural prerequisites for the rule of law given in 1.8 and 1.9 are not met by the parents' rules. A kidnap victim or the victims of extortion can predict harm for not complying with the will of the kidnapper or extortionist, but this does not give the commands of a kidnapper or extortionist the force of law. People can predict being criticized for violating group norms or corporate policy, but the social penalties or disciplinary actions which such violations might bring about do not imply that social norms or corporate policies are laws.

To say that non-compliance with legal obligations will yield penalties is to say that, in this respect, laws are norms or commands that are backed up with the threat of force. In other words, to say that we know what will happen to us if we do not fulfill our legal obligations is not the same as saying that we understand what legal obligations are. We know that if we do not eat, we will die. That does not mean that we understand the biological processes that will culminate in our deaths.

2.5 Legal Sanctions

The descriptive interpretation of the law with its focus on penalties for non-compliance, raises several questions about those penalties. What kinds of penalties can be imposed? Who can justifiably impose them? For what reasons are they imposed? Penalties imposed on those found guilty of breaking the law are called legal sanctions. The concept of a legal sanction includes three elements: the kinds of penalties, the source of the penalty, and the reason for the penalty. The kind of penalty most frequently imposed in America include the loss of property (fines), or the restriction of personal liberties (imprisonment, probation). Some societies use sanctions that include various forms of torture, exclusion from membership, forfeiture of privilege, or the loss of income. Some states use death as a sanction.

The source of the sanction is also important. Legal sanctions can be imposed only by legitimate authorities. The legitimate authority of a society is that society's government. It is the government's legal authority to frame laws, promulgate them, enforce them, and apply sanctions to those guilty of breaking them. It is not the duty of the individual members of a society, such as the private citizens of a state, to apprehend and punish criminals. It is the responsibility of the government of that society to handle such matters. Citizens in general do not have the legal authority to do those things. Even in seeking redress for grievances against one another, citizens must use the legal system. Those who take the law into their own hands (revenge-seekers, vigilantes, or self-appointed "security guards," or "citizen police forces") are acting without proper authority if they seek to punish lawbreakers or if they go outside the legal system to exact punishment for any harm they might have experienced. In many societies such behavior is specifically prohibited. (For a fuller discussion of governmental authority, see Section 3 of Chapter 7.)

Although governments have the authority to impose sanctions, not all governments do impose them. Some systems of law, such as international law, do not always involve sanctions for failure to comply. In other words, it is possible to have laws that carry no sanctions. However, the majority of laws that we encounter or that apply to our daily lives carry sanctions. Sometimes the precise sanction is established by the legislation itself—for example, five years in prison for using a hand gun in committing a felony. Sometimes the sanctions are left to the discretion of the judge or jury within certain limits—for example, an award of punitive damages imposed on a person found guilty of non-criminal negligence such as failing to do something which led directly to harm for another.

Sanctions are to be distinguished from the expenses of coming into compliance with the law. A legal sanction is a penalty imposed for failing to do what one is legally obligated to do (filing a tax return) or for doing what one is legally obligated not to do (speeding). However, not every expense, inconvenience, or restriction of liberty imposed on us by law is considered a sanction. Ramkin in the case study points this out to Ross. The expenses Leisure Industries must incur in order to conform to the law are different from any sanctions imposed for not complying. A tax imposed by legitimate authority is not a sanction, for by definition a sanction is imposed to penalize people for having broken a law. However, failure to pay a tax is failure to comply with a law. The government may, then, collect both the tax and a penalty for the original failure to pay.

2.6 Reasons for Sanctions

Sanctions are imposed because a law has been broken or because harm has been done by one person to another. While that much is clear, there is considerable question about the consequences of sanctioning people and about the justifications for penalizing lawbreakers. In section 1 we detailed many of the advantages of the rule of law. Among other things, the laws make our important social obligations clear. They allow us to better understand and anticipate consequences of noncompliance. The importance of making sure that people abide by the laws is a direct consequence of the value of the rule of law. But, what if the reasons for the sanctions do not fit those penalties we are imposing? Let's look at the different justifications given for using sanctions.

Sanctions applied to those who break the law are intended to play an important role in guaranteeing that the laws are kept. A person may be disinclined to obey even a very clear and important law that is not backed up by the threat of a sanction, because no obvious penalty would arise from disobedience. One reason for sanctions is that they are intended to serve as a coercive force that makes people think twice about breaking the law. In the case study the weak sanction did not seem able to serve this function. Ramkin notes that the vice-president might decide not to obey the smoke-detector law because the attached sanction is so small as to be meaningless to a big company like Leisure Industries. For many years anti-pollution laws were disregarded for similar reasons. Knowing this about people, legislatures often "put teeth" into the law by attaching more significant sanctions. This way, the law's power to deter potential wrongdoers is thought to be enhanced. Whether or not a given sanction in fact has its purported deterrent effect is something which is difficult to prove, but which is essential to determine if one is to justify imposing a given sanction on the basis of this reason.

2.7 Sanctions and the Offender

Two other reasons for sanctions relate to the offender. First, some see sanctions as a way of forcing the offender to make full restitution and of penalizing the offender for having caused the harm in the first place. These ideas seem to work well in civil cases. In a civil case two persons dispute the matter of whether or not one (the defendant) has harmed the other (the plaintiff). If found guilty, the plaintiff must make amends to the person harmed. The offender, in addition to compensating the victim, is often assessed additional fines as a penalty for having caused the harm.

Special problems arise for those determining precisely how restoration is to be made in a variety of cases. It is easiest in financial matters, for the restoration can be on a dollar-for-dollar basis. Even here, however, two serious complications can arise. One is the difficulty of accurately measuring a loss, such as the loss of a work of art, an unpublished novel, or the loss of income that may result from libel. The other is the problem of collecting full restoration from a corporation that may go bankrupt, or from an individual who may lack sufficient resources, or any resources, to make the reimbursements. Collecting in some cases can cause harm to others who are innocent. For example, should the court impose severe fines if it knows that such fines will create significant hardships for the spouse and children of the offender? And, if not, how is proper restitution to be made to the victim?

To protect their families or businesses from such risks, people carry insurance. For example, standard home-owners insurance policies frequently carry liability insurance. Professionals also purchase malpractice insurance. One of the problems involved in liability and malpractice insurance is that people are awarded settlements for damages that are larger than individuals or insurance companies seem to be able to afford to pay. But this raises the problem even more clearly. How does one fix the financial compensation appropriate for sickness, injury, or wrongful death arising out of an accident, foolishness, ignorance, negligence, or malpractice?

Losses other than financial ones are even more problematic. And introducing the criminal dimension—premeditated action based on malicious intentions, for example—creates even more problems.   Most civilizations no longer accept maiming or killing a criminal as a means of restoring to an aggrieved person what is lost through injury or through the death of a loved one.   It is very hard to accurately fix a dollar value on the loss of a limb, the loss of sight, or on death.   The dollar value of being a victim of child abuse, rape, or criminal neglect may be inestimable.

The above suggests that in criminal cases, the concepts of debt and repayment are referred to, but their application is much less evident.   In a criminal case the accused is brought to trial not by the person harmed, there might not even be anyone who was harmed—but by the state acting on behalf of the people as a whole society.   The offense alleged is a violation of the laws of the society, thus implicitly the allegation is that the accused has caused the frustration or endangerment of the society as it attempts to achieve its goals and purposes.   If found guilty the criminal, is penalized.   Recall that in civil cases the penalty was independent of the compensation.   In criminal cases the two are sometimes thought of as one.   We say, for example, that the criminal who has served out a prison sentence has "paid his debt to society."   But the exact application of the concept of a debt in the case of criminal offenses is quite problematic, conceptually.   The victim of the crime, for example rape, is not personally compensated by having the criminal serve time in prison.   And society is not compensated either; in fact, society frequently must assume the costs of such punishments.   Although it should be noted that the costs often go beyond simple incarceration.   For example, because of due-process and the presumption of innocence, when all the legal appeals have been finished a life sentence ends up costing society only one-third what the death penalty costs.   And how does paying with one's life compensate society or the human victim of a crime?

The second view of how sanctions relate to the offender is that sanctions can serve to rehabilitate.   They "teach the offender a lesson" that society will not tolerate certain conduct.   By having to make restitution for the harm,   or by suffering the penalties of fine or imprisonment the offender is, in theory, educated to become a useful and contributing member of society.   As with the potential deterrent effect of sanctions, whether or not a given sanction has its intended rehabilitative effect is a matter of some factual dispute.   Here as well, such factual issues should be resolved before one attempts to justify a given sanction on the basis of this reason.

Whether sanctions are intended as retribution or rehabilitation leads to conflicting views of how sanctions relate, or should relate, to offenders. For a fuller discussion of various theories of punishment, see Section 1 of Chapter 6.

2.8 Sanctions, Society and Those Wronged

There are also tensions between how sanctions relate, or should relate, to the offender and how they relate, or should relate, to the general welfare of society. From the point of view of society, sanctions are intended to protect people from being harmed, either as individual victims, or as a society, by the criminals. But the idea of sanctions as a way of protecting society can come into tension with the idea of sanctions as rehabilitations or as retributions intended to impact on the offender. An important and difficult job for any judge is to balance the welfare of society (its need to be protected from repeated offensive, illegal behavior) against the welfare of the individual offenders (sparing the guilty party from cruel, overly harsh, unusual, or unfair sanctions). There is also a tension between the welfare of society and the welfare of the potential offender. Sometimes harsh mandatory sanctions are imposed by the legislature with a view toward deterring crime—for example, mandatory prison sentences for breaking drug laws. But this can work against the welfare of society. Judges may be moved not to convict people of these crimes, especially if they appear to be first offenders, in order to avoid applying the harsh sanction. But, when that happens, the welfare of society is jeopardized. The dilemma for the judge, however, is in balancing the danger to society against the welfare of the first offender. Our prisons, being what they are, are not places where you would send a person if you really had his welfare in mind.

To all of these tensions another must be added: the tension that arises when we introduce the interests of the wronged or aggrieved person. The aggrieved party has suffered some form of harm at the hands of the lawbreaker. There may have been loss of property (control of resources), loss of life or liberty, physical or economic harm, psychological trauma, or social disadvantage. Whatever it is, there arises a grievance and, so, a claim for restoration. As suggested above, in civil courts a wrongdoer with fiscal resources may be held responsible for making up this loss or rectifying the harm done. Ramkin appreciated this point in the case study. She saw the potential cost of damages should Leisure Industries lose a negligence suit. The cost of restoration would be significantly greater than either the fine for non-compliance or the expenses of compliance. These damages represent efforts to make up to the aggrieved parties what they lost through the fault of the offender.

In civil trials involving the potential to sanction the offender by awarding damages or restitution to the aggrieved, a special tension exists. Too small an award would fail to adequately compensate the person who was wronged. Too large an award might be an unbearable punishment for the offender. Further, for the good of society, the judgment must be universalizable. The judgment will set a precedent that others, not involved in the present case, will follow. If it is too high or too low to suit the circumstances of the present case, it may turn out to be an unfortunate precedent. Many practical problems of malpractice, product liability, and wrongful death suits arise in such connection.

EXERCISES

1. (a) Below is a list of statements, each of which offers either a descriptive or a normative interpretation of some law. Mark each statement *D* or *N* respectively. (2.1–2.4)

___1. If a pedestrian has his or her feet in the intersection, then the motorist may not drive his or her vehicle in such a way as to interfere with the pedestrian's progress.

___2. If you hit a store in the downtown area, the cops are sure to bust you.

___3. When you're on Route 30 between Otisville and Sonnensburgh, you'd better know that it's a speed trap.

___4. No minor is permitted to contract for debts.

___5. A person only does his legal obligation when he reports to the police any knowledge he has of a crime.

___6. Sitting in jail for 30 days is just too steep a price to pay for a little fun one night.

___7. The way the police tail an ex-con, that person's got to know jail's just around the corner for the smallest slip.

___8. If the law is on the books, you ought to respect legal authority and obey it.

(b) Suppose that a law prohibited the sale of heroin under pain of a $15,000 fine for each sale. State the normative interpretation of this law.

(c) State the descriptive interpretation of the law mentioned in (b).

(d) Without reference to any particular law, state the difference between the normative and the descriptive interpretation of a law.

2. (a) Without looking in the glossary first, define sanction by reference to the relationship of a sanction to legal wrongdoing and the relationship between sanction and burden.

(b) State the reasons cited to justify the imposition of legal sanctions.

(c) State which of these reasons are directed toward the potential criminal, which toward the criminal, which toward the victim of the crime, and which toward society in general.

DISCUSSION QUESTIONS

1. Should a practice which the majority of the population finds to be immoral—at least in many cases—be prohibited by law? For example, should abortion be prohibited by law? Notice this is not a question about the morality of abortion, but a question about the relationship between law and morality. What about prostitution?

2. In 2.6 we talked about civil cases where one is trying to find a fair sanction balancing the good of society, the harm done to the person wronged and the ability of the offender to make restitution. But consider the same problem in the case of criminal offenses. What should society do to rectify the harm done to those victimized by criminals who have no financial resources and who commit crimes, such as rape or murder, for which no amount of money can serve as adequate restitution? Does society, as a whole, have any moral responsibilities here? Why ought other taxpayers make restitution for harm which they did not cause? On the other hand, to what extent does accepting that society has the sole duty to enforce its laws entail that when society fails to protect persons it must undertake the financial responsibility for such a failure?

3. Does the death penalty have deterrent effect? What evidence can be brought to bear on this issue? Can you conceive of a way of testing your opinion experimentally? What does the result of your discussion imply for the reasons used to justify capital punishment?

ANSWERS TO SELECTED EXERCISES

1. (a) 1. *N* 2. *D* 3. *D* 4. *N* 5. *N* 6. *D* 7. *D* 8. *N*

(b) Persons have a legal obligation or duty not to sell heroin.

(c) Persons who sell heroin will have to pay a penalty of $5,000 for each such sale.

(d) According to the normative interpretation, a law asserts what one's legal duty is; according to the descriptive interpretation, a law asserts what penalties one will suffer for acting contrary to the law.

9 | CLASHING ETHICAL IDEALS

Unless we stop shooting and start talking, we're all gonna regret it. And we ain't gonna be able to do much about it then!

Koby's Reflections on Justice

We are all familiar with clashing ethical principles. At times self-interest diverges from duty, the ideal of personal freedom is in tension with the ideal of social cooperation, our sense of justice is at odds with social utility, or our respect for law conflicts with our other moral principles. Whatever word we use, the idea is clear: One value is in tension with another. This chapter is devoted to the question, "To what extent and by what strategies is it possible to resolve normative tensions rationally?" The first section explains value tensions in terms of value conflicts and value divergences. Section 2 examines the kinds of value tensions we experience in *personal ethics*. Section 3 does the same for *social ethics*. In both of these sections the emphasis is on value conflicts or value divergencies *between* competing ethical ideals. Section 4 presents three strategies for rationally resolving tensions between different values. We explain the presuppositions, plausibility, limitations, and strengths of each strategy, as well as the problems to which each gives rise. The goal of this chapter is for you to understand the variety of normative tensions and conflicts in personal and social ethics, and to learn the kinds of strategies available for rationally responding to these conflicts.

Section 1
VALUE DIVERGENCE AND VALUE CONFLICT

In this brief section we take a quick look at the three ways value tensions arise and then we sort these tensions into value divergencies and value conflicts. The distinctions developed here are important for several reasons, most importantly, however, because they help us see our conceptual options more clearly. These, then, form the basis for the proposals made later regarding how one might rationally attempt to resolve various sorts of value tensions. After studying this section you should be able to:

- State three sources of value tensions.
- Distinguish value divergencies from essential and non-essential value conflicts.

1.1 Sources of Normative Tensions

Normative thought in both personal and social ethics revolves around a number of normative concepts, such as freedom, duty, justice, respect, utility, and interest. The opening chapter of this book was devoted to providing you with certain central tools and distinctions for understanding these normative concepts more clearly. Throughout the book philosophical analysis has been continually employed, and the standard of universalizability has been invoked and explained. The distinctions between absolute and relative, objective and subjective, and intrinsic and instrumental values have regularly been cited to clarify normative concepts and issues. We have attempted to clarify and to exhibit the value that people intuitively find in individualism, autonomy, security, justice, rule-following, trust, community, respect, happiness, rationality, responsibility, and the explicit articulation of normative expectations in law. That each of these is valuable seems indubitable. Moreover, it seems clear that persons can pursue them with greater certainty once they have knowledge of just what each one is.

In Chapters 2 through 8, as we examined various values, ideals, or ethical principles we noted, through examples, discussion questions, and in the text itself, two kinds of situations out of which normative clashes arise. The first sort was exemplified as we saw how one kind of right might clash with another kind of right, or one sort of freedom with another sort of freedom. In such cases rationally resolving the normative issue requires more than simply saying that all people's rights or freedoms ought to be respected, for the existence of this kind of conflict implies difficulty in respecting all of those rights or freedoms. This first sort of clash might be characterized as being *between a value and itself.*

The second sort arose between one person and another. One person's rights or freedom may have to be restricted in order that rights or freedom for another can be secured. Scarcity of resources may imply that if one person's claim to justice is honored, then the very same claims made by another person cannot be honored. Here the clash is not between one sort of justice, or right, and another, for the same standard of justice or the same right is operative throughout. In such cases the clash is *between persons,* not values.

Having examined values individually, we are now in a good position to explicitly note a third sort of situation in which normative clashes arise. Whereas we have discussed rights, utility, happiness, freedom, and justice as relatively separate topics, it is entirely possible that pursuit of utility may be at odds with the honoring of rights, or the doing of one's duty may be the source of unhappiness. That is, this third type of normative clash is one which arises *between the varieties of values* and concerns we have considered. This sort of clash is often spoken of as a conflict between different ethical theories, principles, or ideas, or a conflict between the different social policies derived from the competing normative theories or principles.

1.2 Forms of Normative Tensions

Before going further, however, we must be more precise about how we are going to use words like *tension, divergence,* and *conflict*. We will use the term *normative tension* to talk generally about all three kinds of situations mentioned above: normative clashes between one value and itself, between persons, or between one value and another value. Regardless of the sources of value tensions, for the purposes of attempting to resolve them rationally they can be classified into two forms. One form of tension, the more moderate and sometimes easier to handle, is *divergence*. Whenever one set of reasons leads to the view that one action should be taken while a second set of reasons suggests that a different action should be taken, the result is divergence. What you would do in following the first set of reasons is *simply different from, but not incompatible with*, what you would do in following the second set of reasons.

Consider an example: Sara, who has been living with a married man, Frank, might conclude on deontological grounds that she should urge Frank not to seek an annulment or a divorce. Then, on grounds of self-interest, Sara might decide that continuing her relationship with Frank could only hurt her in the end. She might decide that if she and Frank were never to marry, then she could not be satisfied with the relationship. From this line of reasoning, Sara might conclude that she ought to break off her relationship with Frank. Here we have an example of divergence. For deontological reasons Sara has concluded that she should admonish Frank not to seek an annulment or a divorce, and for ethical egoistic reasons she has inferred that she should end her relationship with Frank.

It is important to note in this example of divergence that it is quite possible for Sara *both* to urge Frank not to seek an annulment *and* to break off her relationship with him. When two sets of reasons lead us to divergent conclusions, it is often possible for us to resolve any tension by simply doing both of the recommended actions. Sara could both urge Frank not to get a divorce and she could break off her affair with him. Whenever the recommendations implied by two sets of reasons diverge without contradicting each other, only constraints such as lack of opportunity, lack of time, lack of resolve, lack of resources, or lack of cooperation between involved parties will prevent one from following both lines of reasoning and accepting both recommendations.

Sometimes courses of action not only diverge, they *conflict*. Different ethical theories or social policies can lead to recommendations that turn out to be logically contradictory to one another. That is, if you follow the one recommendation, you are thereby prevented from following the other. If Sara, for reasons of self-interest, decided to urge Frank to get a divorce so she could marry him, then it would not be logically consistent for Sara, acting on deontological considerations, to urge Frank not to get a divorce and to refuse to marry him. When two or more values, normative policies, or ethical theories, lead us to draw conclusions which conceptually contradict each other we shall say that these values (policies, principles, theories) *conflict*. In this case, Sara cannot consistently do both—urge Frank to get a divorce and urge Frank not to get a divorce. In such cases, intellectually accepting the conclusion of one value means not being able to accept in a logically consistent manner the conclusion implied by another value. Remember, however, saying that two things logically conflict does not mean that one cannot reject both. Doing neither avoids the conflict to which doing one or the other leads.

Suppose, however, that the conflict is so severe that no matter *how* you go about following one set of recommendations, you are thereby prevented from following another set of recommendations. We will call such a situation an *essential conflict* because the conflict of having to select between inconsistent courses of action is, for all practical purposes, inevitable and unavoidable. For example, a person facing a very difficult decision about abortion may find herself in a situation of essential conflict. The decision she faces is inevitable and unavoidable, and, depending on how she sees the ethics of abortion, she may also infer that acting on the basis of one set of considerations—deciding to carry the fetus to term—precludes acting on the basis of another set of ethical considerations—exercising her right to have the abortion.

In many cases of conflict, however, it is only the strategy or the way a strategy is implemented, not the goal, that leads to conflict. Working alone all evening will preclude spending the evening with your friends. But if you distinguish your goal (finishing your work) from your strategy (working alone) and how it is being implemented (at night), you might see you can use the same strategy to achieve the same goal, but you can implement it differently (in the afternoon). Doing this dissolves the conflict because now you still can spend the evening with your friends. On the other hand, if your goal is to work in the evening, then perhaps you need not be alone in order to achieve this. You might consider the possibility of doing your evening work in the company of your friends—for example, spending the evening studying with friends.

It is often difficult for people to focus their goals and to articulate them with sufficient care so that they can see what is really necessary to achieving those goals as opposed to what is only coincidental or instrumental. Thus what appear to be essential conflicts may turn out to be conflicts, but conflicts that are avoidable. For example, it might be useful for the person agonizing over the abortion decision to clarify her goals. It might be the case that having an abortion is the only way she sees of achieving her goals; or it may turn out, when her aims and goals are brought into sharp focus, that other reasonable options emerge. It might turn out that what was first thought to be an essential conflict is really a conflict of a more manageable sort. Strategies or implementations of strategies which are only coincidental or instrumental to achieving one's goals can potentially be replaced in order to dissolve a conflict.

EXERCISES

1. State three sources of normative tensions and, (by looking back in the text), give examples of each. (1.1)
2. We have sorted normative tensions into "value divergencies" and "value conflicts." Value conflicts were, in turn, sorted into "essential" and, by implication, "non-essential" conflicts. State the contrasts between each sort of value tension. (1.2)

SELF-EXAMINATION QUESTIONS

1. Using your own experience in dealing with value tensions, describe actual cases in your life of value divergence, and value conflicts of the essential and non-essential kind.
2. Just as a thought experiment, select an example of essential value conflict, focus on your goals and attempt to articulate them with as much precision as possible. In thinking about this, what strategies are you conceiving of to achieve those goals? How might a fuller specification of your goals lead to the opening of options which might have seemed closed when your goals were less well conceived?

ANSWERS TO SELECTED EXERCISES

1. Conflicts between persons, as exemplified in Sections 1.2 and 1.3 of the chapter on Justice. Conflicts between a value and itself, as exemplified in Section 4.2 through 4.7 of the chapter on Freedom. Conflicts between values and each other, as exemplified in Section 3.4 of the chapter on Social Utility.
2. In value *divergence* one set of reasons leads to the view that one action should be taken while a second set of reasons suggests that a different action should be taken, however these courses of action are not incompatible. In value *conflict*, values, normative policies, or ethical theories, lead to conclusions which conceptually contradict each other, that is, logically inconsistent courses of action are implied. Value conflict is *essential conflict*, if, for all practical purposes, the conflict is inevitable and unavoidable; that is, no matter how one goes about following one set of values or policies, one is thereby prevented from following the other set of values or policies.

Section 2
PERSONAL ETHICAL CONFLICTS BETWEEN SELF-INTEREST, GENERAL UTILITY, AND ONE'S DUTY

In previous chapters you have had occasion to examine ethical egoism, utilitarianism, and deontological theories of how you ought to go about making ethical decisions on a personal level. Intuitively you were aware that serious tensions might well exist among the values of self-interest, utility, and duty. There are many possible conflicts among the dictates of egoistic, utilitarian, and deontological positions. After studying Section 2, you should be able to:

- Distinguish considerations of self-interest, utility, and deontology.
- Recognize the cluster of meanings that theorists have attached to the ideas of self-interest, happiness, and duty.
- Give examples of cases in which different ethical theories would imply diverging actions.
- Give examples of cases in which different ethical theories would imply conflicting actions.
- State abstractly the features of examples of value divergence and value conflict that lead to those value tensions.

THE CASE OF THE PERPLEXED FRIEND

"Come in, Sara, I'm Dr. Yontek. You mentioned on the phone that you were concerned about your friend. What seems to be the problem?"

"Well, ah, Doctor, you see, ah, I have this friend. She's a good person. Well, ah, ah,....."

"Yes, what about her, Sara?"

"She's been living with a married man. He wants to marry me—I mean her! Oh, no. ..."

"That's all right, Sara, I understand. How do you feel about marrying him?"

"Well—I would personally love it. Life with him would be fantastic for me. We have so much in common, you know. He's a fine father, and I'd want that for any kid I'd have. And with his kind of job, I'd never have to worry about money. I'd even be able to play the stock market like I've always wanted. I mean, if it were just up to me and I had only me to think about I would marry him today. But I can't!"

"What do you mean, 'can't,' Sara?"

"I mean I can't ask him to divorce his wife, and leave his children."

"Say more about that, Sara."

"Divorce would ruin them. She's a sweet innocent woman who adores her husband. Divorce will make her become hard and bitter. And the three children are only in grade school. They need their father. No! Too many people would be hurt if he got a divorce. Why should I make all those people unhappy and risk destroying the future of those children? You know the statistics, Doctor. Kids from broken homes wind up getting divorces themselves when they marry. Doctor, what should I do?"

"Well, Sara, it's not for me to answer that question for you. But have you thought about some options? You and he—what's his name?"

"Frank."

"You and Frank could take the children. Maybe with counseling his wife could make a more satisfactory adjustment. I realize these measures would not solve all the personal problems associated with divorce. But you do have some options."

"No I don't, Doctor. Divorce is wrong. It's against Frank's religion. But Frank seems to think he can get his marriage annulled by his church. Yet, even if he could, I still think that marriage is forever and the annulment would not make me feel any better about it, even if it did help Frank feel better. He made a commitment, and his wife trusts him. I, ah, I just can't bring myself to encourage Frank to get his marriage annulled. Since I believe it's wrong, I would be asking Frank to do something that is wrong. And that's wrong too. Don' t you see, Doctor, I'm stuck. What should I do?"

2.1 Egoism and Social Utility

As Sara talks to Dr. Yontek, she presents a variety of reasons why she should or should not marry Frank. Notice the first set of reasons she gives, which argue in favor of her marrying Frank. She would find married life with him fantastic *for her*. She would be satisfied with the kind of father he would be for her children. She would be contented by his job security and satisfied at the prospect of investing in the stock market. Essentially, in this paragraph Sara describes her own self-perceived self-interest. She tells Dr. Yontek how marrying Frank would, she believes, allow her to further that interest. Her thoughts are self-centered. She does not consider how happy Frank might be because of what they have in common. The kind of father Frank would make pleases her because it coincides with her ideal of what the father of her children should be, not because of any expressed genuine concern about her children's own welfare.

In contrast, the reasons Sara first gives against marrying Frank are of a general utilitarian sort. She brings into play the interests and welfare of Frank's present wife and children, not simply her own interests. She evaluates the probable consequences divorce would have on both the wife and the children. Risks are calculated and both short-term and long-term consequences are brought into play. While, of course, the consideration of long-term consequences is quite compatible with ethical egoism, the reasoning in this passage is definitely not egoistic, since intrinsic value is ascribed to the impact of the consequences upon others besides herself.

The possible tension between egoistic and egalitarian utilitarian considerations is amply demonstrated in this portion of the case study, since these two types of considerations lead Sara to opposite, and contrary conclusions. Abstractly speaking, there is bound to be tension here, because ethical egoism involves treating only one's own happiness as being intrinsically valuable, whereas universal utilitarianism involves egalitarianism, that is, attending to everybody's well-being equally and regarding each person's well-being as intrinsically valuable. Thus, ethical egoism and universal utilitarianism obviously diverge, because utilitarianism understands the happiness of each person as intrinsically valuable, whereas ethical egoism understands the individual's well-being alone being as intrinsically valuable.

2.2 Happiness and Duty

The final set of reasons Sara gives concerning whether to marry Frank has a distinctly deontological character. According to deontological ethical theory, as defined in Chapter 4, Section 3, not only are some states of affairs intrinsically good, but some actions are intrinsically right or wrong and not just instrumentally right or wrong as they conduce to intrinsically valuable states of affairs. While the discussion of deontological theory was presented within the framework of a discussion about rights, deontological theories are not necessarily confined to human rights. The pursuit of justice, the enhancement of freedom, and the maintenance of personal integrity are other examples of goals that may be intrinsically right. Sara's argument in the case study rests on Frank having made a commitment and his wife trusting him. Sara seems to be suggesting that it is keeping one's commitments and not violating the trust that others have in one that are intrinsically right and valuable. In this paragraph of the case study she does not focus on any further aspects or consequences of the keeping of commitments or the respecting of trust.

Such deontological considerations need to be distinguished from the desirability of happiness, which seems to be involved in Sara's earlier comment. In both her egoistic and utilitarian arguments, Sara seems to be concerned ultimately with what will make people happy. There her conflict is between what will make *her* happy and what will lead to the happiness of Frank's *wife and children*. It is important to see, however, that the deontological considerations Sara eventually offers do not rest on the hidden premise that people are necessarily happier when they keep their commitments or do not violate the trust that others have in them. It is possible that Frank would be happier marrying Sara and breaking his commitment to his wife. It is even possible that Frank's wife, after getting over the shock of being betrayed and divorced, would be much happier either living alone or marrying someone else far more compatible with her. Some would say that there is a happiness intrinsic to keeping one's commitments and not betraying the trust that others have, but even if one allows this to be called a form of happiness, it is clearly different from that of good times and pleasant experiences.

Deontologists have also criticized utilitarians for failing to be concerned about the distribution of happiness. Traditionally, utilitarians have attempted to state in quantitative terms how much happiness would be produced for how many people by alternative actions or policies. The right action or policy has then been understood as that most likely to produce the greatest happiness for the greatest number. Deontologists have objected that this conception leaves a very unhappy possibility open: the greatest happiness for the greatest number might be achieved by making some people very happy at the expense of others who would suffer great and undeserved misery, such as slaves or scapegoats. The deontological argument has been that to whatever extent happiness may be intrinsically valuable, its distribution, as well as its amount, must be considered. As long as a utilitarian holds that the greatest amount of happiness should be produced, he can accept the importance of distribution only in the following way: for egalitarian reasons, if two distributions produce equal happiness, then one could decide between *those* alternatives on the basis of the comparative evenness of the distributions.

2.3 Competing Values in Personal Ethics

Thus far we have shown how the case study illustrates conflicts between the values of self-interest, happiness, and duty. The question is how to decide which is the most important value. To better understand the differences between the values, let's examine the benefits that theorists have associated with each. Why have people valued self-interest, happiness, and duty as they have? When divergence and conflict arise among actions dictated by these considerations, how is there plausibly something of importance at stake?

The pursuit of *egoistic self-interest* has been seen as a life of prudence, of foresight and planning, of taking care of one's needs, and of not acting foolishly. The importance of self-knowledge has been emphasized, since the person who knows himself best will know best what his own interests are and will, thus, be advantaged in pursuing them. Efficiency and effectiveness have also been emphasized as virtues. For even if you know yourself well and know what your interest is, still you will be frustrated and dissatisfied if you cannot accomplish what is in your self-interest. Similarly, inefficiency will be a fault, for it means unnecessarily wasting resources in accomplishing one's goals.

Autonomy is generally valued highly by ethical egoists, since (a) rational deliberation is assumed to conduce to one's self-knowledge, effectiveness, and efficiency of action, and (b) freedom from constraint is essential to the pursuit of one's self-interest. Moreover, the development of autonomy is itself a part of one's self-development, and self-development in all respects tends to be highly regarded by theorists advocating the pursuit of one's self-interest.

Happiness has been viewed as the aim of human action by thinkers as divergent as Aristotle and John Stuart Mill. Such different thinkers have conceived happiness in very different ways, associating it with many different things. Human beings, as largely non-instinctual creatures, have a large variety of potentialities; they can learn to and do find happiness in a great variety of activities, including individual projects and social interactions. In fact, most people have more potentialities than they can realize in a lifetime. Part of Aristotle's understanding of human happiness is the development that brings human potentiality to realization, especially in society with others. He also understood the development of these potentialities into an integrated life as part of human happiness.

Happiness has often been associated or equated with sensory pleasure, and unhappiness with pain. The meanings of pleasure and pain, however, have not always been strictly sensory. For pleasure can mean contentment or satisfaction; pain can encompass anxiety and frustration. Since it is clearly possible that a human being can be fulfilled or frustrated, a theory that attempts to encompass such ideas is clearly superior to one that ignores them. Moreover, it is clear that such fulfillment and frustration need not derive only from pursuit of egoistic desires. One might also conceive of variety in human experience as itself a source of pleasure and thus happiness.

The definition of happiness has also been affected by the capacity human beings have for reflecting upon themselves, their actions, their life projects and their patterns of interaction with others. A person can reflect both on herself and on others. When such reflection takes place, a person may like or dislike what she sees, or may be content with herself and with others, or may even despise herself or others. This has led to the suggestion that happiness means accepting oneself and one's world, whereas unhappiness means despising and rejecting oneself or others.

As persons reflect upon themselves, they may find that they have or have not made a careful and rational attempt to live up to their own highest ideals of human life and action. Thus if we think of a person of conscience as one who has made such an attempt, then we can understand the suggestion that the happy person is the person of conscience.

Doing one's *duty* has also been highly prized in human history. Immanuel Kant is famous for emphasizing that to act out of duty is to act out of the only pure moral motive. One acts because it is right, independent of consequentialist concerns. In discussing deontological ethics we have already noted the connection between duties and respect for persons. Thus it is easy to see how a person of duty is conceived as virtuous for maintaining his loyalty to others and upholding the trust they place in him. Because the person follows the commitments she has made, her actions have a consistency that many have found admirable. The purity of actions has seemed noble. Here the idea of an action being noble is that it is an action of principle, an action exhibiting consistency, and, therefore, an action in which one is true to the commitments one has made. It is an action in which one is, therefore, being respectful of oneself by maintaining one's own integrity or, in other words, achieving the integration of one's thoughts or principles with one's actions.

Autonomy also plays a crucial role in deontological ethics. The person who would act out of a pure sense of duty must be self-possessed and rational as only an autonomous person can be. In turn, much of the ground for the assertion that *persons are deserving* of respect consists in the beliefs that those persons are themselves at least potentially autonomous and that their autonomy is intrinsically valuable and worthy of respect.

EXERCISES

1. Below is a list of statements meant to justify various courses of action. Mark the reasons of self-interest S, the reasons of social utility U, and the deontological reasons D. (2.1, 2.2)

    ___(a) When you've made a promise, you ought to keep it.

    ___(b) Any other course of action would have benefited everybody else more than me.

    ___(c) The law is worthy of respect in itself.

    ___(d) We both were only trying to make everybody as happy as possible.

    ___(e) I tried to reassure everybody because I could see they were anxious.

    ___(f) It would have been lying not to tell the court what I knew.

    ___(g) If my testimony helps convict that criminal, it can't hurt, and it might help deter others from committing similar crimes.

    ___(h) I figured that testifying could only help my reputation as a civic-minded citizen.

    ___(i) My integrity was preserved, whatever happened to the others.

2. Below is a list of statements, each of which commends a value traditionally associated with either self-interest, happiness, or doing one's duty. Mark each statement S, H, or D, depending on which the value has been traditionally associated with. In the starred cases more than one answer is plausible.

    ___(a) It's only prudent to think about what you're doing to yourself in the long run.

    ___(b) Her motives were purely principled.

    ___(c) A lot of planning and calculation goes into acting rightly.

    ___(d) Telling people the whole truth just tends to make them discontent.

    ___(e) She abused the trust they had placed in her.

    ___(f) *Tom uses his own wits to make his decisions for himself.

    ___(g) *You can waste a lot of time if you take the wrong approach to a problem.

    ___(h) *A person has a lot of joy in knowing she's lived up to her ideals.

    ___(i) A person who doesn't know what he wants is bound to make a fool of himself.

    ___(j) Even though I didn't know myself what would happen, I spoke in such a way as to try to relieve everybody's anxiety.

    ___(k) *There's a natural sense of fulfillment in developing your abilities.

    ___(l) To the end, her loyalty never wavered.

3. (a) Give an example of where egoism and utilitarianism would imply divergent actions.

    (b) Give an example where egoism and deontological theory would imply divergent actions.

    (c) Give an example where utilitarianism and deontological theory would imply divergent actions.

    (d) In each of (a), (b), and (c), abstractly state the features of the example that give rise to the divergence.

4. (a) Repeat 3 (a), (b), and (c), but supply examples in which the actions are conflicting.
(b) For each example, abstractly state the features that give rise to the conflict.

DISCUSSION QUESTIONS

1. If you were Sara, what would you do? Why?
2. If you were Frank, what would you do? Why?
3. How might a defender of the theories criticized in this section defend their views from the criticisms which have been advanced?

ANSWERS TO SELECTED EXERCISES

1. (a) D (b) S (c) D (d) U (e) U (f) D (g) U (h) S (i) S
   For a discussion of self-interest see Chapter 3; Social Utility is covered in Chapter 2; and deontology is discussed in Chapter 4.
2. (a) S. (b) D (c) S,H (d) H (e) D (f) S,D (g) S,H (h) D,H (i) S (j) H (k) H,S (l) D
3. (d) and 4.(b) Since utilitarianism is egalitarian and egoism is selfish, divergence or conflict can arise when what is in one's own self-interest diverges from or conflicts with the greatest happiness of the greatest number. Since deontological theory is principled while egoism may be calculating, and since deontological theory is committed to respect for all persons whereas egoism is not, divergencies and conflicts can arise on either of these grounds. Since utilitarianism is consequentialist where deontological theory is principled, since utilitarians are committed to happiness as deontologists are not, and since deontology involves respect for every person whereas utilitarianism commends the greatest happiness of the greatest number, whatever may be happening to others, divergence and conflict are possible on each of these grounds.

Section 3
CONFLICTS IN SOCIAL ETHICS BETWEEN JUSTICE, FREEDOM, RIGHTS, UTILITY, LAW, AND THE AIMS OF THE STATE

The normative questions of social ethics are typically those of freedom, justice, utility, rights, law, the goals of society, and sovereignty. As with personal ethical tensions, tensions between values in social ethics can arise between two species of the same value (for example, between two criteria of material justice or two alternative concepts of freedom) or between these basic values. As with personal ethical tensions, tensions in social ethics can take the form of either divergence or conflict. In social ethics, however, a special complication arises, insofar as sovereignty, or ultimate authority, involves the question of who has the authority to adjudicate and resolve tensions within a society. In turn, there is the question of whether the sovereign should exercise its authority through the law or through social customs and mores. As we shall see, social ethics is also complicated by the question of whether the state's aim is to protect its citizens from harm or to promote positive benefits for them. After studying Section 2, you should be able to:

- Describe the kinds of tensions in social ethics arising between each of the following: justice, freedom, human rights, and social utility.
- Explain why these conflicts take different forms, depending upon whether the fundamental aim of the state is avoiding harm or promoting benefits for its citizens.

THE CASE OF WELFARE REFORM LEGISLATION

The Orchard City *Daily Sentinel* recently published a summary of a draft copy of some proposed legislation. It solicited responses and counter-proposals from its readers. Here is what it published :

"Portions of the so-called *Welfare Reform* bill now before the House would give full child support to welfare mothers for all their illegitimate minor children who (a) are alive as of the date the law takes force, or (b) are alive as of the date the welfare mother first becomes a resident of the state, or (c) are born to a welfare mother within 270 days of either of the above dates. All illegitimate children born after that time would receive half support. However, at the second illegitimate birth resulting from a second or subsequent pregnancy following that time, the mother will be sterilized. (The procedure will eliminate reproduction but leave other sexual functioning unimpaired.)"

Here are some of the letters the paper received:

"Dear Editor: I support this legislation. We have to do something to make these women act responsibly. Maybe sterilization will force them to think a little about their morality. Yours, R.F."

"Dear Editor: Sterilization is an outrage. Why do we want to punish those women? It's not fair! You can't legislate morality. Besides, what if they tried to use contraception but it failed? Where is the justice here, I ask you? Why do we sterilize these women but let married women breed litters of children? Yours, J.B."

"Dear Editor: I believe this legislation is the only reasonable solution to a growing financial problem. We cannot afford more money for handouts, but we do owe the less fortunate people of this world an even break. So, okay. Support the ones we have, but that's it. No more. This legislation draws the line right where it belongs. Yours, C.G."

"Dear Editor: Our most treasured American possession is our freedom. This legislation would restrict my freedom. I have the right to have children just like anyone else. What gives the government the right to stop me, to threaten me with sterilization, or to withhold its full support from my child? I'm on welfare not because I want to be, but because I have to be. I have my rights, too. Yours, Anon."

"Dear Editor: If we suppose that our welfare pot is only so big, then we will have to be very careful about how we distribute its resources. We can only support so many children before we either run out of money or lower the levels of support so much as to make it meaningless. So, for the good of those whom we are supporting, we have to set limits on how many we support. Otherwise we deplete our resources and water down our welfare so much that everyone suffers. I support this law, but it does not go far enough. Putting new illegitimate children in foster homes would reduce total government costs and probably give the kids a better home environment too. We could even go further and put these kids up for adoption. Yours, Z. M."

3.1 Conflicts Between Society's Values

In Section 1.1 we showed how value conflicts can arise from three sources: a value may conflict with itself, persons may conflict, or values may conflict with one another. The case study clearly illustrates how conflicts arise concerning fundamental values of social ethics. By relieving the tax burden for welfare, the legislation would tend to enhance the effective freedom of the taxpayers at the expense of that of the welfare mothers and their children. Similarly, not taxing people, allowing them to keep the dollars they have worked for, might be deemed just from the point of view of a work criterion, while providing full payments to welfare mothers and their children would seem just on a need criterion. Without much trouble, you can probably imagine other cases in which there is a conflict between two species or forms of a given value. You probably can also think of cases in which there is conflict between persons concerning the same value. The issues of abortion, hiring quotas, and tax liabilities and exemptions can easily provide you with more examples of such internal conflicts (for more cases review the case studies that begin the sections in Chapters 6, 7, and 8). Our chief focus in this section will be on conflicts which arise between the fundamental values of concern to social ethicists.

3.2 Justice and Social Utility

Let us first consider conflicts between *justice* and *social utility*. When we think about social utilities, we are thinking about benefits minus costs. Many groups in society typically are very costly—for example, children, the elderly, and the handicapped. All of these groups may incur more costs, at least in the short run, than they generate benefits. Therefore, it will tend to be utilitarian to minimize these costs. That, of course, will mean minimizing the benefits to these relatively disadvantaged groups. Yet for one reason or another it may seem unjust to deny a full share of benefits to members of these groups. Often it will seem unjust simply on a need criterion. The educational needs of the young, the medical needs of the old, and the special care required by the handicapped can be easily documented. In some cases an argument about justice might be developed on the basis of a work criterion. For example, it might be argued that the elderly, on the average, have worked hard enough that they ought to be able to avoid the cost of medical treatment during retirement. Their inability to afford that treatment might be used to indicate that they were not sufficiently paid for their labors when they were in the work force. Yet it is quite possible that, however deserved a treatment may be, its cost will be greater than any benefit derived from it. In such cases justice and utility conflict. Reviewing the letters to the editor in the case study, you should now be able to pick out further conflicts suggested by the letter writers between justice and utility as they dispute the merits of the welfare reform legislation.

3.3 Rights and Freedom

These two important values can also be in tension in a society. Ultimately, one cost of many social programs takes the form of restriction upon people's freedom. This, for example, is always true when social programs are paid for through public tax moneys. As some of the letters to the editor argue, the payment of taxes constitutes a restriction of both negative and effective freedom. One's freedom to act is constrained, even though one's action is causing no harm to others, inasmuch as one is constrained to pay her taxes. Once the taxes are paid, of course, one's effective freedom is reduced proportionate to the amount of the tax payment.

In conflict with the undesirability of restricting freedom, however, we often find claims about human rights. In her letter to the editor, the anonymous welfare mother asserts her right to have as many children as she pleases. Similarly, the United Nations Declaration of Human Rights certainly implies the right of each of her children to a nutritious diet and the medical care required for good health. Yet for that right to be secured, it would seem necessary to impose the duty of securing it upon those able to do so. Such a duty, however, inevitably restricts their freedom.

We can easily continue to pair off the fundamental values at issue in social ethics and show how conflicts can arise between them. There is no doubt that there is frequently tension between the values of rights and utility, rights and justice, justice and freedom, and utility and freedom. You may even wish to refer to the case study to see whether you can detect instances of these conflicts of values. We believe it appropriate, however, to examine the remaining possible conflicts within the context of a more broadly based consideration of the underlying social and conceptual factors that lead to such conflicts.

3.4 The Underlying Structure of Normative Social Concepts

Just what are some of the most basic reasons why such tensions so often tend to develop? Consider first the concept of social utility. When one attempts to measure social utility, one is concerned about an aggregate—that is, how great the balance of pleasure over pain, or happiness over unhappiness, is throughout the whole society.

Consequently, questions of social utility pay no attention to the distribution of these benefits within society. In other words, it is quite possible that the greatest balance of pleasure over pain, or whatever, will exist in a situation where some unfortunate individual suffers a great imbalance of pain over pleasure. It is false to assume that because a society as a whole has a fine positive utilitarian balance, each member of the society sustains a similar balance. More likely, some will sustain a better balance while others will sustain a balance not nearly so good. For example, saying that our society is, generally speaking, affluent does not mean that there are no poor people or no economically disadvantaged groups in our society.

Questions of justice, however, are not about the aggregate but about the distribution of benefits and burdens. Moreover, talk of justice presupposes some criterion for the appropriateness of a given distribution. No similar consideration of a criterion is to be found in the discussion of social utility. Thus utility may come into conflict with justice either because the most general question of distribution is not addressed or because the more particular question of the deserts of individual persons is not addressed.

Conflicts between social utility and human rights can arise for similar reasons. Human rights are rights of each individual; it makes little sense to think of them as the rights of the society as an aggregate. (The rights of nations, if there are any, need not be identified with the basic human rights of individuals.) Consequently, the existence of a good balance for the society as a whole is no guarantee that the rights of each of its members are being honored.

It is important, though, to note how considerations of rights are distinct from considerations of justice. This becomes clearest when rights are asserted to be indefeasible and inalienable. An indefeasible right is one that cannot be overridden by another consideration; an inalienable right, one that cannot properly be renounced. An indefeasible and inalienable right belongs to a person simply because he is a person. There is nothing special about him in virtue of which he deserves that right. Moreover, there is no condition under which he might not be deserving of it. Thus, whereas questions of justice are typically questions about what characteristics of persons make them deserving of some benefit or burden, any characteristics that give persons indefeasible and inalienable rights are, of necessity, conditions that all people meet. In this regard many theorists are inclined to speak of human rights as a basic floor, a minimum standard beneath which treatment of human beings may never permissibly fall.

There is a dynamic tension between freedom and all of the foregoing values: social utility, justice, and human rights. On the one hand the pursuit of any of these can imply restriction of freedom. To secure one person's rights may require imposing a duty upon another. To do justice or to achieve the greatest social utility, it may be necessary to require persons to act in certain ways, thus restricting their freedom. On the other hand, the pursuit of these values can also enhance and secure freedom. Sufficient funds may hire, train, and pay a competent police force to secure civil liberties. The more fully rights are respected, the greater the increase in negative human freedom. Paying workers their justly earned wage increases their effective freedom.

The problems of value-conflict resolution may be further complicated by the number of social values that come into tension. Any two, three, or possibly even all four, of utility, justice, rights, and freedom may come into play in given social circumstances, with each value tending to pull in a different direction. The case study illustrates such possible complexity in values conflict. These complexities may be more the rule than the exception in a society where the lives and interests of persons touch one another at many points.

3.5 Divergence, Conflict, and Authority

The question of sovereignty (who ought to have the rightful authority to rule) arises in human society for a variety of reasons. Because human beings have the capacities both to help and to harm each other significantly and because they must make significant choices, ensuring security and freedom is centrally important to human life. The question of sovereignty, however, has another source worth noting. Since tension does exist between fundamental social values, the problem arises of which value should prevail in any given course of action. The problem is especially difficult because decisions have to be made without perfect knowledge. If decisions are not made, sometimes the opportunity to act is lost, and so in effect a decision has been made, even if not formally. For instance, if no reform is instituted in welfare legislation, then automatically, without any formal decision, the present welfare legislation will continue in effect. Undeniably, decisions are going to he made one way or the other. When those decisions need to be made with less than perfect knowledge about a given subject, the question of who should have the ultimate authority to decide becomes especially poignant.

When it comes to questions of social policy, sometimes there is not only ignorance concerning factual matters but also uncertainty about how the tension between fundamental social values ought to be resolved. For example, in the case study we may be both (a) ignorant of what the consequences will actually be if the welfare structure is changed (will the welfare mothers stop having illegitimate children if threatened with sterilization?) and (b) uncertain of which fundamental social values ought to take precedence (the rights of the welfare children present and yet unborn vs. the freedom of the taxpayers, for example). Even if one can successfully argue that having an established authority in such circumstances is desirable in bringing social stability, the question of who ought to have sovereignty is especially important in the light of the need to act upon, and decide between, fundamental conflicting social values.

3.6 The Exercise of Authority and the Aims of the State

Besides the question of who shall be established as legitimate authority, there is also the question of how that authority shall be exercised. Should the legitimate power invested in a sovereign be implemented through use of law or through the force of custom and socially accepted mores not covered by law? At this point social ethical questions as to the legitimate purposes of the law come into play in the matter of values-conflict resolution.

Conflicting fundamental social values are made more problematic on still another count. There remains the question of whether the aim of the state is the avoidance of harm or the promotion of good. Reviewing the case study, you can see how these different aims will redefine the claims that citizens, on the basis of their rights, can make against the state. For example, if the state's goal is to help people avoid harm, welfare mothers can claim the right not to be sterilized, since that procedure would be considered a harm to them. If the state's goal is to promote social good, then on balance the sterilization of a few may be desirable. Similarly redefined is the conception of the justice owed to persons. The task of avoiding harm to the unfortunate and innocent children of the welfare mothers, say by providing them with nutrition adequate for sustaining health, immunizations and other preventive medical measures, and protection against violence is a much different task than that of promoting their good by providing them with special pre-school and tutorial programs, scholarships, opportunities for further enrichment and travel, and the variety of experiences that might add pleasure and potential happiness to their lives.

EXERCISES

1. (a) Give an example of a situation in which conflict would arise between each of the following:
    1. Freedom and justice
    2. Freedom and utility
    3. Freedom and rights
    4. Justice and rights
    5. Justice and utility
    6. Rights and utility
    7. Law and justice
    8. Law and moral rights
    9. Law and freedom
    10. The aims of the state and moral rights
    11. The aims of the state and freedom

    (b) In each case abstractly state the features of the example that give rise to the conflict. (3.4)

2. (a) Below is a list of problem situations that exemplify the ways in which the question of sovereignty gains significance. Identify each situation as one in which one of the following problems arises: (*PH*) people need protection from harm; (*SF*) the freedom of people needs to be secured; (*RI*) resolution of disagreement is necessary in the face of ignorance; (*RT*) resolution of disagreement is necessary in the face of value tension.

    ___1. The occupants of cars disabled on freeways in the city of Troidee are being robbed.

___2. Unemployment and inflation cannot both be reduced quickly.

___3. Although petroleum may become very scarce and expensive to import, automobile companies are not sure they could build vehicles meeting a legislative requirement of 38 miles to the gallon in city driving.

___4. Even though terrorists don't hurt the passengers of the planes they hijack, they do delay the passengers in getting where they want to go.

(b) Explain why sovereignty is important to the resolution of each of these conflicts. (3.5 and 3.6)

3. In discussing the welfare legislation mentioned in the case study, Senator Doolittle Goode made the following speech: "The people on welfare in our state today are largely the children of the people we had on welfare 20 years ago. Welfare reform legislation must reduce the burden on the taxpayer by breaking this cycle. If the children of welfare recipients were raised in an environment where they learned to appreciate taking initiatives, we could break this cycle. What do we want? Just to prevent people from starving, when they could be headed toward a higher standard of living. I think that most people who can work would rather work, and we should give them that chance without penalizing them. Let's have all welfare kids adopted into good working homes at birth, and put their parents to work at jobs where they'll earn their own money." (3.3)

(a) Explain how the senator spoke to the questions of (1) avoiding harm, (2) securing freedom, (3) resolving disagreement in the face of ignorance, and (4) resolving disagreement in the face of value tension, all from the point of view that the sovereign ought to put the promotion of good ahead of the prevention of harm.

(b) After you have checked your answer, write a speech for Senator Doomore Harm containing statements that counter Senator Goode's speech on all four points.

DISCUSSION QUESTIONS

1. In view of all the arguments presented, what is your considered opinion regarding the proposed welfare reform legislation? Why? If you disagree with it, write a superior piece of legislation. Justify your proposal in view of social utility, justice, rights, freedom, and the aims of the state.

2. In a celebrated case the parents of a young man, aged 24, who committed suicide sued the minister to whom the young man had gone for counseling. The parents contended that the minister had the ethical duty to put the distressed young man in contact with a licensed and properly trained psychologist. Identify the conflicting social values operative in such a case. As a start, consider religious freedom, freedom of choice, protection from harm, legal obligations, social utility, etc. Should ministers be required to hold State licenses (which imply some form of minimum standards) before they undertake to offer counseling to those who seek it? Does anyone, professionally trained or not, have a duty to prevent others from committing suicide? Should persons harmed or grieved by the loss of a loved one have the legal right, considering the aims of society, to sue those whom they feel are responsible for their loss and grief?

ANSWERS TO SELECTED EXERCISES

1. For more details about freedom, justice, utility, rights, law, sovereignty, and the aims of society, see Chapters 5, 6, 2, 4, 8, and 7, respectively.

2. (a) 1. *PH* 2. *RT* 3. *RI* 4. *SF*

3. (a) 1. The harm of being in need of welfare assistance would be overcome by reducing the percentage of people requiring welfare.

   2. The restriction on the taxpayer of having to pay higher taxes would be reduced, increasing his freedom.

   3. Without claiming to know, the senator urges action on his belief that most of those who can work want to work.

   4. Leading welfare recipients to a higher standard of living—since that promotes their good—is given the priority over simply providing for basic needs. Similarly, providing an improved environment for the children is given precedence over avoiding the harm of disrupting the welfare families.

Section 4
STRATEGIES FOR RATIONAL RESOLUTION OF VALUES TENSIONS

We have described the fundamental values of personal and social ethics and some of the tensions that tend to arise between them. We offered explanations of why those tensions arise, given the differences in the kinds of values involved. The problem remains, however: How can such tensions be rationally resolved? In our daily experience we are all too aware of non-rational and irrational ways of resolving these conflicts: (1) people ignore the issues, (2) they engage in deceptions, (3) they use manipulative, emotional language, capable of moving persons without providing help with sound reasons, and (4) they all too often engage in the use of force. But are there any *rational* alternatives to these procedures? Yes, indeed there are. They are effective but they are not perfect. They may not resolve all the value tensions, but they are useful in easing and resolving many of them. Similarly, they may work in some but not all circumstances. Nevertheless, even these imperfect procedures are of considerable worth as we try to resolve the value tensions in our lives and our society in rational ways. After studying Section 4, you should be able to:

- Characterize each of the following three strategies for rational resolution of values tensions: setting priorities, finding alternatives, and negotiating compromise.
- For each of these strategies state what makes it plausible and what assumptions it makes.
- For each strategy state its limitations and the problems that it does not fully handle.
- Apply these strategies to real world value tensions.

THE CASE OF KUBULA, JARANKO

The news broadcast was barely audible through the crackle and static of the old radio receiver. But its message was clear. The city of Kubula was beset with riots and the country of Jaranko was on the verge of civil war once more.

"...the soccer match had been played up by the government press as a match between Xororian Leftists and Polaried Rightists. It appears that the government hoped the game would settle the running feud. The government was wrong. A fight erupted in the second half. The crowd of 80,000 poured onto the field and joined the battle. Riots broke out along Lamumbuka Street, which separates Xororian and Polaried sectors of the city. Scores of people are dead, hundreds injured. The police seem unable or unwilling to stop the rioters and street gangs. The military is already arriving in the city. A meeting between Xororian and Polaried leaders is in progress at this moment. This is Joan Fletcher, CNB news, Kubula."

Prime Minister Lukarta snapped the radio off. "There you have it, friends. It is all over the western news services. Every capital in the world knows we are at it again. And is it really so important? I mean, a game of soccer leads to riots, to a revival of the old prejudices. No. Please, friends, consider what is more important. Think of our nation, Jaranko. We need financial and medical aid to improve our economy, raise our people's standard of living, and cure diseases that have been controlled everywhere but here. Is it not better to put aside the old and pointless fights? Let us put down our arms, call back our guerrillas, and make peace."

No sooner had the Prime Minister finished than the insults and recriminations began being hurled back and forth. A Xororian leader cupped his hands to his lips and shouted, "A pretty speech, Minister Lukarta, but no good. We cannot trust the Polaried nor their leaders. They are a band of thieves. Dogs who would take away our jobs and destroy our culture."

To this an outraged Polaried replied, "Not trust us! You're the ones who wish to change the laws, to destroy the old ways of structuring society. You call for 'socialism' when what you really want is anarchy and governmental chaos. Swine!"

The Prime Minister pleaded for reason. "Friends, please, please. This is not the way to settle our problems—yelling, fighting. Soon you will be shooting even here in the high court chamber. Please, I beg you, show control."

When relative calm had been restored to the meeting room, the Prime Minister said, "Good. Now, perhaps we can erase the present tensions in the city first. Having done that much, we will save many lives. Then, later, when we have had more time to reflect, perhaps we can talk again about long-term solutions."

"We Polarieds agree. Too much blood is flowing down sewers. Let us ease back, stop the fighting, then talk."

"That's fine for you to say, but we Xororians are poor. You can talk and talk forever; but no reforms will come from talk. We need action. That is why we are in the streets. That is why we will stay there until the problem is solved. No! You cannot fool us with a smile and a promise to talk tomorrow. Let us talk now. Let it be on your conscience, Abalu, that while we talk people die. So let's talk quickly and let us solve our problem."

"Friends, please once again. At least a ten-hour truce, do you agree to that? Just ten hours to count the dead, tend the wounded, and try to reach accord."

"I'll accept a five-hour truce—a truce until noon. If no solution has been found, we will attack in force on schools, hospitals, and apartment houses."

"Five hours, we too accept. But now, let us begin. Minister, what do you propose?"

"Yes—well, friends, I propose that we discuss a compromise. The Polarieds will give up control of the court system and half the seats in the Parliament in return for access to the Xororian-controlled labor unions. The Xororians may then have equal representation in the Parliament, and equal representation in the unions. The government's executive ministry will assume control of the courts. What do you think?"

4.1 The Strategy of Setting Priorities

The citizens of Kubula face a conflict between social stability and justice for their poorer citizens. The social order that benefits the Polaried Rightists is apparently suppressing the Xororian Leftists unjustly. The threats of the Xororians to continue fighting are the result of their decision that social stability and the utility of the society as a whole are less important than the rectification of the injustices to them. Implicit in their thought is the idea of a set of priorities and its use to resolve or attempt to resolve a social problem. The Xororians perceive two values, social stability and justice, as in conflict. They are convinced it is impossible to achieve both. Being so convinced, they ask: "Which is the more important to achieve?" They then form a ranking from the most important on down:

1. Justice, especially for the Xororians.
2. Social stability.

The implication of the ranking of priorities is that, since justice is more important than social stability, at least in the present circumstances, and since the two are in conflict, justice, the higher value, should be achieved even at the expense of social stability, the lower value.

Put abstractly, then, the strategy of setting priorities amounts to this: it is assumed that two or more values cannot both be realized. Then it becomes appropriate to ask, "Which value should be realized?" The trivial answer, "The more important one, of course," is given substance by ranking the relevant values from most important to least important. From the ranking a decision may be drawn about the course of action to be followed.

4.2 The Plausibility of Setting Priorities

In the case study the Xororians use of a set of priorities is not very persuasive, because you can imagine all too easily that the Polaried Rightists would be inclined to form their own set of priorities and come to a contrary conclusion. The conflict would persist, and nothing would have been gained by forming two contrary sets of priorities. If the setting of priorities is to be a useful strategy for rational conflict resolution, to formulate our ranking we need some objective criterion to which all parties could appeal and that all parties would accept.

The crucial question is what such a criterion might be? A simple example may help to illuminate the kind of criterion that those who favor the strategy have found promising. Suppose that two children go to hear Heifetz play the violin. Each child likes classical music, and after the concert each child claims to have liked the music very much and to have found it very pretty. Is there any way in which we can distinguish the quality of the two children's appreciation? Well, suppose that one child has no training as a musician, while the other child has already spent many years practicing the violin for two hours a day. That child, thus, is aware of the artistry and the technical precision involved in Heifetz's playing. On this supposition we can say objectively that the second child's appreciation of the concert is richer than that of the first. For while both children found the violin music pretty, the second child alone could appreciate the performance for its technical artistry. The other child, by hypothesis, was unaware of the technical difficulty of Heifetz's playing.

What can be extracted from this simple example? Essentially the second child's appreciation is *more encompassing* than the first; it involves everything that the first one's does, *but it also involves more*. Thus if one's action or one's social policy could be said to contain not only one desired value but another value besides, then it could thereby be said to be the better for it encompasses more values.

The nineteenth-century English philosopher John Stuart Mill, in his book *Utilitarianism*, asserted, "It is better to be a human being dissatisfied than a pig satisfied; better to be Socrates dissatisfied than a fool satisfied" (Mill, 1863).This remark is easily interpreted as illustrating the setting of priorities based on the richness of experience. Socrates is able to experience the environmental awareness and the sensations of which the pig is capable, but the pig is not capable of the self-awareness, the abstract thought, the rationality, the awareness of time, and so on, of which Socrates is capable. Socrates' experience is judged the better by Mill because it is richer and more encompassing.

One strategy for setting priorities upon which to base decisions is to identify the *policies or actions* that encompass the greatest number of desirable values. Therefore, those who favor the strategy of setting priorities are very interested in the question, "What kind of action or what kind of social policy has the greatest or most encompassing positive value?" The description of such an ideal would allow them to determine what sort of action or social policy ought to be at the top of their list of priorities. They could then concern themselves with how actions or policies with less of these values might rank in relationship to each other as inferiors to the ideal.

The basic plausibility of such a strategy is that richer actions or policies—that is, actions or policies containing all of the positive value of another plus an additional positive value—are to be valued more highly.

An alternative way of setting priorities to use in decision making allows us to rank values instead of policies. This alternative way is not based on the assumption that some policies allow for greater richness but rather on the assumption that some values are more fundamental. For example, suppose that in Country X there is a labor union, some of whose members hold insecure jobs. These members are frequently laid off and usually they cannot find other work. Country X has no welfare programs for those laid off; they must fend for themselves. The union, however, also has a group of rather wealthy, highly trained, much desired workers whose labor is always in demand. The union is thus faced with a problem. To its first group of members job security is very important, because without a job they literally face starvation. To its second group of members job security is not really an issue, because they are confident they will always have a job. This group of workers wants the union to demand an increased number of four-day weekends for holiday trips as its highest bargaining priority.

The union, of course, wants to keep all of its members. Somehow, though, the leaders recognize that the concerns of the first group of workers are more important. They express this importance as follows: "You can have a job without holiday trips, but you can't have holiday trips without a job."

Stated abstractly, the concept of a fundamental value is such that if the value is not realized, then another, less fundamental value, cannot be realized, while at the same time if the less fundamental value is not realized, the more fundamental value can still be realized. Life, safety, and health could be said to be very fundamental values, because without them many other values, such as having leisure time, developing talents, and engaging in entertainment, cannot be pursued or are at least jeopardized.

4.3 Limitations of Setting Priorities

The problem with the strategy of setting priorities is that conflicting values do not always neatly form hierarchies. That is, it is not always obvious or demonstrable that of two conflicting actions or policies the one guarantees a richer result or reflects a more fundamental value than the other. Often it looks as if they aim at ends that are divergent. If one action aims at peace and another at justice, it is not clear either that peace will involve justice or that justice will involve peace, or that one is the more fundamental.

It is important, however, that we do not overestimate the difficulty in setting priorities among values. The mathematical notion of a partial ranking can be employed. Consider an analogous situation in arithmetic. Suppose we wanted to rank the following from highest to lowest: 2; 16; a number between 1 and 5; 7; and a number between 7 and 10. Some things can be said. Sixteen is the highest; that is, it is higher than 2, higher than the number between 1 and 5, higher than 7, and higher than the number between 7 and 10. Similarly we can say that 2 is lower than

7, lower than the number between 7 and 10, and lower than 16. Thus we can rank some of the numbers from highest to lowest. Others, however, we cannot place in relationship to each other. The number 2 may be higher than the number between 1 and 5, but it may be equal to it, and it may be lower. The number 7 may be either equal to or lower than the number between 7 and 10. Definite higher–lower relationships cannot be stated in these cases. The value of a partial ranking, however, is that some rankings can be definitely and objectively made, even if others cannot. Thus, by analogy, even though there may be cases where it is not clear which alternative is the richer or which value is the more fundamental, still the strategy of setting priorities will be useful wherever a clear and definite partial ranking can be made.

4.4 The Strategy of Finding Alternatives

Many value tensions can be dissolved by finding new alternatives which avoid the problem. As suggested in Section 1.2 if tension is due to divergence without conflict, then it is possible to accommodate the divergence by doing both. If tension is due to undesirable sets of consequences of either of two alternative courses, while still a third or fourth course of action remains, then do neither of the first two. If a conflict arises between two aims owing to present circumstances, then change the circumstances so that, despite divergence, there is no longer conflict between the two aims.

For example, if we serve parsnips, Susan will be unhappy. If we serve eggplant, Roger will be upset. We have no other vegetables on hand. What shall we do? Clearly, given our supply of vegetables, there is tension between pleasing Susan and pleasing Roger. This tension, however, hardly seems inevitable. We could serve both vegetables and please both Susan and Roger. Or, when we went shopping, we could buy other vegetables that both of them like. There doesn't seem to be any necessity that either of them should be displeased by the food served.

Just as it is possible to serve both of two particular vegetables, so it is also possible to pursue both of two complementary, although divergent, aims. The Xororian Leftists are concerned that if a truce is established without negotiations being planned, then no negotiations will take place. But again there is no necessary incompatibility between a truce and negotiation. A plan for negotiations could be built into a truce plan.

Even when aims are not merely divergent but conflicting, it is possible that the conflict only arises because of *present* circumstances. It may be that in other circumstances the conflict would dissolve, and so it may be that changing present circumstances can lead to resolution of a current problem. For examples of this you might glance at Section 1.2 once again.

4.5 The Plausibility of Finding Alternatives

Dissolving tensions is a particularly promising way to handle tensions in situations involving alternative evils. When it seems that no matter which choice we make, we will choose something undesirable, the possibility of not having to choose at all, or the possibility of being able to choose a third alternative, is particularly attractive. Antagonistic parties, for example, may often feel that they can afford neither to trust, nor not to trust, each other. If they trust each other, then they are likely to be taken in and harmed; if they distrust each other, they will be unable to work together to restore peace and the possibility of prosperity for themselves. More promising is a third alternative: working closely with each other without trusting each other but with considerable safeguards to ensure that each side performs up to the other's expectations.

In a word, then, this strategy for the resolution of value tensions is built upon *flexibility and creativity.* It argues for flexibility at all levels. At a material level, the more resources and technological abundance a society or a person has, the easier it becomes to use resources in alternative ways or to create alternatives for people. At a personal level it argues in favor of persons being clearly and distinctly aware of the ends they are seeking. Having a clear idea of one's goals allows one to distinguish them from the means that one is accustomed to using but that one may not need to use in order to accomplish those goals. The more imaginative creative persons are in coming up with alternatives and the more flexible persons are to choose different means to accomplish their ends, the better this strategy works. At a social level flexibility and creativity are again virtues. Whether in developing new kinds of transportation systems, coming up with new ways to finance projects, creating ways for a given resource to serve more than one narrow set of needs, finding new approaches to old problems, the flexibility provides a society with extra alternatives that turn conflicts into divergencies and ultimately dissolve tensions.

The strategy of finding alternatives makes a virtue of *foresight.* Once the Polarieds and the Xororians are at each other's throats, it is difficult to restore peace, much less prosperity, to Jaranko. Keeping alternatives available, not making commitments one may be unable to keep, planning to ensure that divergent aims do not become conflicting but can be accommodated within a single plan—all of these are encompassed within the virtue of foresight so dear to the strategy of finding alternatives.

4.6 Limitations of Finding Alternatives

Simply saying that people ought to be flexible and creatively find new alternatives seems a shallow and inadequate proposal when it comes to two main kinds of cases. In the first place, some conflicts seem to be unavoidable, especially given circumstances over which we have no power and thus under which we are forced to live. For instance, rights, as conceived of in the twentieth century, require a considerable abundance of resources if they are to be honored. Because of resource scarcity, honoring those rights may be impossible, or may require that human freedom be severely curtailed by a tightly organized, centrally controlled society and a government that constrains freedom in order to make society more efficient in its production.

Other conflicts are unavoidable because unwise promises or other commitments have been made. If the Polaried leaders have made commitments to their people, then there is something wrong in their not meeting the expectations they have created, even though meeting them does conflict with the right of the Xororian people to an improved standard of living.

Some theorists would argue that finding alternatives is also limited as a strategy because it does not build character. If it is honorable to keep your commitments, then it is desirable to develop the character traits that will enable you to keep them. Moral fortitude, self-discipline, and nobility of soul are valuable, according to some theorists, not simply as means enabling persons to keep commitments but as ends in themselves. The ability to integrate principle into practice and to be confident and dedicated in following ideals is thought of as intrinsically good. With this thought in mind one may find the strategy of dissolution of conflicts suspect; a strategy of setting priorities may seem much superior. For whereas a setting priorities approach demands that the agent be morally firm and have the moral resolve to follow the highest principle through the gravest of conflicts, the strategy of finding alternatives continually attempts to prevent situations from arising in which moral resolve and fortitude will be needed.

4.7 The Strategy of Negotiating Compromise

Throughout the case study Prime Minister Lukarta advocates a third strategy for conflict resolution, that of compromise. He does so because no mutually acceptable set of priorities is detectable and the problem cannot be made to dissolve by finding an alternative which, astoundingly enough, everyone had managed to overlook before. Lukarta asks first that the present fighting be stopped and time be allowed for reflection on possible long-term solutions. This temporary truce would serve social stability, yet open some prospect for future negotiation on the matter of justice for the Xororians. The proposal goes some way, but not all of the way, toward trying to satisfy both of the principal immediate concerns at stake. A temporary truce is not lasting peace and stability, and postponed justice is not immediate redistribution of benefits and burdens. The other parties to the dispute are too hot, however, to accept this initial compromise proposal. The minister falls back to a proposal for a temporary truce of ten hours to allow for immediate negotiations. Both parties accept a similar proposal with a five-hour limitation. At this point the minister makes a proposal that would give both the Polarieds and the Xororians a part of what they have been seeking to gain through confrontation. As the price for stability the Polarieds are asked to give up control of the courts and half the Parliament seats. On the other hand, the Xororian gains here do not secure immediate redistribution, and the Polarieds are to be granted partial control of the Xororian labor unions. The case study leaves us at a point where this compromise proposal remains to be tested in negotiation and possibly in action.

4.8 Plausibility of Negotiating Compromise

This strategy is a way of providing something for everyone, but not everything for everyone. It is also a way of providing some of each of the values in tension rather than realizing any one of the values to the exclusion of others. Like the strategies of setting priorities and of finding alternatives, the strategy of compromise has its presuppositions. First, since it proposes that everyone should be given something or that each of the values should be actualized in some degree, it assumes that the valuable commodities can be distributed in degrees. It assumes that a right or a freedom as well as a benefit or a burden can be actualized in degrees if not fully.

The second presupposition is that no rational set of priorities is available, either the values that are in conflict or the persons whose interests should take first place. The first clause of this denial means that we cannot apply the strategy of setting priorities. The second clause is, in effect, the assertion of egalitarianism, for if no person can be ranked higher than any other, then all persons must be ranked equally.

The third presupposition is that the tension between the values cannot be dissolved. For if it could be, and thereby all that is valuable could be achieved or all that is undesirable avoided, then there would be no sense in agreeing to a compromise that would accept less. Compromise, then, is a last-ditch strategy, predicated upon failing when trying to set priorities and trying to find alternatives.

4.9 Limitations of Negotiating Compromise

Like the others, this strategy has *limitations.* The strategy of compromise involves two sorts of problems, one theoretical and one practical. Theoretically, the problem involves the presupposition that the contested values can be realized in degree rather than fully. If one is concerned about a benefit that enhances the quality of life but is not essential to a minimal standard of living or even to a good and satisfying life, then it is easy to see how such a compromise would be possible. However, suppose that one of the values in contention is regarded an indefeasible and an inalienable right. How well would Christians be satisfied with a compromise on their right to worship as they chose if it were proposed that they could worship any way they chose, provided that they did not worship on Sunday nor pray to Jesus? How valuable would freedom of assembly be if it were conditioned on never speaking critically about the rulers of one's country? In other words, it is certainly possible that when one compromises a value by achieving the realization of only part of it, the part realized will be insubstantial or of no real value or gain at all, especially in comparison to what was sacrificed in the compromise. As long as all parties are agreed that they are negotiating concerning relative desirables and undesirables, none of which they absolutely must achieve or avoid, there is room for negotiation and for compromise. In fact, however, not all parties may feel that there is such room for compromise. Theoretically, it is not clear that some rights and freedoms could be meaningfully compromised without being substantially destroyed.

A practical problem with the strategy of compromise is that it tends to blur the line between power and authority. In practice one is usually pushed forcefully toward a compromise that favors the more powerful, for they are much more able to enforce their will than are the weak. If fair compromise desired by the weak but unpalatable to the powerful is insisted upon by the weak, the powerful may become totally unwilling to grant even a small compromise that might have been initially acceptable to them. Thus, while the ideal of compromise says that each party will give something and it assumes that all the parties are equal, the realities of power in society suggest that all parties will not be treated equally and that compromise will tend, therefore, regularly to promote a degree of injustice in favor of the powerful.

4.10 Ranking the Three Suggested Strategies

Tensions in which there is no essential conflict can, at least with ingenuity, be resolved by finding an alternative by which everyone can achieve all of his goals. If this is possible, it is more desirable than achieving only the prioritized goal or only some of one's goals to some extent.

If there is an essential conflict between values, at least in this situation, then if one value objectively has a higher priority than the other(s), the value with that priority should be realized and the other value(s) ignored or compromised to some extent.

If there is both an essential conflict and no objective priorities in accord with which one value is of higher priority than the other, then negotiating compromise becomes appropriate if the partial achievement of conflicting values is possible.

These comments suggest that there is an objective ranking of strategies. The ranking suggests: first, try to dissolve the tensions by finding new alternatives; perhaps all values can be realized or other options exist. But if essential conflicts arise, try building a set of priorities, trying to maximize the most important values. And, if no objective ranking is possible, one must try to negotiate compromise.

That these strategies are limited is obvious. That they are much easier to describe than to make work in real situations, is painfully clear. But what other rational choices do we have? As is evident by our efforts to co-exist on this spaceship called Earth with limited resources and under the constant possibility of nuclear war, rational strategies such as these might be all that stands between our continued existence and the irrationality of environmental self-destruction or the nuclear annihilation of the human species.

EXERCISES

1. Characterize each of the following strategies for resolution of values tensions: setting priorities, finding alternatives, negotiating compromise. (4.1, 4.4, and 4.7, respectively)
2. Below is a list of assertions. Some are true of setting priorities, some of finding alternatives, and some of negotiating compromise. Put a T or F in each of the three columns in order to indicate whether an assertion is true or false in each view.
   SP DT C

        (a) This model will work only if there is no essential conflict in the situation.

        (b) This model will work if one of the values in tension is more fundamental than the other.

SP   DT   C

(c) This model assumes that a rational solution is possible even if it is impossible for all parties to achieve everything they originally wanted.

(d) This model can work even if there is an essential conflict between values that cannot be objectively ranked.

(e) If this method is successful, no violence arises out of the resolution of tension.

(f) This model is likely to work in favor of the powerful.

(g) The practicality of this model is improved when there is an increased variety of means available to achieve each goal.

(h) This model requires the choice of one of the values in tension over the other.

(i) This model works toward the full achievement of all goals and values.

(j) This model works toward the partial achievement of central values.

3. Describe three cases such that each is best handled by a different one of the three strategies. Then state the characteristics of each of the cases that make it best handled by a particular strategy.

REAL WORLD APPLICATIONS

1. Privately, then in a group, list the seven things most important to you (individually, and then collectively). State, in terms of the values they realize, why these seven are so important. Rank them and justify the ranking. Repeat this with different groups such as your family, your co-workers, and your close friends.

2. As a group, identify a problem occurring in your institution. Identify the values in tension in that problem. Study the problem, gather relevant factual information, and identify all the well-known options which people have proposed and rejected for solving that problem. Find a new alternative. Propose this alternative to those who are contesting the issue and advocate your proposal seeking to have it accepted as the rational way to solve that problem.

3. Do the same as (b) but this time approach the problem as an unbiased group of persons. After having studied the problem and gathered relevant factual information, invite spokespersons representing the various "sides" of the issue to meet with you. Attempt to negotiate a compromise between them. [This can also be done as a role playing exercise, which might be a useful preliminary to getting involved with the disputing parties.]

ANSWERS TO SELECTED EXERCISES

2. (a)*F,T,F* (b)*T,F,F* (c)*T,F,T* (d)*F,F,T* (e)*T,T,T* (f)*F,F,T* (g)*F,T,T* (h)*T,F,F* (i)*F,T,F* (j)*F,F,T*

Review the plausibility and limitations of each strategy in order to understand each one more fully.

GLOSSARY

ABSOLUTE VALUE: Anything a society deems good or worthy of desire in and of itself.

ACT UTILITARIANISM: The theory that an action is to be judged right or wrong on the basis of the specific consequences of that particular action, that moral rules are rough generalizations based on the accumulation of evidence from individual actions and that moral rules serve only as guidelines.

ALTRUISM: The normative position that one ought act in accord with the maxim that the interests of others should take priority over one's own interests.

ALTRUISTIC UTILITARIANISM: The theory that the extent of the utilitarian consideration of consequences should include all those persons affected but should not include the agent himself or herself.

ANARCHISM: The theory that no form of government (understood as an agency with the sole authority to exercise coercive force over the members of a society) should be established, but that any group needs which arise should be met through the voluntary cooperation of individuals.

AUTHORITY: The right to control or lead a society, particularly as distinguished from power, which is the ability to control a society.

AUTONOMOUS ACTION: An action which is implemented without coercion or constraint and which is the product of a decision made rationally and without coercion or constraint.

CATEGORICAL DUTY: A duty or obligation which exists under all possible circumstances.

CATEGORICAL IMPERATIVE: The statements of one's categorical duty as formulated by Immanuel Kant.

CLASSICAL LIBERALISM: The theory of the state which focuses on the interests of the individual as opposed to the interests of the collective and which stresses minimal interference and maximal personal liberty.

CLASSICAL UTILITARIANISM: *see* UNIVERSALISTIC UTILITARIANISM

COMMUNITY: A society which regularly resides and take meals together.

COMPATIBILISM: The theory that every event has a cause and yet at least some human choices are free.

COMPENSATORY JUSTICE: The corrective distribution of benefits to persons who have experienced undeserved denial of benefit or undeserved suffering or hardship in past distributions of benefits and burdens.

CONCEPTUAL ANALYSIS: The methodical examination of words, ideas, and concepts with a view toward clarifying their meaning.

CONSEQUENTIALIST THEORY: Any normative theory which holds that the ethical character of an action is a function of the intrinsic value of those states of affairs which it brings about.

CONSTRAINT: Any condition such that (a) it prevents a person from finding certain courses of action to be rational, though one might otherwise find them so, or (b) it prevents a person from actually doing what one rationally decided to do.   Type (a) conditions are the limitations that one must take into account as one decides rationally what to do.

CONVENTIONAL RIGHT: Entitlements that come into existence within conventional structures, such as the customs and laws of a given society or culture.

CONVENTIONALIST REASON: The assertion that one has a given duty because of existing social, cultural or legal conventions or standards of moral behavior.

DEMOCRACY: That method of discerning the will of the people who make up a society by either directly involving those persons in voting or deciding issues (participatory democracy), or by electing representatives charged with deciding issues (representative democracy).

DEONTOLOGICAL THEORY: Any normative theory which holds that certain actions are intrinsically valuable in and of themselves.

DICTATORIAL SOVEREIGNTY: That theory of sovereignty which vests ultimate authority in a single person or single group of persons within a society.

DISTRIBUTIVE JUSTICE: The fair distribution of benefits and burdens to persons who have conflicting interests regarding the allocation of those benefits and burdens.

EFFECTIVE FREEDOM: Possession of the means and opportunities necessary to achieve one's aims.

EGALITARIANISM: The normative position that one ought act in accord with the maxim that everyone—one's self and all others—should be regarded as of equal value and importance.

EGOISTIC UTILITARIANISM: The theory that the extent of the utilitarian consideration of consequences should be limited to only those affecting the agent himself or herself, and no other persons—*see* ETHICAL EGOISM.

EQUALITARIANISM: Strict equalitarianism requires that all benefits and burdens be distributed equally to all persons, with each person receiving an equal share; proportional equalitarianism requires that benefits and burdens be distributed in proportion to a person's deserts.

ESSENTIAL CONFLICT: A value conflict such that, for all practical purposes, the conflict is inevitable and unavoidable; that is, no matter how one goes about following one set of values or policies, one is thereby prevented from following the other set of values or policies.

ETHICAL EGOISM: The normative theory that one ought always act so as to maximize one's own self-interest.

ETHICAL EMOTIVISM: The view that all ethical claims are nothing more than expressions of one's emotional reactions to situations or efforts to evoke emotional reactions in others.

ETHICAL NIHILISM: The normative theory that there is nothing which we ought to desire or not desire.

ETHICAL RELATIVISM: The normative view that it is desirable that there should be differences in the ethical standards and values in different societies. Weak-sense ethical relativism relates to a society's relative values. Strong- sense ethical relativism makes its normative claim about absolute values.

ETHICAL SKEPTICISM: The view that ethical claims make sense but cannot be justified.

ETHICS: The rational and disciplined study of normative problems, issues, and principles which aims at achieving unbiased, well-reasoned value judgments at both the practical and theoretical levels.

EXCUSE: A reason presented in order to relieve someone of responsibility or accountability for some action.

FASCISM: That theory of the state which emphasizes the priority of the interests of the state over the interests of any of its individual members.

FORMAL FREEDOM: Equal treatment under the law.

FORMAL JUSTICE: The principle that one should treat relevantly similar cases similarly and relevantly different cases differently in proportion to the difference(s) between them. This principle entails that injustice is done when similar persons are treated differently or when persons who are different are treated similarly. This principle does not specify what respects are to be counted as relevant similarities or differences among persons.

FORMAL VIRTUE: A virtue, like integrity or wisdom, which operates at a second level and is instrumental in any number of goals which a person might have at the material level.

GENETIC FALLACY: Any argument based on the false assumption that all characteristics true of a thing in its original form must remain true of that thing through all of its history and possible transformations.

GOVERNMENT: Any organization of persons vested by the society with the rightful authority to pursue the goals of that society.

HARD DETERMINISM: The theory that every event has a cause and that, if this is so, then no human choice can be free.

HEDONISTIC UTILITARIANISM: The theory that actions or practices are right if they lead to pleasure (or prevent pain), and wrong if they lead to pain (or prevent pleasure).

HYPOTHETICAL IMPERATIVE: A duty which results by virtue of having certain goals or interests.

INALIENABLE RIGHT: Any right which cannot be surrendered or renounced.

INDEFEASIBLE RIGHT: Any right which may not be justifiably overridden or subordinated to any other moral consideration.

INDIVIDUAL SOVEREIGNTY: That theory of sovereignty which vests ultimate authority in each and every individual person, not in any single person or any group of persons.

INSTRUMENTAL VALUE: Anything which is judged desirable (undesirable) as a means to (obstacle to) achieving some end.

INTEGRITY: The ability and disposition to realize and to limit one's own potentialities weaving them into a consistent and balanced way of living.

INTRINSIC VALUE: Anything judged desirable (undesirable) as an end or goal in itself (as something to be avoided in an of itself).

JUSTICE: As a formal principle—the treating of persons alike who are alike in morally relevant respects, and the treating of persons proportionately differently to the extent that they differ in morally relevant respects.

JUSTIFICATION: A reason which would persuade unbiased, informed, rational people that a normative claim is, beyond any reasonable doubt, correct.

LEGAL OBLIGATION: An obligation imposed by the laws of a society which can be interpreted as creating an ethical duty or as describing the penalties or negative consequences to be suffered if the obligation is not fulfilled.

LIBERTARIANISM: The theory that at least some human choices are free and, given that if every event has a cause then no human choices could be free, it must be false that every event has a cause.

LIMITED GOVERNMENT: The theory that the only purposes of government are those minimally necessary to ensure that the most fundamental shared human purposes of the state (such as survival and safety) are met.

LIMITED UTILITARIANISM: The theory that the extent of the utilitarian consideration of consequences should be restricted to only those persons who are members of some identifiable sub-group rather than to all those persons affected.

MATERIAL JUSTICE: Those principles of justice which specify what is to count as morally relevant similarities or differences among persons for purposes of making just discriminations among them.

MATERIAL VIRTUE: Any virtue which is conducive to the achievement of some particular goal, purpose or state of being toward which a person might have decided to strive.

MORAL RIGHTS: Entitlements which are thought to exist independent of and regardless of social, cultural or legal conventions.

NEGATIVE FREEDOM: Freedom from constraint or coercion.

NON-NORMATIVE STATEMENTS: Value neutral claims which do not express, or are not intended to express, value judgments.

NORMATIVE STATEMENTS: Those statements, claims or assertions which express or imply, or are intended to express or imply, value judgments.

NORMATIVE TENSION: The state which arises when value conflicts or value divergence exist between one value and itself, between persons, or between one value and another value.

OBJECTIVE DUTY: In utilitarian theory, the duty to perform those actions or undertake those practices which actually produce the best possible balance of good over bad results.

OBJECTIVIST INTERPRETATION: An interpretation of a normative claim which focuses on characteristics of the object being evaluated as the basis for asserting that the object is or is not worthy of desire independently of the speaker's preferences or feelings concerning that object.

PHILOSOPHICAL DETERMINISM: The thesis that for every event there is some complex set of causal conditions such that, given precisely these conditions, no other event could occur. Also known as the "Principle of Universal Causality."

POPULAR SOVEREIGNTY: That theory of sovereignty which vests ultimate authority in the people of the society taken as a totality.

POSITIVE FREEDOM: Freedom to deliberate and act rationally.

PRESUMPTION: A rule stating how we are to proceed in circumstances where we are not fully informed of all relevant information, yet must decide.

PRESUMPTION OF EQUALITY: Treat all persons as equal unless one has some relevant basis for differentiating among them.

PRESUMPTION OF INEQUALITY: Treat all persons differently unless one has some relevant basis for not making differentiations among them.

PSYCHOLOGICAL EGOISM: The scientific theory that the only motivation out of which people can act is a motivation to serve their own self-interest.

RATIONAL CHOICE: A choice or decision made in accord with the following procedure: (a) set one's own goals, (b) establish one's priorities, (c) identify the means to achieve one's goals, (d) predict the probable consequences of alternative choices, (e) reassess goals and means to goals as necessary, (f) make a choice in light of the above considerations, and (g) evaluate the effort and learn from one's mistakes.

RATIONALIZATION: The process of one's adopting or rejecting reasons because they respectively do or do not support one's preconceived point of view.

RELATIVE VALUE: Anything a society deems desirable as a conventional means of realizing its absolute values.

REPUBLIC: A state governed through representative democracy.

RESPECT: To know and appreciate a creature for its capacity to flourish, that is, for both limitations and its potentials for achievement, and its ways of suffering.

RETRIBUTIVE JUSTICE: The distribution of burdens to correct advantages gained by those persons who have realized undeserved benefit or undeserved avoidance of burden in past distributions of benefits or burdens, or the distribution of burdens to those persons who have inflicted undeserved hardship upon another.

RIGHTS: Entitlements which justify doing or refraining from something.

RULE UTILITARIANISM: The theory that the evaluation of the rightness or wrongness of an action is to be made as a comparative judgment taking into consideration alternative actions, the moral rules which sanction or prohibit the action and each alternative, and the comparative acceptability of those rules as determined by the utility of the practices implied by each rule.

SANCTION, LEGAL: A burden imposed upon a person for the wrong he or she has done in acting contrary to his or her legal obligation.

SELF-RESPECT: Acknowledging and appreciating one's own capacities and limitations, that is, one's own rights as a person.

SOCIALISM: That theory of the state which emphasizes the value and importance of cooperation and collective effort. Atomistic socialism views cooperation primarily as instrumental to the achievement of the purposes of the members of the society. Organic socialism views cooperation as intrinsically valuable in its own right as well as being instrumental to the purposes of individuals and of the society as a totality.

SOCIETY: A group of people engaged in cooperative behavior for the sake of a common purpose or goal.

STATE: That society which directs its cooperative norm-bound behavior toward those shared purposes which are the fundamental shared purposes of human life.

SUBJECTIVE DUTY: In utilitarian theory, the duty to perform those actions or undertake those practices that are likely to produce the best balance of good compared to bad foreseeable consequences.

SUBJECTIVIST INTERPRETATION: That interpretation of a normative claim which treats the claim as a statement regarding the speaker's preferences or emotional responses to the object being evaluated.

TOTALITARIANISM: That theory of government which asserts that the state should maximize its control over all aspects of the lives of its members which might affect the collective good.

UNIVERSALISTIC UTILITARIANISM: The theory that the extent of the utilitarian consideration of consequences should include all who are affected and that each person should count equally in this consideration.

UNIVERSALIZABILITY: The principle that similar agents performing similar acts in similar circumstances ought to be judged in similar ways. The criterion that if R counts as a reason in favor of person A's doing X in situation S, then R also counts as a reason for a similar person to perform a similar act in a similar situation.

UTILITARIANISM: The normative theory that the rightness or wrongness of rules or actions should be determined solely by an evaluation of the net balance of goodness or badness of the consequent states of affairs produced.

VALUE CONFLICT: The state produced when normative policies, or ethical theories, lead to conclusions which conceptually contradict each other, that is, when logically inconsistent courses of action are implied.

VALUE DIVERGENCE: The state produced when one set of reasons leads to the view that one action should be taken while a second set of reasons suggests that a different action should be taken, and these two courses of action are not incompatible.

VIRTUE: A characteristic way of behaving; a habit or character trait which is useful in achieving some goal or purpose; in contrast to a vice, which would be a harmful or negative habit or character trait.

ENDNOTES

Bentham, Jeremy. *An Introduction to the Principles of Morals and Legislation.* First published in London, 1789.

Gilligan, Carol. *In a Different Voice: Psychological Theory and Women's Development.* Cambridge, Mass: Harvard University Press, 1982.

Kant, Immanuel. *Groundwork of the Metaphysic of Morals.* First published in Koenigsberg, East Prussia, 1785.

Kant, Immanuel. *Critique of Practical Reason.* First published in Koenigsberg, East Prussia, 1788.

Kohlberg, Lawrence. "Development of Moral Character and Moral Idealogy," in *Review of Child Development Research,* edited by M. Hoffman and L. Hoffman, Vol. 1, 383–431. New York: Russell Sage Foundation, 1964.

Kohlberg, Lawrence. *The Psychology of Moral Development.* San Francisco: Harper & Row, 1984.

Mill, John Stuart. *Utilitarianism.* First published in London, 1863.

Plato. *Republic.* First published in Athens, 473 B.C.

The sources *Diary of an Urban Freedom Fighter, The Ethical Egoist's Handbook,* Koby's *Reflections on Justice,* and Zio Vincenzo's *Reflections on Cosmic Harmonics,* are fictional and were created by Peter A. Facione, who hereby absolves his two co-authors of all responsibility for their citation in this textbook. Zio Vincenzo, Tiolligni, and Koby are fictional. They were created in *Huck Finn at Forty,* an unpublished manuscript by Peter A. Facione, written in 1987.

The enclosed copy is being sent to you for adoption consideration.

However, if you don't wish to consider it, please use this postage paid label to return the book to us. The book will then be available to send to a colleague for review.

Your cooperation can have considerable impact on the price of textbooks.

Thank you.

(4/88)

A parcel mailed using this label may be mailed at a Post Office or in any mail deposit receptacle.

This label is coated with a dry-gum adhesive. To use, moisten this side and affix label to parcel.

FROM_____

SPECIAL FOURTH CLASS RATE

_____ DELIVERY POST OFFICE
_____ COMPUTE POSTAGE DUE
(See 919.7 Domestic Mail Manual)

POSTAGE _____
MERCHANDISE RETURN FEE _____
TOTAL POSTAGE DUE $ _____

MERCHANDISE RETURN LABEL

PERMIT NO. 29   WEST NYACK, NY 10994

PRENTICE HALL   RTE 59 @ BROOK HILL DR

POSTAGE DUE UNIT

U.S. POSTAL SERVICE
WEST NYACK, NY 10994

INDEX